The Oxford Book of American Literary Anecdotes

The Oxford Book of American Literary Anecdotes

edited by

DONALD HALL

OXFORD UNIVERSITY PRESS
Oxford New York Toronto Melbourne

OXFORD UNIVERSITY PRESS
Oxford London Glasgow
New York Toronto Melbourne Auckland
Delhi Bombay Calcutta Madras Karachi
Kuala Lumpur Singapore Hong Kong Tokyo
Nairobi Dar es Salaam Cape Town

and associate companies in
Beirut Berlin Ibadan Mexico City Nicosia

First published by Oxford University Press, New York, 1981

First issued as an Oxford University Press paperback, 1983

Library of Congress Cataloging in Publication Data
Main entry under title:

The Oxford book of American literary anecdotes.

Includes index.
1. Authors, American—Anecdotes, facetiae,
satire, etc. I. Hall, Donald, 1928–
PS138.096 810'.9 80–27436
ISBN 0–19–502938–0
ISBN 0–19–503388–4 (pbk.)

Printing (last digit): 9 8 7 6 5 4 3 2

Printed in the United States of America

Selections from works by the following were made possible by the kind permission of their respective publishers.

Joseph Adamson: *Groucho, Harpo, Chico and Sometimes Zeppo,* copyright © 1973 by Joseph Adamson III. Reprinted by permission of Simon & Schuster, a Division of Gulf & Western Corporation and by permission of Russell & Volkening, Inc.

Mrs. Thomas Bailey Aldrich: *Crowding Memories.* Reprinted by permission of Judge Bailey Aldrich and Mrs. Vinton Chapin.

Gay Wilson Allen: Reprinted with permission of Macmillan Publishing Co., Inc., from *The Solitary Singer: A Critical Biography of Walt Whitman* by Gay Wilson Allen. Copyright 1955 by Gay Wilson Allen.

Hervey Allen: From *Israfel: The Life and Times of Edgar Allan Poe* by Hervey Allen. Copyright 1926 by Hervey Allen. Copyright 1954 by Ann Andrews Allen. Reprinted by permission of Holt, Rinehart & Winston, Publishers.

Alfred Alvarez: Copyright © 1971 by A. Alvarez. Reprinted from *The Savage God: A Study of Suicide,* by A. Alvarez, by permission of Random House, Inc. and Weidenfeld and Nicholson, Ltd.

Richard E. Amacher: *Franklin's Wit and Folly: The Bagatelles* (New Brunswick, N.J.: Rutgers University Press, 1953). Reprinted by permission of the editor.

Sherwood Anderson: *Sherwood Anderson's Memoirs: A Critical Edition,* ed. Ray Lewis White, copyright © 1969 by the University of North Carolina Press. Reprinted by permission of the publisher and Harold Ober Associates, Inc.

Newton Arvin: *Longfellow: His Life and Work,* copyright © 1963 by Newton Arvin. Reprinted by permission of Little, Brown & Company in association with the Atlantic Monthly Press.

James Atlas: Selections from *Delmore Schwartz* by James Atlas. Copyright © 1977 by James Atlas. Used by permission of Farrar, Straus & Giroux, Inc.

Louis Auchincloss: "Never Leave Me," *American Heritage,* vol. 21. Reprinted by permission of the author and his agent, James Brown Associates, Inc. Copyright © 1973 by Louis Auchincloss.

Carlos Baker: Used by permission of Charles Scribner's Sons from *Ernest Hemingway: A Life Story* by Carlos Baker. Copyright © 1969 by Carlos Baker, copyright © 1969 by Mary Hemingway. Also by permission of William Collins & Sons, Ltd.

William Irving Bartlett: *Jones Very: Emerson's Brave Saint,* copyright 1942 by Duke University Press. Reprinted by permission of the publisher.

Sylvia Beach: *Shakespeare and Co.* Reprinted by permission of Harcourt Brace Jovanovich, Inc. and Faber & Faber, Ltd.

Richard Croom Beatty: *James Russell Lowell.* Reprinted by permission of Vanderbilt University Press.

S. N. Behrman: "They Left 'em Laughing," *New York Times,* Nov. 21, 1965, copyright © 1965 by the New York Times Company. Reprinted by permission.

Saul Bellow: Introduction to *Recovery* by John Berryman, copyright © 1973 by Saul Bellow. Reprinted by permission of Russell & Volkening, Inc., as agents for the author.

Nathaniel Benchley: *Robert Benchley: A Biography,* copyright © 1955 by Nathaniel Benchley. Reprinted by permission of International Creative Management. Originally published by McGraw-Hill Book Company.

A. Scott Berg: *Max Perkins: Editor of Genius.* Reprinted by permission of Elsevier-Dutton Publishing Co., Inc. and Russell & Volkening, Inc.

Burton Bernstein: *Thurber.* Reprinted by permission of Dodd, Mead & Company and Victor Gollancz.

John Berryman: Selection from *Randall Jarrell 1914–1965* by John Berryman. Copyright ©

1967 by Farrar, Straus & Giroux, Inc. Used by permission of Farrar, Straus & Giroux, Inc.

Stephen Birmingham: Specified material from *The Late John Marquand* (J. B. Lippincott), copyright © 1972 by Stephen Birmingham. Reprinted by permission of Harper & Row, Publishers, Inc. and Brandt & Brandt, Literary Agents, Inc.

Paula Blanchard: Excerpted from *Margaret Fuller: From Trancendentalism to Revolution* by Paula Blanchard. Reprinted by permission of Delacorte Press/Seymour Lawrence. A MERLOYD LAWERENCE Book.

Louise Bogan: Reprinted by permission of Harcourt Brace Jovanovich, Inc., from *What the Woman Lived: Letters of Louise Bogan,* edited by Ruth Limmer, copyright © 1973 by Ruth Limmer, Trustee, Estate of Louise Bogan.

Catherine Drinker Bowen: *Yankee From Olympus,* copyright 1944 by Catherine Drinker Bowen. Reprinted by permission of Little, Brown & Company, and Harold Ober Associates, Inc.

Matthew J. Bruccoli: From *The O'Hara Concern,* by Matthew J. Bruccoli. Copyright © 1975 by Matthew J. Bruccoli. Reprinted by permission of Random House, Inc.

W. C. Bruce: *Benjamin Franklin Self-Revealed,* vol. 1. Reprinted by permission of G. P. Putnam's Sons.

Roger Burlingame: From *Of Making Many Books* by Roger Burlingame. Copyright 1946 by Roger Burlingame. Reprinted by permission of Charles Scribner's Sons.

Whit Burnett: *The Literary Life and the Hell With It.* Reprinted by permission of A. Watkins, Inc.

Noel Busch: *T.R.: The Story of Theodore Roosevelt,* copyright © 1963 by Noel F. Busch. Reprinted by permission of William Morrow & Company, Inc. and W. H. Allen Company, Ltd.

Witter Bynner: Selections from *Prose Pieces* by Witter Bynner. Copyright © 1979 by the Witter Bynner Foundation for Poetry, Inc. Used by permission of Farrar, Straus & Giroux, Inc.

Morley Callaghan: *That Summer in Paris,* copyright © 1963 by Morley Callaghan. Reprinted by permission of the Harold Matson Company, Inc.

North Callahan: *Carl Sandburg: Lincoln of Our Literature,* copyright © 1970 by North Callahan. By permission of the author and New York University Press, the publisher.

Virginia Spencer Carr: Excerpts from *The Lonely Hunter: A Biography of Carson McCullers* by Virginia Spencer Carr, copyright © 1975 by Virginia Spencer Carr. Reprinted by permission of Doubleday & Company, Inc. and Peter Owen, Ltd.

Bennett Cerf: From *At Random: Reminiscences of Bennett Cerf* by Bennett Cerf. Copyright © 1977 by Random House, Inc. Reprinted by permission of Random House, Inc.

Margaret Terry Chanler: *Roman Spring: A Memoir,* copyright 1934 by Margaret Terry Chanler. Reprinted by permission of Little, Brown & Company.

Blair Clark: "On Robert Lowell," *Harvard Advocate,* Special Robert Lowell Edition, November 1979. Reprinted by permission of the Harvard Advocate.

David Lee Clark: *Charles Brockden Brown: Pioneer Voice of America,* copyright 1952 by Duke University Press. Reprinted by permission of Duke University Press.

Harold Clurman: From *The Fervent Years: The Story of the Group Theater and the Thirties,* copyright 1945 and renewed 1973 by Harold Clurman. Reprinted by permission of Alfred A. Knopf, Inc.

Daniel Cory: *Santayana: The Later Years,* copyright © 1963 by Daniel Cory. Reprinted by permission of George Braziller, Inc.

Robert Coughlan: Specified material abridged from pp. 109–11 in *The Private World of William Faulkner,* copyright © 1953, 1954 by Robert Coughlan. Reprinted by permission of Harper & Row, Publishers, Inc. and the William Morris Agency.

Malcolm Cowley: From *The Dream of the Golden Mountains,* copyright © 1979 by Malcolm Cowley. Reprinted by permission of Viking Penguin, Inc.

From *Exile's Return,* copyright 1934, 1935, 1941, 1951, renewed 1962, 1963, 1969 by Malcolm Cowley. Reprinted by permission of Viking Penguin, Inc.

"Remembering Allen Tate," *The Georgia Review,* Spring 1980. Reprinted by permission of the author.

From *A Second Flowering,* copyright © 1956 by Malcolm Cowley. Reprinted by permission of Viking Penguin, Inc. and André Deutsch.

Caresse Crosby: *The Passionate Years.* Reprinted by permission of the Ecco Press.

Martin Duberman: *Black Mountain: An Exploration in Community,* copyright © 1972 by Martin Duberman. Used by permission of the Sterling Lord Agency, Inc.

Max Eastman: *Great Companions.* Reprinted by permission of Pitman Publishing Company, Ltd., London.

Leon Edel: Specified material from *Henry James, 1870–1881: The Conquest of London* by Leon Edel, copyright © 1962 by Leon Edel; from *Henry James, 1843–1870: The Untried Years,* by Leon Edel, copyright 1953 by Leon Edel; from *Henry James 1882–1895: The Middle Years* by Leon Edel, copyright © 1962 by Leon Edel; from *Henry James, 1895–1901: The Treacherous Years* by Leon Edel, copyright © 1969 by Leon Edel; from *Henry James, 1901–1916: The Master* by Leon Edel, copyright © 1972 by Leon Edel. All reprinted by permission of Harper & Row, Publishers, Inc. and the William Morris Agency.

Michel Fabre: *The Unfinished Quest of Richard Wright,* copyright © 1973 by William Morrow & Company, Inc. By permission of the publisher.

Andrew Field: From *Nabokov: His Life in Part,* copyright © 1977 by Andrew Field. Reprinted by permission of Viking Penguin, Inc., Hamish Hamilton, Ltd., and Anthony Sheil Associates, Ltd.

Martha Foley: *The Story of Story Magazine: A Memoir by Martha Foley,* with an Introduction and Afterword by Jay Neugeboren. Copyright © 1980 by Francis G. Foley. Reprinted by permission of W. W. Norton & Company, Inc. and the JCA Literary Agency.

Ford Madox Ford: *Return to Yesterday,* copyright 1932 by Ford Madox Ford, copyright renewed 1959 by Janice Biala Brustlien. Reprinted by permission of the Liveright Publishing Corporation and Janice Biala Brustlien.

Robert Francis: *A Time to Talk: Conversations and Indiscretions,* copyright © 1972 by Robert Francis. Reprinted by permission of the University of Massachusetts Press.

Benjamin Franklin: *Franklin's Wit and Folly: The Bagatelles,* ed. Richard E. Amacher (New Brunswick, N.J.: Rutgers University Press 1953). Reprinted by permission of the editor.

Russell Frazer: "Delmore Schwartz," *Michigan Quarterly Review,* Fall 1979. Reprinted by permission of the author.

Otto Friedrich: *Clover,* copyright © 1978 by Otto Friedrich. Reprinted by permission of the author and Simon & Schuster, a Division of Gulf & Western Corporation.

Hamlin Garland: From *My Friendly Contemporaries* and from *Roadside Meetings.* Reprinted by permission of Isabel Garland Lord and Constance Garland Doyle.

Brendan Gill: From *Here at the New Yorker* by Brendan Gill. Copyright © 1975 by Brendan Gill. Reprinted by permission of Random House, Inc. and Michael Joseph, Ltd.

E. Stanley Godbold: *Ellen Glasgow and the Woman Within.* Reprinted by permission of Louisiana State University Press.

Malcolm Goldstein: From *George S. Kaufman: His Life, His Theater* by Malcolm Goldstein. Copyright © 1979 by Oxford University Press, Inc. Reprinted by permission.

Richard Goldstone: *Thornton Wilder: An Intimate Portrait.* Reprinted by permission of the author.

Jean Gould: Reprinted by permission of Dodd, Mead & Company, from *Amy: The World of Amy Lowell and the Imagist Movement* by Jean Gould. Copyright © 1975 by Jean Gould. And from *Edna St. Vincent Millay: The Poet and Her Book,* by permission of Dodd, Mead & Company.

Gertrude M. Graves: "A Cousin's Memories of Emily Dickinson," *Boston Globe,* January 12, 1930. Reprinted courtesy of the Boston Globe.

James Grossman: *James Fenimore Cooper,* copyright 1949 by William Sloan Associates, Inc. By permission of William Morrow & Company, Inc.

Hermann Hagedorn: *E. A. Robinson: A Biography,* copyright 1938 by Hermann Hagedorn, renewed 1966 by Dorothy Hagedorn. Reprinted by permission of Macmillan Publishing Co., Inc. and Dorothea Hagedorn Parfit and Mary Hagedorn DuVall.

Donald Hall: Specified material from *Remembering Poets,* copyright © 1977, 1978 by Donald Hall. Reprinted by permission of Harper & Row, Publishers, Inc. "A Visit with Robert Giroux," *New York Times Book Review,* January 6, 1980, copyright © 1980 by the New York Times Company. Reprinted by permission.

Walter Harding: *The Days of Henry Thoreau.* Reprinted by permission of the author.

Leon Harris: Specified material from pp. 30, 130, and 240 in *Upton Sinclair: American Rebel* (T. Y. Crowell), copyright © 1975 by Leon Harris. Reprinted by permission of Harper & Row, Publishers, Inc. and Julian Bach Literary Agency, Inc.

James S. Haskins: *Always Movin' On: The Life of Langston Hughes,* copyright © 1976 by James S. Haskins. Used by permission of the publisher, Franklin Watts, Inc.

Ben Hecht: *A Child of the Century,* copyright 1954 by Ben Hecht. Reprinted with permission of Simon & Schuster, a Division of Gulf & Western Corporation.

Lillian Hellman: *An Unfinished Woman: A Memoir,* copyright © 1969 by Lillian Hellman. Reprinted by permission of Little, Brown & Company and Harold Matson Company, Inc.

Ernest Hemingway: *A Moveable Feast,* copyright © 1964 by Ernest Hemingway, Ltd. Reprinted by permission of Charles Scribner's Sons, Jonathan Cape, Ltd., and the Executors of the Ernest Hemingway Estate.

Josephine Hendin: *The World of Flannery O'Connor.* Reprinted by permission of Indiana University Press.

C. David Heymann: From *American Aristocracy,* copyright © 1980 by C. David Heymann. Reprinted by permission of Dodd, Mead & Company. *Ezra Pound: The Last Rower,* copyright © 1976 by C. David Heymann. Reprinted by permission of Viking Penguin, Inc. and Literistic, Ltd.

Helen Howe: *The Gentle Americans, 1864–1918: Biography of a Breed.* Reprinted by permission of the Executors of the Estate of Helen Howe.

Mark Anthony DeWolfe Howe: *Holmes of the Breakfast Table.* Reprinted by permission of Paul Appel, Publishers. *John Jay Chapman and His Letters.* Reprinted by permission of Houghton Mifflin Company. *Memories of a Hostess: A Chronicle of Eminent Friendships.* Reprinted by permission of the Estate of Mark Anthony DeWolfe Howe.

Mark DeWolfe Howe: From *Justice Oliver Wendell Holmes: The Shaping Years 1841–1870* (Cambridge, Mass.: Harvard University Press, 1963). Reprinted by permission of the publisher.

William Dean Howells: *My Mark Twain.* Reprinted by permission of Professor William White Howells.

Edwin P. Hoyt: From *Horatio's Boys: The Life and Works of Horatio Alger, Jr.* Copyright © 1974 by the author, Edwin P. Hoyt. Reprinted with the permission of the publisher, Chilton Book Company, Radnor, Pa.

Nancy Hoyt: From *The Portrait of An Unknown Lady* by Nancy Hoyt, copyright 1935 by the Bobbs-Merrill Company, Inc. Reprinted by permission of the publisher.

Langston Hughes: Reprinted from *Selected Poems of Langston Hughes,* by Langston Hughes, by permission of Alfred A. Knopf, Inc. Copyright 1942 by Alfred A. Knopf, Inc., and renewed 1970 by Anna Bontemps and George Houston Boss.

Alice James: *The Diary of Alice James,* ed. Leon Edel. Reprinted by permission of Dodd, Mead & Company.

Mrs. Randall Jarrell: Selection from "The Group of Two" by Mrs. Randall Jarrell, from *Randall Jarrell 1914–1965.* Copyright © by Farrar, Straus & Giroux, Inc. Used by permission of Farrar, Straus & Giroux, Inc.

Robinson Jeffers: *Selected Letters of Robinson Jeffers,* ed. Ann M. Ridgeway, copyright © 1968 by the Johns Hopkins Press. Reprinted by permission of the Johns Hopkins Press.

James Weldon Johnson: From *Along This Way.* Copyright 1933 by the Viking Press, renewed 1961 by Grace Nail Johnson. By permission of Viking Penguin, Inc.

Matthew Josephson: *Life Among the Surrealists.* Reprinted by permission of Harold Ober Associates, Inc.

Justin Kaplan: *Lincoln Steffens,* copyright © 1974 by Justin Kaplan. *Mr. Clemens and Mark Twain,* copyright © 1966 by Justin Kaplan. *Walt Whitman: A Life,* copyright © 1980 by Justin Kaplan. All reprinted by permission of Simon & Schuster, a division of Gulf & Western Corporation.

Alfred Kazin: From *New York Jew* by Alfred Kazin. Copyright © 1978 by Alfred Kazin. Reprinted by permission of Alfred A. Knopf, Inc. Also by permission of Martin Secker and Warburg, Ltd.

John Keats: *You Might as Well Live: The Life and Times of Dorothy Parker,* copyright © 1970 by John Keats. Reprinted by permission of Simon & Schuster, a Division of Gulf & Western Corporation. Also reprinted by permission of the Sterling Lord Agency, Inc.

Richard Kennedy: *Dreams in the Mirror.* Reprinted by permission of the Liveright Publishing Corporation.

Hugh Kenner: *The Pound Era.* Reprinted by permission of the University of California Press.

Jack Kerouac: *Jack's Book: An Oral Biography,* eds. Barry Gifford and Lawrence Lee. Reprinted by permission of St. Martin's Press.

Dale Kramer: *Chicago Renaissance.* Reprinted by permission of the Evelyn Singer Agency, Inc.

Stanley Kunitz: "The Sense of a Life," *New York Times Book Review,* October 16, 1977, copyright © 1977 by the New York Times Company. Reprinted by permission.

H. S. Lathan: *Margaret Mitchell and Her Novel, Gone With the Wind* (New York: Macmillan, 1936). Reprinted by permission of Macmillan Publishing Co., Inc.

Aaron Lathem: From *Crazy Sundays,* copyright © 1970, 1971 by John Aaron Lathem. Reprinted by permission of Viking Penguin, Inc. and Martin Secker and Warburg, Ltd.

R.W.B. Lewis: Specified material pp. 498 and 499 in *Edith Wharton,* copyright © 1975 by R.W.B. Lewis. Reprinted by permission of Harper & Row, Publishers, Inc. and A. Watkins, Inc.

Robert Lowell: "Robert Frost" and "Ezra Pound" from *History* by Robert Lowell. Copyright © 1967, 1968, 1969, 1970, 1973 by Robert Lowell. Used by permission of Farrar, Straus & Giroux, Inc. Reprinted by permission of Faber & Faber, Ltd. from *History* by Robert Lowell. "To Delmore Schwartz" from *Life Studies* by Robert Lowell. Copyright © 1956, 1959 by Robert Lowell. Used by permission of Farrar, Straus & Giroux, Inc. Reprinted by permission of Faber & Faber, Ltd., from *Life Studies* by Robert Lowell. Interview by Fredrick Seidel in *Writers at Work,* 2nd series, by permission of Viking Penguin, Inc.

Percy Lubbock: *Portrait of Edith Wharton.* Reprinted by permission of the executors of the Percy Lubbock Estate.

Frank MacShane: From *The Life of Raymond Chandler* by Frank MacShane. Copyright © 1976 by Frank MacShane. Reprinted by permission of the publisher E. P. Dutton and Brandt and Brandt Literary Agents, Inc.

David Madden (ed.): *Remembering James Agee.* Reprinted by permission of Louisiana State University Press.

Pierre Marambaud (ed.): *William Byrd of Westover, 1674–1744.* Reprinted by permission of the University of Virginia Press.

Richard March and Tambimuttu (eds.): *T. S. Eliot: A Symposium.* All rights reserved. First published in the U.S. by Henry Regnery Co., 1949. Reprinted by permission of Contemporary Books, Inc.

Norman Mailer: From *The Armies of the Night* by Norman Mailer. Copyright © 1968 by

Norman Mailer. Reprinted by arrangement with the New American Library, Inc., New York. Reprinted by permission of the author and the author's agents, Scott Meredith Literary Agency, Inc., 845 Third Avenue, New York, New York 10022.

Jay Martin: Selections from *Nathanael West: The Art of His Life* by Jay Martin. Copyright © 1970 by Jay Martin. Reprinted by permission of Farrar, Straus & Giroux, Inc. and the author.

Cotton Mather: *The Diary of Cotton Mather for the Year 1712*, ed. William R. Manierre. Reprinted by permission of the University of Virginia Press.

T. S. Matthews: Specified material from *Great Tom: Notes Toward the Definition of T. S. Eliot*, copyright © 1973, 1974 by T. S. Matthews. Reprinted by permission of Harper & Row, Publishers, Inc. and Deborah Owen, Ltd.

Sara Mayfield: Excerpted from the book *The Constant Circle: H. L. Menken and His Friends* by Sara Mayfield. Copyright © 1968 by Sara Mayfield. Reprinted by permission of Delacorte Press and Lurton Blassingame.

Robert McAlmon: *Being Geniuses Together.* Reprinted by permission of Michael Joseph.

Philip McFarland: *Sojourner.* Reprinted by permission of Atheneum Publishers.

Suzi Mee: "The Double Life of Wallace Stevens," *Harvard Magazine*, Sept.–Oct. 1979. Reprinted by permission of Harvard Magazine.

Cornelia Meigs: From *Invincible Louisa* by Cornelia Meigs, copyright 1933, © 1961, 1968, by permission of Little, Brown & Company. *The Story of Louisa May Alcott*, by permission of George C. Harrap and Company, Ltd.

James K. Mellow: From *Charmed Circle* by James K. Mellow, copyright © 1974 by James K. Mellow. Reprinted by permission of Holt, Rinehart & Winston, Publishers.

Margaret Mitchell: *Margaret Mitchell's Gone With the Wind Letters, 1936–1949*, ed. Richard Harwell. Reprinted by permission of Stephens Mitchell.

John S. Morgan: *Noah Webster.* Reprinted by permission of Mason/Charter Publishers, Inc.

Willie Morris: Excerpts from *James Jones: A Friendship* by Willie Morris, copyright © 1978 by Willie Morris. Reprinted by permission of Doubleday & Company, Inc. and the Sterling Lord Agency, Inc.

Kathleen Morrison: From *Robert Frost: A Pictorial Chronicle* by Kathleen Morrison. Copyright © 1974 by Kathleen Morrison. Reprinted by permission of Holt, Rinehart & Winston, Publishers.

Vladimir Nabokov: From *Strong Opinions* by Vladimir Nabokov. Copyright © 1973 by McGraw-Hill International. Used with the permission of McGraw-Hill Book Company.

Charles Norman: *The Magic Maker: E. E. Cummings* by Charles Norman, copyright © 1958 by Charles Norman. Reprinted by permission of Macmillan Publishing Co.
Poets & People. Reprinted by permission of the author.

Simon Nowell-Smith: *Henry James: The Legend of the Master.* Reprinted by permission of Constable and Company, Ltd. and the author.

Richard O'Connor: *Ambrose Bierce: A Biography*, copyright © 1967 by Richard O'Connor. *Jack London: A Biography*, copyright © 1964 by Richard O'Connor. Both reprinted by permission of McIntosh and Otis, Inc.

William Van O'Connor: *Ezra Pound*, University of Minnesota Pamphlets on American Writers, #26. Reprinted by permission of the University of Minnesota Press.

Mary Oppen: *Meaning: A Life.* Reprinted by permission of Black Sparrow Press.

Charles Osborne: Excerpted from *W. H. Auden: The Life of a Poet*, copyright © 1979 by Charles Osborne. Reprinted by permission of Harcourt Brace Jovanovich, Inc. Also by permission of the publisher, Eyre Methuen.

Frances Thomas Osborne: "Herman Melville Through a Child's Eyes," *Bulletin of the New York Public Library*, #69, December 1965. Reprinted by permission of the *Bulletin of the New York Public Library.*

Hesketh Pearson: *Tom Paine: Friend of Mankind.* Reprinted by permission of the Estate of

Hesketh Pearson. From *The Man Whistler* by Hesketh Pearson (Taplinger, 1978). Copyright © by Michael Holroyd. Reprinted by permission. Also by permission of the Estate of Hesketh Pearson.

Marjorie Perloff: *Frank O'Hara: A Critical Introduction*, copyright © 1977 by Marjorie Perloff. Reprinted by permission of George Braziller, Inc.

George Plimpton: Reprinted by permission of the Berkley Publishing Corporation from *Shadow Box* by George Plimpton, copyright © 1977 by George Plimpton. Also by permission of Russell & Volkening, Inc.

Ezra Pound: *The Cantos of Ezra Pound.* Copyright © 1934 by Ezra Pound. Reprinted by permission of New Directions Publishing Corporation. Reprinted by permission of Faber & Faber, Ltd., from *The Cantos of Ezra Pound.*

Henry Rankin: Specified material from *Intimate Character Sketches of Abraham Lincoln.* Copyright © 1924 by Henry B. Rankin. Renewed 1952 by Emma R. Barber. Reprinted by permission of Harper & Row, Publishers, Inc.

Theodore Roosevelt: *The Letters of Theodore Roosevelt*, volume IV, *The Square Deal 1903–1905*, edited by Elting E. Morison (Cambridge, Mass.: Harvard University Press, 1951). Reprinted by permission of the publisher.

Michael Ryan: "A Talk on Wallace Stevens," *Poetry*, September 1979. Reprinted by permission of the author.

Mark Schorer: *Sinclair Lewis: An American Life* by Mark Schorer. Copyright © 1961 by Mark Schorer. Reprinted by permission of Brandt & Brandt Literary Agents, Inc.

Winfield Townley Scott: Excerpts from "John Wheelwright and His Poetry," copyright 1954, "To See Robinson," © 1956, are reprinted from *New Mexico Quarterly* published by the University of New Mexico Press, Albuquerque, in *Exiles and Fabrications* by Winfield Townley Scott. Reprinted by permission of Doubleday & Company, Inc.

Allen Seager: *The Glass House.* Reprinted by permission of the McGraw-Hill Book Company and Mrs. Beatrice Roethke Lushington.

Robert Sencourt: *T. S. Eliot: A Memoir.* Reprinted by permission of Dodd, Mead & Company and the Garnstone Press.

Elizabeth Shepley Sergeant: Specified excerpts from pp. 168–69, 201–2 in *Willa Cather: A Memoir* by Elizabeth Shepley Sergeant (J. B. Lippincott). Copyright © 1953 by Elizabeth Shepley Sergeant. Reprinted by permission of Harper & Row, Publishers, Inc.

Anne Sexton: Interview in *Writers at Work*, 4th series, copyright © 1974, 1976 by Paris Review, Inc. Reprinted by permission of Viking Penguin, Inc.

Louis Sheaffer: From *O'Neill: Son and Artist* by Louis Sheaffer. Copyright © 1973 by Louis Sheaffer. By permission of Little, Brown & Company and Granada Publishing Ltd.

Odell Shepard: *Pedlar's Progress: The Life of Bronson Alcott.* Reprinted by permission of Willard O. Shepard.

Louis Simpson: Excerpts of about 517 words from pp. 118, 189, and 217 in *Three on the Tower* by Louis Simpson. Copyright © by Louis Simpson. By permission of William Morrow & Company, Inc.

Chard Powers Smith: Reprinted with permission of Macmillan Publishing Co., Inc. from *Where the Light Falls: A Portrait of Edwin Arlington Robinson* by Chard Powers Smith. Copyright © 1965 by Chard Powers Smith.

Logan Pearsall Smith: *Unforgotten Years.* Reprinted by permission of Constable Publishers.

Stephen Spender (ed): *W. H. Auden: A Tribute* edited by Stephen Spender. Copyright © 1974, 1975 by George Weidenfeld & Nicholson, Ltd. Reprinted by permission of Weidenfeld & Nicholson, Ltd. and Macmillan Publishing Co., Inc.

R. W. Stallman: *Stephen Crane*, copyright © 1968, by R. W. Stallman. Reprinted by permission of George Braziller, Inc.

Aubrey Harrison Starke: From *Sidney Lanier: A Biography and Critical Study* by Aubrey Harrison Starke. Copyright 1933 by the University of North Carolina Press. Reprinted by permission of the University of North Carolina Press.

John Steinbeck: From *Steinbeck: A Life in Letters,* edited by Elaine Steinbeck and Robert Wallsten. Copyright © 1975 by Elaine A. Steinbeck and Robert Wallsten. Copyright © 1952 by John Steinbeck. Copyright © 1969 by the Executors of the Estate of John Steinbeck. Reprinted by permission of Viking Penguin, Inc. and McIntosh and Otis, Inc.

Nancy Hunter Steiner: *A Closer Look at Ariel: A Memoir of Sylvia Plath.* Reprinted by permission of Harper & Row, Publishers, Inc.

Elizabeth Stevenson: *Henry Adams: A Biography,* copyright © 1955 by Elizabeth Stevenson. Reprinted by permission of Macmillan Publishing Co., Inc.

Randall Stewart: *Nathaniel Hawthorne.* Reprinted by permission of Yale University Press.

W. A. Swanberg: Used by permission of Charles Scribner's Sons from *Dreiser* by W. A. Swanberg. Copyright © 1965 by W. A. Swanberg. Also by permission of McIntosh and Otis, Inc.

Allen Tate (ed): From *T. S. Eliot: The Man and His Work* edited by Allen Tate. Copyright © 1966 by The University of the South (Publisher of *Sewanee Review*). Reprinted by permission of Delacorte Press/Seymour Lawrence. Also by permission of Brandt & Brandt Literary Agents, Inc. and the *Sewanee Review.*

Peter Taylor: From *Randall Jarrell: 1914–1965* ed. Robert Lowell, Peter Taylor, and Robert Penn Warren. Reprinted by permission of the author.

Howard Teichmann: From *Smart Aleck* by Howard Teichmann. Copyright © 1976 by Howard Teichmann and Evelyn Teichmann. By permission of William Morrow & Company, Inc. Also by permission of Deborah Rogers, Ltd.

Walter Teller: *Walt Whitman's Camden Conversations,* ed. Walter Teller. Reprinted by permission of Walter Teller.

John Thompson: "Robert Lowell," *New York Review of Books,* October 27, 1977. Reprinted with permission from the New York Review of Books. Copyright © 1977 Nyrev, Inc.

Lawrance Thompson: From *Robert Frost: The Early Years 1874–1915* by Lawrance Thompson. Copyright © 1966 by Lawrance Thompson. Copyright © 1966 by the Estate of Robert Frost. From *Robert Frost: The Later Years* by Lawrance Thompson and R. H. Winnick. Copyright © 1976 by Holt, Rinehart & Winston. Copyright © 1976 by the Estate of Robert Frost. Both reprinted with permission of Holt, Rinehart & Winston, Publishers.

James Thurber: Copyright 1943 by James Thurber. Copyright © 1973 by Helen W. Thurber and Rosemary T. Sauers. From *The Thurber Carnival,* published by Harper & Row. Originally printed in *The New Yorker.* Reprinted by permission of Mrs. Helen Thurber. Copyright © 1959 James Thurber. From *The Years with Ross,* published by Atlantic Little, Brown. Originally printed in somewhat different form in *The Atlantic Monthly.* Reprinted by permission of Hamish Hamilton, Ltd. and Mrs. Helen Thurber.

Eunice Tietjens: *The World at My Shoulder.* Reprinted with permission of Marshall Head.

Mabel Loomis Todd: Mabel Loomis Todd Papers, Yale University Library Archives. Reprinted by permission of Yale University Library.

Andrew Turnbull: Used by permission of Charles Scribner's Sons from *F. Scott Fitzgerald: A Biography* by Andrew Turnbull. Copyright © 1962 by Andrew Turnbull. From *F. Scott Fitzgerald: A Biography* by Andrew Turnbull published by the Bodley Head. Used by permission of Charles Scribner's Sons from *Thomas Wolfe: A Biography* by Andrew Turnbull. Copyright © 1967 Charles Scribner's Sons. From *Thomas Wolfe: A Biography* by Andrew Turnbull published by the Bodley Head.

Clara Newman Turner: "My Personal Acquaintance with Emily Dickinson," Millicent Todd Bingham Papers, Yale University Library. Reprinted by permission of the Yale University Library.

John Eugene Unterecker: From *Voyager: A Life of Hart Crane* by John Eugene Unterecker. Copyright © 1969 by John Eugene Unterecker. Used by permission of Farrar, Straus & Giroux, Inc.

Jean Starr Untermeyer: *Private Collection,* copyright © 1965 by Jean Starr Untermeyer. Reprinted by permission of Alfred A. Knopf, Inc.

Carl Van Doren: By permission of Viking Penguin, Inc. From *Benjamin Franklin* by Carl Van Doren. Copyright 1938 by Carl Van Doren, copyright renewed 1966 by Margaret Van Doren Bevans, Barbara Van Doren Klaw, Anne Van Doren Ross.

Edward Wagenknecht: *Washington Irving: Moderation Displayed.* Copyright © 1962 by Edward Wagenknecht. Reprinted by permission of Oxford University Press, Inc.

Franklin Walker: *San Francisco's Literary Frontier.* Reprinted by permission of Mrs. Imogen B. Walker.

Constance Webb: Reprinted by permission of G. P. Putnam's Sons from *Richard Wright: A Biography* by Constance Webb. Copyright © 1968 by Constance Webb. Also reprinted by permission of Joan Daves.

Stanley Weintraub: Excerpted from *London Yankees,* copyright © 1979 by Stanley Weintraub. Reprinted by permission of Harcourt Brace Jovanovich, Inc. and W. H. Allen and Co., Ltd.

Edith Wharton: *A Backward Glance.* Reprinted by permission of Charles Scribner's Sons and A. Watkins, Inc.

Elizabeth Wade White: *Anne Bradstreet: "The Tenth Muse."* Copyright © 1971 by Elizabeth Wade White. Reprinted by permission of Oxford University Press, Inc.

Walt Whitman: *Walt Whitman's Camden Conversations,* ed. Walter Teller. Reprinted by permission of Walter Teller. *Walt Whitman and the Civil War,* ed. Charles T. Glicksberg. Reprinted by permission of the University of Pennsylvania Press.

Richard Wilbur: Copyright © 1972 by Richard Wilbur. Reprinted from his volume *The Mind-Reader* by permission of Harcourt Brace Jovanovich, Inc. Reprinted by permission of Faber & Faber, Ltd., from *The Mind-Reader* by Richard Wilbur.

William Carlos Williams: *The Autobiography of William Carlos Williams.* Copyright 1951 by William Carlos Williams. Reprinted by permission of New Directions Publishing Corporation.

Edmund Wilson: Selections from *Letters on Literature and Politics* by Edmund Wilson. Copyright © 1957, 1973, 1974, 1977 by Elena Wilson, Executrix of the Estate of Edmund Wilson. Used by permission of Farrar, Straus & Giroux, Inc. and Routledge and Kegan Paul, Ltd. Selections from *The Shock of Recognition* by Edmund Wilson. Copyright 1943 by Doubleday, Doran & Company, Inc. Copyright © 1955 by Edmund Wilson. Reprinted by permission of Farrar, Straus & Giroux, Inc. and W. H. Allen and Company, Ltd. Selections from *The Twenties* by Edmund Wilson. Edited with an Introduction by Leon Edel. Copyright © 1975 by Elena Wilson, Executrix of the Estate of Edmund Wilson. Reprinted with the permission of Farrar, Straus & Giroux, Inc.

R. H. Winnick: From *Robert Frost: The Later Years* by Lawrance Thompson and R. H. Winnick. Copyright © 1976 by Holt, Rinehart & Winston. Copyright © 1976 by the Estate of Robert Frost. Reprinted by permission of Holt, Rinehart & Winston, Publishers.

Ola E. Winslow: Reprinted with permission of Macmillan Publishing Co., Inc. from *Jonathan Edwards* by Ola E. Winslow. Copyright 1940 by Macmillan Publishing Co., Inc., renewed 1968 by Ola Elizabeth Winslow.

Geoffrey Wolff: From *Black Sun: The Brief Transit and Violent Eclipse of Harry Crosby* by Geoffrey Wolff. Copyright © 1976 by Geoffrey Wolff. Reprinted by permission of Random House, Inc. and the Robert Lescher Agency.

Marjorie Worthington: Excerpts from *Miss Alcott of Concord* by Marjorie Worthington. Copyright © 1958 by Marjorie Worthington. Reprinted by permission of Doubleday & Company, Inc. and the William Morris Agency.

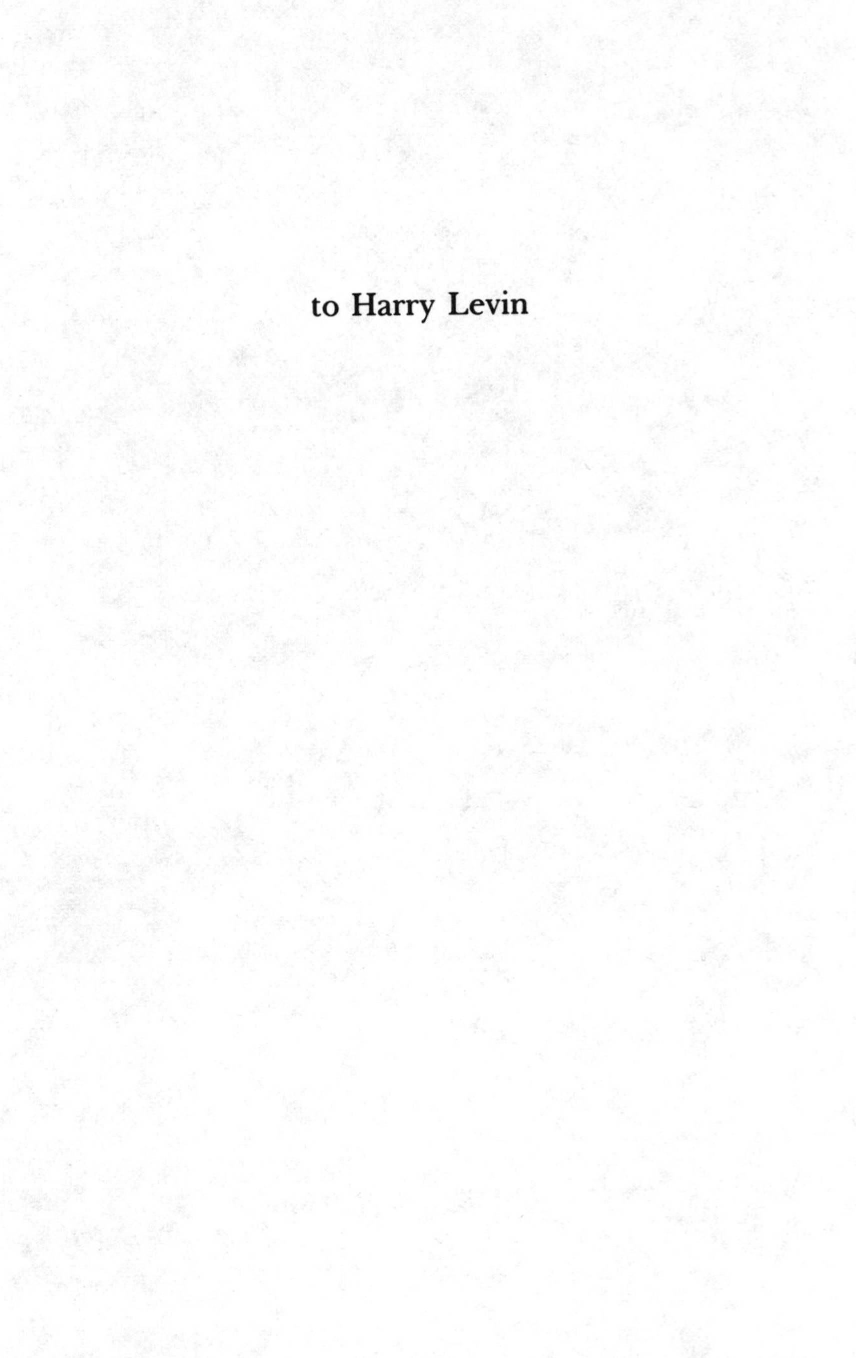

to Harry Levin

Preface

This book is first indebted to James Sutherland's *Oxford Book of Literary Anecdotes,* which restricted itself to English authors. (The present collection shares with Sutherland's two writers of ambiguous nationality, Henry James and T. S. Eliot, and adds W. H. Auden.) In his introduction, Sutherland spoke of the history of the word "anecdote," which Johnson defined in the first edition of his *Dictionary* as "something yet unpublished; secret history." By the fourth edition of the *Dictionary* (1773) Johnson needed to add the new meaning: "a biographical incident; a minute passage of private life."

Sutherland endeavored to keep his anecdotes literary, to tell the stories from writers' lives that touched upon their lives as writers. Here I have allowed myself more latitude and include stories not directly connected with authorship. Although most of my material is narrative, I have also collected the curious item of information and the *bon mot.* Without the witticism this book would have impoverished itself, lacking both the *fin de siècle* epigram and the wisecrack of the twenties and thirties, lifework of Dorothy Parker and George S. Kaufman.

For my purposes I have defined an anecdote as a story or a quotation that answers the question we ask about someone we do not know: "What is she *like?*" We may answer with abstractions or physiognomy—she is brave, with cheekbones of alabaster—or by quoting a remark or telling a story.

The richest moment of the American anecdote is the nineteenth century. Earlier pickings are sparse, but then colonial America was sparse, not to mention its literature. The anecdotal nineteenth century begins with accounts of Washington Irving and James Fenimore Cooper and ends with stories about Mark Twain and Henry James; each could be the subject of a book of anecdotes. Midcentury is the heyday of New England anecdotage, as Bostonian hostesses and editors note the behavior of Emerson, Thoreau, Longfellow, Whittier, Lowell, and Holmes. Often it is women who are the great rememberers—from Mrs. Hawthorne with her epistolary description of a skating party through Annie T. Fields writing the journal of her hospitality down to Mrs. Thomas Bailey Aldrich who describes in her memoirs a visit from Harriet Beecher Stowe . . . and Mrs. Stowe's drunken lapse . . . and Mrs. Stowe's underwear.

The reader will find here some authors known best for unliterary accomplishments. Abraham Lincoln's written words, nobly assembled, reside in the American consciousness. Do we therefore call him "literary"? I do not pretend to answer the question when I include anecdotes about him and Thomas Jefferson and several less presidential public figures whom we know for their prose as well as for other matters. If William James is not so literary a figure as his brother, I nonetheless repeat Logan Pearsall Smith's anecdote of public outrage.

In the matter of accuracy, I have been careful to be unscrupulous; if a story achieves print it is grist for this mill. Only once or twice has my sense of propriety raised itself to censor an obvious lie. On the other hand, when I have found different versions of a story, I have allowed the greater authenticity to decide the choice. In the absence of such reasons, I have chosen the version best told. On rare occasions, acknowledged, I have amalgamated several versions into my own.

Often we lack stories about writers we wish to know of and find anecdotal gold mines about writers who excite us less. Among one's friends, there are those who provide a continual fund of stories; others equally worthy give us a few tales to tell. One might wish to know more of Kate Chopin and less of Joaquin Miller.

I have modernized some seventeenth- and eighteenth-century spelling and punctuation. I have silently corrected a few obvious errors. I have shortened anecdotes by piece-cutting them with ellipses. I have given sources for each anecdote, not attempting scholarly form but providing information that may lead a curious reader to the original. Instead of using footnotes and bracketed insertions, I have introduced and annotated these anecdotes with passages in italics. Oxford University Press suggested as a model Jan Morris's anecdote book, *The Oxford Book of Oxford*—which is of course another source of indebtedness.

The reader will find two indices in the back of this book. One lists authors, both main subjects and those whose names occur within anecdotes about others. (Sometimes it was difficult to decide under which of two or three names an anecdote belonged.) There is also an index of topics illustrated, a list which often sounds like the seventy-seven deadly sins: vanity, drinking, greed, jealousy. . . .

I owe much to many helpers. Nancy Heffernan told me a story about Faulkner. Robert Wilson allowed me to use his memories of Marianne Moore. Robert Giroux not only recounted some tales for me, but also recommended Witter Bynner's reminiscent essays. Philip Booth, X. J. Kennedy, and James Camp told me stories. Justin Kaplan gave me a list of books, mainly nineteenth century, that provided many of my favorite anecdotes. Ben Franklin, professor of English at the University of South Carolina, checked the manuscript for me.

For thirty-some years I have talked with my friends about writers, hearing stories or hearing recommendations of books rich with anecdotes. Working on this book for six years, I have sought help in every company. From all who have helped me, whose names escape me now, I ask forgiveness.

Two Oxford editors guided and counseled me: James Raimes (now of Ticknor & Fields) and Sheldon Meyer. An Oxford copy-editor, Kim Lewis, helped me to avoid embarrassments. Frank Barham modernized spelling. Lois Fierro, Dorothy Foster, and Sharon Giannotta helped to prepare the manuscript. Linda Howe researched and proofed with great resourcefulness.

But my greatest debt is to Pat Wykes, who read Baker Library at Dartmouth for me, who prospected for anecdotes and found gold among iron pyrites, who inhabited stacks and tormented Interlibrary Loan, who read and reread and copied and consulted and accomplished the ten thousand things. Then it was she who undertook the frustrating task of securing permissions to reprint these stories: after the ten thousand things the ten thousand letters.

This book is dedicated to a great teacher who years ago instructed me as lecturer and tutor. Neither Harry Levin nor the other people whom I thank are responsible for my errors and omissions.

Wilmot, N.H. D. H.
April 15, 1981

Contents

Anne Bradstreet	3
Michael Wigglesworth	3
Edward Taylor	5
Samuel Sewall	5
Cotton Mather	6
William Byrd	8
Jonathan Edwards	9
Benjamin Franklin	10
Mather Byles	13
Thomas Paine	14
Thomas Jefferson	16
Philip Freneau	25
Timothy Dwight	26
Joel Barlow	28
Noah Webster	29
Charles Brockden Brown	29
Daniel Webster	30
Washington Irving	33
James Fenimore Cooper	35
William Cullen Bryant	36
Bronson Alcott	36
Ralph Waldo Emerson	40
Nathaniel Hawthorne	46
Henry Wadsworth Longfellow	51
John Greenleaf Whittier	55
Abraham Lincoln	57
Oliver Wendell Holmes	67
Edgar Allen Poe	68

Margaret Fuller 71
Harriet Beecher Stowe 76
Horace Greeley 80
Jones Very 81
Henry David Thoreau 82
Frederick Douglass 89
Herman Melville 91
Walt Whitman 93
James Russell Lowell 102
Emily Dickinson 103
Horatio Alger, Jr. 106
Louisa May Alcott 107
James Abbott McNeill Whistler 109
Samuel Clemens (Mark Twain) 112
Bret Harte 119
William Dean Howells 120
Henry Adams 122
Joaquin Miller 125
Oliver Wendell Holmes, Jr. 126
Sidney Lanier 128
William James 128
Henry James 130
James Whitcomb Riley 137
Henry Cabot Lodge 138
Booker T. Washington 139
Frank Harris 141
Theodore Roosevelt 142
John Dewey 143
George Lyman Kittredge 144
Edith Wharton 144
W. S. Porter (O. Henry) 147
George Santayana 147
Lincoln Steffens 148
Edwin Arlington Robinson 149
Frank Norris 153
Stephen Crane 153
Theodore Dreiser 156
James Weldon Johnson 159
Willa Cather 159
Ellen Glasgow 160

Amy Lowell 161
Gertrude Stein 165
Robert Frost 170
Sherwood Anderson 178
Jack London 180
Upton Sinclair 183
Carl Sandburg 184
Vachel Lindsay 187
Wallace Stevens 189
Carl Van Vechten 192
H. L. Mencken 192
Witter Bynner 193
Ludwig Lewisohn 195
William Carlos Williams 196
Maxwell Perkins 199
Ring Lardner 201
Sinclair Lewis 202
Ezra Pound 206
Elinor Wylie 211
Hilda Doolittle (H. D.) 212
Alexander Woollcott 213
Marianne Moore 216
Robinson Jeffers 223
Raymond Chandler 223
T. S. Eliot 224
Eugene O'Neill 230
Robert Benchley 232
George S. Kaufman 234
Harold Ross 235
Elmer Rice 237
Edna St. Vincent Millay 238
Dorothy Parker 239
John P. Marquand 241
E. E. Cummings 242
Dashiell Hammett 246
James Thurber 247
Ben Hecht 248
Edmund Wilson 253
John Dos Passos 255
F. Scott Fitzgerald 255

Louise Bogan 264
William Faulkner 265
Thornton Wilder 268
John Wheelwright 270
Harry Crosby 271
Vladimir Nabokov 273
Ernest Hemingway 275
Hart Crane 282
Allen Tate 289
Thomas Wolfe 289
Margaret Mitchell 292
Langston Hughes 295
John Steinbeck 297
Nathanael West 298
Louis Zukofsky 300
John O'Hara 300
Clifford Odets 303
W. H. Auden 304
Theodore Roethke 308
Richard Wright 312
James Agee 315
Charles Olson 316
Delmore Schwartz 317
Randall Jarrell 320
John Berryman 321
Carson McCullers 323
Robert Lowell 324
Shirley Jackson 329
James Jones 330
Jack Kerouac 334
Flannery O'Connor 336
Frank O'Hara 336
Anne Sexton 338
Sylvia Plath 339

Name Index 345
Topic Index 355

The Oxford Book of American Literary Anecdotes

Anne Bradstreet 1612–1672

Anne Bradstreet was born in England, married at sixteen, and in 1630 emigrated to the Massachusetts Bay Colony on board the Arbella. *Twenty years later in London her brother-in-law published a book of her poems without her knowledge or consent, under the title* The Tenth Muse Lately Sprung Up in America, "By a Gentlewoman in those parts." *In an epistle to the reader, he felt obliged to emphasize two points:*

". . . I doubt not but the reader will quickly find more than I can say, and the worst effect of his reading will be unbelief, which will make him question whether it be a woman's work, and ask, Is it possible? If any do, take this as an answer from him that dares avow it; it is the work of a woman, honored, and esteemed where she lives, for her gracious demeanor, her eminent parts, her pious conversation, her courteous disposition, her exact diligence in her place, and discreet managing of her family occasions; and more than so, these poems are the fruit but of some few hours, curtailed from her sleep, and other refreshments. . . ."

—Elizabeth Wade White, *Anne Bradstreet: "The Tenth Muse,"* 1971.

Cotton Mather praised her. John Norton, Puritan divine renowned for persecuting Quakers, celebrated her in couplets:

Her breast was a brave Pallace, a Broad-street,
Where all heroick ample thoughts did meet,
Where nature such a Tenement had tane,
That other Souls, to hers, dwelt in a lane.

Michael Wigglesworth 1631–1705

Many New England preachers wrote verse in which piety loomed larger than poesy. Michael Wigglesworth's rhymed theology included The Day *of* Doom *(1662) and* Meat out of the Eater *(1670). In 1679 Wigglesworth, who was prematurely aged and frail at forty-eight, suffered the loss of his wife. Despite his physical frailty, his bereavement resulted in new interests, about which Increase Mather wrote him in some agitation.*

Reverend Sir,—Since I saw you the last in B. [Boston ?] one that doth unfeignedly desire your welfare hath been with me, expressing grief of heart with reference unto a matter wherein yourself is concerned. I owe you that respect (& much more) as to inform you what I have been told. The report is, that you are designing to marry with your servant maid, & that she is one of obscure parentage, & not 20 years old, & of no church, nor so much as baptized. If it be as is related, I would humbly entreat you (before it be too late) to consider of these arguments in opposition.

1. For you to do this, which will be a grief of heart to your dear relations, if it be not a matter which God doth command to be done (for no man will deny but one ought rather to grieve his friends, than to provoke the Lord), is not advisable. Now I hear that they are much troubled at your intended proceedings, & I suppose there is no divine precept requiring your marrying with such an one. Is it not then better to desist?

2. I doubt that considering her youth, & your age, & great bodily infirmities, such a change of your condition, if that which is intimated by the Holy Apostle, 1 Corinthians 7, 3, should be attended, your days would be shortened, & consequently the 5th Commandment broken.

3. Such general rules as those, Philippians 4, 8, do concern as all Christians, so most eminently Ministers of Church. And doubtless it will *male audire* for you to do this thing, yea, I fear it will leave a blot upon your name after you shall cease to be in this world.

4. The ministry will be blamed, which we should be very careful to prevent. 2 Corinthians 6, 3. The mouths of carnal ones will be opened, not only to censure you, but your brethren in the ministry will be condemned also. The world will say, there's such an one, he was as justified a man as any of them, & yet we see unto what his affectations have carried him.

5. I am afraid that if you should proceed, that rule, 2 Corinthians 6, 14, will be transgressed. It useth to be said *nube pari,*

but to marry with one so much your inferior on all accounts, is not *nubere pari.* And to take one that was never baptized into such nearness of relation, seemeth contrary to the gospel; especially for a Minister of Christ to do it. The like never was in New England. Nay, I question whether the like hath been known in the Christian world.

—*Collections of the Massachusetts Historical Society,* 1868.

Although Mather went on to abjure Wigglesworth to "put the object out of your sight," Wigglesworth married his former maidservant; Martha Mudge bore him six children before she died at twenty-eight in 1690, fifteen years before her husband.

Edward Taylor c. 1642–1729

Best of the Puritan poets was Edward Taylor, who recollected in his diary an embarrassment of his Harvard years. Mr. Graves was his teacher.

Mr. Graves, not having his name for nought, lost the love of the undergraduates by his too much austerity, whereupon they used to strike a nail above the hall door-catch while we were reciting to him, and so nail him in the hall. At which disorder I was troubled, whereupon being desired by him to go into the buttery privily and watch who did it, one morning I did so; but being spied by the scholars I was fain to haste out and make haste to Boston before I spake to Mr. Graves, the better to cloak over the business that so the scholars might conclude it was accidental and not *ex proposito* (for I was fearful of incensing them against me), for which, notwithstanding the hazard I was in of setting them against me and the love I expressed to Mr. Graves in putting myself for his sake into such hazard, I was checked by him when I came up again. . . .

—*Proceedings of the Massachusetts Historical Society,* 1881.

Samuel Sewall 1652–1730

Greatest of diarists was Samuel Sewall, the colonial Pepys. Sewall was a tutor at Harvard, held many political positions in Massachusetts, petitioned William III to restore the colony's abrogated charter, and eventually became chief justice of the superior court of judicature. In an earlier and darker moment he served as a special commissioner in the Salem witchcraft trials, an act for which he later did public penance. Like his contemporaries, he read religious significance into life's smallest occasions.

March 27th. Set out homeward, lodged at Cushing's. *Note.* I prayed not with my servant, being weary. Seeing no chamber pot called for one; a little before day I used it in the bed, and the bottom came out, and all the water run upon me. I was amazed, not knowing the bottom was out till I felt it in the bed. The trouble and disgrace of it did afflict me. As soon as it was light, I called up my man and he made a fire and warmed me a clean shirt and I put it on, and was comfortable. How unexpectedly a man may be exposed! There's no security but in God, who is to be sought by prayer.

—*Collections of the Massachusetts Historical Society,* 1878–82.

He gives us accounts of Puritan party talk.

Last night at Mr. Thomas's had discourse about the body. Mr. Dudley maintained the belly should not be raised, because he knew no use of it. I maintained the contrary, because Christ saw no corruption. Saints shall be conformed to Him. The Creator in his infinite wisdom will know what use to make of them.

Dudley. What use of tasting, smelling?

Sewall. 'Tis possible the bodies of the Saints may have a fragrancy attending them.

Dudley. Voice is laborious.

Sewall. As much labor as you please, the more the better, so it be without toil, as in Heaven it will be. I dare not part with my belly. *Christ* has redeemed it; and there is danger of your breaking in further upon me, and cutting off my hand or foot.

—*Collections.*

Cotton Mather 1663–1728

Cotton Mather was the eldest son of Increase, who wrote so eloquently to Michael Wigglesworth (page 4). His two grandfathers, Richard Mather and John Cotton, had been leaders of the Puritan colonists, and their namesake determined to revive the faltering spirit of Calvinism in

New England. At twelve he was the youngest student ever admitted to Harvard, and by all accounts the worst prig. He became, however, a remarkable preacher and prolific author of texts both religious and political. The Wonders of the Invisible World *(1693) recounted some of the Salem witchcraft trials; he concurred in the verdicts but disagreed with the sentences of execution.*

Mather was a paradoxical figure. A scholar of seven languages, probably the most learned American of his time, in part he was progressive: he promoted inoculation for smallpox; yet the more than four hundred works he left behind—poems, sermons, essays, biographies, and seven formidable volumes of a diary—for the most part reflect an ingenious conservative Calvinism. From his diaries come these meditations on excretory functions, on revenge, and on marriage.

Formerly I resolved, that my attendance on the excretory necessities of nature, should be still accompanied, with some holy thoughts of a repenting and an abased soul. I will now make some addition to that projection of piety. The urinary excretions occur often every day. I have seen such tragical instances of nephritic and ischuriac miseries, in others that I cannot be enough thankful for my own deliverance from such things. And then also, an action that carries humiliation with it, how justly may it lead me, to think with wonderment on what my Savior will do for me, in the advancements of the future state. Wherefore, when I am at any time obliged into the urinary discharges, I would have one or both of these thoughts, formed in my mind; on that mean occasion. *My God, I bless thee for saving me from the terrible diseases of the wheel broken at the cistern.* And, *O my dear JESUS; wilt thou even bring this vile body, to the glories and blessings of the heavenly places?*

An horrid fellow, who is one of the wickedest of men, formerly made me the object of his malice, and his fury, and his libels. He has lately endeavored a cursed slander, and a subornation of mischief, against a pious and faithful magistrate, my very good friend Mr. *Bromfield.* The wretch goes on with such boisterous pride, and mischievous wickedness and restlessness, that it appeared unto me, time for us to carry him unto the Lord, with *united supplications.* . . . Accordingly, that gentleman, at my desire, joined with me, in part of the duties of this day. Having him with me in my study, we together entered before the Lord our complaint concerning that child of Belial.

We first, forgave him, and renounced with abhorrence all thoughts of a personal revenge upon him. We asked the Lord also to forgive him, and make him a new creature, and bring him to the tempers and actions of goodness, and that he might share with us in all the blessings of goodness. But yet we asked that he might be stopped in the perverse way wherein he is going on before the Lord. . . .

But if this might not be granted, we entreated that our glorious and enthroned *JESUS,* Who has all angels at His command, would in His own time, and His own way, interpose for our deliverance from that persecutor. . . . Particularly, we requested that the guilty monster may be stricken with some sense of his guilt, and smitten with such a remorse and horror of conscience as may be a warning unto other people.

My consort, from whose hand I most choose it, obliges me with bringing me my short breakfast herself, and sitting with me, while I am drinking of it. I will endeavor, that whenever she so comes to me, and sits with me, I will communicate some useful thought unto her.

—*The Diary of Cotton Mather for the Year 1712,* ed. William R. Manierre, 1964.

William Byrd 1674–1744

The Virginia diarist was acutely aware of the struggle between spirit and flesh. He could accommodate married love. "In the afternoon," he once noted, "I took a flourish with my wife, and then read a sermon in Tillotson."

But his "combustible matter"—as he put it—led him astray from home, and these fires used up the water he put on them.

The struggle between . . . the King and the Parliament in England was never half so violent as the Civil War between this hero's principles and his inclinations. . . .

I neglected to say my prayers, which I should not have done, because I ought to beg pardon for the lust I had for another man's wife. . . .

Endeavoured to pick up a woman, but could not, thank God. . . .

—*William Byrd of Westover, 1674–1744,* ed. Pierre Marambaud, 1971.

Jonathan Edwards 1703–1758

Forty years younger than Cotton Mather, Jonathan Edwards entered Yale at twelve. Like Mather he was partly scientific in temper; he excelled at natural observation. As an undergraduate he read Locke's Essay Concerning Human Understanding *and developed philosophical ideas that resembled Berkeley's idealism. But when he succeeded his grandfather in the Congregational pulpit at Northampton, Massachusetts, Edwards revealed his theological conservatism. His extraordinary eloquence compelled a Great Awakening of Calvinist piety.*

A contemporary diarist recorded Mr. Edwards's effect on the community.

"We went over to Enf[ie]l[d] where we met dear Mr. E[dwards] of N[ew] H[aven] who preached a most awakening sermon from these words—Deuteronomy 32–35 and before sermon was done—there was a great moaning & crying out through the whole house—What shall I do to be saved—oh I am going to Hell—Oh what shall I do for Christ etc., etc. So that the minister was obliged to desist—the shrieks & cries were piercing & amazing—after some time of waiting the congregation were still so that a prayer was made by Mr. W. & after that we descended from the pulpit and discoursed with the people—some in one place and some in another—and amazing and astonishing the power God was seen—& several souls were hopefully wrought upon that night & oh the cheerfulness and pleasantness of their countenances that received comfort—oh that God would strengthen and confirm—we sung an hymn & prayed & dismissed the assembly."

—Ola E. Winslow, *Jonathan Edwards 1703–1758,* 1940.

The Great Awakening aroused what might better have been left sleeping.

Late in the spring of 1735 the first sinister note was struck in the attempted suicide of Thomas Stebbins, a man of weak mentality. Several weeks later Joseph Hawley, one of the chief men of the town and uncle to Jonathan Edwards, "cut his throat on Lord's Day morning" and died immediately. The community was aghast. "An awful Providence," wrote Ebenezer Hunt in his *Journal.* A fast was appointed, and the congregation prostrated itself before God. But the turning point had come: the spell was broken, the emotional climate changed at once, and the long-delayed reaction set in. For the first time sobered men and women began to question the wholesomeness of the excitement under which they had been living. As a matter of fact, the limit of endurable ecstasies had been reached; but before equilibrium could be established and life could proceed normally once more there were to be many blots on the record. Hawley's death proved to be only the beginning, even in suicides. "Multitudes," to quote the pastor's own word, were impelled to do likewise, feeling it "urged upon them as if somebody had spoke to them *'Cut your own throat. Now is a good opportunity.'* "

—Winslow.

Benjamin Franklin 1706–1790

There were also Enlightenment temperaments which remained scientific and came to represent the forthcoming nation more nearly than Mather and Edwards did. Benjamin Franklin was scientist and magus, mountebank and moralist, joker and miracle worker. This story comes from a visit to England.

One day when they were walking in the park at Wycombe [Franklin] said that he could quiet the waves on a small stream which was being whipped by the wind. He went two hundred paces above where the others stood, made some magic passes over the water, and waved his bamboo cane three times in the air. The waves gradually sank and the stream became as smooth as a mirror. After they had marvelled Franklin explained. He carried oil in the hollow joint of his cane, and a few drops of it spreading on the water had caused the miracle.

—Carl Van Doren, *Benjamin Franklin,* 1938.

Franklin noticed Thomas Jefferson's discomfort as a committee revised the prose of his Declaration of Independence. Franklin consoled the distraught author with a story which Jefferson remembered later.

. . . "I was sitting by Dr. Franklin, who perceived that I was not insensible to these mutilations. 'I have made it a rule,' said he, 'whenever in my power, to avoid becoming the draftsman of papers to be reviewed by a public body. I took my lesson from an incident which I will relate to you. When I was a journeyman printer one of my companions, an apprentice hatter, having served out his time was about to open shop for himself. His first concern was to have a handsome signboard with a proper inscription. He composed it in these words: "John Thompson, hatter, makes and sells hats for ready money," with a figure of a hat subjoined. But he thought he would submit it to his friends for their amendments. The first he showed it to thought the word "hatter" tautologous, because followed by the words "makes hats" which show he was a hatter. It was struck out. The next observed that the word "makes" might as well be omitted, because the customers would not care who made the hats. If good and to their mind, they would buy, by whomever made. He struck it out. A third said he thought the words "for ready money" were useless, as it was not the custom of the place to sell on credit. Everyone who purchased expected to pay. They were parted with, and the inscription now stood: "John Thompson sells hats." "Sells hats?" says his next friend. "Why, nobody will expect you to give them away. What then is the use of that word?" It was stricken out; and "hats" followed it, the rather as there was one painted on the board. So his inscription was reduced ultimately to "John Thompson" with the figure of a hat subjoined.' "

—Van Doren.

Although he lived in France for some years, Franklin's cleverness did not extend to the French language.

On one occasion, when at the theatre with Mme. de Boufflers, from whom he took his cue in helping to swell the plaudits of the evening, he was chagrined to find that his most vigorous applause had been bestowed on flattering allusions to himself.

—W. C. Bruce, *Benjamin Franklin Self-revealed,* 1923.

His cleverness did extend, however, to the game of chess.

When Dr. Franklin went to France on his revolutionary mission, his eminence as a philosopher, his venerable appearance, and the cause on which he was sent, rendered him extremely popular—for all ranks and conditions of men there entered warmly into the American interest. He was, therefore, feasted and invited to all the court parties. At these he sometimes met the old Duchess of Bourbon, who being a chess-player of about his force, they were very generally played together. Happening once to put her king into prise, the Doctor took it. "Ah," says she, "we do not take kings so." "We do in America," said the Doctor.

—Sarah Randolph, *The Domestic Life of Thomas Jefferson,* 1871.

. . . Chaumont tells of one all-night bout Franklin had with the *"Abbé Catholique,"* presumably Morellet or de la Roche. The game was begun in the wing of the Hôtel de Valentinois which the older de Chaumont's wife occupied. When it came time to retire, the game being still in progress, Franklin proposed they go to his wing of the building to finish it. As soon as the game was ended, another was speedily begun. This procedure was repeated *ad infinitum.* In the middle of one game the last wax candle in the Franklin establishment was discovered to be burning perilously low. The abbé momentarily considered stopping, but Franklin would not hear of it. "My dear abbé," he protested, "it is impossible for two men such as us to stop merely because of lack of light." The abbé then remembered that he had some extra candles *chez lui.* He would run back and get them, he excitedly told Franklin. "Go, then," the doctor replied, "and may the goddess of the night protect you in your adventurous course." Chaumont says that when the abbé had disappeared, Franklin profited by the last flicker in the candlelight to rearrange the pieces so that he would win. When the abbé returned, it was dawn. Still pretending to be absorbed in the game, Franklin said, "What's the matter, dear abbé? You have the face of a man who is about to lose two games of chess. The goddess of night has just answered my prayers and has sent one of Mercury's agents here to aid me while you were gone."

"Ah, well, my dear doctor," the abbé responded, "darkness is appropriate to him and to thieves! But it is Phoebus, or at least the rosy fingers of Aurora, that reign at this moment."

Drawing the blinds and for the first time noticing that the

new day had actually arrived, Franklin said, "All Passy awakes, it is time for us to go to sleep!"

—*Franklin's Wit and Folly: The Bagatelles*, ed. Richard E. Amacher, 1953.

He lived to a fine age, and although he suffered from a kidney stone at eighty, his ingenuity comforted him.

He studiously read even while taking the long hot baths which were his relief from the stone. His tub was copper, shaped like a shoe. "He sits in the heel," Jeremy Belknap gossiped, "and his legs go under the vamp; on the instep he has a place to fix his book; and here he sits and enjoys himself."

—Van Doren.

Before he died he suggested an epitaph for himself.

The body of
Benjamin Franklin, printer,
(Like the cover of an old book,
Its contents worn out,
And stript of its lettering and gilding)
Lies here, food for worms!
Yet the work itself shall not be lost,
For it will, as he believed, appear once more,
In a new
And more beautiful edition,
Corrected and amended
By its Author!

—*Dictionary of Biographical Quotation*, eds. Richard Kenin and Justin Wintle, 1978.

Mather Byles 1707–1788

Mather Byles—grandson of Increase, nephew of Cotton—was a minister and versifier whose puns and pranks outlived his poetry. Byles was a Tory during the Revolution, and subject to prosecution.

In his trial before the justices of the peace a certain Ebenezer ____________, commonly known as "Ebby," was summoned to give evidence. The man was probably giving his testimony in too low a tone for the doctor to hear, when suddenly the old wit leaning forward, with his hand to his ear called out: "What does that Ebby-dunce say?" "Who is that man in uniform before your house?" once queried someone of the doctor while he was being guarded by a sentinel. "O," said Doctor Byles quickly, "that is my observe-a-Tory!"

—Arthur W. Eaton, *The Famous Mather Byles,* 1914.

Thomas Paine 1737–1809

The English revolutionary arrived in Philadelphia in 1774, where Benjamin Franklin befriended him. Common Sense *advocated separation from England at a time when political realists would have settled for reform.*

The effect of Paine's pamphlet, published on January 10, 1776, was swift and universal. Its sale was prodigious. In less than three months 120,000 copies had been sold, and Paine refused to take a penny of the profits, half of which he offered to the publisher, who ran some risk in printing such a revolutionary work, the other half being intended to purchase mittens for the troops. But the publisher, a Scottish republican named Robert Bell, collared the lot; and Paine, who ought to have made a fortune, was actually out of pocket over the venture, because he paid the printer's bill of a later and enlarged edition and the sum was never refunded.

—Hesketh Pearson, *Tom Paine: Friend of Mankind,* 1937.

Not everyone approved of Common Sense. *John Adams called it "a poor ignorant, malicious, short-sighted, crapulous mass. . . ."*

Denounced by Coleridge, damned in a Byronic epigram, his private life gossiped over, his deism considered blasphemous, Paine returned to England in 1787; he was—according to an American critic—"cocksure of bringing about a revolution." In London in 1792, a great poet saved him from probable execution.

On September 12th he attended a meeting of the "Friends of Liberty" and in a state that would now be called paranoiac he let forth a stream of "inflammatory eloquence." The next evening he was at the house of his friend Johnson, the publisher, in St. Paul's Churchyard, where he repeated what he had said to certain well-wishers, among them the poet, William Blake, who, however mystical in his writings, was realistic enough in everyday matters. When Paine got up to go, Blake rose too and, putting his hand on Tom's shoulder, said: "You must not go home, or you are a dead man." Blake showed extraordinary prevision, for the substance of Paine's speech had been digested by the authorities, who had already determined to act. The pleadings of his friends, backed by the promptings of a Frenchman who had been sent by the municipality of Calais to bring him over, had the desired effect, and Paine left London that night for Dover, going a round about way, through Rochester, Sandwich, and Deal, in order to evade the officers of the law, who had first gone to arrest him at Rickman's house. At Dover the customs official was on the lookout for suspicious characters and vigilantly attended to the luggage and pockets of Paine and his two companions. Several letters in Paine's trunk would have given the official courage if he had read them, for they were from French republican bodies; but fortunately he began with a letter from President Washington, in which that warrior prayed for the happiness of future generations, and the sight of so famous a signature attached to so proper a sentiment produced a spasm of timidity in the breast of the official, whose curiosity was quickly suppressed. Paine was allowed to go on board, and twenty minutes after the packet had sailed two steaming horses came clattering through the streets of Dover. The warrant for Paine's arrest had arrived.

—Pearson.

Although an outlaw in England, Paine was imprisoned in France as an enemy Englishman. He wrote The Age of Reason *(1794–95) in a French jail. He returned to the United States in 1802.*

His journey northwards passed without incident, except at Baltimore, where Mr. Hargrove, a minister of the sect founded by Swedenborg, accosted him:

"You are Mr. Paine?"

"Yes."

"My name is Hargrove, sir. I am minister of the New Jerusalem

Church here. We, sir, explain the Scripture in its true meaning. The key has been lost above four thousand years, and we have found it."

"Then it must have been very rusty," said Paine.

—Pearson.

When he was an old man, sick and poor, with few friends and many enemies, he kept his wit and his ill-humor. An artist named John Wesley Jarvis, who was visiting Paine, remembered a story.

His after-dinner snooze was still a regular feature of his day's program. One afternoon an old lady dressed in a scarlet cloak knocked at the door and inquired for him. Jarvis said that he was asleep.

"I am very sorry for that, as I want to see him very particularly," said the old lady.

Jarvis took her into Paine's room and woke him up. He hated being disturbed on these occasions and looked so fiercely at the lady in scarlet that she retreated a step or two.

"What do you want?" he demanded.

"Is your name Paine?"

"Yes."

"Well, then, I come from Almighty God, to tell you that if you do not repent of your sins and believe in our blessed Saviour, Jesus Christ, you will be damned, and - - - - -"

"Poh, poh! it is not true. You were not sent with any such impertinent message. Jarvis, make her go away. Pshaw! God would not send such a foolish ugly old woman as you about with his messages. Go away—be off—and shut the door."

—Pearson.

Thomas Jefferson 1743–1826

The third President of the United States and author of the Declaration of Independence, Jefferson graduated from William and Mary College in 1762 and went on to study law. When his great-granddaughter collected stories about him, she found this testimony to his courtroom prowess.

An idea of the impression made by him as an advocate in the court-room is given in the following anecdote, which we have from his eldest grandson, Mr. Jefferson Randolph. Anxious to learn how his grandfather had stood as a pleader, Mr. Randolph once asked an old man of good sense who in his youth had often heard Jefferson deliver arguments in court, how he ranked as a speaker, "Well," said the old gentleman, in reply, "it is hard to tell, because he always took the right side."

—Sarah Randolph, *The Domestic Life of Thomas Jefferson,* 1871.

When he was almost thirty he married Martha Wayles Skelton, a twenty-three-year-old widow whom his great-granddaughter described as "beautiful, with a lithe and excellently formed figure, a model of graceful and queenlike carriage."

So young and so beautiful, she was already surrounded by suitors when Jefferson entered the lists and bore off the prize. A pleasant anecdote about two of his rivals has been preserved in the tradition of his family. While laboring under the impression that the lady's mind was still undecided as to which of her suitors should be the accepted lover, they met accidentally in the hall of her father's house. They were on the eve of entering the drawing-room, when the sound of music caught their ear; the accompanying voices of Jefferson and his lady-love were soon recognized, and the two disconcerted lovers, after exchanging a glance, picked up their hats and left.

—Randolph.

He lived the life of a Virginia gentleman even as he wrote the documents of our political history.

It was his habit to the day of his death, no matter what his occupation, nor what office he held, to spend the hours between one and three in the afternoon on horseback. Noted for his bold and graceful horsemanship, he kept as riding-horses only those of the best blood of the old Virginia stock. In the days of his youth he was very exacting of his groom in having his horses always beautifully kept; and it is said that it was his habit, when his riding-horse was brought up for him to mount, to brush his white cambric handkerchief across the animal's shoulders and send it back to the stable if any dust was left on the handkerchief.

—Randolph.

An old friend remembered one of Jefferson's stories, of horses and horse-flies.

"While the question of Independence was before Congress, it had its meetings near a livery-stable. The members wore short breeches and silk stockings, and, with handkerchief in hand, they were diligently employed in lashing the flies from their legs. So very vexatious was this annoyance, and to so great an impatience did it arouse the sufferers, that it hastened, if it did not aid, in inducing them to promptly affix their signatures to the great document which gave birth to an empire republic.

"This anecdote I had from Mr. Jefferson at Monticello, who seemed to enjoy it very much, as well as to give great credit to the influence of the flies. He told it with much glee, and seemed to retain a vivid recollection of an attack, from which the only relief was signing the paper and flying from the scene."

—Randolph.

After not quite eleven years of marriage and six children, Martha Jefferson died. Their daughter, also named Martha, who was ten, remembered her father's devotion and his despair.

"For four months that she lingered he was never out of calling; when not at her bedside, he was writing in a small room which opened immediately at the head of her bed. A moment before the closing scene, he was led from the room in a state of insensibility by his sister, Mrs. Carr, who, with great difficulty, got him into the library, where he fainted, and remained so long insensible that they feared he never would revive. . . .

"He kept [to] his room three weeks, and I was never a moment from his side. He walked almost incessantly night and day, only lying down occasionally, when nature was completely exhausted, on a pallet that had been brought in during his long fainting-fit. . . . When at last he left his room, he rode out, and from that time he was incessantly on horseback, rambling about the mountain, in the least frequented roads, and just as often through the woods. In those melancholy rambles I was his constant companion—a solitary witness to many a burst of grief."

—Randolph.

He took his children's education in hand. In 1783 he wrote a letter to eleven-year-old Martha, who was attending school in Philadelphia while Jefferson participated in Congress at Annapolis.

"With respect to the distribution of your time, the following is what I should approve:

"From 8 to 10, practice music.

"From 10 to 1, dance one day and draw another.

"From 1 to 2, draw on the day you dance, and write a letter next day.

"From 3 to 4, read French.

"From 4 to 5, exercise yourself in music.

"From 5 till bed-time, read English, write, etc. . . .

"I expect you will write me by every post. Inform me what books you read, what tunes you learn, and inclose me your best copy of every lesson in drawing. . . . Take care that you never spell a word wrong. Always before you write a word, consider how it is spelt, and, if you do not remember it, turn to a dictionary. It produces great praise to a lady to spell well."

—Randolph.

He continued to write his children from France, where he followed Benjamin Franklin as minister from the United States to the Court of Saint-Germain. ("You replace Dr. Franklin," said the Count de Vergennes, the French foreign minister. "I succeed him; no one could replace him," answered Jefferson.)

It was on this visit that he contended with the great naturalist Georges Buffon. Daniel Webster repeated the story.

"It was a dispute in relation to the moose—the moose-deer, as it is called in New Hampshire—and in one of the circles of *beaux-esprits* in Paris. Mr. Jefferson contended for certain characteristics in the formation of the animal which Buffon stoutly denied. Whereupon Mr. Jefferson, without giving any one notice of his intention, wrote from Paris to General John Sullivan, then residing in Durham, New Hampshire, to procure and send him the whole frame of a moose. The General was no little astonished at a request he deemed so extraordinary; but, well acquainted with Mr. Jefferson, he knew he must have sufficient motive for it; so he made a hunting-party of his neighbors, and took the field. They captured a moose of unusual proportions, stripped it to the bone, and sent the skeleton to Mr. Jefferson, at a cost of fifty pounds sterling. On its arrival Mr. Jefferson invited Buffon and some other *savants* to a supper at his house, and exhibited his dear-bought specimen. Buffon immediately acknowledged his error, and expressed his great admiration for Mr. Jefferson's energetic determination to establish the truth. 'I should have consulted you, Monsieur,' he said, with usual French civility, 'before publishing my book on Natural History, and then I should have been sure of my facts.' "

—Randolph.

Jefferson's accomplishments ranged from the architecture of democracy to the architecture of architecture. He designed Monticello as well as the University of Virginia. He invented the dumbwaiter, the swivel chair, and decimal coinage. When John Kennedy honored forty-nine Nobel Prize winners in 1962, he called them "the most extraordinary collection of human talent, of human knowledge, that has ever been gathered at the White House—with the possible exception of when Thomas Jefferson dined alone." Of course he did not lack for detractors.

He was riding along one of the highways leading into Washington, when he overtook a man wending his way towards the city. Jefferson, as was his habit, drew up his horse and touched his hat to the pedestrian. The man returned the salutation, and began a conversation with the President—not knowing, of course, who he was. He at once entered upon the subject of politics—as was the habit of the day—and began to abuse the President, alluding even to some of the infamous calumnies against his private life. Jefferson's first impulse was to say "good-morning" and ride on, but, amused at his own situation, he asked the man if he knew the President personally?

"No," was the reply, "nor do I wish to."

"But do you think it fair," asked Jefferson, "to repeat such stories about a man, and condemn one whom you dare not face?"

"I will never shrink from meeting Mr. Jefferson should he ever come in my way," replied the stranger, who was a country merchant in high standing from Kentucky.

"Will you, then, go to his house to-morrow at - - o'clock and be introduced to him, if I promise to meet you there at that hour?" asked Jefferson, eagerly.

"Yes, I will," said the man, after a moment's thought. With a half-suppressed smile, and excusing himself from any further conversation, the President touched his hat and rode on.

Hardly had Jefferson disappeared from sight before a suspicion of the truth, which he soon verified, flashed through the stranger's mind. He stood fire, however, like a true man, and at the appointed hour the next day the card of Mr. ______, "Mr. Jefferson's yesterday's companion," was handed to the President. The next moment he was announced and entered. His situation was embarrassing, but with a gentlemanly bearing, though with some confusion, he began, "I have called, Mr. Jefferson, to apologize for having said to a stranger—"

"Hard things of an imaginary being who is no relation of mine," said Jefferson.

In going from Washington to Monticello, Jefferson generally left the city in the afternoon, and spent the first night of his journey with his friend Mr. William Fitzhugh, of Ravensworth, who lived nine or ten miles from Washington. It so happened that there lived near Ravensworth a Doctor Stuart, of Chantilly, who was a bitter Federalist, and consequently a violent hater of Jefferson, in whom he could not believe there was any good whatever. He was intimate, however, with Mr. Fitzhugh, and, being a great politician, generally found his way over to Ravensworth the morning after Jefferson's visit, to inquire what news he had brought from the capital.

On the occasion of one of these visits, while Mr. Fitzhugh and his distinguished guest were strolling round the beautiful lawn at Ravensworth enjoying the fresh morning air, a servant ran up to tell them that a negro man had cut himself severely with an axe. Mr. Fitzhugh immediately ordered the servant to go for a physician. Jefferson suggested that the poor negro might bleed to death before the doctor could arrive, and, saying that he himself had some little skill and experience in surgery, proposed that they should go and see what could be done for the poor fellow. Mr. Fitzhugh willingly acquiesced, and, on their reaching the patient, they found he had a severe cut in the calf of his leg. Jefferson soon procured a needle and silk, and in a little while had sewed up the wound and carefully bandaged the leg.

As they walked back from the negro's cabin, Jefferson remarked to his friend that, though the ways of Divine Providence were all wise and beneficent, yet it had always struck him as being strange that the thick, fleshy coverings and defenses of the bones in the limbs of the human frame were placed in their rear, when the danger of their fracture generally came from the front. The remark struck Fitzhugh as being an original and philosophical one, and served to increase his favorable impressions of his friend's sagacity.

Jefferson had not long departed and resumed his journey, before Dr. Stuart arrived, and greeted Mr. Fitzhugh with the question of, "What news did your friend give you, and what new heresy did the fiend incarnate attempt to instill into your mind?" "Ah! Stuart," Mr. Fitzhugh began, "you do Jefferson injustice; he is a great man, a very great man"; and then went on to tell of the accident which had befallen the negro, Jefferson's skill in dressing the wound, and his remark afterwards, which had made such an impression upon him.

"Well," cried Dr. Stuart, raising his hands with horror, "what is the world coming to! Here this fellow, Jefferson, after turning upside down every thing on the earth, is now quarrelling with God Almighty himself!"

—Randolph.

Jefferson's two terms as President were over and he had returned to Virginia when the War of 1812 broke out. His Monticello overseer, Captain Edmund Bacon, told this story.

"Mr. Jefferson had a very large library. When the British burnt Washington, the library that belonged to Congress was destroyed, and Mr. Jefferson sold them his. He directed me to have it packed in boxes and sent to Washington. John Hemings, one of his servants, made the boxes, and Burwell and I packed them up mostly. Dinsmore helped us some, and the girls, Ellen, Virginia, and Cornelia would come in sometimes and sort them out, and help us a good deal. There was an immense quantity of them. There were sixteen wagon loads. I engaged the teams. Each wagon was to carry three thousand pounds for a load, and to have four dollars a day for delivering them in Washington. If they carried more than three thousand pounds, they were to have extra pay. There were all kinds of books—books in a great many languages that I knew nothing about. There were a great many religious books among them—more than I have ever seen anywhere else."

—Rev. Hamilton W. Pierson, *Jefferson at Monticello,* 1862.

Jefferson took the time to found the University of Virginia. In 1817 he laid it out.

As we passed through Charlottesville, I went to old Davy Isaacs' store, and got a ball of twine, and Dinsmore found some shingles and made some pegs, and we all went on to the old field together. Mr. Jefferson looked over the ground some time, and then stuck down a peg. He stuck the very first peg in that building, and then directed me where to carry the line, and I stuck the second. He carried one end of the line, and I the other, in laying off the foundation of the University. He had a little rule in his pocket that he always carried with him, and with this he measured off the ground, and laid off the entire foundation, and then set the men at work. . . .

After the foundation was nearly completed, they had a great time laying the corner-stone. The old field was covered with carriages and people. There was an immense crowd there. Mr. Monroe laid the corner-stone. He was President at that time. He held the instruments, and pronounced it square. He only made a few remarks, and Chapman Johnson and several others made speeches. Mr. Jefferson—poor old man!—I can see his white head just as he stood there and looked on.

—Pierson.

His red hair turned sandy and then white, but his health remained excellent; when he died at eighty-four he had never lost a tooth. Captain Bacon admired his habits.

"Mr. Jefferson was always an early riser—arose at daybreak, or before. The sun never found him in bed. I used sometimes to think, when I went up there *very* early in the morning, that I would find him in bed; but there he would be before me, walking on the terrace.

"He never had a servant make a fire in his room in the morning, or at any other time, when he was at home. He always had a box filled with nice dry wood in his room, and when he wanted fire he would open it and put on the wood. He would always have a good many ashes in his fireplace, and when he went out he would cover up his fire very carefully, and when he came back he would uncover the coals and make on a fire for himself.

"He did not use tobacco in any form."

—Pierson.

But his old age was not tranquil. He was besieged by correspondence, by visitors, and partly in consequence by debt. He wrote John Adams:

"I do not know how far you may suffer, as I do, under the persecution of letters. . . .

". . . the year before the last. I found the number to be one thousand two hundred and sixty-seven, many of them requiring answers of elaborate research, and all to be answered with due attention and consideration. Take an average of this number for a week or a day, and I will repeat the question suggested by other considerations in mine of the 1st. Is this life?"

—Randolph.

His great-granddaughter wrote about the visitors, as many as fifty at a time. Captain Bacon suspected that many of them saved themselves the price of a tavern, although he acknowledged the power of curiosity.

No one could have been more hospitable than he was, and no one ever gave a more heartfelt or more cordial welcome to friends than he did; but the visits of those who were led by curiosity to Monticello was an annoyance which at times was almost painful to one of as retiring a disposition as he was. These visitors came at all hours and all seasons, and when unable to catch a glimpse of him in any other way, they not unfrequently begged to be allowed to sit in the hall, where, waiting until the dinner-hour arrived, they saw him as he passed through from his private apartments to his dining-room. On one occasion a female visitor, who was peering around the house, punched her parasol through a windowpane to get a better view of him.

—Randolph.

One visitor late in life was most welcome. Jefferson's grandson told the story.

"The lawn on the eastern side of the house at Monticello contains not quite an acre. On this spot was the meeting of Jefferson and Lafayette, on the latter's visit to the United States. The barouche containing Lafayette stopped at the edge of this lawn. His escort—one hundred and twenty mounted men—formed on one side in a semicircle extending from the carriage to the house. A crowd of about two hundred men, who were drawn together by curiosity to witness the meeting of these two venerable men, formed themselves in a semicircle on the opposite side. As Lafayette descended from the carriage, Jefferson descended the steps of the portico. The scene which followed was touching. Jefferson was feeble and tottering with age—Lafayette permanently lamed and broken in health by his long confinement in the dungeon of Olmutz. As they approached each other, their uncertain gait quickened itself into a shuffling run, and exclaiming, 'Ah, Jefferson!' 'Ah, Lafayette!' they burst into tears as they fell into each other's arms. Among the four hundred men witnessing the scene there was not a dry eye—no sound save an occasional suppressed sob. The two old men entered the house as the crowd dispersed in profound silence."

—Randolph.

Jefferson was eighty-two, Lafayette sixty-seven.

Bankrupt, in debt, with old friends unwilling or unable to help him, Jefferson began to fail in health. On the second of July, 1826, he fell into a coma; on the third he awoke to ask, "Is it the fourth?" He died on the fourth of July, on the fortieth anniversary of Independence Day, a few hours before his old rival John Adams, whose last words—"Thomas Jefferson still survives"—were mistaken.

Philip Freneau 1752–1832

The author of "The Indian Burying Ground," often called "the poet of the American Revolution," writing a friend in 1819, sounded the eternally plaintive note of the neglected author.

[I am] not a little out of humor that my two little volumes seemed to have fallen nearly deadborn from the Press, owing to the enmity of some, the politics of others, and the general inattention of all. I suppose, however, the truth is, that almost every person in your city has other and more serious matters to think of than mine, or at least such poetry as mine happens to be. . . .

After all, as I take it, the genius of the City of New York is so entirely commercial, that I suspect it swallows up all ideas of poetry, or refuses any attention to poetical productions, further than what is calculated for the fly market stalls, or to be sung at some Tammany Convivial Meeting or the Bacchanian Sons of the Hotels.

—*Unpublished Freneauana,* ed. Charles Heartman, 1918.

Timothy Dwight 1752–1817

Grandson of Jonathan Edwards, Dwight matriculated at Yale when he was thirteen, where he set an example by his self-discipline.

In those days, the ancient superstition touching the peculiar virtue of early-rising was still rampant at the college. The students were, indeed, not required to be at their morning devotions in the chapel earlier than half-past five o'clock in winter, or than half-past four in summer; but young Dwight, unable to sanction by his example the sluggish habits thus engendered, proudly betook himself from bed every morning in time to read and construe, before chapel, a hundred lines of Homer. Moreover, no day could at all justify itself in his eyes, unless it had yielded to him fourteen hours for close study. When he came to be a tutor at the college, his demands upon himself grew still more strict. Covetous of time, he determined to avoid all waste of it through so base a thing as bodily exercise, by extinguishing the need of bodily exercise; and this he expected to accomplish by gradually lessening the quantity of his food. His success was very striking. He so far reduced his diet that he was able to dine on just twelve mouthfuls. That, of course, was his most luxurious meal; but for breakfast and supper he deemed it his duty to be less abandoned to gluttony. Just how many mouthfuls he permitted to himself at those minor repasts, history does not record. However, having continued for about six months this system of diet, he was still unsatisfied with himself; he felt "less clearness of apprehension than was desirable"; and suspecting that the effect complained of might be due to the animal food which had thus far been a part of his daily regimen, he resolved thenceforth to confine himself to a vegetable diet, but without any increase in the number of mouthfuls allotted to each meal. By the summer of 1774, he had so far prospered in his hygienic experiments, that he had nineteen hard attacks of bilious colic in the course of two months. Being by that time reduced nearly to a skeleton, and having scarcely strength enough left to raise his head from the pillow, his father was summoned, and with the greatest difficulty took him home to Northampton, apparently to die.

—Moses Coit Tyler, *Three Men of Letters,* 1895.

But he did not die for some years, and was president of Yale University from 1795 through 1817. He also wrote poems, tried to bring contemporary literature into Yale's curriculum, and was first of the Connecticut Wits. Perhaps his greatest talent was as dictator.

". . . during the most of his life, all his writing of whatever sort, in prose or verse, was done by the hand of another; and in this act of dictation, his utterance was so ready and so sure, that no amanuensis could ever keep pace with it and no sentence thus produced was in need of amendment thereafter. While engaged in literary composition, he had no objection to the presence of company, and could 'proceed with two trains of thought by the hour together, conversing with the company, and also dictating to the amanuensis.'

". . . His mind took such firm hold of the subject which principally occupied it, that no ordinary force could separate it from its grasp. He was always conscious of the exact progress which he had made in every subject. When company, or any other occurrence, compelled him to break off suddenly, it would sometimes happen that he did not return to his employment until after the expiration of several days. On resuming his labors, all he required of his amanuensis was, to read the last word, or clause, that had been written; and he instantly would proceed to dictate as if no interruption had occurred. In several instances he was compelled to dictate a letter at the same time that he was dictating a sermon. In one, a pressing necessity obliged him to dictate three letters at the same time. He did so. Each amanuensis was fully occupied; and the letters needed no correction but pointing."

—Tyler.

Joel Barlow 1754–1812

Connecticut Wit and author of The Columbiad *(1807), Barlow published not only epic poetry but political theory and a new translation of the Psalms. Appointed minister to France in 1811, he died near Cracow in Poland on his way to conclude a treaty with Napoleon.*

He is remembered for a humble effort, of which his biographer describes the genesis. At this time Barlow had lived abroad for many years.

. . . At Chambery he remained several weeks, captivated by its scenery, finding great refreshment in the simple life of its people, and every day, amid its green mountain slopes and its pretty farmhouses, reminded of his own early life among the hills of western Connecticut. Writing to his wife, he said: "With you and a little farm among these romantic mountains and valleys, I could be happy, content; I would care no more for the pleasures of the plain. But America—the word is sweetness to my soul; it awakens all the tenderness of my nature." In this mood of patriotic reminiscence and of longing for home, it happened to him, one evening, as he sat down to supper "under the smoky rafters of a Savoyard inn," to find steaming hot upon the table the favorite dish of his own New England—"Hasty-Pudding,"—a dish for which he had many a time enquired in vain in London and Paris. The exile's heart was touched; and with genuine enthusiasm, and in lucky disregard of his usual poetic stilts, he then produced the one really popular poem he ever wrote,—the famous mock pastoral which bears the name of the dish that had so inspired him, and which in its opening lines preserves a glimpse of the romantic Italian scene wherein it was written, even as it is pervaded throughout by the homely tones and tints of domestic life in colonial New England:

> Ye Alps audacious, through the Heavens that rise,
> To cramp the day and hide me from the skies;
> Ye Gallic flags that, o'er their heights unfurled,
> Bear death to kings and freedom to the world,
> I sing not you. A softer theme I choose,
> A virgin theme, unconscious of the Muse,

But fruitful, rich, well suited to inspire
The purest frenzy of poetic fire.
. . .
Dear Hasty-Pudding . . .

—Moses Coit Tyler, *Three Men of Letters,* 1895.

Noah Webster 1758–1843

When Webster published his spelling book in 1783—his full dictionary would not appear until 1828—he ran afoul of religious usage by insisting that the suffixes -tion, -sion, and -cion be pronounced as single syllables. Supporters of the old two-syllable pronunciation showed a partisan wrath.

The story goes that a Scottish Presbyterian elder in western Pennsylvania rode furiously into town one morning and called out: "Have ye heard the news, mon? Do ye ken what's gaen on? Here's a book by a Yankee lad called Webster, teaching the children clean against the Christian religion!"

"How so?"

"Why, ye ken ye canna sing the psalms of David without having salvation and such words in four syllables, sal-va-si-on, and he's making all the children say salvashun."

—John S. Morgan, *Noah Webster,* 1975.

Webster's self-esteem was legendary, and the subject of legend.

William Cobbett, a writer who was to plague Noah for many years, probably invented one piece of Websterian apocrypha. Dr. Benjamin Rush, whom Noah had cultivated, supposedly met him upon his arrival and said: "How do you do, my dear friend. I congratulate you on your arrival in Philadelphia."

"Sir," Webster allegedly replied, "you may congratulate Philadelphia on the occasion."

—Morgan.

Charles Brockden Brown 1771–1810

Our first native professional author, Brown imported Grubb Street to American shores. His biographer tells us that an admiring English visitor found him

. . . wearing the typical dress of an author, "a great coat and shoes run down at the heel," and making his pen fly before him; in Brown's living quarters Davis saw a "dismal room in a dismal street"; being asked if he could not write with more facility were his window to command the prospect of Lake Geneva, Brown answered, "Good pens, thick paper, and ink well diluted would facilitate my composition more than the broadest expanse of water, or mountains rising above the clouds."

—David Lee Clark, *Charles Brockden Brown: Pioneer Voice of America,* 1952.

Daniel Webster 1782–1852

As boys, Daniel and his brother Ezekiel were famous for their laziness and for Daniel's wit.

Their father had given them directions to perform a specific labor during his temporary absence from home, but on his return at night, he found the labor unperformed, and, with a frown upon his face, questioned the boys in regard to their idleness. "What have you been doing, Ezekiel?" said the father. "Nothing, sir," was the reply. "Well, Daniel, what have *you* been doing?" "Helping Zeke, sir."

On another occasion, Daniel was put to mowing. He made bad work of it. His scythe was sometimes in the ground, and sometimes over the tops of all the grass. He complained to his father that his scythe was not hung right. Various attempts were made to hang it better, but with no success. His father told him, at length, he might hang it to suit himself; and he therefore hung it upon a tree, and said, "There, that's just right." His father laughed, and told him to let it hang there.

—Charles Lanman, *The Private Life of Daniel Webster,* 1858.

Tales were told of great powers of memory. An old schoolteacher—"Master Tappan"—in his eighty-sixth year recalled his celebrated pupil.

"Daniel was always the brightest boy in the school," said Master Tappan, "and Ezekiel the next; but Daniel was much quicker at his studies than his brother. He would learn more in five minutes than another boy in five hours. One Saturday, I remember, I held up a handsome new jack-knife to the scholars, and said, the boy who would commit to memory the greatest number of verses in the Bible by Monday morning should have it. Many of the boys did well; but when it came to Daniel's turn to recite, I found that he had committed so much that, after hearing him repeat some sixty or seventy verses, I was obliged to give up, he telling me that there were several chapters yet that he had learned. Daniel got that jack-knife. Ah! sir, he was remarkable even as a boy."

At this period of his life it was, too, that his eyes first fell upon the Constitution of the United States, of which he subsequently became the *chief expounder and defender*. And what is truly remarkable, is the fact that this particular copy was printed upon an imported cotton pocket handkerchief, according to a fashion of the time, which he chanced to stumble upon in a country store, and for which he paid, out of his own pocket, all the money he had, twenty-five cents. The evening of the day on which he obtained the document was wholly devoted to its close and attentive perusal, while seated before the fire, and by the side of his father and mother. What dreamer, on that night, in the wildest flights of his imagination, could have seen the result of that accident, or marked out the future career of that New Hampshire boy?

—Lanman.

His intelligence recognized, Webster attended Phillips Exeter Academy and Dartmouth College, unusual opportunities for a farm boy from the backwoods. His graduation from Dartmouth made a famous occasion.

Mr. Webster went through college in a manner that was highly creditable to himself and gratifying to his friends. He graduated at Dartmouth in 1801, and though it was universally believed that he ought to have received, and would receive the valedictory, that honor was not conferred upon him, but upon one whose name has since passed into forgetfulness. The ill-judging faculty of the college, however, bestowed upon him a diploma, but instead of pleasing, this commonplace compliment only disgusted him, and at the conclusion of the commencement exercises the disappointed youth asked a number of his classmates to accompany him to the green behind the college, where, in their presence, he deliberately *tore up* his honorary document, and threw it to the winds, exclaiming, "My industry may make me a great man, but this miserable parchment can not!" and immediately mounting his horse, departed for home.

—Lanman.

It was a time of political giantism, when leaders were gods or devils. In a lyrical outburst of grief over the death of the great one, Theodore Parker ennumerated the hero's qualities of soul.

He was a powerful man physically, a man of a large mould,—a great body and a great brain: he seemed made to last a hundred years. Since Socrates, there has seldom been a head so massive huge, save the stormy features of Michael Angelo,—

The hand that rounded Peter's dome,
And groined the aisles of Christian Rome;

he who sculptured Day and Night into such beautiful forms,—looked them in his face before he chiselled them in stone. The cubic capacity of his head surpassed all former measurements of mind. Since Charlemagne, I think there has not been such a grand figure in all Christendom. A large man, decorous in dress, dignified in deportment, he walked as if he felt himself a king. Men from the country, who knew him not, stared at him as he passed through our streets. The coal-heavers and porters of London looked on him as one of the great forces of the globe: they recognized a native king. In the Senate of the United States, he looked an emperor in that council. Even the majestic Calhoun seemed common compared with him. Clay looked vulgar, and Van Buren but a fox. His countenance, like Strafford's, was "manly black." His mind—

Was lodged in a fair and lofty room.
On his brow
Sat terror, mixed with wisdom; and, at once,
Saturn and Hermes in his countenance.

What a mouth he had! It was a lion's mouth; yet there was a sweet grandeur in his smile, and a woman's softness when he would. What a brow it was! what eyes! like charcoal fires in the bottom of a deep, dark well. His face was rugged with volcanic fires. . . .

—Theodore Parker, *A Discourse Occassioned by the Death of Daniel Webster,* 1853.

Others held divergent views. In his poem "Ichabod," Whittier took him to task as a fallen angel for appeasing the slave owners. With unaccustomed frankness of idiom, Emerson said that the "word 'honor' in the mouth of Mr. Webster is like the word 'love' in the mouth of a whore." It remained to John Quincy Adams to enumerate "the gigantic intellect, the envious temper, the ravenous ambition, and the rotten heart of Daniel Webster."

Washington Irving 1783–1859

With the publication of The Sketch Book *(1819–20) Washington Irving became the first American author to achieve international fame, a success in England as well as in America. When Charles Dickens first visited the United States in 1842, Irving presided over a dinner in New York at which Dickens rose to his feet and declared:*

"Washington Irving! Why, gentlemen, I don't go upstairs to bed two nights out of the seven . . . without taking Washington Irving under my arm; and when I don't take him, I take his own brother, Oliver Goldsmith. . . . Washington Irving—Diedrich Knickerbocker—Geoffrey Crayon—why, where can you go that they have not been there before? Is there an English farm—is there an English stream, an English city, or an English country-seat, where they have not been? Is there no Bracebridge Hall in existence? Has it no ancient shades or quiet streets?"

—Edward Wagenknecht, *Washington Irving: Moderation Displayed,* 1962.

A little later the two men met by accident in Baltimore, conversed—and were gifted by a watching admirer with what Dickens described as "a most enormous mint julep, wreathed with flowers." In later life Dickens remembered the occasion.

"We sat, one on either side of it, with great solemnity (it filled a respectably sized round table), but the solemnity was of very short duration. It was quite an enchanted julep, and carried us among innumerable people and places that we both knew. The julep held out far into the night, and my memory never saw him afterwards otherwise than as bending over it, with his straw, with an attempted air of gravity (after some anecdote involving some wonderfully droll and delicate observation of character), and then, as his eye caught mine, melting into that captivating laugh of his, which was the brightest and best I have ever heard."

—Wagenknecht.

After Irving had written his Spanish histories, in 1838 he undertook a related subject.

With his materials assembled and the writing three months along, the author was at work one winter day in the New York Society Library on Chambers Street when he was accosted by an acquaintance, a friend of the historian William Hickling Prescott, whose *History of the Reign of Ferdinand and Isabella* had recently been published in Boston. Irving's present interlocutor was sounding him, on behalf of Prescott, to discover what subject America's most famous author was then occupied with, as the younger historian in Boston "did not wish to come again across the same ground with him"—Irving's *Columbus* and *Conquest of Granada* having treated two of the most interesting aspects of Prescott's own subsequent book. "Mr. Irving asked: 'Is Mr. Prescott engaged upon an American subject?'

" 'He is,' was the reply.

" 'What is it? Is it the Conquest of Mexico?' Mr. Irving rapidly asked.

" 'It is,' answered Cogswell.

" 'Well, then,' said Mr. Irving, 'I *am* engaged upon that subject, but tell Mr. Prescott I abandon it to him. . . .' "

—Philip McFarland, *Sojourners,* 1979.

Irving often had difficulty getting down to the work of writing; and like so many authors, he continued to find difficulty with what he had written, even after he had written it.

Late in life, Irving told N. P. Willis that "he was always afraid to open the first copy that reached him of a new book of his own. He sat and trembled, and remembered all the weak points where he had been embarrassed and perplexed, and where he felt he might have done better—hating to think of the book, indeed, until the reviewers had praised it." In the year of his death, when he was asked which book he valued most highly, he replied, "I scarcely look with full satisfaction upon any; for they do not seem what they might have been. I often wish that I could have twenty years more, to take them down from the shelf one by one, and write them over."

—Wagenknecht.

James Fenimore Cooper 1789–1851

The author of the Leatherstocking novels undertook his first fiction as a challenge.

One evening when his wife was unwell he was reading aloud the latest English novel of family life. After a chapter or two he threw it aside in disgust, saying, "I could write you a better book than that myself." Susan turned what could have been merely conventional and inherently modest criticism into a challenge: it was absurd, he hated writing even a letter. He set to work almost immediately. . . .

—James Grossman, *James Fenimore Cooper,* 1949.

Universally read, Cooper has not remained universally popular. Mark Twain, in "Fenimore Cooper's Literary Offenses," found in "two-thirds of a page, Cooper has scored 114 offenses against literary art out of a possible 115. It breaks the record." And in England William Hazlitt noted that he "strutted through the streets with a very consequential air . . . as if he never relaxed in the assumption nor wished it to be forgotten by others, that he was the American Walter Scott."

Ivanhoe met Deerslayer in Paris, their dialogue recorded for all time:

"Est-ce Monsieur Cooper que j'ai l'honneur de voir?"
"Monsieur, je m'appelle Cooper."
"Eh bien, donc, je suis Walter Scott."

—M. A. DeWolfe Howe, *American Bookmen,* 1898.

William Cullen Bryant 1794–1878

The poetry began early. "Thanatopsis" was composed at eighteen or nineteen, but was not published until the poet's father discovered it among papers in a desk. Although Bryant continued to write and translate throughout the rest of his life, most of his energy was devoted to politics, newspaper editing, and controversy.

The diary of a New York gentleman tells us that he was shaving one morning, in 1831, when he saw Bryant, across the street, striking a fellow-editor, William L. Stone, with a cowhide, which Stone bore off when the bystanders had separated the combatants; and the incident is confirmed in a volume of reminiscences more recently published. It is the more to Bryant's credit that with a natural temper, to which, under the old amenities of journalism, he could give such vigorous utterance, he attained so true a poise and dignity as time went on.

—M. A. DeWolfe Howe, *American Bookmen,* 1898.

Bronson Alcott 1799–1888

Eldest of Transcendentalists was Bronson Alcott—and by all accounts the most unworldly. He was Emerson's friend, Thoreau's sometime colaborer *(see page 38)**, and father of* Little Women. *Everyone spoke a word about Bronson Alcott. Emerson called him "a tedious archangel," Carlyle "a venerable Don Quixote, whom nobody can laugh at without loving," Thoreau "a blue-robed man, whose fittest roof is the over-arching sky," and his daughter Louisa a "man up in a balloon, with his family and friends holding the ropes which confine him to earth, and trying to haul him down."*

There was no keeping him down for long.

. . . Bronson Alcott was always gentle with mosquitoes. As a vegetarian he probably deplored their carnivorous, or rather their "sanguinary" habits, but, on the other hand, as a Pythagorean he disliked to destroy life. Self-defense might extend to waving a mosquito aside, but never to slaughter. And the same forbearance was shown toward other insects. The legend still lives in Concord that when Alcott was residing at Hillside and was keeping a vegetable garden in the meadow across the road he used always to collect his potato bugs in a can, being careful not to injure them in any way, and then to dump them tenderly over the fence into Sam Staples' garden—Sam Staples being the famous deputy-sheriff who had an annual argument with Alcott about the propriety of his paying his poll tax, and who could never see any connection between the paying of such taxes and what the Federal Government was doing to Mexico, or was refusing to do for the slaves. He and Bronson Alcott remained always on the best of terms.

—Odell Shepard, *Pedlar's Progress: The Life of Bronson Alcott,* 1937.

When Fredrika Bremer reported her "Impressions of America" in her The Homes of the New World *(1854), she took special notice of Alcott.*

He himself has lived for many years only on bread, fruits, vegetables, and water; and this is what he wishes all other people to do; and, thus fed, they would become, according to his theory, beautiful, good, and happy beings. Sin is to be driven out by diet; and the sacred flood of enthusiasm would constantly flow in the human being purified and beautified by diet. Both the proposition and the conversation were in the clouds, although I made a few attempts to draw them forth. Alcott drank water, and we drank—fog. He has paid me a few visits, and has interested me as a study. He passed last evening with me and Benzon, and entertained us with various portions of his doctrine. Every bland and blue-eyed person, according to him, belongs to the nations of light, to the realm of light and goodness. I should think Lowell would be Alcott's ideal of a son of light; all persons, however, with dark eyes and hair are of the night and evil. I mentioned Wilberforce, and other champions of the light with dark hair. But the good Alcott hears an objection as if he heard it not. . . .

—Bremer.

. . . he took no great pleasure in the dinners Emerson often gave for persons of distinction who visited Concord. On one of these occasions the host is said to have dilated at considerable length, while carving a roast, upon the horrors of cannibalism. Bronson Alcott's face was working with amusement and barely suppressed glee until he suddenly burst forth with "But Mr. Emerson, if we are to eat meat at all why should we *not* eat the *best?*"

—Shepard.

Emerson told a story about him.

"Once an admirer sent him a twenty-dollar gold piece from Boston. About a week after, a mendicant, passing his door, asked alms.

" 'I have nothing,' said Alcott, answering from habit—'or yes, stay; I have, too; wait a minute!'

"And, running into his house, he returned with the gold coin, which he handed to the beggar. He took it and vanished. I believe a week or so afterwards he returned it to Mr. Alcott, with the remark that he found he was not able to either keep or spend it."

—Charles Woodbury, *Talks with Ralph Waldo Emerson,* 1890.

Emerson instigated the collaboration between Alcott and Thoreau.

In the summer of 1847, just before Thoreau left Walden, Emerson purchased two and a half acres of land on the eastern side of his property on Lexington Road and, tearing down the boundary fence hired Bronson Alcott for fifty dollars to build a summerhouse. It was undoubtedly one more example of Emerson's kindly ingenuity in providing an income for the improvident Alcott's family. Alcott was to be the architect of the projected summerhouse, but Emerson readily recognized that it would need Thoreau's practicality if it ever were to get built. . . .

On July 15 Alcott, Thoreau, and Emerson trekked out to Emerson's Walden woodlot and cut down and brought home twenty hemlock posts for the frame. Alcott, inept as ever, dreamily felled a tree without looking where it was going, and Thoreau, seeing that it was about to land in some neighboring trees, rushed at it while it was falling and by main strength carried out the trunk until it fell where he wanted it to.

On August 12 Alcott, with Thoreau's assistance, laid the timbers for the floor and some of the planks. The next day, having completed the planking, they set up nine corner joists—nine not for any practical purpose but because Alcott wished to honor the nine muses. . . .

As the structure grew, so did Alcott's plans. He kept Thoreau busy searching the woods for strangely gnarled branches and shoots, for they made up most of its skeletonic structure. . . . Thoreau's Aunt Maria reported to Prudence Ward:

> H_______ is building an arbour for Mr. Emerson, but H_______ says, A_______ pulls down as fast as he builds up, (quite characteristic) but it is rather expensive [and] somewhat tedious to poor Henry, to say nothing of endangering life and limbs for if there had not been a comfortable haystack near that he availed himself of by jumping into, when the top rafter was knock'd off, it might have been rather a serious affair. I do not know but I exaggerate a little, but at any rate jump he had to, and I believe it *was* in a hay mow. . . .

But Alcott was not perturbed in the least. Despite all the appended bric-a-brac and gingerbread, he boasted in his journal that the one merit of the structure was its simplicity. So enthralled with the project was he that he seldom reached home before dark, dreamed about it all night long, and awoke in the morning filled with an urgency to get immediately back to the task. . . .

It became the standard amusement of the townsfolk to make a daily examination of the weird progress of the building. . . . Only the coming of cold weather brought the project to a stop. Then he resumed work in the spring, and it was mid-summer before he was finally satisfied that it was completed. Emerson's mother promptly dubbed it "The Ruin" and the name stuck. The open architecture kept out neither the rain nor the mosquitoes, so it was never used. . . .

—Walter Harding, *The Days of Henry Thoreau,* 1965.

Thomas Carlyle, who spoke of the inevitability of loving this Don Quixote, also found Alcott a "terrible old bore," as Henry James, Sr., told it.

"It was almost impossible to be rid of him, and impossible also to keep him, for he would not eat what was set before him. Carlyle had potatoes for breakfast and sent for strawberries for Mr. Alcott, who, when they arrived, took them with the potatoes upon the same plate, where the two juices ran together and fraternized. This shocked Carlyle, who would eat nothing himself, but stormed up and down the room instead."

—M. A. DeWolfe Howe, *Memories of a Hostess,* 1922.

Ralph Waldo Emerson 1803–1882

Emerson started as conventionally as anyone, minister's son following father into pulpit. But soon his reputation altered. John Jay Chapman remembered, "My grandmother told me that the first time she ever heard Emerson's name was when a neighbor said to her: 'Oh have you heard? The new minister of the Second Church has gone mad.' "

He resigned his position when he found himself unable in good conscience to serve communion. In 1835, established as a professional lecturer, he settled in Concord where he would be among Alcott, Thoreau, Jones Very, Orestes Brownson, Margaret Fuller, and Nathaniel Hawthorne.

It became a story in Concord village that

. . . one night, before his wife had become completely accustomed to his habits, she awoke suddenly, and hearing him groping about the room, inquired anxiously,—

"My dear, are you unwell?"

"No, my love, only an idea."

—*Homes of American Authors,* 1852.

More practical than Alcott, Emerson seems nonetheless to have kept himself at a little distance from the reality of things. Once when he made gestures toward digging in his garden, his son spoke out in anxiety: "Look out, papa! you'll dig your leg." He therefore hired his young friend Thoreau, who imitated him in speech and manner, to dig his garden, perform handyman chores, and assist his wife during his frequent absences on lecture tours.

Apparently he was emotionally absent even when physically present: friends like Margaret Fuller resented his coldness, and he himself lamented that he could not show more affection to his wife: he said that he was better as a father than as a stove.

It is true that he was besieged by people who wanted to meet him. ("Whom God hath put asunder," he protested, "why should man join together?") His friends and peers praised him to the point of blasphemy. Holmes called him "an exotic transplanted from some angelic nursery," and Lowell added, "When one meets him the Fall of Adam seems a false

report." Herman Melville, more cynical and perhaps more shrewd, had another notion of Emerson's putative relationship to deity: "I could readily see in Emerson, not withstanding his merit, a gaping flaw. It was the insinuation that had he lived in those days when the world was made, he might have offered some valuable suggestions."

Charles J. Woodbury called him "a punctual man."

I remember one afternoon we were going to drive. As I came into his room, prompt to the moment, I saw that he was already waiting. Every book and manuscript were put out of reach, not even the newspaper before him; but there he sat on the edge of the lounge, his coat on his arm, his hat in his hand.

—*Talks with Ralph Waldo Emerson,* 1890.

An anonymous writer recollected coming to tea at Emerson's.

I had driven up with some friends to an esthetic tea at Mr. Emerson's. It was in the winter, and a great wood fire blazed upon the hospitable hearth. There were various men and women of note assembled, and I, who listened attentively to all the fine things that were said, was for some time scarcely aware of a man who sat upon the edge of the circle, a little withdrawn, his head slightly thrown forward upon his breast, and his bright eyes clearly burning under his black brow. As I drifted down the stream of talk, this person, who sat silent as a shadow, looked to me, as Webster might have looked, had he been a poet,—a kind of poetic Webster. He rose and walked to the window, and stood quietly there for a long time, watching the dead white landscape. No appeal was made to him, nobody looked after him, the conversation flowed steadily on as if every one understood that his silence was to be respected. It was the same thing at table. In vain the silent man imbibed esthetic tea. Whatever fancies it inspired did not flower at his lips. But there was a light in his eye which assured me that nothing was lost. So supreme was his silence that it presently engrossed me to the exclusion of every thing else. There was very brilliant discourse, but this silence was much more poetic and fascinating. Fine things were said by the philosophers, but much finer things were implied by the dumbness of this gentleman with heavy brows and black hair. When he presently rose and went, Emerson,

with the "slow, wise smile" that breaks over his face, like day over the sky, said:

"Hawthorne rides well his horse of the night."

—*Homes of American Authors.*

As Emerson and Whittier were driving in a carriage one day, Whittier asked a question.

. . . "What does thee pray for, friend Emerson?"

"Well," said Mr. Emerson, "when I first open my eyes upon the morning meadows, and look out upon the beautiful world, I thank God that I am alive, and that I live so near Boston."

—Mary B. Claflin, *Personal Recollections of John Greenleaf Whittier,* 1893.

The acquaintance between Emerson and Walt Whitman began when Whitman mailed Emerson a proof copy of the first edition of Leaves of Grass *in 1855. Emerson's magnanimous response, to a man of whom he knew nothing, was this famous letter.*

Concord, Massachusetts, 21 July, 1855

Dear Sir—I am not blind to the worth of the wonderful gift of *Leaves of Grass.* I find it the most extraordinary piece of wit and wisdom that America has yet contributed. I am very happy in reading it, as great power makes us happy. It meets the demand I am always making of what seemed the sterile and stingy Nature, as if too much handiwork, or too much lymph in the temperament, were making our Western wits fat and mean.

I give you joy of your free and brave thought. I have great joy in it. I find incomparable things said incomparably well, as they must be. I find the courage of treatment which so delights us, and which large perception only can inspire.

I greet you at the beginning of a great career, which yet must have had a long foreground somewhere, for such a start. I rubbed my eyes a little, to see if this sunbeam were no illusion; but the solid sense of the book is a sober certainty. It has the best merits, namely, of fortifying and encouraging.

I did not know until I last night saw the book advertised in a newspaper that I could trust the name as real and available for a post-office. I wish to see my benefactor, and have felt much like striking my tasks and visiting New York to pay you my respects.

R. W. Emerson

—Edmund Wilson, *The Shock of Recognition,* 1955.

Without asking Emerson's permission, Whitman arranged for the letter to be printed in the New York Tribune. *Emerson's friend Frank Bellew called on him later in the year and heard Emerson speak enthusiastically about the new poet.*

" 'I wrote at once,' he said, 'a letter to the author, congratulating him.' 'Yes,' I replied, 'I read it.' 'How? When? Have you been to New York?' 'No, I read it in the New York *Tribune.*' 'In the New York *Tribune?* No, no! Impossible! He cannot have published it!' he exclaimed, with much surprise. I assured him that I had read it a few weeks before in that paper.

" 'Dear! dear!' he muttered, 'that was very wrong, very wrong indeed. That was merely a private letter of congratulation. Had I intended it for publication I should have enlarged the *but* very much—enlarged the *but,*' repeating 'enlarged the *but*' twice and biting the 'but' off with his lips, and for a moment looking thoughtfully out of the window."

—Wilson.

The next year a new edition of Leaves of Grass *arrived in Concord. Josiah Quincy was visiting Emerson.*

"Mr. Emerson came into his study at Concord where I was sitting, bearing in his hand a book which he had just received. This was the new edition of Whitman's book with the words 'I greet you at the beginning of a great career. R. W. Emerson,' printed in gold letters upon the cover. Emerson looked troubled, and expressed annoyance that a sentence from a private letter should be wrenched from its context and so emblazoned. He afterwards gave me the book, saying that the inside was worthy attention even though it came from one capable of so misusing the cover. I noted the incident because at no other time had I seen a cloud of dissatisfaction darken that serene countenance."

—Wilson.

In 1860, for a third edition, published in Boston, Whitman entrained north to Massachusetts and met with Emerson for the first time. Whitman remembered how Emerson tried to persuade him to omit poems certain to excite outrage.

"Up and down this breadth by Beacon Street, between these same old elms, I walk'd for two hours, of a bright sharp February mid-day twenty-one years ago, with Emerson, then in his prime, keen, physically and morally magnetic, arm'd at every point, and when he chose, wielding the emotional just as well as the intellectual. During those two hours he was the talker and I the listener. It was an argument-statement, reconnoitring, review, attack, and pressing home, (like an army corps in order, artillery, cavalry, infantry) of all that could be said against that part (and a main part) in the construction of my poems, *Children of Adam.* More precious than gold to me that dissertion—it afforded me, ever after, this strange and paradoxical lesson; each point of E.'s statement was unanswerable, no judge's charge ever more complete or convincing, I could never hear the points better put—and then I felt down in my soul the clear and unmistakable conviction to disobey all, and pursue my own way."

—Wilson.

Emerson's advice, Whitman told Horace Traubel years later, was "neither moral nor literary" but "given with an eye to my worldly success." Emerson did not, said Whitman without petulance, "see the significance of the sex element."

Emerson called on Whitman in Brooklyn—"I can easily see how Carlyle should have likened Emerson's appearance in their household to the apparition of an angel"—and on another occasion invited Whitman to dinner at the Astor House in New York City; but from this visit Emerson returned to Boston irritated: Whitman had come to dine at the Astor House without a coat!

It was probably the latter meeting which turns up—perhaps distorted by Emerson's aging memory, perhaps by the storyteller—in an account given by the Englishman Edward Carpenter who spoke with Emerson in 1877.

"When I spoke of Whitman and asked what he thought of him, he laughed (a little nervously, I thought) and said, 'Well, I thought he had some merit at one time: there was a good deal of promise in his first edition—but he is a wayward fanciful man.' (He used a third epithet beside *wayward* and *fanciful,* something like *violent,* but I hardly think as strong as that.) 'I saw him in

New York and asked him to dine at my hotel. He shouted for a "tin mug" for his beer. Then he had a noisy fire-engine society. And he took me there, and was like a boy over it, as if there had never been such a thing before.' He went on, in words which I do not recall, to object to the absence of meter in *Leaves of Grass. . . .*"

—Wilson.

Although most reports of Emerson emphasize his benignity, there are moments when he behaved like any other writer. William Dean Howells, editing the Atlantic Monthly, *observed a moment less than Olympian:* genus irritabile vatum.

Sometimes my utmost did not avail, or more strictly speaking it did not avail in one instance with Emerson. He had given me upon much entreaty a poem which was one of his greatest and best, but the proof-reader found a nominative at odds with its verb. We had some trouble in reconciling them, and some other delays, and meanwhile Doctor Holmes offered me a poem for the same number. I now doubted whether I should get Emerson's poem back in time for it, but unluckily the proof did come back in time, and then I had to choose between my poets, or acquaint them with the state of the case, and let them choose what I should do. I really felt that Doctor Holmes had the right to precedence, since Emerson had withheld his proof so long that I could not count upon it; but I wrote to Emerson, and asked (as nearly as I can remember) whether he would consent to let me put his poem over to the next number, or would prefer to have it appear in the same number with Doctor Holmes's; the subjects were cognate, and I had my misgivings. He wrote me back to "return the proofs and break up the forms." I could not go to this iconoclastic extreme with the electrotypes of the magazine, but I could return the proofs. I did so, feeling that I had done my possible, and silently grieving that there could be such ire in heavenly minds.

—William Dean Howells, *Literary Friends and Acquaintances,* 1902.

Loss of memory came early for Emerson. James Elliot Cabot observed him when he was only sixty-one, with eighteen more years to live.

"I remember his getting up at a dinner of the Saturday Club, on the Shakespeare anniversary in 1864, to which some guests had been invited, looking about him tranquilly for a moment or two, and then sitting down; serene and unabashed, but unable to say a word upon a subject so familiar to his thoughts from boyhood."

—M. A. DeWolfe Howe, *Holmes of The Breakfast Table,* 1939.

In the year of his death—of the New Englanders only Holmes would survive him—he attended Longfellow's funeral.

. . . and the body was then carried, "under the gently falling snow," to Mount Auburn Cemetery, where it was buried. One of the few friends present was Emerson, who had himself only a few weeks more to live, and whose hold on the factual had almost entirely failed him. Howells, who was also present, tells us that, after the services were over, Emerson turned to his daughter Ellen and said: "The gentleman we have just been burying was a sweet and beautiful soul; but I forget his name."

—Newton Arvin, *Longfellow: His Life and Work,* 1962.

Nathaniel Hawthorne 1804–1864

Nathaniel Hawthorne attended Bowdoin College, classmate of Henry Wadsworth Longfellow and Franklin Pierce, who became the fourteenth President of the United States.

Hawthorne finished *The Scarlet Letter* on February 3, 1850. On the evening of that day he read the latter part of the book to his wife who—as always—had religiously refrained from any inquiry or intermeddling during the process of composition. "It broke her heart," Hawthorne wrote . . . "and sent her to bed with a grievous headache, which I look upon as a triumphant success."

—Randall Stewart, *Nathaniel Hawthorne,* 1948.

Fame brought its usual annoyances. Hawthorne wrote in a letter:

"I forgot to mention that I was recognized in some inscrutable way by a gentleman in the train, who brought us to the door in his carriage, and put his house, his beach, and everything else, at our disposal. O ye Heavens! How absurd that a man should spend the best of his years in getting a little mite of reputation, and then immediately find the annoyance of it more than the profit."

—Julian Hawthorne, *Nathaniel Hawthorne and His Wife,* 1884.

Hawthorne enjoyed some company, under some circumstances. His wife described a scene on the Concord River, three monsters of literature at their play. . . .

"One afternoon Mr. Emerson and Mr. Thoreau went with him [Hawthorne] down the river. Henry Thoreau is an experienced skater, and was figuring dithyrambic dances and Bacchic leaps on the ice—very remarkable, but very ugly, methought. Next him followed Mr. Hawthorne, wrapped in his cloak, moved like a self-impelled Greek statue, stately and grave. Mr. Emerson closed the line, evidently too weary to hold himself erect, pitching headforemost, half lying on the air."

—Rose Hawthorne Lathrop, *Memories of Hawthorne,* 1897.

Ordinarily he was not a social being. "I doubt whether I have ever really talked with half a dozen persons in my life," he wrote, "men or women." Henry James, Sr., said that he had "the look all the time . . . of a rogue who suddenly finds himself in the company of detectives." Even with his skating companions, he could be ill at ease under other circumstances.

Once Emerson and Thoreau arrived to pay a call. They were shown into the little parlor upon the avenue, and Hawthorne presently entered. Each of the guests sat upright in his chair like a Roman Senator. . . . The host sat perfectly still, or occasionally propounded a question which Thoreau answered accurately, and there the thread broke short off. Emerson delivered sentences that only needed the setting of an essay, to charm the world; but the whole visit was a vague ghost of the Monday Evening Club at Mr. Emerson's,—it was a great failure. Had they all been lying idly upon the river brink, or strolling in Thoreau's blackberry pastures, the result would have been utterly different. But imprisoned in the proprieties of a parlor, each a wild man in his way, with a necessity of talking inherent in the nature of the occasion, there was only a waste of treasure. This was the only "call" in which I ever knew Hawthorne to be involved.

—*Homes of American Authors,* 1852.

Out of the silence, certain episodes speak of the Puritan's continual self-examination.

At one time, in his younger days, he was accustomed to sup frequently at a friend's table, where the lady of the house made very excellent tea, which the guest was very fond of. One evening, in sending down to replenish his cup, she remarked, "Now, Mr. Hawthorne, I am going to play Mrs. Thrale to your Johnson. I know you are a slave to my tea." Mr. Hawthorne made no reply, but contented himself with mentally noting that he had been guilty of a personal indulgence; and during five years, dating from that evening, he never touched another cup of tea. Every aspect of his life reflects the same principle; he could not endure the thought of being in the thraldom of any selfish or sensuous habit.

—Julian Hawthorne.

He once described a gentleman inspecting a workhouse in the English city of Liverpool, who was followed by a child.

This child—this sickly, wretched, humor-eaten infant, the offspring of unspeakable sin and sorrow, whom it must have required several generations of guilty progenitors to render so pitiable an object as we beheld it—immediately took an unaccountable fancy to the gentleman just hinted at. It prowled about him like a pet kitten, rubbing against his legs, following everywhere at his heels, pulling at his coat-tails, and, at last, exerting all the speed that its poor limbs were capable of, got directly before him and held forth its arms, mutely insisting on being taken up.

—Nathaniel Hawthorne, *Our Old Home,* 1863.

Hawthorne ventured the opinion that this gentleman "did a heroic act and effected more than he dreamed of toward his final salvation when he took up the loathsome child." He did not add that he was himself the gentleman. His third-person account appeared in Our Old Home, *essays about England published after his term as American consul in Liverpool. After his death, his wife published the notebooks on which he had based his essays, where he speaks firsthand about "the loathsome child."*

. . . this little sickly, humor-eaten fright . . . expressed such perfect confidence that it was going to be taken up and made much of, that it was impossible not to do it. It was as if God had promised the child this favor on my behalf . . . and that I must needs fulfill the contract.

—Nathaniel Hawthorne, *Passages from the English Notebooks,* 1870.

After England the Hawthornes spent two years in Italy. Their son Julian, writing a biography many years later, told a story that began in Italy.

. . . In the year 1858 Nathaniel Hawthorne was living with his family in the Villa Montauto, just outside the walls of Florence. Among his near neighbors during that summer . . . were Mr. and Mrs. Robert Browning; and they were often visitors at Montauto. Mrs. Browning was at that time deeply interested in spiritualism; and in the course of some discussions on the subject, it was accidentally discovered that the governess in Mr. Hawthorne's family, a young American lady of great attainments and lovely character, was a medium,—the manifestation of her capacities in this direction being by writing. If she held a pencil over a sheet of paper for a minute or so, her hand would seem to be seized, or inspired with motion, and words, sentences, or pages would be written down, sometimes rapidly, sometimes slowly, and in various totally dissimilar styles of handwriting, none of which bore any resemblance to the lady's own. . . .

One day, in the midst of some heavenly-minded disquisition from the dead mother of one of the onlookers, the medium's hand seemed to be suddenly arrested, as by a violent though invisible grasp, and, after a few vague dashes of the pencil, the name of "Mary Rondel" was written across the paper in large, bold characters. . . . at last somebody put the question, who Mary Rondel was? Hereupon the medium's hand was again seized as before, and some sentences were rapidly dashed off, to the effect that Mary Rondel had no rest, and demanded the sympathy of Nathaniel Hawthorne. Subsequent inquiries elicited from Mary Rondel the information that she had been, in her lifetime, connected in some way with the Hawthorne family; that she had died in Boston about a hundred years previous, and that nothing could give her any relief but Nathaniel Hawthorne's sympathy. . . .

From this time forth, Mary Rondel, violent, headstrong, often ungrammatical, and uniformly eccentric in her spelling, was the chief figure among the communicants from the other world. She would descend upon the circle like a whirlwind, at the most unexpected moments, put all the other spirits unceremoniously to flight, and insist upon regaling her audience with a greater or less number of her hurried, confused, and often obscure utterances. But the burden of them all was, that at last, after her long century of weary wandering, she was to find some relief and consolation in the sympathy of Nathaniel Hawthorne. . . .

Before long . . . the seances were discontinued. . . . Mr. Hawthorne moved his family to Rome, where other interests soon put Mary Rondel and the rest of her tribe out of their heads. In 1859 Hawthorne returned to England, whence, after a year's sojourn, he sailed for America; and there, in 1864, he died.

. . . after Nathaniel Hawthorne's death his son [the author of this narrative] came into possession of a number of letters, documents, manuscripts, books, and other remains. . . . Among these was a large, old-fashioned folio volume, bound in brown leather, and much defaced in binding and paper by the assiduous perusal of half a dozen generations. It was a copy of an early edition of Sir Philip Sidney's "Arcadia," and had been brought to New England for Major William Hathorne, whose autograph appeared upon the margin of one or two pages. In turning over these venerable leaves, brown with age and immemorial thumb-marks, there appeared, written in faded ink, the name of Mary Rondel; and opposite to it, in the same chirography, that of Daniel Hathorne.

This unexpected discovery interested the finder not a little; and his interest was increased when, on coming to the latter part of the volume, which is mainly taken up with love-sonnets and other amatory versification, he found certain verses underlined, or surrounded by a wavy mark in ink, together with such inscriptions (also in bold Daniel's handwriting) as "Lucke upon this as if I my own self spacke it," "Pray mistris read this," and so forth. . . .

Conceiving that some information on the subject might be forthcoming from certain elder connections of the family, resident in Salem, application was made to them, but without saying anything about the spiritualistic communications in Florence. The following facts were elicited: that, in 1755 or thereabouts, when Daniel was over twenty-one years old, he fell in love with a young woman named Mary Rondel, who lived in Boston. She returned his love; but, somehow or other, the affair ended unhappily, and Mary soon after died.

—Julian Hawthorne.

Hawthorne returned from England and Italy to Concord for the last four years of his life. The Liverpool consulship had been a political spoil, repayment by President Franklin Pierce (Hawthorne's old Bowdoin roommate) for the only campaign biography ever composed by a major novelist. It was on a trip with Franklin Pierce, who failed to win re-election for a second term, that Hawthorne died suddenly in Plymouth, New Hampshire.

Henry Wadsworth Longfellow 1807–1882

Longfellow was already a famous poet and a professor at Harvard when he married Frances Appleton in 1843. Her father gifted the newlyweds with Craigie House, their mansion on Brattle Street. Emerson did not approve of this affluence. He wrote in his journal:

"If Socrates were here, we could go and talk with him; but Longfellow, we cannot go and talk with; there is a palace, and servants, and a row of bottles of different coloured wines, and wine glasses, and fine coats."

—Newton Arvin, *Longfellow: His Life and Work,* 1962.

After eighteen years of marriage and five children, the life at Craigie House was canceled in one minute.

George William Curtis once told Howells that, one summer day in 1861, he had been driving past the Craigie House with Dr. Holmes, and that the latter had said he trembled to look at the house, "for those who lived there had their happiness so perfect that no change, of all the changes which must come to them, could fail to be for the worse." It was a strangely premonitory thought. Only a short time later, that perfect happiness was destroyed by a peculiarly cruel and shocking blow. Fanny Longfellow, sitting one day in the library before an open window, dropped some burning wax, or perhaps a lighted match, on her summer dress, and in a moment she was wrapped in flames. Though Longfellow, awakened from a nap in his study nearby, attempted to put out the flames by throwing a small rug about her, she was already too terribly burned to be saved, and on the following day she died. Longfellow himself had been so badly burned about his face and hands that he was unable to attend her funeral at Mount Auburn three days later. It was the anniversary of their wedding day.

—Arvin.

This abrupt reversal shocked the world. Nathaniel Hawthorne summed up the general notion.

I cannot at all reconcile this calamity to my sense of fitness. One would think that there ought to have been no deep sorrow in the life of a man like him; and now comes this blackest of shadows, which no sunshine hereafter can ever penetrate!

—M. A. DeWolfe Howe, *Memories of a Hostess,* 1922.

Out of the horror came the patriarch of American letters with the white beard, for Longfellow's facial burns kept him from shaving. For years he endured depression. Friends urged upon him the task of translating Dante's Divine Comedy. *This "dandy Pindar," in Margaret Fuller's phrase, noted of himself:*

"Most of the time am alone; smoke a great deal; wear a broad-brimmed black hat, black frock-coat, a black cane. Molest no one. Dine out frequently. In winter go much into Boston society."

—*Dictionary of Biographical Quotation,* eds. Richard Kenin and Justin Wintle, 1978.

Oxford and Cambridge gave him honorary degrees, and the Queen received him. At home he entertained traveling dignitaries and was besieged in person and by post.

Hardly an English man of letters, traveling in America, failed to pay his respects to this most beloved of American writers, and often they were entertained at meals. Dickens, on his first trip to this country, had been given "a bright little breakfast"—the brightness of which seems not to have been dimmed by the presence of "the Unitarian pope," Andrews Norton—and the two young writers struck up a lifelong friendship. Such men as Trollope, Charles Kingsley, Wilkie Collins, and Monckton Milnes arrived on Brattle Street as a matter of course. When Dom Pedro II, Emperor of Brazil, was traveling in this country, not officially but privately—like a modern Haroun al Raschid, said Longfellow—he expressed his desire to dine with the poet, and rather imperially named the persons—Emerson, Lowell, and Holmes—whom he wished also to have invited. Perhaps the most unlikely visitor, from our point of view, was the Russian anarchist Mikhail Bakunin, who had escaped from Siberia a few months earlier and, having made his way eastward across the Pacific, en route to Europe, had reached the northern United States, and came to call at the Craigie House. He stayed so long, Ernest Longfellow tells us, that he had to be invited to lunch; "Yiss," he answered, "and I will dine with you too"—as he did. He may have proved a somewhat fatiguing guest—his vehemence was notorious—but Longfellow seems to have been charmed by him, and describes him in his journal as "a giant of a man, with a most ardent, seething temperament."

These were distinguished visitors, but they did not outnumber the succession of simple, often touching, and sometimes afflicting callers, mostly Americans, who came to constitute a serious problem for Longfellow, but who were invariably received with courtesy and consideration—though some of them belonged in that category of "books, bores, and beggars" which even he came to count as one of the principal vexations of daily life. Fortunately his humor was usually equal to the occasion, and he could describe some of his guests with characteristic good nature. There was the Englishman who remarked that, in other countries, you know, we go to see ruins and all that—"but you have no ruins in your country, and I thought I would call and see *you.*" There was the young Westerner who asked Longfellow how old he was, and when the poet answered "Seventy," rejoined, "I have seen a good many men of your age who looked much younger than you." A German woman, with a strong accent, called to talk with him about "The Building of the Ship," which she was planning to read in public, and which she called "The Lunch of the Sheep." As he was standing at the front door one August morning, a woman in black came up to him and inquired whether this was the house in which Longfellow had been born; when he explained that is was not, she went on to ask, "Did he die here?"

His correspondence, too, had assumed appalling proportions, and his kindness was too genuine to allow him to turn a deaf ear to any of it. Most of the appeals he received, of course, were requests for his autograph, sometimes for *quantities* of autographs to be sold at benefits and the like; perhaps there were not many appeals, however, though there was one, for "your autograph in your own handwriting." Many of these demands came from people who wished Longfellow to read and criticize their manuscripts, like the man in Maine who had written an epic poem on the Creation, and had "done up" the six days' work "in about six hundred lines." Other appeals were for original poems; a stranger in the West put in an order for two poems "on friendship, or a subject like that, for the album of a young lady who is a very particular friend"; he also directed Longfellow to "send the bill with the articles."

—Arvin.

Longfellow himself paid a courtesy call on a poet whose work he could not approve.

On a visit to the Centennial Exposition in Philadelphia in 1876, Longfellow was taken by his host, the wealthy George W. Childs, over the river to Camden to call on Whitman, as he could easily have declined to do. Their colloquy, it appears, had to be brief, owing to delays in transportation, but it must have been friendly enough; four years later, during his last visit to Boston, Whitman felt free and even obliged to go out to Cambridge and call on Longfellow. He said later that he would not soon forget "his lit-up face and flowing warmth and courtesy, in the modes of what is called the old school."

—Arvin.

John Greenleaf Whittier 1807–1892

Born in the same year as Longfellow, the Quaker poet came from a different class in the new country—from farming people without money and largely without education. Whittier wished to write a people's poetry, and loved Robert Burns except for his "lawless passion," as an early critic put it. A fierce abolitionist, he devoted much of his life to writing on its behalf.

Unlike the Bostonian poets, Whittier did not enjoy society. His friend Mary Claflin told a story.

On one occasion I invited some of his old acquaintances to an afternoon tea. Knowing his aversion to meeting people, and fearing he might flit, I did not speak to him of my plan, but contrived by some artifice to keep him in the house till the guests should arrive.

He was so shy that he could not be counted upon, and often, if he suspected company had been invited to meet him, he would slip away. With his keen perception and insight, he discovered that something a little out of the ordinary course was going on, and he said, "What is thee going to do? I think thee is going to do something."

I replied, "Why do you think so, Mr. Whittier?"

"Oh, I know thee is going to have some kind of a fandango."

When the guests came he received them most cordially, and treated them as though they were conferring a great favor upon him. After they had left, he said, with a boy's shyness, "I think thee managed that very well."

—Mary B. Claflin, *Personal Recollections of John Greenleaf Whittier,* 1893.

Occasionally his beliefs clashed with his affections.

Mr. Whittier loved beautiful things, though he was careful not to express much admiration of pictures and statuary, because that would be inconsistent with his Quaker ideas. He called everything in the way of statuary, from a tiny figure to a colossal bust, "a graven image." In the house of one of his friends whom he frequently visited, there was a life-size figure of Ruth, which turned on a pivot. He was often seen examining this in private, and evidently admiring it, and he was quite disturbed one day when the figure was by accident turned in such a way as to present the back, rather than the face, to those who approached it, and he said to his hostess, "Thy graven image appears to be backing folks t' much. I think thee better turn her round."

—Claflin.

Nor was he wholly without vanity. One day Mary Claflin found him after he had read unfavorable remarks about his work in an English magazine.

He stood before the fire, with his hands clasped behind him, looking, as it were, into space, and after a long silence he said, with a sigh: "Tennyson has written a perfect poem. It is a great thing to write a *perfect* poem. *Tennyson* is so grand."

—Claflin.

*Matthew Arnold journeyed from Boston to Amesbury to visit. And a world traveler encountered earlier among these anecdotes (**see page 53**) paid him tribute.*

When Dom Pedro, the Emperor of Brazil, was visiting Boston, he was invited one morning to a private parlor to meet some of the men who have made this city famous in the world of letters. As one after another was presented to him, he received each one graciously, but without enthusiasm. But when Mr. Whittier's name was announced his face suddenly lighted up, and, grasping the poet's hand, he made a gesture as though he would embrace him; but seeing that to be contrary to the custom of the Friends, he passed his arm through that of Mr. Whittier's, and drew him gently to a corner where he remained with him, absorbed in conversation, until the time came to leave. The Emperor, taking the poet's hand in both his own again, bade him a reluctant farewell, and turned to leave the room, but still unsatisfied, he was heard to say, "Come with me," and they passed slowly down the staircase, his arm around Mr. Whittier.

—Claflin.

As Mary Claflin told it, Whittier left this world in a benignant spirit.

The beautiful life finished its earthly course on a perfect summer's morning, and he entered the life for which he longed. His last words were characteristic. He was breathing out his life; his eyes were closed, and his friends stood around the bed about which had clustered so much loving interest, waiting and watching for the last look, or the last word, when he opened those eyes which had often seemed to look into the mysteries of eternity, and said with labored breath: "My—love—to—the—world."

—Claflin.

Abraham Lincoln 1809–1865

The sixteenth President, born in a log cabin to illiterate parents, is the subject of more tales than any other American. Some are apocryphal, but many are genuine. Many do not concern Lincoln's actions but recount anecdotes he told to make his points. He spoke in the voice of the people (vulgarity was a common charge against him) and won his way by wit—"fox populi," a contemporary called him.

He rose to the presidency through diligent study, reading by the dim light of a wood fire, as we all know. His campaign biographer, John Locke Scripps, told how he had damaged a book, Ramsay's Life of Washington, *and worked out the book's cost in three days' hard labor for the farmer from whom he had borrowed it. Scripps also described Lincoln's reading of Plutarch.*

Not long after this incident, he was fortunate enough to get possession of a copy of Plutarch's *Lives.* What fields of thought its perusal opened up to the stripling, what hopes were excited in his youthful breast, what worthy models of probity, of justice, of honor, and devotion to great principles he resolved to pattern after, can be readily imagined by those who are familiar with his subsequent career, and who have themselves lingered over the same charmed page.

—J. L. Scripps, *Life of Abraham Lincoln,* 1860.

But Scripps was myth-making. Shortly after writing his book he addressed a letter to its subject:

I believe the biography contains nothing that I was not fully authorized to put into it. In speaking of the books you read in early life, I took the liberty of adding Plutarch's *Lives.* I take it for granted that you have read that book. If you have not, then you must read it at once to make my statement good.

—David C. Mearns, *The Lincoln Papers,* 1948.

Lincoln never answered Scripps, but the White House withdrew from the Library of Congress an edition of Plutarch's Lives.

When he practiced law with William Herndon, Lincoln annoyed his partner by reading aloud from the newspaper when he arrived at the office each morning. A young clerk remembered him reading something else aloud.

We were discussing with some heat Walt Whitman's "Leaves of Grass," a volume then just published. Lincoln was at work in a corner of the room, deeply engrossed, taking no part in the talk and apparently giving it no attention. . . .

After a while, Lincoln, whom we had supposed not to be listening, arose and took up the book. His capacity to write and listen at the same time, independently, I often had cause to be aware of. That was the first time he had seen Whitman's "Leaves of Grass," although its publication had already created a furor of discussion, and in some quarters a violence of disapprobation which it is difficult for the reader of this day to comprehend. Lincoln read and turned the pages leisurely. Evidently he was enjoying them. After some time he did an unusual thing. He began to read aloud without having made any comment before doing so. He continued from poem to poem with a growing relish.

—Henry Rankin, *Intimate Character Sketches of Abraham Lincoln,* 1924.

Many Lincoln stories are probably just tales to which the tellers added his name, like salt to meat. There are people in every generation whose names make a good story better.

Whenever the people of Lincoln's neighborhood engaged in dispute; whenever a bet was to be decided; when they differed on points of religion or politics; when they wanted to get out of trouble, or desired advice regarding anything on the earth, below it, above it, or under the sea, they went to "Abe."

Two fellows, after a hot dispute lasting some hours, over the problem as to how long a man's legs should be in proportion to the size of his body, stamped into Lincoln's office one day and put the question to him.

Lincoln listened gravely to the arguments advanced by both contestants, spent some time in "reflecting" upon the matter, and then, turning around in his chair and facing the disputants, delivered his opinion with all the gravity of a judge sentencing a fellow-being to death.

"This question has been a source of controversy," he said, slowly and deliberately, "for untold ages, and it is about time it should be definitely decided. It has led to bloodshed in the past, and there is no reason to suppose it will not lead to the same in the future.

"After much thought and consideration, not to mention mental worry and anxiety, it is my opinion, all side issues being swept aside, that a man's lower limbs, in order to preserve harmony of proportion, should be at least long enough to reach from his body to the ground."

Lincoln was, naturally enough, much surprised one day, when a man of rather forbidding countenance drew a revolver and thrust the weapon almost into his face. In such circumstances "Abe" at once concluded that any attempt at debate or argument was a waste of time and words.

"What seems to be the matter?" inquired Lincoln with all the calmness and self-possession he could muster.

"Well," replied the stranger, who did not appear at all excited, "some years ago I swore an oath that if I ever came across an uglier man than myself I'd shoot him on the spot."

A feeling of relief evidently took possession of Lincoln at this rejoinder, as the expression upon his countenance lost all suggestion of anxiety.

"Shoot me," he said to the stranger; "for if I am an uglier man than you I don't want to live."

—Col. Alexander K. McClure, *Abe Lincoln's Yarns and Stories,* 1901.

Ugliness is a theme in many Lincoln stories. So is horse trading.

When Lincoln was a young lawyer in Illinois, he and a certain Judge once got to bantering one another about trading horses; and it was agreed that the next morning at nine o'clock they should make a trade, the horses to be unseen up to that hour, and no backing out, under a forfeiture of $25. At the hour appointed, the Judge came up, leading the sorriest-looking specimen of a horse ever seen in those parts. In a few minutes Mr. Lincoln was seen approaching with a wooden saw-horse upon his shoulders.

Great were the shouts and laughter of the crowd, and both were greatly increased when Lincoln, on surveying the Judge's animal, set down his sawhorse, and exclaimed:

"Well, Judge, this is the first time I ever got the worst of it in a horse trade."

—McClure.

In many stories the President responds to a problem with his ready wit or with an appropriate anecdote.

When he first came to Washington he was inundated with office-seekers. One day he was particularly afflicted; about twenty place-hunters from all parts of the Union had taken possession of his room with bales of credentials and self-recommendations ten miles long. The President said:

"Gentlemen, I must tell you a little story I read one day when I was minding a mudscow in one of the bayous near the Yazoo.

"Once there was a certain king," he said, "who kept an astrologer to forewarn him of coming events and especially to tell him whether it was going to rain when he wanted to go on hunting expeditions. One day he had started off for the forest with his train of ladies and lords for a grand hunt, when the cavalcade met a farmer, riding a donkey, on the road. 'Good morning, Farmer,' said the king. 'Good morning, King,' said the farmer. 'Where are you folks going?' 'Hunting,' said the king. 'Lord, you'll get wet,' said the farmer. The king trusted his astrologer, of course, and went to the forest, but by midday there came on a terrific storm that drenched and buffeted the whole party. When the king returned to his palace he had the astrologer decapitated and sent for the farmer to take his place. 'Law's sake,' says the farmer when he arrived, 'it ain't me that knows when it's goin' to rain, it's my donkey. When it's goin' to be fair weather that donkey always carries his ears forward so.' 'Make the donkey the court astrologer!' shouted the king. It was done. But the king always declared that that appointment was the greatest mistake he ever made in his life."

Lincoln stopped there. "Why did he say it was a mistake?" we asked him. "Didn't the donkey do his duty?" "Yes," said the President, "but after that time every donkey in the country assembled in front of the palace and wanted an office."

—*Leslie's Weekly,* 1863.

Three or four days after the battle of Bull Run, some gentlemen who had been on the field called upon the President.

He inquired very minutely regarding all the circumstances of the affair, and, after listening with the utmost attention, said, with a touch of humor:

"So it is your notion that we whipped the rebels and then ran away from them?"

When Governor Curtin of Pennsylvania described the terrible butchery at the battle of Fredericksburg, Mr. Lincoln was almost broken-hearted.

The Governor regretted that his description had so sadly affected the President. He remarked: "I would give all I possess to know how to rescue you from this terrible war." Then Mr. Lincoln's wonderful recuperative powers asserted themselves and this marvelous man was himself.

Lincoln's whole aspect suddenly changed, and he relieved his mind by telling a story.

"This reminds me, Governor," he said, "of an old farmer out in Illinois that I used to know.

"He took it into his head to go into hog-raising. He sent out to Europe and imported the finest breed of hogs he could buy.

"The prize hog was put in a pen, and the farmer's two mischievous boys, James and John, were told to be sure not to let it out. But James, the worst of the two, let the brute out the next day. The hog went straight for the boys, and drove John up a tree. Then the hog went for the seat of James's trousers, and the only way the boy could save himself was by holding on to the hog's tail.

"The hog would not give up his hunt, nor the boy his hold! After they had made a good many circles around the tree, the boy's courage began to give out, and he shouted to his brother, 'I say, John, come down, quick, and help me let go this hog!'

"Now, Governor, that is exactly my case. I wish some one would come and help me to let the hog go."

—McClure.

There were stories of pardons.

An Ohio Senator had an appointment with President Lincoln at six o'clock, and as he entered the vestibule of the White House his attention was attracted toward a poorly clad young woman, who was violently sobbing. He asked her the cause of her distress. She said she had been ordered away by the servants, after vainly waiting many hours to see the President about her only brother, who had been condemned to death. Her story was this:

She and her brother were foreigners, and orphans. They had been in this country several years. Her brother enlisted in the army, but, through bad influences, was induced to desert. He was captured, tried and sentenced to be shot—the old story.

The poor girl had obtained the signatures of some persons who had formerly known him, to a petition for a pardon, and alone had come to Washington to lay the case before the President. Thronged as the waiting-rooms always were, she had passed the long hours of two days trying in vain to get an audience, and had at length been ordered away.

The gentleman's feelings were touched. He said to her that he had come to see the President, but did not know as he should succeed. He told her, however, to follow him upstairs, and he would see what could be done for her.

Just before reaching the door, Mr. Lincoln came out, and, meeting his friend, said good-humoredly, "Are you not ahead of time?" The gentleman showed him his watch, with the hand upon the hour of six.

"Well," returned Mr. Lincoln, "I have been so busy to-day that I have not had time to get a lunch. Go in and sit down; I will be back directly."

The gentleman made the young woman accompany him into the office, and when they were seated, said to her: "Now, my good girl, I want you to muster all the courage you have in the world. When the President comes back, he will sit down in that armchair. I shall get up to speak to him, and as I do so you must force yourself between us, and insist upon his examination of your papers, telling him it is a case of life and death, and admits of no delay."

These instructions were carried out to the letter. Mr. Lincoln was at first somewhat surprised at the apparent forwardness of the young woman, but observing her distressed appearance, he ceased conversation with his friend, and commenced an examination of the document she had placed in his hands.

Glancing from it to the face of the petitioner, whose tears had broken forth afresh, he studied its expression for a moment, and then his eye fell upon her scanty but neat dress. Instantly his face lighted up.

"My poor girl," said he, "you have come here with no Governor, or Senator, or member of Congress to plead your cause. You seem honest and truthful; and you don't wear hoopskirts—and I will be whipped but I will pardon your brother."

—McClure.

Chief telegrapher Thomas Eckert described Lincoln working.

". . . the President came to the office every day and invariably sat at my desk while there. Upon his arrival early one morning in June, 1862, shortly after McClellan's 'Seven Days' Fight,' he asked me for some paper, as he wanted to write something special. I procured some foolscap and handed it to him. He then sat down and began to write. I do not recall whether the sheets were loose or had been made into a pad. There must have been at least a quire. He would look out of the window a while and then put his pen to paper, but he did not write much at once. He would study between times and when he had made up his mind he would put down a line or two, and then sit quiet for a few minutes. After a time he would resume his writing, only to stop again at intervals to make some remark to me or to one of the cipher-operators, as a fresh dispatch from the front was handed to him.

"Once his eye was arrested by the sight of a large spiderweb stretched from the lintel of the portico to the side of the outer window-sill. This spiderweb was an institution of the cipher-room and harbored a large colony of exceptionally big ones. We frequently watched their antics, and Assistant Secretary Watson dubbed them 'Major Eckert's Lieutenants.' Lincoln commented on the web, and I told him that my lieutenants would soon report and pay their respects to the President. Not long after a big spider appeared at the crossroads and tapped several times on the strands, whereupon five or six others came out from different directions. Then would follow what appeared to be a conference among the spiders, all of which the President noted. Scanning what he already had written, the President would remain motionless for a minute or two as he buckled his mind to what he wanted to pen next. Another glance at the spiders, a hitch to the chair, a glance out of the window, and then, with the right words in mind, he'd write a few lines, pausing to read over the document as far as he'd gone.

"He didn't write much at a time, and he didn't write rapidly, but what he did write was beautifully done, with few or no interlineations or erasures. After the first day or two of this kind of work all four cipher men knew what he was doing, as he made no secret about it. . . .

"That's the way the Emancipation Proclamation grew under Lincoln's hand. . . ."

—David Homer Bates, *Lincoln Stories,* 1926.

Walt Whitman recalled the figure the President made in wartime Washington.

"August 12th—I see the President almost every day, as I happen to live where he passes to or from his lodgings out of town. I saw him this morning about eight coming in to business, riding on Vermont avenue, near L street. He always has a company of twenty-five or thirty cavalry, with sabres drawn and held upright over their shoulders. They say this guard was against his personal wish, but he let his counselors have their way. The party makes no great show in uniform or horses. Mr. Lincoln on the saddle generally rides a good-sized, easy-going gray horse, is dressed in plain black, somewhat rusty and dusty, wears a black stiff hat, and looks about as ordinary in attire, etc., as the commonest man.

"I see very plainly Abraham Lincoln's dark-brown face, with the deep-cut lines, the eyes, always to me with a deep, latent sadness in the expression. We have got so that we exchange bows and very cordial ones. . . .

"None of the artists or photo-pictures have caught the deep, though subtle and indirect expression of this man's face. There is something else there. One of the great portrait painters of two or three centuries ago is needed. As it is impossible to depict a wild perfume or fruit-taste, or a passionate tone of the living voice—such was Lincoln's face, the peculiar color, the lines of it, the eyes, mouth, expression. Of technical beauty it had nothing—but to the eye of a great artist it furnished a rare study, a feast and a fascination. The current portraits are all failures—most of them caricatures.

"April 16, '65—Of all the days of the war there are two especially I can never forget. Those were the days following the news, in New York and Brooklyn, of that first Bull Run defeat and the day of Abraham Lincoln's death. I was home in Brooklyn on both occasions. The day of the murder we heard the news very early in the morning. Mother prepared breakfast—and other meals afterward—as usual; but not a mouthful was eaten all day by either of us. We each drank half a cup of coffee; that was all. Little was said. We got every newspaper, morning and evening, and the frequent extras of that period, and passed them silently to each other."

—Rankin.

After the assassination, people remembered warnings and premonitions. The following story is attributed to "a soldier."

One night I was doing sentinel duty at the entrance to the Soldiers' Home. This was about the middle of August, 1864. About eleven o'clock I heard a rifle shot, in the direction of the city, and shortly afterwards I heard approaching hoof-beats. In two or three minutes a horse came dashing up. I recognized the belated President. The President was bareheaded. The President simply thought that his horse had taken fright at the discharge of the firearms.

On going back to the place where the shot had been heard, we found the President's hat. It was a plain silk hat, and upon examination we discovered a bullet hole through the crown.

The next day, upon receiving the hat, the President remarked that it was made by some foolish marksman, and was not intended for him; but added that he wished nothing said about the matter.

The President said, philosophically: "I long ago made up my mind that if anybody wants to kill me, he will do it. Besides, in this case, it seems to me, the man who would succeed me would be just as objectionable to my enemies—if I have any."

One dark night, as he was going out with a friend, he took along a heavy cane, remarking, good-naturedly:

"Mother (Mrs. Lincoln) has got a notion into her head that I shall be assassinated, and to please her I take a cane when I go over to the War Department at night—when I don't forget it."

—McClure.

Cipher-operator Tinker, of the White House telegraph office, told about the "last time I saw Mr. Lincoln alive."

"On April 14, 1865, the day Lincoln was shot, he came to the telegraph office while I was transmitting a cipher dispatch that was couched in very laconic terms. Lincoln read the dispatch, and after taking in the meaning of the terse phrases, he turned to me and with his accustomed smile said, 'Mr. Tinker, that reminds me of the old story of the Scotch lassie on her way to market with a basket of eggs for sale. She had just forded a small stream with her skirts well drawn up, when a wagoner on the opposite side of the stream called out, "Good morning, my lassie; how deep's the brook and what's the price of eggs?" She answered, "Knee deep and a sixpence."'

"Mr. Lincoln, still with a smile, lifted his coat tails in imitation of the maiden and passed into Secretary Stanton's room adjoining."

—Bates.

Oliver Wendell Holmes 1809–1894

Poet, physician, autocrat of the breakfast table, sire of a future Supreme Court Justice, Oliver Wendell Holmes was noted for the honest intensity of his self-regard. "I was always patient with those who thought well of me," he said, "and accepted all their tributes with something more than resignation."

William Dean Howells:

I remember the delight Henry James, the father of the novelist, had in reporting to me the frankness of the doctor, when he had said to him, "Holmes, you are intellectually the most alive man I ever knew." "I am, I am," said the doctor. "From the crown of my head to the sole of my foot, I'm alive, I'm alive!"

—*Literary Friends and Acquaintances,* 1902.

N. P. Willis writing in 1858 describes the doctor as an artful conversationalist.

"Holmes talks very nearly all the time, but the secret of the charm of the monopoly is the fact that he is, all this time, *broidering on your woof*—apparently dwelling only on what you have suggested, and reading your mind very truly to yourself, only that he makes it seem a good deal clearer than you thought it! Then his perpetual and exceeding brilliancy of wit is so pointed, and so outlined with nice science and universal reading, that you keep pocketing his good things to think them over with more leisure—sighing perpetually as he glances off, that he had not dwelt on *that* a little longer. There is a curious effect while he is conversing with you—arising from his continual *surprises* of forethought and construction. He travels telegraph, in fact, while you think him stage-coaching at your side—. . ."

—M. A. DeWolfe Howe, *Holmes of the Breakfast Table,* 1939.

Many attempted to describe his conversational manner, including Charles Kingsley who stammered the epithet "an insp-sp-sp-ired j-j-j-ack-daw." President Charles Eliot of Harvard called him

. . . "simple-hearted in a charming way, with a sort of natural vanity which he expressed without reserve. I was sitting beside him one day at the Club when I mentioned that I had just parted from an Englishman who had spoken of him with great reverence and admiration. Dr. Holmes inquired instantly, 'What did he say? What did he say, Mr. President? You know I like to have it laid on thick.' "

—Howe.

His sallies were repeated.

. . . while Holmes was still practicing medicine he met a priest leaving the house of a poor patient, a boy he was on the point of visiting.

"Good morning, doctor," said the priest, "your patient is very ill—he is going to die."

"Yes," said Holmes, "and he's going to hell."

"No, I have just given extreme unction—and you must not say such things!"

"Well," came the reply, "you expressed a medical opinion, and I have just as much right to a theological opinion."

—Howe.

He attended a dinner party late in his life in Washington; President Grover Cleveland had arrived before him.

. . . [Holmes] thought himself unseen, but a daughter of the house, not yet old enough to come to her father's formal dinners, watched him from above stairs, as he came to the hat-rack on which the President's large hat had been left, solemnly putting it on his own head, and inspecting himself in a mirror.

—Howe.

Edgar Allan Poe 1809–1849

During his brief stay at the University of Virginia, Poe was already writing fiction.

On one occasion Poe read a story of great length to some of his friends who, in a spirit of jest, spoke lightly of its merits, and jokingly told him that his hero's name "Gaffy" occurred too often. His proud spirit would not stand such open rebuke, so in a fit of anger, before his friends could prevent him, he had flung every sheet into a blazing fire, and thus was lost a story of more than ordinary parts which, unlike most of his stories, was intensely amusing, entirely free from his usual somber coloring and sad conclusions merged in a mist of impenetrable gloom. He was for a long time afterwards called by those in his particular circle "Gaffy" Poe, a name that he never altogether relished.

—Hervey Allen, *Israfel: The Life and Times of Edgar Allan Poe,* 1926.

When Poe married his thirteen-year-old cousin Virginia, the couple lived in poverty with Virginia's mother Maria Clemm, who was also Poe's aunt. A visitor—Mrs. Gove Nichols—recollected the cottage, its ménage, and a strange athletic contest.

"The cottage had an air of gentility that must have been lent to it by the presence of its inmates. So neat, so poor, so unfurnished, and yet so charming a dwelling I never saw. The floor of the kitchen was white as wheaten flour. A table, a chair, and a little stove it contained seemed to furnish it completely. The sitting room was laid with check matting; four chairs, a light stand, and a hanging bookshelf completed its furniture. There were pretty presentation copies of books on the little shelves, and the Brownings had posts of honor on the stand. With quiet exultation Poe drew from his inside pocket a letter he had recently received from Elizabeth Barrett Browning. He read it to us. It was very flattering. . . . On the bookshelf there lay a volume of Poe's poems. He took it down, wrote my name in it and gave it to me. . . . He was at this time greatly depressed. Their extreme poverty, the sickness of his wife, and his own inability to write sufficiently accounted for this. We spent half an hour in the house, when some more company came, which included ladies, and then we all went to walk.

"We strolled away into the woods, and had a very cheerful time, till someone proposed a game at leaping. I think it must have been Poe, as he was expert in the exercise. Two or three gentlemen agreed to leap with him, and though one of them was tall and had been a hunter in times past, Poe still distanced them all. But alas! his gaiters, long worn and carefully kept, were both burst in the grand leap that made him victor. . . .

I was certain he had no other shoes, boots, or gaiters. Who amongst us could offer him money to buy a new pair? . . . When we reached the cottage, I think all felt that we must not go in, to see the shoeless unfortunate sitting or standing in our midst. I had an errand, however—and I entered the house to get it. The poor old mother looked at his feet with a dismay that I shall never forget. 'Oh, Eddie!' said she, 'how did you burst your gaiters?' Poe seemed to have come into a semi-torpid state as soon as he saw his mother. 'Do answer Muddie,' now said she coaxingly—I related the cause of the mishap, and she drew me into the kitchen.

" 'Will you speak to Mr. _______, [an editor]' she said, 'about Eddie's last poem? . . . If he will only take the poem, Eddie can have a pair of shoes. He has it—I carried it last week, and Eddie says it is his best. You will speak to him about it, won't you?'

"We had already read the poem in conclave, and Heaven forgive us, we could not make head or tail of it. It might as well have been in any of the lost languages, for any meaning we could extract from its melodious numbers. I remember saying that I believed it was only a hoax that Poe was passing off for poetry, to see how far his name would go in imposing upon people. But here was a situation. The reviewer had been actively instrumental in the demolition of the gaiters.

" 'Of course, they will publish the poem,' said I, 'and I will ask C________ to be quick about it.'

"The poem was paid for at once and published soon after. I presume it is regarded as genuine poetry in the collected poems of its author, but then it bought the poet a pair of gaiters, and twelve shillings over."

—Allen.

Virginia's tuberculosis grew worse. A neighbor named Miss Cromwell, quoted as saying "They were awful *poor," remembered the colors of a tableau.*

Miss Cromwell lived a little beyond the Poes. In the Spring of 1846, as she was passing by the cottage up the Kingsbridge Road, she noticed Poe up in the cherry tree gathering the red, ripe fruit, and tossing it to Virginia, who caught it in her lap, laughing and calling back, as she sat dressed in white on a green sod bank beneath. Poe was standing on a branch above her, about to toss another bunch of cherries into the bright red pile already gathered in Virginia's apron, when white and crimson suddenly became one in the tide which leaped from her lips.

—Allen.

For a moment, Poe enjoyed celebrity. "The Raven" was enormously popular. In addition, Poe had attacked the irreproachable Longfellow as a plagiarist, which drew attention to the accuser.

As dramatic critic of the *Broadway Journal* he was now much at the theater. One night at the Park, an actor who knew him saw him sitting in the audience. Into the lines of his part as the scene progressed, he interpolated, "Nevermore, Nevermore."

—Allen.

Margaret Fuller 1810–1850

Margaret's father, Timothy Fuller, had unusual ambition in the education of his daughter. He

. . . set up a lesson plan for the child, which his wife helped her to follow during the day, and when he came home in the evening he would ask for a report of how she had spent the day and what she had learned. By the time she visited her grandparents in Canton, Massachusetts, in the spring of her fourth year, her father's affection had become firmly associated in her mind with intellectual achievement, and he was closing his letters to his wife with such conditional endearments as, "My love to the little Sarah Margarett. I love her if she is a good girl and learns to read."

—Paula Blanchard, *Margaret Fuller: From Transcendentalism to Revelation,* 1978.

Margaret Fuller was most celebrated as a speaker. W. E. Channing described her at a meeting of the Transcendental Club.

When her turn came, by a graceful transition she resumed the subject where preceding speakers had left it, and, briefly summing up their results, proceeded to unfold her own view. Her opening was deliberate, like the progress of some massive force gaining its momentum; but as she felt her way, and moving in a congenial element, the sweep of her speech became grand. The style of her eloquence was sententious, free from prettiness, direct, vigorous, charged with vitality. Articulateness, just emphasis and varied accent, brought out most delicate shades and brilliant points of meaning, while a rhythmical collocation of words gave a finished form to every thought. She was affluent in historic illustration and literary allusion, as well as in novel hints. She knew how to concentrate into racy phrases the essential truth gathered from wide research, and distilled with patient toil; and by skilful treatment she could make green again the wastes of commonplace. Her statements, however rapid, showed breadth of comprehension, ready memory, impartial judgment, nice analysis of differences, power of penetrating through surfaces to realities, fixed regard to central laws and habitual communion with the Life of life. Critics, indeed, might have been tempted to sneer at a certain oracular grandiloquence, that bore away her soberness in moments of elation; though even the most captious must presently have smiled at the humor of her descriptive touches, her dextrous exposure of folly and pretension, the swift stroke of her bright wit, her shrewd discernment, promptitude, and presence of mind. The reverential, too, might have been pained at the sternness wherewith popular men, measures, and established customs, were tried and found guilty, at her tribunal; but even while blaming her aspirations as rash, revolutionary and impractical, no honest conservative could fail to recognize the sincerity of her aim. And every deep observer of character would have found the explanation of what seemed vehement or too high-strung, in the longing of a spirited woman to break every trammel that checked her growh or fettered her movement.

In conversations like these, one saw that the richness of Margaret's genius resulted from a rare combination of opposite qualities. To her might have been well applied the words first used as describing George Sand: "Thou large-brained Woman, and large-hearted Man." She blended in closest union and swift interplay feminine receptiveness with masculine energy.

—Blanchard.

She was truthful, but not altogether modest, when she said, "I now know all the people worth knowing in America, and I find no intellect comparable to my own." Hawthorne was ambivalent, admiring her intelligence and calling her "a great humbug." To complain of her conduct at Brook Farm, he called a heifer after her and complained of the heifer. William James, in his The Varieties of Religious Experience *(1902), recounted the most famous Margaret Fuller anecdote.*

"I accept the universe" is reported to have been a favorite utterance of our New England transcendentalist Margaret Fuller; and when someone repeated this phrase to Thomas Carlyle, his sardonic comment is said to have been, "Gad! she'd better."

—*Dictionary of Biographical Quotation,* eds. Richard Kenin and Justin Wintle, 1978.

She was despised because she was a woman who did not know her place.

. . . her [book] reviews are frank and occasionally even angry, they are free of personal spite. But they betrayed the sex of their writer not at all, and this offense was not easily forgiven. A lady reviewer (supposing such an anomalous creature existed) was expected to praise or be silent, as she would in society; if absolutely driven to find fault, she would have to do so in a timid, self-deprecatory way which could not be taken seriously. Margaret's reviews were based on an assumption of competence which, though it would not have been remarkable in a man, was thought by many to be intolerable in a woman. If roused the witch-hunting instincts of men who were ready to see in any negative comment of Margaret's, no matter how disinterested, evidence of that kind of spitefulness they expected from a woman who "unsexed" herself by writing like men. Hence Poe's revealing observation that humanity could be divided into three classes: "men, women, and Margaret Fuller."

—Blanchard.

In her famous conversations with women of Boston and Cambridge, she did her utmost to encourage the intellectual ambitions of American women. Yet such were the ambiguities of her time and character that she never advocated woman suffrage. A woman of considerable passion, she found her Transcendentalist male friends cold and removed, most frustratingly

Emerson with his reluctance even to undertake friendship. When she went to Italy, during its struggle for independence, she found new fulfillment. Elizabeth Barrett Browning wrote of her in a letter:

"The American authoress, Miss Fuller, with whom we had had some slight intercourse by letter, and who has been at Rome during the siege, as a devoted friend of the republicans and a meritorious attendant on the hospitals, has taken us by surprise at Florence, retiring from the Roman field with a husband and child above a year old. Nobody had even suspected a word of this underplot, and her American friends stood in mute astonishment before this apparition of them here. The husband is a Roman marquis, appearing amiable and gentlemanly, and having fought well, they say, at the siege, but with no pretension to cope with his wife on any ground appertaining to the intellect. She talks, and he listens."

—Blanchard.

Margaret Fuller Ossoli, her son Nino, and her husband sailed for home on a sailing ship because a steamer cost too much money. The ship grounded off Fire Island, New York, in a great storm. In the biographer's account that follows, Horace Sumner and Celeste Paoline are fellow passengers, Mrs. Hasty is widow of the captain who died on the voyage, Davis is second mate and Mr. Bangs first mate.

In the forecastle, wrapped in coats and blankets and strengthened by the food, the passengers began to think there was some chance of rescue. As the light grew stronger figures could be seen on the beach—beachcombers, looking for debris from the wreck—but they seemed oblivious to any sign of life on board. It was decided that someone would try to bring help. The ship's boats were all smashed or lost, but Margaret had brought two life preservers, one of which was still usable, and a sailor took it and dived in. He was carried far up the beach by the current but eventually was seen to reach shore. Another sailor followed with a spar. Encouraged by their example, Horace Sumner took a plank and jumped in, but he sank almost immediately. After that, numbed and sickened, the others sat down to wait for help.

But although the activity on the beach increased, none of it seemed directed at rescue. Carts were seen to arrive, but only to be loaded with the scraps of exotic cargo which were already being tossed on the beach: bolts of silk and wool, flasks of oil, boxes of almonds and juniper berries, Leghorn hats. To those aboard it appeared that no one intended to help them, although in fact a lifeboat and a mortar gun with a line were on their way from a life-saving station two miles or more away. Meanwhile the tide, which had ebbed at nine, was coming back in, and the officers urged the passengers to trust themselves to planks, each rigged with ropes and propelled by a swimming sailor. Celeste refused, and Margaret insisted she would not be separated from her son and husband. Finally Mrs. Hasty and Davis, in order to prove it could be done, jumped in together. After a long struggle during which the plank was overturned twice, they were dragged half-conscious from the surf some distance up the beach, but it is not certain whether those on board saw them. Bangs now turned again to Margaret, offering to take Nino himself, but she again refused to let him go. Having seen Sumner drown so quickly she must have realized that a very young child would have no chance at all, and with the beach only a few hundred yards off she still hoped for rescue. And in fact the carts carrying the lifeboat and mortar did finally arrive, but no one was willing or able to launch the boat in a hurricane surf. The mortar, which had to be fired against the wind, was found to be useless. For another two hours or more the life-saving team stood around on the beach and stared at the wreck and the survivors stared back, while the scavengers went about their business. Bangs renewed his arguments, but the passengers would not listen to him. Finally, exasperated, he shouted, "Save yourselves!" and jumped overboard, followed by most of the crew. Four stayed on board: the steward Bates, who had a son Nino's age home in England; the carpenter; the cook; and a very old, sick sailor.

About three o'clock the ship began to break up. The cabin had been swept away, and now the forecastle was flooded and the last remaining mast was beginning to loosen, prying the deck up with it. The eight people on board gathered around it, and Bates made a last desperate effort to persuade Margaret to part with Nino. Even as he succeeded, Ossoli was washed overboard, but Margaret, intent on her child, did not see him go. A moment later a last, mountainous wave broke over the vessel, carrying off the mast and everyone remaining on board. The cook and the carpenter, thrown clear, saw Ossoli and Celeste cling for a moment to the rigging, then disappear. There was no sign of Margaret. The bodies of Nino and the steward were washed up on the beach a few minutes later.

—Blanchard.

Harriet Beecher Stowe 1811–1896

On the day Uncle Tom's Cabin *was published in 1852 it sold three thousand copies; within a year more than three hundred thousand were purchased in the United States. As the author's son put it, "Almost in a day the poor professor's wife had become the most talked-about woman in the world. . . ." However, Stowe resisted taking credit for the book. Annie Fields recalled a conversation.*

At last she spoke, and said, "I have just received a letter from my brother Edward from Galesburg, Illinois. He is greatly disturbed lest all this praise and notoriety should induce pride and vanity, and work harm to my Christian character." She dropped her brush from her hand and exclaimed with earnestness, "Dear soul, he need not be troubled. He doesn't know that I did not write that book."

"*What!*" said I, "you did not write 'Uncle Tom'?"

"No," she said, "I only put down what I saw."

"But you have never been at the South, have you?" I asked.

"No," she said, "but it all came before me in visions, one after another, and I put them down in words."

But being still skeptical, I said, "Still you must have arranged the events."

"No," said she, "your Annie reproached me for letting Eva die. Why! I could not help it. I felt as badly as any one could! It was like a death in my own family, and it affected me so deeply that I could not write a word for two weeks after her death."

"And did you know," I asked, "that Uncle Tom would die?"

"Oh yes," she answered, "I knew that he must die from the first, but I did not know *how*. When I got to that part of the story, I saw no more for some time. I was physically exhausted, too.

"I was very tired when we returned to our boarding house to the early midday dinner. After dinner we went to our room for rest. Mr. Stowe threw himself upon the bed; I was to use the lounge; but suddenly arose before me the death scene of Uncle Tom with what led to it—and George's visit to him. I sat down at the table and wrote nine pages of foolscap paper without pausing, except long enough to dip my pen into the inkstand. Just as I had finished, Mr. Stowe awoke. 'Wife,' said he, 'have not you lain down yet?' 'No,' I answered. 'I have been writing, and I want you to listen to this, and see if it will do.' I read aloud to him with the tears flowing fast. He wept, too, and before I had finished, his sobs shook the bed upon which he was lying. He sprang up, saying. 'Do! I should think it would do!' And folding the sheets he immediately directed and sent them to the publisher, without one word of correction or revision of any kind."

—Annie Fields, *The Life and Letters of Harriet Beecher Stowe,* 1897.

Abraham Lincoln met her in 1862. He took her by the hand and said, "Is this the little woman who made this great war?"

At the height of her fame she traveled to England where Queen Victoria received her. In the United States she lectured and accepted homage. She wrote her husband:

"God has given me strength as I needed it, and I never read more to my own satisfaction than last night. . . .

"One woman in Portland the other night, . . . totally deaf, came to me afterwards and said: 'Bless you. I come jist to see you. I'd rather see you than the Queen.' Another introduced her little girl named Harriet Beecher Stowe, and another, older, named Eva. She said they had traveled fifty miles to hear me read. An incident like that appeals to one's heart, does it not?"

—Fields.

When Mrs. Thomas Bailey Aldrich, wife of the novelist and editor, wrote her memoirs in 1920, she told a story about Harriet Beecher Stowe—which featured a potent wine punch and some closely observed undergarments.

. . . Mr. Aldrich, laden with books and manuscripts, returned from the city of his editorial cares, and said, with perplexed face and whimsical manner: "We are, *nolens volens,* to have a visitor, 'O'ermaster it as you may.' This morning Mrs. Harriet Beecher Stowe came to the office, and without preamble said, 'I should like to make you and Mrs. Aldrich a little visit; the personality of your wife strongly attracts me.' " Then followed the startling intelligence that the distinguished guest would arrive early the next day.

For the châtelaine of the humble château there was little sleep that night. What would befall her in the next few hours when Mr. Aldrich was in town, and she alone with the distinguished guest—a guest who at the tender age of twelve years had chosen for her theme, "Can the Immortality of the Soul be proved by the Light of Nature?" . . .

The next morning Mr. Aldrich was adamant to the prayer that he would forego all editorial duties for that day, but giving his promise to return from the city as early as possible, and to bring with him a man rich in the lore of theology and kindred matters, he hurried to the train, leaving his laughing advice, if there seemed danger of being swept beyond the depths, to call to the rescue the jocund sprites, with their trumpets and drums, their rattling wagons, their squeaking carts—the armament with which they so frequently had silenced conversation in the small house. . . .

Mr. Aldrich was speaking of their children.

At dinner the night before the memorable visit Mr. Aldrich had suggested that as the next day would probably be warm, a claret cup, served with its clinking ice, its ruby color, and its bit of mint, would be a refreshment for body and soul. . . .

The morning was half over before a carriage stopped at the door, and a reluctant hostess went forward to greet her distinguished guest. What was a personality that attracts? Whatever it was it certainly was not an unconscious personality, but a very conscious one, that waited at the door. The day was excessively warm, the train from the city overcrowded, making Mrs. Stowe look worried and frail, like a last rose of summer. With the first look at the wilted flower, personality fled, and there was but one thought: what can be done for this guest's comfort?

She was brought into the house, placed in the easiest chair, a fan put in her hand, her bonnet taken off. With her sigh of relief and gratitude for these ministrations came the request for something to drink that would quench her inordinate thirst. Almost before Mrs. Stowe had finished speaking, to her young hostess came the remembrance of the ruby cup cooling in the ice chest, and with the remembrance a feeling of deep thankfulness that she had something so refreshing to offer. A little tray on which was a plate holding a biscuit and a glass pitcher filled with the delectable mixture was quickly brought and placed on a stand by Mrs. Stowe's chair. . . .

[She] drank, and very shortly afterwards complained of the unsettled character of the room, which seemed to the visitor to be stationary at an angle of forty-five degrees. And the sea turn—everything is in a blue mist—did we often have such sudden fogs? She would lie down if the sofa had not such a momentum; to her eye it was misbehaving as badly as her berth at sea.

It was with penitent and contrite heart that the hapless sinner, whose want of concentration of her errant thoughts in the brewing of the cup had brought about this dire mischance, assisted her guest; and fervent was her prayer that the recumbent position would prove recuperative and restore speedily the equilibrium that through her fault had gone so far astray.

In the days of the sixties women still wore hoops or reeds in their skirts, and in lying on the sofa Mrs. Stowe's skirts, like Hamlet's words, "flew up," revealing very slender ankles and feet encased in prunella boots; the elastic V at the sides no longer elastic, but worn and loose. The stockings were white, and the flowery ribbon of the garter knots was unabashed by the sunlight. . . .

Mrs. Aldrich realized that her husband would soon return bringing a male guest. Her thoughts ran to cover-up.

On a distant chair lay a gossamer scarf which would drape the unconscious form. But if in the getting of it she wake the sleeper? Which was the kindest thing—to wait for "Nature's sweet restorer" or to drape the scarf and run the risk of waking her poor victim? If Mr. Aldrich was only coming alone, she could bar the door and banish him. But in this long, low house there was but one living-room, and what could be done with the stranger guest who was coming with him? For this reason the venture must be made. With stealthy steps the goal was won, and light as a butterfly's wing the gossamer scarf slowly descended, only to rise again with accelerated motion, for Mrs. Stowe at the first touch sat straight upright, and with dim, reproachful eyes asked: "Why did you do it? I am weak, weary and warm as I am—let me sleep." There was given a gentle hint that there was drapery to be rearranged, but the negative was firm, and the answer decisive: "I won't be any properer than I have a mind to be. Let me sleep."

—*Crowding Memories,* 1920.

As luck would have it, Mr. Aldrich was delayed.

Horace Greeley 1811–1872

Horace Greeley advocated the homestead law and said "Go West, Young Man!" in support of it. Anti-slavery, pro-labor, anti-monopoly, pro-temperance, he was a great editor and editorial-writer of his time.

One of the civic leaders of New York City . . . entered the editorial office one day and exploded in curses and screams over Greeley's back, the latter being bent over a desk, engrossed in preparing a column for the presses. Greeley continued to write, apparently not heeding the party leader, whom his columns had not actively supported, until at length the angered man had exhausted his repertoire of recriminations; then, as the man was turning to leave, his wrath fully spent, the editor looked up from his work with his frequently seen childlike smile, remarking casually over his shoulder, "Don't go! don't go! come back and free your mind!"

—James H. Trietsch, *The Printer and the Prince,* 1955.

He was known for his intolerance of inaccuracy and for his illegible handwriting. A reporter named Joseph Bucklin Bishop mistakenly reported a Republican majority of twelve thousand votes in a particular county.

When Greeley saw the story, he called Bishop to him, told him that "any fool should know that there were not even twelve thousand people in that county who were eligible to vote," and then gave him an illegible note of dismissal. Trembling and frightened at the man's wrath, Bishop carried the scribbled note to the managing editor who, unable to decipher the hieroglyphics, told Bishop to be more careful in the future and to continue working, remembering in reporting election returns that Greeley knew the voting strength of virtually every city, county, and state in the North and East. Bishop treasured this advice, and Greeley did not seem to remember that he ever had fired this faithful employee. In fact, Greeley often dismissed his employees dozens of times, while they continued working for him; the handwriting of his dismissal notes was often so illegible that the dismissed persons took the notes to neighboring newspapers and used them as recommendations from Greeley.

—Trietsch.

Jones Very 1813–1880

A friend of Emerson, Very was more a mystic than a Transcendentalist. He transcribed sonnets dictated to him during visions. He tutored in Greek at Harvard while he studied at the Divinity School—until Harvard authorities began to doubt his sanity.

His body was emaciated from lack of recreation and food, his nerves frayed and broken by super-excitement and abnormal exertion. Only the spirit seemed thoroughly and constantly alive. One day early in the term, as he stood before his Greek class, the increasing consciousness of his prophetic powers outgrew all further restraint. His eyes burned with a strange and intense light. Suddenly he startled his students with the apocalyptic cry, "Flee to the mountains, for the end of all things is at hand."

—William Irving Bartlett, *Jones Very: Emerson's Brave Saint,* 1942.

He was committed for a time to McLean's private insane asylum in Belmont, Massachusetts, where other poets would follow him. (Robert Lowell speaks of McLean's in Life Studies.*) Emerson described him in his journal.*

"Here is Simeon the Stylite, or John of Patmos in the shape of Jones Very, religion for religion's sake, religion divorced, detached from man, from the world, from science and art; grim, unmarried, insulated, accusing; yet true in itself, and speaking things in every word. The lie is in the detachment; and when he is in the room with other persons, speech stops as if there were a corpse in the apartment."

—Bartlett.

Henry David Thoreau 1817–1862

When Thoreau graduated from Harvard he refused to take his degree. "It isn't worth five dollars," he said. Later, he overheard Emerson remarking that Harvard taught all branches of learning. "Yes, indeed," Thoreau interjected, "all the branches and none of the roots."

He was Emerson's young friend and follower, and to many seemed a mere imitator. Charles J. Woodbury wrote of him

Emerson called him "My Spartan-Buddhist, Henry," "My Henry Thoreau." With no one was he so intimate, until the disciple became as his master, adopting his accent and form, realizing his attractions and antipathies, and knowing his good and evil. The development of this sturdy bud into its sturdier flower was a perpetual delight to the philosopher. In Thoreau, he lived himself over again. He said he liked Thoreau because "he had the courage of his convictions," but I think he meant his own convictions.

—*Talks with Ralph Waldo Emerson,* 1890.

Emerson was often away from Concord, traveling to lecture at lyceums. In his absence he employed Thoreau as handyman about the house, who also provided companionship for the lonely Lidian Emerson.

Emerson was delighted. His garden got planted, his apple trees grafted, and the chimneys burned out. When Mrs. Emerson needed a place to store her Sunday-go-to-meeting gloves, Thoreau built a special little drawer under the seat of one of the diningroom chairs. When she complained that the hens were invading her gardens and scratching out the flowers, Thoreau, with a straight face but a twinkle in his eye, made gloves for their claws.

—Walter Harding, *The Days of Henry Thoreau,* 1965.

When Hawthorne moved to the Old Manse, he arrived to discover that Thoreau had plowed and planted a garden in anticipation of the Hawthorne family's arrival.

After meeting him, Hawthorne wrote in his diary that "Mr. Thorow" was a young man with much of wild original nature . . . as ugly as sin, long-nosed, queer mouthed. . . ." (It is alleged that Thoreau could swallow his nose.) His manner and his independence, if not his beauty, fascinated his Concord acquaintances.

In an essay Emerson wrote for the Atlantic Monthly *after the younger man's death, he told about the manufacture of pencils.*

His father was a manufacturer of lead-pencils, and Henry applied himself for a time to this craft, believing he could make a better pencil than was then in use. After completing his experiments, he exhibited his work to chemists and artists in Boston, and having obtained their certificates to its excellence and to its equality with the best London manufacture, he returned home contented. His friends congratulated him that he had now opened his way to fortune. But he replied, that he should never make another pencil. "Why should I? I would not do again what I have done once."

—*Atlantic Monthly,* 1862.

This lover of nature, who could talk to animals, found difficulty educating woodchucks.

"My enemies," he said, "are worms, cool days, and most of all woodchucks. They have nibbled for me an eighth of an acre clean. I plant in faith, and they reap."

Thoreau was at a loss for a time what to do. The woodchucks, he felt, had prior claims as residents, but if they remained, there would be no garden. He finally consulted a veteran trapper for advice. "Mr. W., is there any way to get woodchucks without trapping them with—?" "Yes; shoot 'em, you damn fool," was the reply. But Thoreau ignored that sage advice and matters got worse instead of better. Finally, in desperation, he procured a trap and captured the grandfather of all the woodchucks. After retaining it for several hours, he delivered it a severe lecture and released it, hoping never to see it again. But it was a vain delusion. Within a few days it was back at its old stand, nibbling as heartily as ever at his beans. Accordingly he set the trap again, and this time when he caught the villain he carried it some two miles away, gave it a severe admonition with a stick, and let it depart in peace.

—Harding.

Years later he recorded another woodchuck encounter.

"I squatted down and surveyed him at my leisure. . . . When I moved, it gritted its teeth quite loud, sometimes striking the under jaw against the other chatteringly, sometimes grinding one jaw on the other, yet as if more from instinct than anger. Whichever way I turned, that way it headed. I took a twig a good long one and touched its snout, at which it started forward and bit the stick, lessening the distance between us by two feet, and still it held all the ground it gained. I played with it tenderly awhile with the stick, trying to open its gritting jaws. . . . We sat looking at one another about half an hour, till he began to feel mesmeric influences. . . . I walked round him; he turned as fast and fronted me still. I sat down by his side within a foot. I talked to him *quasi* forest lingo, baby-talk, at any rate in a conciliatory tone, and thought that I had some influence on him. He gritted his teeth less. . . . With a little stick I lifted one of his paws to examine it, and held it up at pleasure. I turned him over to see what color he was beneath (darker or more purely brown), though he turned himself back again sooner than I could have wished. . . . I spoke kindly to him. I reached checkerberry leaves to his mouth, I stretched my hands over him, though he turned up his head and still gritted a little. I laid my hand on him, but immediately took it off again, instinct not being wholly overcome. If I had had a few fresh bean leaves, thus in advance of the season, I am sure I should have tamed him completely. . . . I finally had to leave him without seeing him move from the place."

—Harding.

There was a famous mouse.

The favorite of all his wild pets was a mouse, which Thoreau said had a nest under his house, and came when he took his luncheon to pick the crumbs at his feet. It had never seen the race of man before, and so the sooner became familiar. It ran over his shoes and up his pantaloons inside, clinging to his flesh with its sharp claws, and it would run up the side of the room by short impulses like a squirrel, which it resembled. When he held it a piece of cheese, it came and nibbled between his fingers, and then cleaned its face and paws like a fly.

—Harding.

In his Atlantic Monthly *piece, Emerson told stories of Thoreau in the natural world, his ability to measure, to observe, to experiment.*

When I was planting forest-trees, and had procured half a peck of acorns, he said that only a small portion of them would be sound, and proceeded to examine them, and select the sound ones. But finding this took time, he said, "I think, if you put them all into water, the good ones will sink"; which experiment we tried with success.

And those pieces of luck which happen only to good players happened to him. One day, walking with a stranger, who inquired where Indian arrow-heads could be found, he replied, "Everywhere," and, stooping forward, picked one on the instant from the ground.

He could pace sixteen rods more accurately than another man could measure them with rod and chain. He could find his path in the woods at night, he said, better by his feet than his eyes. He could estimate the measure of a tree very well by his eye; he could estimate the weight of a calf or a pig, like a dealer. From a box containing a bushel or more of loose pencils, he could take up with his hands fast enough just a dozen pencils at every grasp.

It was a pleasure and a privilege to walk with him. He knew the country like a fox or a bird, and passed through it as freely as paths of his own. He knew every track in the snow or on the ground, and what creature had taken this path before him. One must submit adjectly to such a guide, and the reward was great. Under his arm he carried an old musicbook to press plants;

in his pocket, his diary and pencil, a spy-glass for birds, microscope, jack-knife, and twine. He wore straw hat, stout shoes, strong gray trousers, to brave shrub-oaks and smilax, and to climb a tree for a hawk's or a squirrel's nest. He waded into the pool for the water-plants, and his strong legs were no insignificant part of his armor. On the day I speak of he looked for the Menyanthes, detected it across the wide pool, and, on examination of the florets, decided that it had been in flower five days. He drew out of his breast-pocket his diary, and read the names of all the plants that should bloom on this day, whereof he kept account as a banker when his notes fall due.

Snakes coiled round his leg; the fishes swam into his hand, and he took them out of the water; he pulled the woodchuck out of its hole by the tail, and took the foxes under his protection from the hunters. Our naturalist had perfect magnanimity; he had no secrets; he would carry you to the heron's haunt, or even to his most prized botanical swamp,—possibly knowing that you could never find it again, yet willing to take his risks.

—*Atlantic Monthly,* 1862.

His books did not sell. In his journal he told a famous story.

For a year or two past, my *publisher,* falsely so called, has been writing from time to time to ask what disposition should be made of the copies of "A Week on the Concord and Merrimack Rivers" still on hand, and at last suggesting that he had use for the room they occupied in his cellar. So I had them all sent to me here, and they have arrived to-day by express, filling the man's wagon—706 copies out of an edition of 1000 which I bought of Munroe four years ago and have ever since been paying for, and have not quite paid for yet. The wares are sent to me at last, and I have an opportunity to examine my purchase. They are something more substantial than fame, as my back knows, which has borne them up two flights of stairs to a place similar to that to which they trace their origin. Of the remaining two hundred and ninety and odd, seventy-five were given away, the rest sold. I have now a library of nearly nine hundred volumes, over seven hundred of which I wrote myself.

—*Journal V,* Oct. 27, 1853.

Through Emerson Thoreau came to know Walt Whitman, who spoke of him to Horace Traubel.

Thoreau had his own odd ways. Once he got to the house while I was out—went straight to the kitchen where my dear mother was baking some cakes—took the cakes hot from the oven. . . . But Thoreau's great fault was disdain—disdain for men (for Tom, Dick and Harry): inability to appreciate the average life—even the exceptional life: it seemed to me a want of imagination. He couldn't put his life into any other life—realize why one man was so and another man was not so: was impatient with other people on the street and so forth. We had a hot discussion about it—it was a bitter difference: it was rather a surprise to me to meet in Thoreau such a very aggravated case of superciliousness. It was egotistic—not taking that word in its worst sense. . . . We could not agree at all in our estimate of men—of the men we meet here, there, everywhere—the concrete man. Thoreau had an abstraction about man—a right abstraction: there we agreed. We had our quarrel only on this ground. Yet he was a man you would have to like—an interesting man, simple, conclusive. . . .

—*Walt Whitman's Camden Conversations,* ed. Walter Teller, 1973.

Thoreau knew himself well enough to reject the notion of Brook Farm. ("I think I had rather keep bachelor's hall in hell," he said, "than go to board in heaven.") Yet he would play and fool with children, or comfort them in their afflictions, as if superiority or disdain were alien to him.

When little Edward Emerson, carrying a basket full of his harvest, tripped and spilled them all and burst into tears, none of the others could console him with offers of berries from their baskets. But Thoreau came up, put his arm around the boy, explained that if the crop of huckleberries were to continue, it was necessary that some should be planted and that nature had provided for little boys now and then to stumble and sow the berries. If Eddy would come back in a few years, he would find a grand lot of bushes and berries on this very spot. And Edward's tears turned to smiles.

—Harding.

On occasion he entertained family or friends with displays of solo dancing. One visitor to the Thoreau house

recalled that on the evening of a day too stormy for Thoreau to take his customary outdoor exercise, he came flying down from his study and amazed them all by suddenly breaking into a dance all by himself, "spinning airily around, displaying most remarkable litheness and agility and . . . finally [springing] over the center-table, alighting like a feather on the other side—then, not in the least out of breath [continuing] his waltz until his enthusiasm abated." His mother boasted to the guest that she had taken care to see that he had had dancing lessons as a child as one of "the usual accomplishments of well-bred children."

—Harding.

When he was dying his Aunt Louisa asked him if he had made his peace with God, and he answered, "I did not know we had ever quarreled." When another friend ventured to approach him on the subject of religion he replied, "One world at a time." It remained to his mentor and friend Emerson to summarize his character.

He was a protestant *à l'outrance,* and few lives contain so many renunciations. He was bred to no profession; he never married; he lived alone; he never went to church; he never voted; he refused to pay a tax to the State; he ate no flesh, he drank no wine, he never knew the use of tobacco; and, though a naturalist, he used neither trap nor gun.

It cost him nothing to say No; indeed, he found it much easier than to say Yes. It seemed as if his first instinct on hearing a proposition was to controvert it, so impatient was he of the limitations of our daily thought. This habit, of course, is a little chilling to the social affections; and though the companion would in the end acquit him of any malice or untruth, yet it mars conversation. Hence, no equal companion stood in affectionate relations with one so pure and guileless. "I love Henry," said one of his friends, "but I cannot like him; and as for taking his arm, I should as soon think of taking the arm of an elm-tree."

—*Atlantic Monthly,* 1862.

Frederick Douglass 1817–1895

Frederick Douglass was born a slave in Maryland, escaped to Massachusetts in 1838, lectured against slavery, and wrote three autobiographies. Brought up by a grandmother while his mother worked in the fields, Douglass remembered that his mother's "visits to me . . . were few in number, brief in duration, and mostly made in the night."

My mother was hired out to a Mr. Stewart, who lived about twelve miles from old master's, and, being a field hand, she seldom had leisure, by day, for the performance of the journey. The nights and the distance were both obstacles to her visits. She was obliged to walk. . . . It was a greater luxury than slavery could afford, to allow a black slave-mother a horse or a mule, upon which to travel twenty-four miles, when she could walk the distance. Besides, it is deemed a foolish whim for a slave-mother to manifest concern to see her children, and, in one point of view, the case is made out—she can do nothing for them. She has no control over them; the master is even more than the mother, in all matters touching the fate of her child. Why, then, should she give herself any concern? She has no responsibility. Such is the reasoning, and such the practice. The iron rule of the plantation, always passionately and violently enforced in that neighborhood, makes flogging the penalty of failing to be in the field before sunrise in the morning, unless special permission be given to the absenting slave. "I went to see my child," is no excuse to the ear or heart of the overseer.

One of the visits of my mother to me, while at Col. Lloyd's, I remember very vividly, as affording a bright gleam of a mother's love, and the earnestness of a mother's care.

I had on that day offended "Aunt Katy" (called "Aunt" by way of respect), the cook of old master's establishment. I do not now remember the nature of my offense in this instance, for my offenses were numerous in that quarter, greatly depending, however, upon the mood of Aunt Katy, as to their heinousness; but she had adopted, that day, her favorite mode of punishing me, namely, making me go without food all day—that is, from after breakfast. The first hour or two after dinner, I succeeded pretty well in keeping up my spirits; but though I made an excellent stand against the foe, and fought bravely during the afternoon, I knew I must be conquered at last, unless I got the accustomed reenforcement of a slice of corn bread, at sundown. Sundown came, but *no bread,* and, in its stead, there came the threat, with a scowl well suited to its terrible import, that she "meant to *starve the life out of me!"* Brandishing her knife, she chopped off the heavy slices for the other children, and put the loaf away, muttering, all the while, her savage designs upon myself. Against this disappointment, for I was expecting that her heart would relent at last, I made an extra effort to maintain my dignity; but when I saw all the other children around me with merry and satisfied faces, I could stand it no longer. I went out behind the house, and cried like a fine fellow! When tired of this, I returned to the kitchen, sat by the fire, and brooded over my hard lot. I was too hungry to sleep. While I sat in the corner, I caught sight of an ear of Indian corn on an upper shelf of the kitchen. I watched my chance, and got it, and, shelling off a few grains, I put it back again. The grains in my hand, I quickly put in some ashes, and covered them with embers, to roast them. All this I did at the risk of getting a brutal thumping, for Aunt Katy could beat, as well as starve me. My corn was not long in roasting, and, with my keen appetite, it did not matter even if the grains were not exactly done. I eagerly pulled them out, and placed them on my stool, in a clever little pile. Just as I began to help myself to my very dry meal, in came my dear mother. And now, dear reader, a scene occurred which was altogether worth beholding, and to me it was instructive as well as interesting. The friendless and hungry boy, in his extremest need—and when he did not dare to look for succor—found himself in the strong, protecting arms of a mother; a mother who was, at the moment (being endowed with high powers of manner as well as matter) more than a match for all his enemies. I shall never forget the indescribable expression of her countenance, when I told her that I had had no food since morning; and that Aunt Katy said she "meant to starve the life out of me." There was pity in her glance at me, and a fiery indignation at Aunt Katy at the same time; and, while she took the corn from me, and gave me a large ginger cake, in its stead, she read Aunt Katy a lecture which she never forgot. My mother threatened her with complaining to old master in my behalf; for the latter, though harsh and cruel himself, at times, did not sanction the meanness, injustice, partiality and oppressions enacted by Aunt Katy in the kitchen. That night I learned the fact that I was not only a child, but *somebody's* child. The "sweet cake" my mother gave me was in the shape of a heart, with a rich, dark ring glazed upon the edge of it. I was victorious, and well off for the moment; prouder, on my mother's knee, than a king upon his throne. But my triumph was short. I dropped off to sleep, and waked in the morning only to find my mother gone, and myself left at the mercy of the sable virago, dominant in my old master's kitchen, whose fiery wrath was my constant dread. I do not remember to have seen my mother after this occurrence.

—Frederick Douglass, *My Bondage and My Freedom*, 1855.

Herman Melville 1819–1891

The sea-going Melville, an adventurer who traveled light, astounded the quiet Hawthornes, whose son Julian remembered Melville decades later.

". . . when the narrative inspiration was on him, he looked like all the things he was describing—savages, sea-captains, the lovely Fayaway in her canoe, or the terrible Moby Dick himself."

—*Dictionary of Biographical Quotation*, eds. Richard Kenin and Justin Wintle, 1978.

Writing his biography of his parents, Julian Hawthorne recounted a particular storytelling.

. . . one evening . . . [Herman Melville] came in, and presently began to relate the story of a fight which he had seen on an island in the Pacific, between some savages, and of the prodigies of valor one of them performed with a heavy club. The narrative was extremely graphic; and when Melville had gone, and Mr. and Mrs. Hawthorne were talking over his visit, the latter said, "Where is that club with which Mr. Melville was laying about him so?" Mr. Hawthorne thought he must have taken it with him; Mrs. Hawthorne thought he had put it in the corner; but it was not to be found. The next time Melville came, they asked him about it; whereupon it appeared that the club was still in the Pacific island, if it were anywhere.

—*Nathaniel Hawthorne and His Wife*, 1884.

In Hawthorne's journals, Melville is the object of wonder and admiration—

He sailed from Liverpool in a steamer on Tuesday, leaving his trunk behind him at my consulate, and taking only a carpet-bag to hold all his traveling gear. This is the next best thing to going naked; and as he wears his beard and mustache, and so needs no dressing case—nothing but a tooth-brush—I do not know a more independent personage. He learned his traveling habits by drifting about, all over the South Sea, with no other clothes or equipage than a red flannel shirt and a pair of duck trousers.

—Nathaniel Hawthorne, *Passages from the English Notebooks,* 1870.

—admiration perhaps limited by one famous clause of qualification.

He is a person of very gentlemanly instincts in every respect, save that he is a little heterodox in the matter of clean linen.

—Hawthorne.

The author of Moby-Dick *fit in oddly at Concord, and agreed not at all with Emerson's notions of human nature. In a copy of Emerson's essays, where the Sage had written "Trust men, and they will be true to you; treat them greatly, and they will show themselves great," Melville wrote in the margin, "God help the poor fellow who squares his life according to this."*

After early success as the author of sea stories like Typee *and* Omoo, *Melville's reputation declined with the sales of his books. The New York correspondent of the* Boston Literary World *reported that he had seen "an old gentleman with white hair in a bookstore" who was identified as the Herman Melville who had once written "romances of the South Sea." He concluded*

Had he possessed as much literary skill as wild imagination his works might have secured for him a permanent place in American literature.

—1885.

Years after his death his granddaughter (Mrs. Frances Cuthbert Thomas Osborne) remembered a game the old man played with her.

Grandpa had one delightful custom. Sometimes he would ask me to lend him five cents. It would always be when he knew I had that amount in my possession, having just been paid for picking stones from Grandma's little garden, a penny for every time I filled a certain small gill measure. The first time Grandpa asked me for a loan I gave up my nickel rather reluctantly for it had just been earned, but he returned it in the form of a dime. I had to have it explained that it was twice as much, for the dime looked so small and thin compared to my nickel. After that I was always ready to lend my money whenever he asked for it, for it always came back with interest.

—"Herman Melville Through a Child's Eyes," *Bulletin of the New York Public Library*, 1965.

Walt Whitman 1819–1892

Whitman set the type for the first edition of Leaves of Grass, *which sold poorly. The* Boston Intelligencer *did not conceal its feelings about the new author.*

The beastliness of the author is set forth in his own description of himself, and we can conceive of no better reward than the lash for such a violation of decency. The author should be kicked from all decent society as below the level of the brute. He must be some escaped lunatic raving in pitiable delirium.

—1855.

Not all reviews were hostile, for Whitman reviewed Leaves of Grass *himself and was more kindly disposed than the* Boston Intelligencer. *In the* Brooklyn Times, *Whitman anonymously wrote:*

Very devilish to some, and very divine to some, will appear these new poems, the Leaves of Grass, an attempt as they are, of a live, naieve *[sic]*, masculine, tenderly affectionate, rowdyish, contemplative, sensual, moral, susceptible and imperious person, to cast into literature not only his own grit and arrogance, but his own flesh and form, undraped, regardless of foreign models, regardless of modesty or law, and ignorant or silently scornful, as at first appears, of all except his own presence and experience, and all outside the fiercely loved land of his birth, and the birth of his parents for several generations before him.

—1855.

A year later, when Emerson had spread the news about Leaves of Grass, *Whitman welcomed guests from Concord. Bronson Alcott and Henry Thoreau arrived accompanied by a Mrs. Sara Tyndale from New York.*

Walt showed them up the narrow stairs at Classon Avenue to the attic room he shared with Eddy [his brother]. Their common bed was still unmade; the chamber pot beneath sat practically in full sight. Walt, it was clear, exhibited the insouciance and rectitude he cherished in animals. A rough worktable and chair stood by the single window; there was a small pile of books on the mantelpiece. Pasted on the bare wall were prints of Hercules, Bacchus, and a satyr. "Which, now, of the three, particularly, is the new poet here?" Alcott asked. Walt declined to be questioned about the pictures, hinting, as Alcott understood, that perhaps he saw himself as Hercules, Bacchus and satyr combined, a sort of pantheon.

Pictures aside, he seemed not only eager to talk about himself but reluctant to have the conversation stray from the subject for long. While his visitors tried to accommodate themselves in this cheerless coop, Walt told them a great deal about himself, his daily baths (even in the coldest weather), his passion for the opera, Broadway omnibuses, their drivers and, above all, his writing. He lived for nothing else but to "make poems," he told them, pronouncing the word "pomes," . . .

—Justin Kaplan, *Walt Whitman: A Life,* 1980.

Whitman's service during the Civil War needs his own telling.

During the Union War I commenced at the close of 1862, and continued steadily through '63, '64, '65, to visit the sick and wounded of the Army, both on the field and in the Hospitals in and around Washington. From the first I kept little notebooks for impromptu jottings in pencil to refresh my memory of names and circumstances, and what was specially wanted, &c. In these I brief'd cases, persons, sights, occurrences in camp, by the bedside, and not seldom by the corpse of the dead. Of the present Volume most of the pages are *verbatim* renderings from such pencillings on the spot. Some were scratch'd down from narratives I heard and itemized while watching or waiting, or tending somebody amid these scenes. I have perhaps forty such little note-books left, forming a special history of those years, for myself alone, full of associations never to be possibly said or sung. I wish I could convey to the reader the associations that attach to these soil'd and creas'd little livraisons, each composed of a sheet or two of paper, folded small to carry in the pocket, and fastn'd with a pin. I leave them just as I threw them by during the War, blotch'd here and there with more than one blood-stain, hurriedly written, sometimes at the clinique, not seldom amid the excitement of uncertainty, or defeat, or of action, or getting ready for it, or a march. Even these days, at the lapse of many years, I can never turn their tiny leaves, or even take one in my hand, without the actual sights and hot emotions of the time rushing like a river in full tide through me. Each line, each scrawl, each memorandum, has its history. Some pang of anguish—some tragedy, profounder than ever poets wrote. Out of them arise active and breathing forms.

Sunday Evening, May 3, '63. Armory Sq. Hosp. Ward D. to 5 wounded or sick with fever &c. distributed a small pot of nice apple jelly—fed 2 who were very weak with a spoon.

April 7th 1863.

Joseph Armstrong, quiet Pennsylvania boy, very low with dysentery—I write this sitting by his bed—tells me, he can't help thinking of the time when his mother died—(dysentery)—both of us are crying and very much ashamed & mad about it afterward.

Henry D. Boardman—Co. B. 27th Conn. Vol.—Young man from Northford, Conn. (near 7 miles from New Haven).—Bed 25—Camp. H.W.6—wants a rice pudding, not very sweet.

July 22, 1863.—Oscar F. Wilber, Co. G. 154th N.Y.—Ward K. Bed 47—talk with him July 22d '63 afternoon. Asked me to read a chapter in the New Testament—I complied, asking him what. "Make your own choice," said he. I opened at the close of one of the Evangelists in the first part testament describing the latter hours & crucifixion of Christ—he asked me to read the following chapter, how he rose again. It pleased him very much, the tears were in his eyes—he asked me if I "enjoyed religion"—I said probably not my dear, in the way you mean.

Wm. Von Vliet, Co. #. 89th New York. Bed 37,—shell wound in the arm—Gave 20 cts.—Wants some smoking tobacco & pipe—arm amp.—turn out bad—died poor boy.

Hiram Scholis—bed 3—Ward E.—26th N. York—wants some pickles—a bottle of pickles.

—*Walt Whitman and the Civil War,* ed. Charles I. Glicksberg, 1933.

In 1871 it was not common for poets to read their poems aloud.

On August 1 a committee representing the American Institute in New York invited [Whitman] to deliver a poem celebrating the opening of the fortieth National Industrial Exhibition on September 7, 1871. They offered to pay him $100 and his expenses, and requested the privilege of supplying copies of the poem to the metropolitan press "for publication with the other proceedings." Whitman lost no time in accepting these terms. Fairs and exhibitions had always fascinated him, and aside from the liberal honorarium, the publicity would be a real windfall. . . .

On the scheduled day Whitman appeared and delivered his poem "After All, Not to Create Only." Horace Greeley was usually the main attraction on opening day, but he was away on a lecture tour, and Walt Whitman attempted to put on a show in his place. He not only supplied some two dozen copies of his poem for the newspapers of New York and Brooklyn, but he also provided what would later have been called "press releases," and he succeeded in getting publicity, though not much of it to his liking. Twelve out of seventeen metropolitan papers printed his poem next day, and a few printed his "handouts" either before or after the performance. But the papers were for the most part satirical or downright hostile after the event.

On opening day of the exhibition the workmen were still noisily building or arranging the exhibits, and several papers reported that of the two or three hundred in the audience scarcely anyone could hear a word the poet said. . . .

Whitman replied to the slurs and attacks with anonymous articles in the Washington *Chronicle* and *Evening Star.* In the former a purported correspondent from New York reported that when the poet began reading, five or six hundred carpenters, machinists, and other workmen paused with their tools in their hands to listen, and that the audience of two or three thousand people several times interrupted with applause.

—Gay Wilson Allen, *The Solitary Singer,* 1955.

Although his work was reviled, it was also loved—and pilgrims arrived to pay homage. Whitman had a considerable following in England, and even Tennyson invited him to call.

Oscar Wilde, wearing his brown velvet suit, crossed over to Camden with J. M. Stoddard, the publisher. They were admitted to the Whitman home on Stevens Street by Walt's sister-in-law, who offered them elderberry wine. Wilde drank it off as if it "were the nectar of the gods," and confided to Stoddard later that, "If it had been vinegar, I would have drunk it all the same, for I have an admiration for that man which I can hardly express." The two poets got along splendidly together. Walt called him "Oscar," and the younger man sat at his feet on a low stool, with his hand on the poet's knee. Next day to a Philadelphia *Press* reporter Whitman stated for publication that he thought Wilde "was glad to get away from lecturing, and fashionable society, and spend a time with an 'old rough.' We had a very happy time together. I think him genuine, honest, and manly."

—Allen.

One visitor arrived in mid-morning.

Two mornings later Trowbridge called again at Walt's garret. He had been warned not to come before ten o'clock, and it was after ten. Walt was partly dressed and was preparing his breakfast on the sheet-iron stove. With his jackknife he cut slices of bread, which his guest kindly toasted for him on a sharpened stick. He made tea in a tin kettle, dipped sugar out of a brown paper bag, and used another piece of brown paper for a butter plate. For cupboard he used an oblong pine box standing against the wall. Breakfast over, he burned his butter plate. Besides the teakettle, his entire housekeeping equipment consisted of a tin cup, a bowl, and a spoon.

—Allen.

Logan Pearsall Smith's sister Mary came home to Germantown from Smith College, announcing that a great poet was living in Camden, New Jersey. Therefore her family paid a visit, as her brother remembered it.

We flashed along through Fairmont Park, we drove across Philadelphia, we embarked in the ferry and crossed the Delaware, and dashed up before the little two-story wooden house in Camden to which we had been directed. An elderly woman who answered the doorbell ushered us into a little parlour and shouted upstairs, "Walt, here's some carriage folk come to see you." We heard a stirring above us as of a slow and unwieldy person, and soon through the open door we saw two large feet in carpet slippers slowly descending the stairs, and then the bulky form of the old man appeared before us. Walt Whitman greeted us with friendly simplicity; he had no notion who we were, and we had no introduction to him, but the unannounced appearance of these "carriage folk" from across the river—this portly and opulent-looking gentleman with his tall son and beautiful tall daughter—did not seem to surprise him in the least. My sister informed him that our name was Smith, that she had read his *Leaves of Grass,* and had come to express her immense admiration for that volume, and this explanation was received with great complacency; we were all invited to follow him upstairs to his den, where we sat down on what chairs could be hastily provided, and were soon engaged in lively talk.

My father, who at first held himself aloof in the most disapproving manner, soon, to the surprise of my sister and myself, began to join in this friendly conversation, and we were still more surprised, when we got up to take our departure, to hear our impulsive parent invite the object of his grave disapprobation to drive back with us to Germantown and spend the night. The afternoon was, he urged, a fine one, the drive across the Park would be pleasant, and it would be a pity to bring to a premature end so agreeable a confabulation. "No, Mr. Smith, I think I won't come," the poet answered; but when he had hobbled to the window and seen, waiting in the street outside, my father's equipage, he said that he thought he might as well come after all, and, hastily putting a nightshirt and a few other objects in a little bag, he hobbled downstairs and we all drove off together. It was, as my father had said, a pleasant afternoon; we crossed again the ferry, we drove through Philadelphia and through the Park to our home in Germantown, where Walt Whitman remained with us for a month, and whither he would often afterwards return. He became indeed a familiar and friendly inmate of the house, whose genial presence, even when we did not see him, could hardly pass unnoticed, for he had the habit of singing "Old Jim Crow" when not occupied in conversation, and his loud and cheerful voice could be heard echoing every morning from the bathroom or the water closet. His arrivals were always unannounced; he would appear when he liked, stay as long as he liked; and then one morning we would find at breakfast a pencilled note to say that he had departed early, having had for the present enough of our society.

—Logan Pearsall Smith, *Unforgotten Years,* 1938.

Smith adds a tale of another encounter.

My sister Mary recalls how once, when she was on the Camden ferry, she saw an Englishman also on the boat. He must, she rightly concluded, be on a pilgrimage like herself to visit Walt Whitman, for how otherwise account for the presence of that Englishman? She, therefore, accosted the correct and dapper figure, who confessed, with some surprise, that this was in fact his purpose. My sister offered to show him the way to Walt Whitman's house, and they proceeded thither, to find, however, that the door was locked and they could get no answer to their knockings. "I'm sure he's upstairs," my sister said; "he always is, so the best thing is for me to boost you up to the window, which you can open, and then come down and let me in." Edmund Gosse (for the Englishman was Edmund Gosse) seemed considerably surprised, my sister says, by the unconventionality of this proposal, but as he had come a long way to visit Walt

Whitman, and did not wish to be baffled in his object, he finally allowed my sister to boost him up; and then he descended to open the front door to her, and they found Walt Whitman as usual in his study. . . .

—Smith.

Gosse denied the story.

When Whitman was old, he had many visitors, some of whom set down his words.

[Whitman, said:] "What lies behind 'Leaves of Grass' is something that few, very few, only one here and there, perhaps oftenest women, are at all in a position to seize. It lies behind almost every line; but concealed, studiedly concealed; some passages left purposely obscure. There is something in my nature *furtive* like an old hen! You see a hen wandering up and down a hedgerow, looking apparently quite unconcerned, but presently she finds a concealed spot, and furtively lays an egg, and comes away as though nothing had happened! That is how I felt in writing 'Leaves of Grass.' Sloan Kennedy calls me 'artful'—which about hits the mark. I think there are truths which it is necessary to envelop or wrap up."

—Edward Carpenter, *Days with Walt Whitman,* 1906.

A young man named Horace Traubel visited him regularly, asked questions, and wrote down the replies. Whitman showed him some of the correspondence and manuscripts that he kept around in trunks, boxes, and heaps. Here are some of Traubel's records, quoting Whitman; the interjections without quotation marks are Traubel's own words.

". . . there in Brooklyn: we were coming down what was called Washington Hill together . . . one of the many walks I delighted to take with my dear, dear mother. I can see it all, all, even now: the two of us there, the man approaching—my mother's voice: her hand as it was laid on my arm. . . . The fellow came up—asked me for ten cents: he had not eaten, &c. I growled out: 'I'll give you nothing': turned away. The man was drunk then: was evidently now far along in a week of dissipation—perhaps trying to get rid of the effects of it: anyway, in bad condition. I was certain the ten cents more would but go . . . for drink. We passed on. My mother spoke to me: she said (laid her hand on my arm): 'I know what you are thinking—I know you feel it would only add to his misery to give him ten cents more now: I know about such men: when they get into that state then nothing can be done for the moment but give them the drink: it is but mercy to give it to them.' . . . She was quiet, tender: I looked at her as if to ask, What? she continuing: 'I wish you had given him the money: I would have you go back and give it to him yet.' So I went back, complied—we resumed our walk."

"No one of my people—the people near to me—ever had any time for Leaves of Grass—thought it more than an ordinary piece of work, if that." Not even his mother? "No—I think not—even her: there is, as I say, no one in my immediate family who follows me out on that line. My dear mother had every general faith in me: that is where she stopped. She stood before Leaves of Grass mystified, defeated."

"What a sweat I used to be in all the time," said W., "over getting my damned books published! When I look back at it I wonder I didn't somewhere or other on the road chuck the whole business into oblivion. Editions! Editions! Editions! like the last extra of a newspaper: an extra after an extra: one issue after another: fifty-five, fifty-six, sixty-one, sixty-seven—oh! edition after edition. Yes, I wonder I never did anything violent with the book, it has so victimized me!"

8 P.M. W. reading the Mrs. Carlyle letters. Held the book sort of in the air as he read. Eyes wide open. Hat on. Entire attitude one of great interest. Light burned brightly. Saw me—laid the book down: "Howdy? Howdy?" extending his right hand. They had cleared the room up a bit today. Complains some of his eyes. Fire burns in his room. Very hot but calls the room "just about comfortable." Likes to keep the stove door open—to feed the fire from time to time. Still hates to be helped. "I'd rather die helping myself than live being helped."

—*Walt Whitman's Camden Conversations,* ed. Walter Teller, 1973.

James Russell Lowell 1819–1891

Although one of the New England Pantheon welcomed Whitman, and others were polite, a few were unreconciled—especially James Russell Lowell, who succeeded Longfellow as a lecturer at Harvard. As a teacher he answered a clergyman's letter about Leaves of Grass *in 1863.*

I am obliged to you, however, for calling my attention to a part of this book of which I knew nothing, and I will take care to keep it out of the way of the students.

—Richard Croom Beatty, *James Russell Lowell,* 1942.

Lowell had his eccentric moments: he was prone to depression and complementary manic extravagance.

On one occasion he hoisted himself up a lamppost, where for hours he perched and crowed like a rooster. Acquaintances recalled Lowell unconcernedly removing and proceeding to eat with knife and fork a bouquet of flowers from the centerpiece at a literary supper in one of Boston's great houses. At an important meeting of poets he astounded everyone by gathering up his coattails and galloping around the room to illustrate the movements of a horse. He was known to accost strangers on the street and swing them about as though they were his closest friends, whom he had not seen in years. Nor was the stone wall built that he could resist mounting and conquering, balancing himself along its edge with the finesse of a tightrope artist. People who knew him took Lowell at these instances for a rowdy showoff or a violent madman, rather than the intellectual hero and cultural ideologue he prided himself on being. Had he been any less accomplished a poet he would surely have been handcuffed and led off, never to be heard from or seen again.

—C. David Heymann, *American Aristocracy,* 1980.

Even on the heights of a Bostonian Parnassus, the gods sometimes offended each other. Annie Fields recorded an episode in which Emerson revealed ignorance and Lowell took revenge.

Parkman said to Lowell, and a more strange evidence of lapse of tact could hardly be discovered, "Lowell, what did you mean by 'the land of broken promise'?" Emerson, catching at this last, said, "What is this about the land of broken promise?" clearly showing he had never read Lowell's Ode upon the death of Agassiz—whereat Lowell answered not at all, but dropped his eyes and silence succeeded, although Parkman made some kind of futile attempt to struggle out of it. Emerson said, "We have met two great losses in our Club since you were last here—Agassiz and Sumner." "Yes," said Lowell, "but a greater than either was that of a man I could never make you believe in as I did—Hawthorne." This ungracious speech silenced even Emerson. . . .

—M. A. DeWolfe Howe, *Memories of a Hostess,* 1922.

Lowell was appointed minister to Spain (1877–80) and to England (1880–85). In London he became an avuncular friend of the younger Henry James. It was James who recollected an incident at the table of the Poet Laureate.

"Luncheon began with an embarrassing silence, broken finally by the Bard's growling at Lowell: 'Do you know anything about Lowell?' Mrs. Tennyson had to come to the rescue with a 'Why, my dear, this *is* Mr. Lowell!' "

—Leon Edel, *Henry James: The Conquest of London 1870–1881,* 1962.

Emily Dickinson 1830–1886

A few years younger than Whitman and the Bostonians, the poet of Amherst lived an apparently narrow and secluded life—energetic with poems, gregarious with letters. Because her family was prominent in the town and its college, Dickinson's privacy made her a local myth, long before anyone realized her genius. In 1881, before Mabel Todd met Emily Dickinson—though she later became her close friend and her brother's mistress—she wrote a letter full of local rumor.

"I must tell you about the *character* of Amherst. It is a lady whom the people call the *Myth.* She is a sister of Mr. Dickinson, & seems to be the climax of all the family oddity. She has not been outside of her own house in fifteen years. . . . No one who calls upon her mother & sister ever see her, but she allows little children once in a great while, & one at a time, to come in, when she gives them cake or candy, or some nicety, for she is very fond of little ones. But more often she lets down the sweetmeat by a string, out of a window, to them. She dresses wholly in white, & her mind is said to be perfectly wonderful. She writes finely, but no one *ever* sees her. Her sister, who was at Mrs. Dickinson's party, invited me to come & sing to her mother some time and I promised to go & if the performance pleases her, a servant will enter with wine for me, or a flower, & perhaps her thanks; but just probably the token of approval will not come then, but a few days after, some dainty present will appear for me at twilight. People tell me that the *myth* will hear every note—she will be near, but unseen. . . . Isn't that like a book?"

—Richard B. Sewall, *Emily Dickinson,* 1974.

There were stories the family told.

On one Sunday in particular the dignified lawyer [Emily's father] had assembled his family for divine worship in the village church and Emily was summoned with the rest of the group. But she had disappeared, nor could search reveal her hiding place. Late in the afternoon Vinnie [her sister Lavinia] discovered her rocking away peacefully in the cellar bulkhead, reading a favourite book. "Oh yes," she replied calmly, to exclamations of wonder at her chosen place of immolation, "Why should I argue? I did not wish to go to church."

—Sewall.

There were years when she went nowhere.

. . . she . . . crept out one evening with her brother as far as a certain tree in the hedge in order to see the new church which her brother had been the most instrumental in building. Old College Hall had been the church which she knew before the new stone Gothic building had arisen; so she went out actually from the house as far as would allow her a view of what she had heard about for months, but had not seen until the wonderful night which took her out into its view.

—Sewall.

Her brother's house was next door, and Dickinson was especially fond of her brother's small son.

Her little nephew, boy-like, had a way of leaving anything superfluous to his immediate needs at Grandma's. After one of these little "Sins of Omission," over came his high-top rubber boots, standing erect and spotless on a silver tray, their tops running over with Emily's flowers. At another time the little overcoat was returned with each velvet pocket pinned down, and a card with "Come in" on one, and "Knock" on the other. The "Come in" proved to be raisins:—the "Knock," cracked nuts.

—Clara Newman Turner, "My Personal Acquaintance with Emily Dickinson," 1894 [quoted in Sewall].

She cultivated many friends, especially through correspondence. Several encouraged her in her work—although none of them, understandably, had the critical talent to detect her poetic genius. Only six of her poems appeared in her lifetime, and none with her consent.

Thomas Wentworth Higginson, editor of the Atlantic Monthly, *feared that her verbal eccentricities might have been encouraged by a reading of* Leaves of Grass. *"You speak of Mr. Whitman—" she answered him, "I never read his book—but was told that he was disgraceful—."*

Another friend was the newspaper editor Samuel Bowles, who came calling in Amherst.

This is the time when, according to a familiar story, Emily had at first declined to see him, and he had shouted upstairs, "Emily, you damned rascal! No more of this nonsense! I've traveled all the way from Springfield to see you. Come down at once." Down she came, we are told, and was charming and sociable.

—Gertrude M. Graves, "A Cousin's Memories of Emily Dickinson," *Boston Sunday Globe,* Jan. 12, 1930.

She took pleasure in routine. When an old servant departed the Dickinson household, Emily wrote, "I winced at her loss, because I was in the habit of her, and even a new rolling pin has an embarrassing element." Yet if we pity her solitude, we may mistake the matter. She so organized her life that she produced an enormous oeuvre, *unequaled in value and in size by any American poet besides Whitman. And she is the first great female poet of the English language.*

Still, her anecdotal presence remains apart from the poems—as the legend dressed in white inhabiting an attic room. Nine years before she died, when Emily was forty-seven, Clara Bellinger Green visited the Dickinson house with her brother and sister. The three visitors sang for Emily Dickinson, who listened upstairs. Green told what happened next.

At the close of the singing a light clapping of hands, like a flutter of wings, floated down the staircase, and Miss Lavinia came to tell us that Emily would see us—my sister and myself—in the library. . . . In the library, dimly lighted from the hall, a tiny figure in white darted to greet us, grasped our hands and told us of her pleasure in hearing us sing.

"Except for the birds," she said, "yours is the first song I have heard for many years. I have long been familiar with the voice and the laugh of each one of you, and I know, too, your brother's whistle as he trudges by the house." She spoke rapidly, with the breathless voice of a child and with a peculiar charm I have not forgotten.

. . . As she stood before us in the vague light of the library we were chiefly aware of a pair of great, dark eyes set in a small, pale, delicately chiseled face, and a little body, quaint, simple as a child and wholly unaffected.

—*The Bookman,* Nov. 1924.

Horatio Alger, Jr. 1832–1899

Horatio Alger, Jr., published one hundred and thirty books which sold twenty million copies, mostly stereotyped tales in which young men moved from rags to riches, from beggary to business: Ragged Dick, Luck and Pluck, Tattered Tom. Before he turned to literature, he had been a minister, a calling which he left in disgrace. As a rich novelist, in later years, he kept close association with the Newsboys' Lodging House in New York City.

For it was boys, boys, boys that interested the Reverend Mr. Alger. He organized the Cadets for Temperance, which drew boys from his Sunday School classes. Unlike other adults he was never too busy for a walk in the woods or a game of ball or a songfest. He organized games and entertainments and events that would appeal to boys in a quiet rural community where so little was available for amusement. His love for boys and the boys' attraction to him were well known. Now, the rueful committee members wished they had been warned by this inordinate fondness for boys, for recently the most dreadful rumors regarding Horatio Alger, Jr. and boys of the parish had been making their way around the community.

. . . the parish committee adjourned.

A week later Thomas Crocker, Elisha Bangs and Moderator Gould came in with a dreadful report. Crocker had started at home with his own son, Thomas S. Crocker, and from him had learned that the Reverend Mr. Alger had been buggering him. Not only him, but John Clark too, and perhaps there were others. The shocked senior Crocker wished to go no further. "We learn from John Clark and Thomas S. Crocker that Horatio Alger, Jr. has been practicing on them at different times deeds that are too revolting to relate," Crocker, Bangs and Gould reported to the parishioners. Further, they had called Horatio Alger to appear before them and repeated the accusations of their boys, half hoping that the boys were up to some devilment and that the whole dreadful matter was a mistake.

But no. Braced by the committee, Horatio Alger, Jr. did not deny the charges. He had been "imprudent," he said.

—Edwin P. Hoyt, *Horatio's Boys,* 1974.

Louisa May Alcott 1832–1888

Alcott wrote in Little Women *a happy account of her Concord childhood, where her father, Bronson Alcott, was Emerson's close friend. As a young girl, she cherished hidden feelings for the philosopher.*

She was tremendously moved, just as other girls were then, by *Goethe's Correspondence with a Child,* which she had discovered while browsing in Emerson's library. This was published in 1835, and tells of the romantic passion a young girl, Bettina von Arnim, conceived for the poet when he was nearly sixty years old. Louisa immediately imagined herself the Bettina of the letters, and replaced Goethe, whom she had always adored, with her father's friend, Mr. Emerson.

She wrote passionate letters to Ralph Waldo Emerson, but never sent them. She sat in the tall walnut tree in front of his house, at midnight, singing to the moon—until an owl scared her back to bed. She left wild flowers at the door of her "master's" study and sang songs under his window in very bad German.

Of course, Emerson was totally unaware of this devotion from the nice child who ran in and out of his house as freely as his own daughter, Ellen.

—Marjorie Worthington, *Miss Alcott of Concord: A Biography*, 1958.

Her romantic imagination reached to include Nathaniel Hawthorne's eldest son.

Julian Hawthorne, who was attending the Sanborn School, went past the house every day, and always stopped for talk and laughter. He was somewhat younger than May, the youngest Alcott; but it was one of Louisa's family jokes that he had developed a tender passion for this younger sister. Louisa used to hold forth on the hopelessness of poor Julian's attachment, since a mythical "cousin from England," a vague person of highest rank and fortune, was to arrive some day and carry May away to pursue life in the exalted ranks of the titled great.

One evening, just at dusk, Julian was walking down the road past the house when a strange and horrifying sight met him. May was standing at the gate, and beside her was a tall stranger, carrying a foppish cane, dressed with a slight eccentricity which must be foreign, possessed of bold, dark eyes and a small black moustache. The astounding thing was that his arm was about May's waist, evidently without her protest or objection.

Julian approached, his eyes fairly starting from his head, and was introduced to "our cousin." The foreigner stepped forward, bowed, and acknowledged the introduction with an insolent patronage of manner which the boy could not endure.

"Well, well, so this is our young friend Julian; quite a well-grown boy!"

Intolerable talk to a lad who had cast something in the nature of adoring eyes at May! Julian stepped up to the stranger and was received by a flourish of the cane in his face, twirled with apparent carelessness by the English youth, but none the less uncomfortably and threateningly near. The American boy clenched his fists, and suddenly May, apparently overcome, turned and took flight towards the house. The Englishman took one more provocative step forward, then, amazingly, snatched off the black moustache and threw it over Julian's head, following it with the black felt hat which had created such a rakish, foreign impression. The removal of the hat brought down a flood of dark hair. Julian Hawthorne said of the scene, long afterwards:

"Then Louisa turned and pursued May up the path, whooping like a Comanche, but with a feminine consciousness, I fancied, of the pantaloons."

—Cornelia Meigs, *The Story of Louisa May Alcott,* 1935.

In later years she devoted herself to the struggle for woman suffrage, and found her fame as an author both boon and burden.

She recalls that during the Woman's Congress in Syracuse one energetic lady in the crowd grasped her hand and gushed, "If you ever come to Oshkosh, your feet will not be allowed to touch the ground: you will be borne in the arms of the people. Will you come?"

"Never," responded Miss Alcott. . . .

—Worthington.

James Abbott McNeill Whistler 1834–1903

The painter and polemicist dropped ten thousand bons mots, some of which were printed in The Gentle Art of Making Enemies—*a collection of ripostes and letters to editors denouncing critics. One of the book's items is headed, "A Correction."*

A supposititious conversation in *Punch* brought about the following interchange of telegrams:—

From Oscar Wilde, Exeter, to J. McNeill Whistler, Tite Street—*Punch* too ridiculous—when you and I are together we never talk about anything except ourselves.

From Whistler, Tite Street, to Oscar Wilde, Exeter.—No, no, Oscar, you forget—when you and I are together, we never talk about anything except me.

—1906.

Wilde was an old friend, therefore subject of much vituperation; Whistler's gentle art kept friendships brief. It was Wilde to whom Whistler directed his most famous line. Wilde had applauded one of Whistler's witticisms and innocently added that he wished he had said it himself. Whistler replied, "You will, Oscar, you will."

If tact was not Whistler's strongest quality, neither was fact.

An American accosted Whistler in the Carlton Restaurant, London: "You know, we were both born in Lowell, Massachusetts, and at very much the same time. There is only the difference of a year: you are sixty-seven and I am sixty-eight." Whistler raised his eyeglass, secured the attention of the other diners with his sharp "Ha-ha!" and replied: "Very charming! And so you are sixty-eight and were born at Lowell! Most interesting, no doubt, and as you please. But I shall be born when and where I want, and I do not choose to be born at Lowell, and I refuse to be sixty-seven!"

—Hesketh Pearson, *The Man Whistler,* 1952.

On other occasions he had named Baltimore, Maryland, as his birthplace, and St. Petersburg, Russia. He was born in Lowell.

One need have no worries about its veracity to enjoy the story of early poverty, which Whistler performed for Robert Ross, who repeated it to Whistler's biographer.

"I had no money, and fish was cheap, so I lived on fish. Fish for breakfast, fish for dinner, always fish. My landlady could only think in fish. The lodgings reeked of fish. Even the Thames, which I had beautified, became for me merely the home of fish. I tried to paint a portrait, but the face of my subject seemed scaly. Then one day I looked out of my window and up at the clouds, and behold! a mackerel sky. So I looked down. Could I believe my eyes? At least I could believe my nose. There, in a bowl of water on my landlady's window sill, were three goldfish swimming tauntingly at their ease. I resolved to teach her a lesson. Soon she would be bringing me a meal of fish. She, too, should have fish for her meal. I affixed a bent pin to a piece of string, baited the pin with bread, and let it down from my window into the bowl beneath. I am not a skilled fisherman, and I had to play for my fish a long time before they could see the joke. But at last I was rewarded with a bite. I hooked my first fish. After that the other two wanted to come up. I helped them to come. I am a good cook, as you know, and I fried them to a turn. Then I lowered them, one by one, into the bowl, with a charming note: "Madam, you have cooked so many fish for me that I have ventured to cook some for you.' She was cured. She gave me no more fish. She gave me notice instead."

—Pearson.

Whistler stories demonstrate his self-esteem.

To the question: "Do you think genius is hereditary?" he once replied: "I can't tell you, madam. Heaven has granted me no offspring."

When someone, annoyed by his bragging, grumbled: "It's a good thing we can't see ourselves as others see us," he rejoined: "Isn't it! I know in my case I should grow intolerably conceited."

. . . his reply to the gushing lady who said that she had just come up from the country along the Thames, "and there was an exquisite haze in the atmosphere which reminded me so much of some of your little things. It was really a perfect series of Whistlers." "Yes, madam," he returned with the utmost gravity: "Nature is creeping up."

—Pearson.

When Whistler grew older and received acclaim, he acquired disciples. One was the English painter Walter Sickert.

For a while he was a sort of chosen disciple. "Nice boy, Walter!" said Whistler; but the boy had to pay for being nice. In the evenings they would go in a cab to the Café Royal or elsewhere, accompanied by a weighty lithographic stone in case inspiration should visit the Master either during or after dinner. Sickert was charged with the care of the stone, and the waiter was ordered to bring an extra table for it. The evening over, and the stone untouched, Sickert bore it back again. In 1883 Whistler's portrait of his mother was exhibited at the *Salon,* and Sickert was graciously permitted to take it across the Channel, see it through the Customs, travel with it on the railway journeys, and be wholly responsible for its safe arrival. This was an honor which he fearfully undertook but fully appreciated. During his stay in Paris he was Oscar Wilde's guest at the Hôtel du Quai Voltaire, and he presented letters of introduction to Degas and Manet, to both of whom he explained that Whistler was "amazing," having been instructed to tell them so by Whistler. Dictatorial and exigent though the Master could be, there was always a twinkle in his eyes when he made his most outrageous claims and assertions. Once, when Sickert dropped a plate that he was working on, Whistler snapped: "How like you, Walter!" Shortly afterward Whistler himself dropped one. "How unlike me!" he drawled.

—Pearson.

Samuel Clemens (Mark Twain) 1835–1910

As a boy learning to be a Mississippi steamboat pilot, Clemens was not encouraged in literary pursuits. One day the master caught him where he had hidden to read a book.

"I've seen it over and over agin," he said, "You needn't tell me anythin' about it; if ye're going to be a pilot on this river yer needn't ever think of reading, for it just spiles all. Yer can't remember how high the tides was in Can's Gut three trips before the last now, I'll wager." "Why no," said Mark, "that was six months ago." "I don't care if't was," said the man. "If you hadn't been spiling yer mind by readin' ye'd have remembered."

—M. A. DeWolf Howe, *Memories of a Hostess,* 1922.

When he was thirty-two years old, the young Westerner was accorded the singular honor of an invitation to address Brahmin Boston at Whittier's seventieth birthday party, December 17, 1877. It was to be an occasion for East to honor West, by allowing West to honor East. In this case, East was an extraordinary collection of aging sages and their Bostonian admirers. Clemens's friend described the disaster.

He had jubilantly accepted our invitation and had promised a speech, which it appeared afterward he had prepared with unusual care and confidence. It was his custom always to think out his speeches, mentally wording them, and then memorizing them by a peculiar system of mnemonics which he had invented. On the dinner-table a certain succession of knife, spoon, salt-cellar, and butter-plate symbolized a train of ideas, and on the billiard-table a ball, a cue, and a piece of chalk served the same purpose. With a diagram of these printed on the brain he had full command of the phrases which his excogitation had attached to them, and which embodied the ideas in perfect form. He believed he had been particularly fortunate in his notion for the speech of that evening, and he had worked it out in joyous self-reliance. It was the notion of three tramps, three dead-beats, visiting a California mining-camp, and imposing themselves upon the innocent miners as respectively Ralph Waldo Emerson, Henry Wadsworth Longfellow, and Oliver Wendell Holmes. The humor of the conception must prosper or must fail according to the mood of the hearer, but Clemens felt sure of compelling this to sympathy, and he looked forward to an unparalleled triumph.

But there were two things that he had not taken into account. One was the species of religious veneration in which these men were held by those nearest them, a thing that I should not be able to realize to people remote from them in time and place. They were men of extraordinary dignity, of the thing called *presence,* for want of some clearer word, so that no one could well approach them in a personally light or trifling spirit. I do not suppose that anybody more truly valued them or more piously loved them than Clemens himself, but the intoxication of his fancy carried him beyond the bounds of that regard, and emboldened him to the other thing which he had not taken into account—namely, the immense hazard of working his fancy out before their faces, and expecting them to enter into the delight of it. If neither Emerson, nor Longfellow, nor Holmes had been there, the scheme might possibly have carried, but even this is doubtful, for those who so devoutly honored them would have overcome their horror with difficulty, and perhaps would not have overcome it at all.

The publisher, with a modesty very ungrateful to me, had abdicated his office of host, and I was the hapless president, fulfilling the abhorred function of calling people to their feet and making them speak. When I came to Clemens I introduced him with the cordial admiring I had for him as one of my greatest contributors and dearest friends. Here, I said, in sum, was a humorist who never left you hanging your head for having enjoyed his joke; and then the amazing mistake, the bewildering blunder, the cruel catastrophe was upon us. I believe that after the scope of the burlesque made itself clear, there was no one there, including the burlesquer himself, who was not smitten with a desolating dismay. There fell a silence, weighing many tons to the square inch, which deepened from moment to moment, and was broken only by the hysterical and blood-curdling laughter of a single guest, whose name shall not be handed down to infamy. Nobody knew whether to look at the speaker or down at his plate. I chose my plate as the least affliction, and so I do not know how Clemens looked, except when I stole a glance at him, and saw him standing solitary amid his appalled and appalling listeners, with his joke dead on his hands. From a first glance at the great three whom his jest had made its theme, I was aware of Longfellow sitting upright, and regarding the humorist with an air of pensive puzzle, of Holmes busily writing on his menu, with a well-feigned effect of preoccupation, and of Emerson, holding his elbows, and listening with a sort of Jovian oblivion of this nether world in that lapse of memory which saved him in those later years from so much bother. Clemens must have dragged his joke to the climax and left it there, but I cannot say this from any sense of the fact. Of what happened afterward at the table where the immense, the wholly innocent, the truly unimagined affront was offered, I have no longer the least remembrance. I next remember being in a room of the hotel, where Clemens was not to sleep, but to toss in despair, and Charles Dudley Warner's saying, in the gloom, "Well, Mark, *you're* a funny fellow." It was as well as anything else he could have said, but Clemens seemed unable to accept the tribute.

I stayed the night with him, and the next morning, after a haggard breakfast, we drove about and he made some purchases of bric-à-brac for his house in Hartford, with soul as far away from bric-à-brac as ever the soul of man was. He went home by an early train, and he lost no time in writing back to the three divine personalities which he had so involuntarily seemed to flout. They all wrote back to him, making it as light for him as they could. I have heard that Emerson was a good deal mystified, and in his sublime forgetfulness asked, Who was this gentleman who appeared to think he had offered him some sort of annoyance? But I am not sure that this is accurate. What I am sure of is that Longfellow, a few days after, in my study, stopped before a photograph of Clemens and said, "Ah, he is a *wag!*" and nothing more. Holmes told me, with deep emotion, such as a brother humorist might well feel, that he had not lost an instant in replying to Clemens's letter, and assuring him that there had not been the least offense, and entreating him never to think of the matter again. "He said that he was a fool, but he was God's fool," Holmes quoted from the letter, with a true sense of the pathos and the humor of the self-abasement.

To me Clemens wrote a week later, "It doesn't get any better; it burns like fire." But now I understand that it was not shame that burnt, but rage for a blunder which he had so incredibly committed. That to have conceived of those men, the most dignified in out literature, our civilization, as impersonable by three hoboes, and then to have imagined that he could ask them personally to enjoy the monstrous travesty, was a break, he saw too late, for which there was no repair.

—William Dean Howells, *My Mark Twain,* 1910.

Howells edited the Atlantic Monthly *and recollected Clemens's troubles with Mrs. Clemens over his language.*

. . . Now and then he would try a little stronger language than *The Atlantic* had stomach for, and once when I sent him a proof I made him observe that I had left out the profanity. He wrote back: "Mrs. Clemens opened that proof, and lit into the room with danger in her eye. What profanity? You see, when I read the manuscript to her I skipped that."

—Howells.

He enjoyed outrage. Visiting a friend, he was confronted at breakfast with an infant in the arms of its aunt.

"Don't you adore babies, Mr. Clemens?" she asked unsuspectingly. "No, I hate them," he answered, and he told her how once, when he was convalescing from typhoid, his own sister's infant son had climbed on his bed and kissed him. "I made up my mind, if I lived I would put up a monument to Herod," he said. . . .

—Justin Kaplan, *Mr. Clemens and Mark Twain*, 1966.

In his years of prosperity, Clemens entertained lavishly in his chosen city of Hartford, Connecticut. A typical occasion included Mr. Thomas Bailey Aldrich.

On a bright winter day in March 1874, Howells, Thomas Bailey Aldrich and his wife, and James R. Osgood started out on a visit to Nook Farm. They took the morning train from Boston to Springfield. In a characteristic gesture of Nook Farm hospitality, Clemens and Charles Dudley Warner, their hosts, met them there and rode with them the rest of the way to Hartford. At the Hartford station they found waiting the Clemens carriage, driven by a liveried coachman and the Clemens butler as footman. This equipage was one of many evidences of an almost magical prosperity that these visitors, accustomed to a more frugal tradition, observed with wonderment during two days and nights at Nook Farm. They drove past the site on Farmington Avenue where Clemens' new house was going up. At dinner at the Warners' the first night the heavy scent of flowers in the conservatory and the plash of a fountain surrounded by lilies seemed to transform winter into summer.

While the Aldriches were dressing for breakfast the next morning Clemens rapped on their door and, in a voice lacking in its usual gentleness, said, "Aldrich, come out. I want to speak to you." Lilian Aldrich, wrapped in her kimono, put her ear to the door and listened in horror as Clemens complained about the noises they had made in their bedroom. "Our bedroom is directly under yours, and poor Livy and her headache . . ." (Livy's delicate health was well known; she was also entering her sixth month of pregnancy.) "Do try to move more quietly, though Livy would rather suffer than have you give up your game on her account." Battered and subdued, the Aldrich couple crept timidly downstairs, where they found Livy pouring coffee from a silver urn. "I have no headache," she explained with some puzzlement after they had apologized. And as for those disgraceful noises, "We have not heard a sound. If you had shouted we should not have known it, for our rooms are in another wing of the house." "Come to your breakfast, Aldrich, and don't talk all day," Clemens broke in, and then, in an equally bewildering turnabout, he pronounced grace. . . . Later on, in December, as part of his implicit warfare of egos with Aldrich himself, he answered Aldrich's request for a photograph by sending him one each day for two weeks; on New Year's Day Aldrich's mail included twenty photographs of Mark Twain in separate envelopes.

Their last night in Hartford, the Aldriches and the other Boston visitors saw another aspect of their extraordinary host. After dinner, with a log fire blazing in the red-curtained drawing room, he sang "Swing Low, Sweet Chariot," "Golden Slippers," "Go Down, Moses" (he sang them in Florence, thirty years later, the night Livy died). He swayed gently as he stood, his voice was low and soft, a whisper of wind in the trees; his eyes were closed, and he smiled strangely. Through the sadness and exultation of these songs which he had known since boyhood, he transported himself far from the circle of polite letters and from the New England snowscape, and he found it difficult to come back. He wanted to go for a walk. They had run out of ale, and though he could call on the servants to run errands for him, he put on his winter costume of sealskin cap and sealskin coat and low evening slippers and left for the village. (In present-day Hartford he could have bought his ale by walking a few blocks from Farmington Avenue to the Mark Twain Package Store.) He tried the whiskey at the saloon where he bought the ale. He came back excited, hilarious, distinctly overheated. His feet were wet, and somewhere along the route he had thrown away his sealskin cap. This time the butler was sent out to look for it, while Clemens changed from his evening slippers into something considerably odder for Hartford, white cowskin moccasins with the hair on the outside. And, in a crowning act of confident alienation from his guests, he twisted his body into the likeness of a crippled uncle or a Negro at a hoedown and danced strange dances for them. Howells always remembered that evening, the joy and disoriented surprise of the guests, Livy's first reaction of dismay and "her low, despairing cry of, 'Oh, Youth!' "

"The vividest impression which Clemens gave us two ravenous

young Boston authors," Howells said, "was of the satisfying, the surfeiting nature of subscription publishing." He described for them the army of agents that was busy selling his books by the thousands all over the country. "It sells right along just like the Bible," he said about *The Innocents Abroad*, and he lectured them on the folly of publishing books the way Boston was accustomed to publishing books: "Anything but subscription publication is printing for private circulation." He tried to talk them into a three-man collaboration that would earn them all, he said, a fortune in the subscription market. And in the weeks after, he kept up his barrage, offered to negotiate contracts for them with Elisha Bliss, urged them to buy and settle at Nook Farm. "You can do your work just as well here as in Cambridge, can't you?" By the end of the visit Howells had been so infected by Clemens' visions of opulence that he found it difficult to follow his usual thrifty practice of walking in order to save carfare.

—Kaplan.

There were years in Germany, and difficulties with the German language: Clemens decided he would rather decline two drinks than one verb. There were years in England, and contact with other expatriates: Henry James asked Clemens if he knew Bret Harte; "Yes," said Clemens, "I know the son of a bitch."

He also encountered the natives.

As young Winston Churchill strolled off with Clemens into another room for a few moments of private talk, each with his inevitable cigar, other guests wondered which one would do the talking. Each was known to prefer a monologue to a conversation, but experienced listeners predicted that the old veteran would prevail. The pair returned, and Churchill, asked if he had enjoyed himself, answered with an eager "Yes!" Clemens, taken aside privately, answered the same question with "I have had a smoke."

—Stanley Weintraub, *The London Yankees*, 1979.

In England he made a famous rejoinder.

. . . a reporter named White, representing the *New York Journal*, arrived at 23 Tedworth Square with two cablegrams from his paper, which he showed Clemens:

IF MARK TWAIN DYING IN POVERTY, IN LONDON, SEND 500 WORDS.

IF MARK TWAIN HAS DIED IN POVERTY SEND 1000 WORDS.

Clemens suggested, in substance, a shorter response: James Ross Clemens, a cousin, was seriously ill here two or three weeks ago, but is well now. The report of my illness grew out of his illness; the report of my death was an exaggeration.

—Weintraub.

When he returned to the United States for his last years, he was celebrated as few men live to be. Thirty-eight years after his failing at Whittier's seventieth birthday, a banquet celebrated his own seventieth.

After meeting the guest of honor at a reception, they filed into Delmonico's red room to the music of a forty-piece orchestra from the Metropolitan Opera House. Surrounded by potted palms and huge gilt mirrors, they dined on fillet of kingfish, saddle of lamb, Baltimore terrapin, quail, and redhead duck washed down with sauterne, champagne, and brandy. Then they settled back to absorb five hours of toasts, poems, and speeches, every word of which, together with photographs of the guests by Byron, was preserved in a special thirty-two-page supplement to the Christmas issue of *Harper's Weekly.* In the small hours the guests started for home carrying as souvenirs of the occasion foot-high plaster busts of Mark Twain.

—Kaplan.

His old friend Howells told his old friend Aldrich, "I hate to see him eating so many dinners and writing so few books."

Bret Harte 1836–1902

The first literary voice of the American West, even earlier than Clemens, was Bret Harte. His poem, "The Heathen Chinee," and his stories, collected in The Luck of Roaring Camp and Other Sketches *(1870), made him briefly the most famous living American author. When he came east in triumph the* Atlantic Monthly *contracted for twelve contributions at the fabulous price of ten thousand dollars. William Dean Howells remembered Harte's arrival in Cambridge.*

In those days, the men whose names have given splendor to Cambridge were still living there. I shall forget some of them in the alphabetical enumeration of Louis Agassiz, Francis J. Child, Richard Henry Dana, Jun., John Fiske, Dr. Asa Gray, the family of the Jameses, father and sons, Lowell, Longfellow, Charles Eliot Norton, Dr. John G. Palfrey, James Pierce, Dr. Peabody, Professor Parsons, Professor Sophocles. The variety of talents and of achievements was indeed so great that Mr. Bret Harte, when fresh from his Pacific slope, justly said, after listening to a partial rehearsal of them, "Why, you couldn't fire a revolver from your front porch anywhere without bringing down a two-volumer!"

—William Dean Howells, *Literary Friends and Acquaintances,* 1902.

Harte continued eastward, to end his days in London where he supported himself by writing increasingly distant fantasies of a California past.

One afternoon . . . my attention was drawn to a man whose appearance was almost precisely that of the typical English clubman of the American stage. He was tall, and his hair parted in the middle was white. He wore gray-striped trousers, a cutaway coat over a fancy vest, and above his polished shoes glowed lavender spats. In his hand he carried a pair of yellow gloves.

"Who is that?" I asked of Zangwill.

"Don't you know who that is?" he asked. "That is your noble compatriot, Francis Bret Harte."

"Bret Harte!" I started at him in amazement. Could that dandy, that be-monocled, be-spatted old beau be the author of "The Luck of Roaring Camp" and "Two Men of Sandy Bar"?

—Hamlin Garland, *Roadside Meetings,* 1930.

William Dean Howells 1837–1920

Howells was born in Ohio, wrote for newspapers, and published poems before becoming a novelist. Like many other literary men from the provinces, he came to Boston.

When William Dean Howells came to Boston in 1860, at the age of twenty-three, he was a pilgrim from the Midwest worshiping at the feet of New England's literary great. It was with a sense of entering another world altogether that this postulant sat through a four-hour dinner in a private room at the Parker House with Dr. Oliver Wendell Holmes, who had given the *Atlantic* its name, James T. Fields, its publisher, and James Russell Lowell, its editor in chief. With an informality Howells would never have guessed in Columbus, Ohio, these eminences addressed each other as "James" and "Wendell," as if they were all still boys together. About the time the coffee came in, the dapper little doctor cast a smiling glance at Howells and, turning to Lowell, said, "Well, James, this is something like the apostolic succession; this is the laying on of hands."

—Justin Kaplan, *Mr. Clemens and Mark Twain,* 1966.

Editor of the Atlantic Monthly *and later of* Harper's, *the novelist was capable of critical incisiveness. John Jay Chapman told a story in a letter.*

"Did you hear what Howells once said to a boring author who was trying to wring a compliment out of him? 'I don't know how it is,' said the author, 'I don't seem to *write* as well as I used to do.' 'Oh, yes you do—indeed you do. You write as well as you ever did;—But your *taste* is improving.' "

—M. A. DeWolfe Howe, *John Jay Chapman and His Letters,* 1937.

His move to New York as editor of Harper's *recognized the shift of eastern literary power from the old city to the new one. Friend of the Boston old guard, of Mark Twain, and of the young, by the time the century turned he was no longer champion of everything new.*

Meeting Theodore Dreiser in the office of *Harper's* in 1900, William Dean Howells said, "You know, I don't like *Sister Carrie,*" and moved on.

—[Editor's paraphrase].

He lived out his life in Maine, with the fortuitous comfort of an automobile.

"I have a new Ford car," he said. . . .

"In going over some boxes of old papers, I came upon two bankbooks each of which indicated an unused balance. . . . I verified these records and drew the money which in most marvelous manner exactly equaled the cost of a car!"

—Hamlin Garland, *My Friendly Contemporaries,* 1932.

Henry Adams 1838–1918

Great-grandson of the second President, grandson of the sixth, Henry Adams grew up among friends named James and Holmes. He taught at Harvard, he edited, he wrote essays on politics and history. He published two political novels, concealing his authorship. In 1885 his wife Clover committed suicide after thirteen years of marriage; he never mentioned this horror which clearly dominated his life. He traveled extensively in Asia and Europe and wrote of his travels, his life, and his ideas in works including: Mont-Saint-Michel and Chartres *(1913; privately published, 1904) and* The Education of Henry Adams *(1918; privately published, 1906).*

Many writers have shown drafts of their work to friends for help, but in the years before photocopying there were problems in making clear copies.

Henry adopted the luxurious practice of privately publishing a few copies of each of his books and then circulating them among his closest friends. Henry designed these preliminary copies with very wide margins so that his friends could write down their observations, and he took those observations into consideration in his final revisions before the formal publication.

—Otto Friedrich, *Clover,* 1979.

He concealed the authorship of his novel, Democracy, *so successfully that he was allowed the rare privilege of hearing what his own brother Charles thought of it.*

When John Hay's *Bread-Winners* appeared anonymously in 1883, Charles wrote to E. L. Godkin, who knew the secret of *Democracy* but not of *The Bread-Winners,* with a remarkable suggestion. "Who the author is . . . I am sure I do not know," he declared, "but one thing is to me very plain. It is written by the same hand that wrote the novel 'Democracy' some years ago. . . . It has the same coarse, half-educated touch; and the Nast-like style of its portrait and painting is unmistakable. . . ." Godkin promptly forwarded the letter to Henry, with a note at the bottom, asking, "What shall I say to this?" Henry was delirious. "I want to roll on the floor," he wrote to Hay, "to howl, kick and sneeze; to weep silent tears of thankfulness to a beneficent providence which has permitted me to see this day. I want to drown my joy in oceans of Champagne and lemonade. Never, No, never, since Cain wrote his last newspaper letter about Abel was there anything so droll." He concluded by signing himself "Ever your poor, coarse and half-educated friend, Henry Adams," adding "My coarse and half-educated wife has had a fit over her brother-in-law's Nast-like touch."

—Friedrich.

Majorie Terry remembered that Adams "was delightful with children."

I took my youngest son, Theodore, to lunch with him one day, and as I was presenting him I said, "This is your Uncle Henry (all my children called him that), and he knows everything." Teddy looked at him in round-eyed silence through part of the meal, watching his opportunity. During a pause in the conversation of the grownups the little boy leaned forward respectfully and said, "Uncle Henry, how do you feed a chameleon?"

—Marjorie Terry Chanler, *Roman Spring: Memoirs*, 1934.

A biographer told of Adams on his travels.

Even in the South Seas, Adams characteristically preferred the company of women. He enjoyed their familiarities and their impudence and gave them extravagant presents. He tried to look "as solemn as a Justice of the Supreme Court" among the chiefs, who were tremendously dignified men. (He called one of them John Adams.) But "when the giants have dismissed me, and I can sprawl on the mats among the girls, I begin to be happy, and when the handsomest one peels sugar-cane with her teeth, and feeds me with chunks of it, I have nothing more to ask."

—Elizabeth Stevenson, *Henry Adams: A Biography*, 1955.

In Europe when he was an old man he defined Eden.

My idea of paradise is a perfect automobile going thirty miles an hour on a smooth road to a twelfth-century cathedral.

—Stevenson.

The company of his niece Aileen Tone sustained him during his last five years, which were spent largely in Washington, D.C. He wanted her always to be near. "He never dined out," she recollected, "even when asked to the White House—'I'm in bed with a nurse' was his invariable excuse— . . ." They dressed for dinner every night, even when they were alone. Louis Auchincloss wrote:

He would have adored to have been surrounded by a crowd of disciples as was Justice Holmes, of whom in this respect he was very jealous. Judge Learned Hand told me once how vividly he remembered Adams' snort and his "Very interesting, very interesting" when Hand told him that Holmes was the man he admired most in the world.

—"Never Leave Me," *American Heritage,* Feb. 1970.

Marjorie Terry told another story from these later years.

My youngest daughter went to stay with him in Washington and tells of a strange evening she spent alone with "Uncle Henry." Miss Tone, the "niece in residence," was dining out, and the sixteen-year-old Gabrielle, better known to the family and friends as "Bebo" (the first two syllables of her Roman nursery name of Bebolina), was rather afraid of him. She need not have been, since he was amused with her and soon made her feel at home. During the meal they chatted cheerily of places and people they had known, and then settled in the low armchairs of the library for the rest of the evening. There was a pause; Uncle Henry leaned back with his eyes half closed and his two hands joined at the upturned fingers. Then he began to talk, softly at first as if to himself; then, gathering momentum from his surging thoughts, he went on to speak of all that lay on his mind, the mysteries of time and eternity, man and destiny, his aspiration and helplessness. It was all way over her head, but she listened breathless, feeling that something great and wonderful was happening, though she could not understand it. At last he paused and came back to earth, looked at her, and said: "Do you know why I have told you all this?" Of course she had no answer. "It is because you would not understand a word of it and you will never quote me."

—Chanler.

Miss Tone remembered her last absence.

"But at last I did go away—just for a weekend. I had been asked to stay with Mr. and Mrs. Nelson Fell in Virginia. It was a small house party, and Mrs. Fell made such a point of my coming that I agreed to go. I worried about Uncle Henry every minute. Finally I became so nervous that I called the house in Washington. Elsie Adams answered the telephone and tried to reassure me about Uncle Henry. I told her I was coming straight home. She insisted that it was not necessary, but I came anyway. When I got to the house I hurried upstairs, where I found Uncle Henry sitting with Elizabeth Hoyt, who was reading aloud to him. I went straight over to his side and knelt down by the low chair and put my arms around him. He was a little man, you know, and I could feel his whole body trembling. 'Never leave me, never leave me,' he murmured, and I replied, 'I never will.' Two days later, when I went into his room in the morning, I found him dead."

—Auchincloss.

Joaquin Miller 1841–1913

One of the great frauds of American letters, author of the immortal "Columbus," Miller abandoned his wife Minnie Myrtle—also a poet—declaring:

"A man never becomes famous until he leaves his wife, or does something atrocious to bring himself into notice; and besides, literary men never get along well with their wives. Lord Byron separated from his wife, and some of my friends think I am a second Lord Byron. Farewell."

—Franklin Walker, *San Francisco's Literary Frontier,* 1939.

In London Miller became a sensation, wearing cowhide boots and a sealskin greatcoat while dining with Edmund Gosse. When he added sombrero and red shirt to the costume, he explained, "It helps sell the poems, you know, and it tickles the duchesses."

He could prove an embarrassment to other Americans abroad. In 1873 he was guest of honor, along with Samuel Clemens, at a dinner for Ambrose Bierce.

Miller showed up in music-hall regalia, hair flowing to the shoulder, buckskin jacket, red sash, huge knife in his belt as though he might have to hack his way through savage tribesmen to reach Mitre Court. While the others goggled—and Bierce and Twain tried to ignore him as they would a child showing off for his elders—Miller picked up a fish by the tail and swallowed it whole.

—Richard O'Connor, *Ambrose Bierce: A Biography,* 1967.

Oliver Wendell Holmes, Jr. 1841–1935

The future justice of the Supreme Court grew up in Cambridge, Massachusetts—son of the poet, boyhood friend of William and Henry James. Apparently the young men shared a regard for a young woman named Minnie Temple, who died young, and whom Henry James used as a fictional model.

Wounded three times in the Civil War, young Wendell was nothing if not literary.

"At Ball's Bluff, Tremlett's boy George told me, I was hit at 4½ P.M., *the heavy firing having begun about an hour before, by the watch*—I felt as if a horse had kicked me and went over—1st Sergt. Smith grabbed me and lugged me to the rear a little way & opened my shirt and ecce! the two holes in my breasts & the bullet, which he gave me. George says he squeezed it from the right opening. Well—I remember the sickening feeling of water in my face—I was quite faint—and seeing poor Sergt. Merchant lying near—shot through the head and covered with blood—and then the thinking begun. (Meanwhile hardly able to speak—at least, coherently.) Shot through the lungs? Lets see—and I spit. Yes—already the blood was in my mouth. At once my thoughts jumped to 'Children of the New Forest' (by Marryatt) which I was fond of reading as a little boy, and in which the father of one of the heroines is shot through the lungs by a robber. I remembered he died with terrible haemorrhages & great agony. What should I do? Just then I remembered and felt in my waist coat pocket—Yes there it was—a little bottle of laudanum which I had brought along. But I won't take it yet; no, see a doctor first. It may not be as bad as it looks. At any rate wait till the pain begins—

"When I had got to the bottom of the Bluff the ferry boat (the scow), had just started with a load—but there was a small boat there. Then, still in this half conscious state, I heard somebody groan. Then I thought 'Now wouldn't Sir Philip Sydney have that other feller put into the boat first?' "

—Mark DeWolfe Howe, *Justice Oliver Wendell Holmes: The Shaping Years 1841–1870*, 1963.

As Sir Philip Sydney lay dying in battle, he passed a cup of water to another wounded man, and said, "Thy necessity is greater than mine." When Holmes recovered from his near-fatal wound, he discovered that someone had made off with his bottle of laudanum.

The third time, he was wounded in the heel, and later confessed his regret that his foot did not require amputation: the young captain had had enough of war.

On the battlefield, he once yelled at someone.

Holmes's eye was caught by the outrageous sight of a tall civilian blandly surveying the battlefield while bullets smashed into the Fort. In the heat of the moment Holmes shouted "Get down, you damn fool, before you get shot." At the moment when the explosive order came from his lips Holmes "was wholly unaware of who it was" but "a sharp look after his exclamation made him aware."

—Howe.

It was the President.

As Holmes grew older his dignity and detachment became more pronounced, until some observers found him cold and indifferent. Henry James, who had grown up with him, compared Holmes's demeanor to "a full glass carried without spilling a drop."

In her fictionalized biography, Catherine Drinker Bowen told the story of a young president and an old Justice.

Franklin D. Roosevelt, a few days after his inauguration in 1933, came round to call. He found Holmes in his library, reading Plato. The question rose irresistably. "Why do you read Plato, Mr. Justice?"

"To improve my mind, Mr. President," Holmes replied.

—*Yankee from Olympus*, 1944.

Sidney Lanier 1842–1881

Mrs. Mattie Montgomery, a motherly friend of Lanier, remembered his poetical behavior.

"Often when I saw his horse tied in the grounds below the house, I went out in search of him. In some arbor I was sure to find him, or under the branches of some spreading shade trees, prone upon his back, gazing up through the leaves, lost in reverie.

" 'Well, son what is it?' I would ask.

" 'O little mother!' he would exclaim, 'isn't it superb? Listen to their music'; at which I would chide him for his vain dreaming and laughing, would say that I should not be surprised at any time to see him vanish from my sight, and be lost in the depths of the sky into which his fancy so often soared."

—Aubrey H. Starke, *Sidney Lanier: A Biography and Critical Study*, 1933.

William James 1842–1910

Elder brother of the novelist Henry James, psychologist William James grew up in New York, but spent most of his adult life in the environs of Harvard. Logan Pearsall Smith retold an anecdote which James had confided to him, asking Smith only that he not repeat it in Cambridge.

He had gone, he told me, by tram that afternoon to Boston; and as he sat and meditated in the Cambridge horse-car two strains of thought had occupied his mind. One of these was the notion, which Mrs. James had recently derived from the perusal of Kipling's writings, that our civil order, that all the graces and amenities of our social life, had for their ultimate sanction nothing but force, however much we might disguise it—the naked fist, in fact, the blow of the sword, the crack of the pistol, or the smoke and roar of guns. Superimposed upon this meditation began to recur, with greater and greater persistence, the memory of certain remarks of his brother Henry, who, on a recent visit to America had indignantly protested against the outrageous pertness of the American child and the meek pusillanimity with which the older generation suffered the behaviour of their children without protest.

It was not long, William James said, before he became aware of what had aroused this second line of thought; it was the droning sound which filled the horse-car—the voice, in fact, of an American child, who was squeaking over and over again an endless, shrill, monotonous singsong. Growing more and more irritated by this squeaking, William James resolved that he at least would not suffer it without protest; so, addressing the mother of the vocal infant, he said politely, "I think, madam, you can hardly be aware that your child's song is a cause of annoyance to the rest of us in this car." The lady thus addressed paid no attention; but a gallant American, who had heard it, turned on him and said with great indignation, "How dare you, sir, address a lady in this ungentlemanly fashion!" At this insult William James, recalling the doctrine of naked force which his wife had impressed upon him, replied with manly promptness, "Sir, if you repeat that remark, I shall slap your face." The remark, to his consternation, was repeated, and the professor was compelled to make good his word. The slap was conscientiously administered; the occupants of the horse-car arose in indignation, pressing their cards upon the victim of the assault, and protesting their willingness to be witnesses at any legal proceedings which might ensue. Then they all sat down; and as the car clattered along through the dust towards Boston, with the child still shrilly singing, the grave burden of the public disapproval which William James had encountered became almost more, he said, than he could bear.

He looked from hostile face to hostile face, longing for some sign of sympathy and comprehension, and fixed at last all his hopes on a lady who had taken no part in the uproar, and whose appearance suggested foreign travel perhaps, or at any rate a wider point of view. He felt that she at least understood the motive of his action; and so great was his longing for sympathy that when at last the car reached Boston and they all got out he committed the error of trying to make sure of her approbation. "You, madam," he said, addressing her, "you, I feel sure, will understand. . . ." Thereupon the lady drew back from him and exclaimed, "You brute!"

—Logan Pearsall Smith, *Unforgotten Years,* 1938.

Henry James 1843–1916

When Henry James, Jr., was born, his mother received congratulations from Emerson: "Tell Mrs. James," he wrote the father, "that I heartily greet her on the new friend. . . ." As William and young Henry grew older, they took part with their younger brothers Garth Wilkinson and Robertson in disputatious mealtimes.

Garth Wilkinson makes a remark and is challenged by his younger brother Robertson. Henry Junior emerges from his silence to defend Wilky. William joins in. Finally the father seeks to act as moderator. Ralph Waldo Emerson's son Edward, who describes this scene as he saw it at Newport, goes on to say that the voice of the moderator "presently would be drowned by the combatants and he soon came down vigorously into the arena, and when, in the excited argument the dinner knives might not be absent from eagerly gesticulating hands, dear Mrs. James, more conventional, but bright as well as motherly, would look at me, laughingly reassuring, saying, 'Don't be disturbed, Edward; they won't stab each other. . . .' "

—Leon Edel, *Henry James: The Untried Years 1843–1870,* 1953.

The elder brothers found themselves frequently at odds. H. G. Wells told a story which occurred many decades later.

I once saw James quarrelling with his brother William James, the psychologist. He had lost his calm; he was terribly unnerved. He appealed to me, to me of all people, to adjudicate on what was and what was not permissible behaviour in England. William was arguing about it in an indisputably American accent, with an indecently naked reasonableness. I had come to Rye with a car to fetch William James and his daughter to my home at

Sandgate. William had none of Henry's passionate regard for the polish upon the surfaces of life and he was immensely excited by the fact that in the little Rye inn, which had its garden just over the high brick wall of the garden of Lamb House, G. K. Chesterton was staying. William James had corresponded with our vast contemporary and he sorely wanted to see him. So with a scandalous directness he had put the gardener's ladder against that ripe red wall and clambered up and peeped over! Henry had caught him at it.

It was the sort of thing that isn't done. It was most emphatically the sort of thing that isn't done. . . . Henry had instructed the gardener to put away that ladder and William was looking thoroughly naughty about it. To Henry's manifest relief I carried William off and in the road just outside the town we ran against the Chestertons. . . . William got his coveted impression.

—Simon Nowell Smith, *Henry James: The Legend of the Master,* 1948.

Henry's sister Alice told of an "eccentric accident" that befell her brother Henry in Florence in 1890.

The evening he arrived he was seized after dinner with a very severe pain in his throat; having had a bad tooth-ache he supposed it had to do with that. The next day he spent with the dentist, and went in the afternoon from the hotel to stay with Dr. Baldwin, his throat becoming more and more sore so that he immediately said to the Doctor, "You must look at my throat"—"Why, you have got something sticking in it and it's green!" He tugged and tugged and brought out a long haricot vert which had wound itself about the root of his tongue.

—*The Diary of Alice James,* ed. Leon Edel, 1964.

James frequently visited France, where he made many friends. When Guy de Maupassant returned his visit in London, there was a clash of trans-channel cultures.

Maupassant, dining in a restaurant with James, pointed to a woman sitting at a table and asked Henry to "go over and get her for me." Henry carefully explained that in England there was the matter of being properly introduced. Maupassant tried again. Pointing to another woman he said: "Surely you know her at least? Ah, if I only spoke English!" When James had refused, with full explanation, for about the fifth time, Maupassant was said to have remarked irritably: "Really, you don't seem to know anyone in London."

—Leon Edel, *Henry James: The Middle Years 1882–1895*, 1962.

James's prose was praised and blamed for its ambiguity. His sexual proclivities were similarly indefinite. A story current in England asserted that, when James was an old man, the young novelist Hugh Walpole offered his body to the master in homage; James answered, "I cannot, my dear, I cannot."

When he began to dictate his fiction, his prose style changed to incorporate further qualification and nuance.

During the autumn of 1896, when he was working on *What Maisie Knew*, his wrist condition became chronic. In February 1897 he accordingly engaged a stenographer, William MacAlpine, a silent Scot from Aberdeen and Edinburgh, who worked regularly as shorthand reporter for medical societies, but had his mornings free to take James's dictation. The novelist began by letting him take his letters in shorthand; and James's typewritten letters from the first announced themselves in elaborate apologies for "this cold-blooded process," this "fierce legibility"—"the only epistolary tongue of my declining years." By the end of the first month, he was dictating directly to the typewriter; it saved time and enabled him to do much more. "I can address you only through an embroidered veil of sound," he dictated to his Parisian friend Morton Fullerton of the *Times*. "The sound is that of the admirable and expensive machine that I have just purchased for the purpose of bridging our silences." He added: "The hand that works it, however, is not the lame *patte* which, after inflicting on you for years its aberrations, I have now definitely relegated to the shelf, or at least to the hospital." . . .

A certain number of letters continued to be typewritten; but the machine in the end was reserved for his art. He became so accustomed to its sound that he was unable to dictate one day when his own typewriter broke down and an alien machine temporarily replaced it.

—Leon Edel, *Henry James: The Treacherous Years 1895–1901*, 1969.

Someone asked his brother William about Henry's later changes in style; William answered that there was no change in style, only a new amanuensis who actually recorded all of Henry's clauses.

Henry James was the great dictator of modern times, as Timothy Dwight had been for the eighteenth century (see pages 27–28). He dictated the massive fictions of The Ambassadors *(1903),* The Wings of the Dove *(1902), and* The Golden Bowl, *(1904) and his prose became more like his speech. For decades his friends had been recording his extraordinary conversation.*

Henry James, once standing with Father at the head of Marlboro Street, looked down its long expanse of similar brick houses and sighed, "Marlboro Street cannot be said to be precisely"—time out for the Jamesian pause—"*passionate.*"

—Helen Howe, *The Gentle Americans, 1864–1960: Biography of a Breed,* 1965.

Seldom was he so succinct. Alfred Sutro described the more typical manner.

"One had to wait a long time for the thought to be expressed; one watched the process of its germination and development; but when it came one felt that it had been tremendously worth waiting for, and that it was a thought peculiarly his own and expressed as no other man could have expressed it. . . . He talked as if every sentence had been carefully rehearsed; every semicolon, every comma, was in exactly the right place, and his rounded periods dropped to the floor and bounced about like tiny rubber balls."

—Leon Edel, *Henry James: The Master, 1901–1916,* 1972.

Perhaps Witter Bynner, meeting him on his 1904 trip to New York, has committed to print the most exquisite of Jamesian spoken utterances—on the subject of a common cold. According to Brynner, James said:

I had brought availably with me two overcoats, one somewhat heavier and one somewhat lighter, and in Boston I had worn with comfort the somewhat lighter overcoat and was carrying, for possible immediate need in New York, the slightly warmer overcoat on my arm. All had gone well, until I found myself here, seated in a cab beside my friend, David Munroe, known to you doubtless as a fellow-editor, albeit much older, editing, yes, *The North American Review,* and so faithfully replete with welcome and so instantly exacting of responses that I was only vaguely, though venially, aware of my impulse and need to doff the somewhat lighter overcoat and to don the slightly heavier overcoat, which I by all means should have done, to be sure, on account of a rapid change in temperature, or else a difference in temperatures at the place where my journey began and the place where it ended, or perhaps merely a change in hour, but a change all in all,—and, as I have noted, my good friend, David, so engrossed me in greetings and reminiscences and interrogations that I continued, despite a disquieting chill in my marrow, to wear the somewhat lighter overcoat, protecting only one arm with the slightly thicker overcoat, which I should assuredly have been wearing in order to avoid this probably thus avoidable touch of influenza with which I must begin my—under otherwise auspicious aspects—visit to New York, and all, let me charge, on account of your beastly, and by me long foresworn, climate."

—Witter Bynner, *Prose Pieces,* 1979.

His most famous utterance was recorded by his friend and fellow novelist Edith Wharton, who often took him motoring.

Mrs. Wharton and her motorcar—he was fond of both of them—exhausted the aging James, who called her an "angel of devastation." Once he wrote of a visit: "Her powers of devastation are ineffable, her repudiation of repose absolutely tragic, and she was never more brilliant and able and interesting."

On another occasion she remembered him asking directions in the town of Windsor, England.

While I was hesitating and peering out into the darkness James spied an ancient doddering man who had stopped in the rain to gaze at us. "Wait a moment, my dear—I'll ask him where we are"; and leaning out he signalled to the spectator.

"My good man, if you'll be good enough to come here, please; a little nearer—so," and as the old man came up: "My friend, to put it to you in two words, this lady and I have just arrived here from *Slough;* that is to say, to be more strictly accurate, we have recently *passed through* Slough on our way here, having actually motored to Windsor from Rye, which was our point of departure; and the darkness having overtaken us, we should be much obliged if you would tell us where we now are in relation, say, to the High Street, which, as you of course know, leads to the Castle, after leaving on the left hand the turn down to the railway station."

I was not surprised to have this extraordinary appeal met by silence, and a dazed expression on the old wrinkled face at the window; nor to have James go on: "In short" (his invariable prelude to a fresh series of explanatory ramifications), "in short, my good man, what I want to put to you in a word is this: supposing we have already (as I have reason to think we have) driven past the turn down to the railway station (which in that case, by the way, would probably not have been on our left hand, but on our right) where are we now in relation to . . ."

"Oh, please," I interrupted, feeling myself utterly unable to sit through another parenthesis, "do ask him where the King's Road is."

"Ah—? The King's Road? Just so! Quite right! Can you, as a matter of fact, my good man, tell us where, in relation to our present position, the King's Road exactly *is*?"

"Ye're in it," said the aged face at the window.

—Edith Wharton, *A Backward Glance,* 1934.

Earlier, James had visited Wharton in the United States and read Walt Whitman aloud to her.

At any rate, "his voice filled the hushed room like an organ adagio" as he read from the "Song of Myself" and "When lilacs last in the dooryard bloomed" and "Out of the Cradle" which he crooned rather than read. "We talked long that night of *Leaves of Grass,*" Mrs. Wharton remembered, "tossing back and forth to each other treasure after treasure." At the end, the Master flung his hands upward, a characteristic gesture, and with eyes twinkling said: "Oh, yes, a great genius; undoubtedly a very great genius! Only one cannot help deploring his too-extensive acquaintance with the foreign languages."

—Edel, *The Master.*

In England he met Stephen Crane, who became a great favorite. He met Ford Madox Hueffer (later Ford Madox Ford), who claimed a great closeness to the Master; other witnesses have recalled a reticence on James's part; an amanuensis remembered James hiding behind a tree in order to avoid Hueffer. Ezra Pound—in a passage in the Cantos*—remembered a meeting and a voice.*

And the great domed head, *con gli occhi*
onesti e tardi
Moves before me, phantom with weighted motion,
Grave incessu, drinking the tone of things,
And the old voice lifts itself
weaving an endless sentence.

—Ezra Pound, *A Draft of XXX Cantos,* 1930.

The Italian is Dante's, "with eyes grave and slow." The Latin means "with slow movement." Another meeting with a young man was apparently less successful.

"Winston," said one who was present, "was at his very worst." He had never read Henry James; he was impatient at the respect and deference shown this old man who was so slow-spoken, even though his rhetoric was so remarkable when he finally got it out. Everyone listened to Henry James in awe. Winston was impatient, irritable; he could not wait for the end of such long and intricate sentences. He disregarded the Master; or he interrupted him. He showed him "no conversational consideration." He used a great deal of slang.

—Edel, *The Master.*

Near the end of his life, James composed his autobiography.

He dictated that summer the passage in *A Small Boy* in which Thackeray admired the buttons on James's boyhood jacket; he held in his hand the daguerreotype by Brady of the small boy wearing the jacket which would later be the frontispiece to the book. Suddenly in the midst of dictating the passage he left the room and returned. He was carrying the original jacket, buttons and all—those buttons which had fascinated Thackeray more than half a century before in New York.

—Edel, *The Master.*

When his first stroke felled him, he told a friend that he had had the thought: "So it has come at last—the Distinguished Thing." He lingered, intermittently confused, for almost three months before he died. "I have a curious sense," he said once, "that I'm not the bewildering puzzle to all of you that you are to me." His mind held to its old habits.

On the afternoon of Saturday, December 11, he called once more for the typewriter and dictated words about touching "the large old phrase into the right amplitude . . . we simply shift the sweet nursling of genius from one maternal breast to the other and the trick is played, the false note averted." Then he exclaimed: "Astounding little stepchild of God's astounding young stepmother!" There followed a passage that seemed to contain a recall of the war, and to become confused with his reading of Napoleonic memoirs. He was back in the Paris of the Second Empire which he had known in his boyhood: back in the Louvre. This was his dictation; sometimes Miss Bosanquet missed a word; sometimes there was discontinuity of thought:

> . . . on this occasion moreover that, having been difficult to keep step . . . we hear of the march of history, what is remaining to that essence of tragedy, the limp?
>
> . . . mere patchwork transcription becomes of itself the high brave art. We . . . five miles off at the renewed affronts that we see coming for the great, and that we know they will accept. The fault is that they had found themselves too easily great, and the effect of that, definitely, had been, within them, the want of long provision for it. It wasn't why they [were] to have been so thrust into the limelight and the uproar, but why they [were] to have known as by inspiration the trade most smothered in experience. They go about shivering in the absence of the holy protocol—they dodder sketchily about as in the betrayal of the lack of early advantages; and it is upon *that* they seem most to depend to give them distinction. . . .

"After luncheon," Miss Bosanquet noted at the time (this was on December 12), "he wanted me again and dictated, perfectly clearly and coherently two letters from Napoleon Bonaparte to one of his married sisters. . . ."

—Edel, *The Master.*

James Whitcomb Riley 1849–1916

While Henry James perfected his clauses and qualifications, another American literary figure polished his act to a shine of absolute artifice. In this account, a young writer visited the Hoosier poet in Boston.

Generals, senators, and bankers put up at the Parker House and the fact that Riley could spend several days in much splendor quite overwhelmed me, and, after sending up my name, I awaited his answer with a sense of uncertainty. Was I justified in doing this? He had written to me pleasantly, but suppose he should refuse to see me?

"Come right in, p'fessor," he called in a drawl which was as characteristic of Indiana as Mark Twain's utterance was of Missouri. "Take a cheer and don't mind my 'dishabilly.' I'm just dressin' fer dinner." His smile was cordial, but his mouth was puckered at one corner for the reason, as I soon discovered, that he was carrying a quid of tobacco in that cheek, and while he went on with his toilet he proceeded in a quaintly querulous monotone. "Yas, I'm dressin' fer dinner—'pears like I'm always dressin' fer dinner nowadays. When I was young and had a good digestion, could eat anything at any time, no one asked me to dine, but now when I'm old and feeble, stomach all gone, can't eat a thing but crackers and milk—look at that!"—Here he put his hand on a heap of invitations. "Don't it beat hell?"

. . . he rambled along in a most amusing, poetic and individual monologue, now quoting some of his own lines, now uttering a droning stream of shrewd comment on Western writers and Western literature. He described comical incidents of his lecture tour, and quoted criticisms of his recent verse. . . . Taking from his dresser a manuscript, he read with frank delight "Knee Deep in June," keeping one eye fixed upon me obliquely as if enjoying the effect of his performance, and I, keenly sensitive to dramatic reading, was a delighted auditor. He talked of the country fiddler, of the tin peddler, and called my attention to certain phrases which he had caught from life. . . .

"You and I are voices cryin' in the Western wilderness," he said. "We're obliged to keep neighborly," and his smile, now that he was rid of his quid, displayed fine, even teeth. "So long!"

His success on the platform that night was phenomenal.

—Hamlin Garland, *Roadside Meetings*, 1930.

Henry Cabot Lodge 1850–1924

Lodge took his Ph.D. in Political Science at Harvard, studying under Henry Adams. Two years after his graduation, he became editor of the

North American Review *and later, a senator and foe of the League of Nations.*

I was once staying with the Lodges, during Roosevelt's Presidency. Cabot came home for dinner tired and irritated; he was Senator then and had been wrangling with his fellow legislators all day. After trying various subjects of conversation I mentioned a book I had lately come across, *The Lives of the Dukes of Urbino.* Cabot flew out at me: "A pack of unmitigated ruffians and blackguards!" (Which of course they were.) "I would rather read the lives of the Selectmen of Nahant."

—Marjorie Terry Chanler, *Roman Spring: Memoirs,* 1934.

Booker T. Washington 1856–1915

Washington was born a slave and after the Civil War worked in coal mines while attending school part-time. After graduating from Hampton Institute in Virginia, he became a teacher and in 1891 founded Tuskegee Institute in Alabama.

He remembered servitude.

I remember that at one time I saw two of my young mistresses and some lady visitors eating ginger-cakes, in the yard. At that time those cakes seemed to me to be absolutely the most tempting and desirable things that I had ever seen; and I then and there resolved that, if I ever got free, the height of my ambition would be reached if I could get to the point where I could secure and eat ginger-cakes in the way that I saw those ladies doing.

—Booker T. Washington, *Up from Slavery,* 1901.

He remembered emancipation.

The night before the eventful day, word was sent to the slave quarters to the effect that something unusual was going to take place at the "big house" the next morning. There was little, if any, sleep that night. All was excitement and expectancy. Early the next morning word was sent to all the slaves, old and young, to gather at the house. In company with my mother, brother, and sister, and a large number of other slaves, I went to the master's house. All of our master's family were either standing or seated on the veranda of the house, where they could see what was to take place and hear what was said. There was a feeling of deep interest, or perhaps sadness, on their faces, but not bitterness. As I now recall the impression they made upon me, they did not at the moment seem to be sad because of the loss of property, but rather because of parting with those whom they had reared and who were in many ways very close to them. The most distinct thing that I now recall in connection with the scene was that some man who seemed to be a stranger (a United States officer, I presume) made a little speech and then read a rather long paper—the Emancipation Proclamation, I think. After the reading we were told that we were all free, and could go when and where we pleased. My mother, who was standing by my side, leaned over and kissed her children, while tears of joy ran down her cheeks.

—Washington.

He struggled to educate himself, to find an identity—and a name.

From the time when I could remember anything, I had been called simply "Booker." Before going to school it had never occurred to me that it was needful or appropriate to have an additional name. When I heard the school-roll called, I noticed that all of the children had at least two names, and some of them indulged in what seemed to me the extravagance of having three. I was in deep perplexity, because I knew that the teacher would demand of me at least two names, and I had only one. By the time the occasion came for the enrolling of my name, an idea occurred to me which I thought would make me equal to the situation; and so, when the teacher asked me what my full name was, I calmly told him "Booker Washington," as if I had been called by that name all my life; and by that name I have since been known. Later in my life I found that my mother had given me the name of "Booker Taliaferro" soon after I was born, but in some way that part of my name seemed to disappear and for a long while was forgotten, but as soon as I found out about it I revived it, and made my full name "Booker Taliaferro Washington." I think there are not many men in our country who have had the privilege of naming themselves. . . .

—Washington.

Frank Harris 1856–1931

The author of a three-volume pornographic autobiography, My Life and Loves *(1923–27), Harris was known for the obstinacy of his obsessions. Sylvia Beach, proprietor of the Parisian bookstore Shakespeare and Co., once played a trick on him.*

Once, when he was rushing to catch a train to Nice, he stopped at the bookshop for something to read on the long journey. Could I suggest something exciting? My eye wandered along the shelf where I kept a few Tauchnitz volumes. I asked him if he had read *Little Women.* He jumped at the title, which to someone with an obsession like his could have only the French meaning of *petites femmes.* He grabbed the two volumes of Louisa Alcott's "hot book" and off he dashed to the station.

—Sylvia Beach, *Shakespeare and Co.,* 1959.

Harris was a customer of Henry Miller's father, a tailor in Brooklyn—Frank Harris was the first writer Miller ever met. The pornographer-to-be helped the old pornographer put his trousers on, while Harris discoursed on Jesus, Shakespeare, and Oscar Wilde.

Whit Burnett, knowing Harris as an old man, heard him reveal the secret of his vigor.

Until the last, Mr. Harris kept a ruddy interest in the flesh, as well as the spirit. He was an Irishman and a Westerner. He insisted, when I marveled at his long life and hearty appetite, that I feel the biceps of his good right arm.

"Just like steel," he said.

"Just like steel," I said.

We went in to dinner. We ate.

"I can eat anything," said Mr. Harris. "At 70-odd, too."

There was roast duck and *pommes soufflés,* Chablis with the *hors-d'oeuvres* and a good solid Chateauneuf du Pape with the duck. Afterward there were ices and coffee, and then armagnac and cognac. I think Frank took Calvados, which is stronger and more decisive as a drink than any apogee of applejack. It is a lovely, clearing drink. It is the white-heat poker of the spirits.

"Do you know how I do it?" asked Mr. Harris.

I confessed I did not.

"Every night," said Mr. Harris, "at ten o'clock, I take an enema."

—*The Literary Life and the Hell with It,* 1938.

Theodore Roosevelt 1858–1919

Roosevelt enjoyed caricatures of himself.

When he was Police Commissioner in New York . . . he came to dine one evening in great glee. He had gone to his office that morning and found the personnel at Police Headquarters gathered around a letter delivered by the postman; clerks and stenographers were tittering nervously, and hesitated to show it. "And here it is," he said, pulling it out of his pocket. It bore no other address than a pair of glasses over a double row of clenched teeth. He was enchanted. "Few men," he said, "live to see their own hieroglyph."

—Marjorie Terry Chanler, *Roman Spring: Memoirs,* 1934.

His thick glasses and Harvard accent misled bullies. As a young politician in Albany he had used his fists; after the death of his first wife he went west, and proved himself again in Mingusville, Montana.

When Roosevelt, wearing his steel-rimmed spectacles, entered the hotel lobby which also served as a bar, one of its several patrons, far gone in his cups, was flourishing a pistol. "Four Eyes is going to treat," shouted this individual, and, as Roosevelt made his way to a table in the corner, pursued him and repeated his remark for the benefit of the entire company:

"Maybe you didn't hear me. Four Eyes is going to treat!"

Glancing modestly down beside his chair, Roosevelt observed that his self-appointed adversary was standing with his feet placed close together. He rose, as though to comply with instructions, and let go with a short right to the jaw. On the way to the floor, the recipient hit the back of his head against the bar. Totally unconscious, he was dragged outdoors to recover.

—Noel F. Busch, *T.R.: The Story of Theodore Roosevelt,* 1963.

Roosevelt's daughter Alice was married in the White House in 1906, and not a moment too soon for the President.

Between her debut and her wedding, the conduct of the President's oldest daughter had not always been of a sort to set her father's mind at rest. Escapades like setting an automobile speed record between Newport and Boston and letting her name be used with that of the young actress, Ethel Barrymore, to advertise a charity bazaar indicated a mettlesome disposition but also led to a plethora of headlines. When "Princess Alice" popped in and out of her father's office three times during a call at the White House by Owen Wister, the latter felt emboldened to ask: "Theodore, isn't there anything you can do to control Alice?"

"I can do one of two things," replied T.R. "I can be President of the United States or I can control Alice. I cannot possibly do both."

—Busch.

He was more literary than most of our presidents. (See the story about him and Edwin Arlington Robinson on pages 149–50.) When Henry James came to Washington during Roosevelt's presidency and stayed with Henry Adams, Roosevelt invited the novelist to dinner. In public they were polite to each other, but in private they expressed reservations; Roosevelt referred to James as "a miserable little snob," while James described Roosevelt as the "monstrous embodiment of unprecedented and resounding noise."

John Dewey 1859–1952

Dewey was both philosopher and educator, whose influential philosophy of education derived from his pragmatism and democratic thought. Ideas of education began at home.

Dewey's study was directly under the bathroom, and he was sitting there one day, absorbed in a new theory of arithmetic, when suddenly he felt a stream of water trickling down his back. He jumped out of his chair and rushed upstairs to find the bathtub occupied by a fleet of sailboats, the water brimming over, and his small boy Fred busy with both hands shutting it off. The child turned as he opened the door, and said severely:

"Don't argue, John—get the mop!"

—Max Eastman, *Great Companions,* 1959.

George Lyman Kittredge 1860–1941

Philologist and long-time English professor at Harvard, Kittredge was for decades the subject of anecdotes emphasizing his forthright self-regard. He never took a doctorate. When someone asked him, perhaps facetiously, if he would get himself a Ph.D., he asked: "Who would examine me?"

Invited to afternoon tea in Cambridge, Kittredge, whose appearance was formidable, alarmed the maid who opened the door to his knock. "My God!," said the maid.

"Not God, Madam," said Kittredge. "Kittredge."

—[Editor's paraphrase].

Edith Wharton 1862–1937

Socially, Edith Wharton was the starchiest of American writers. A young Englishwoman recorded an example of her hauteur.

Mr. Wharton had preceded us after dinner to the hall, to order coffee and secure a comfortable corner, and when we followed we found him talking in the passage to two middle-aged ladies, clearly American. To my surprise Edith seemed not to perceive them, and she was passing without any sign of recognition when her husband called out, "Oh, Pussy, don't you see the duchess?" Then indeed she did pause, gave a stiff bow in the direction of the group, and without further greeting proceeded, not to the hall but into the lift, beckoning to us to follow her. My husband did, but I lingered for a moment, desirous to see the end of the little scene. Mr. Wharton was all confused apology—that was easily seen. "While she is taking the cure, my wife," he said, "has to rest a great deal—she feels the cold too." "Yes," said the duchess serenely, "I noticed the chill in the air." . . . In the Wharton's sitting-room the air was still a little chilly. "Those dreadful women," she said as her husband entered: "we don't see them at home—why should we here?"

—Percy Lubbock, *Portrait of Edith Wharton,* 1947.

Nor was anyone likely to succeed in placing her in an awkward position—not even Isabella Gardner, the Boston art collector.

No one was more quick-witted than Edith, nor more intolerant of pretentiousness. She happened to be stopping in Boston just at the moment when Mrs. Gardner was arranging the interior of Fenway Court. Mrs. Gardner loved to veil her proceedings with an air of mystery, and she permitted people to have a peep at her house, admitted by a "postern" (which was merely a side-door) at some precise and generally rather inconvenient moment. If this appointment was not exactly met, the "postern" was closed and the unfortunate late-comer left without. I think Mrs. Gardner rather enjoyed these early morning appointments, and perhaps also the failure of tardy guests to enjoy her hospitality. Knowing that Mrs. Wharton was in town, she sent word to her that if she wished to see the house and would arrive promptly at twelve minutes past eight in the morning, Mrs. Gardner would consent to show it to her. Mrs. Wharton replied that she was never up at that hour, and the invitation was declined.

—Lubbock.

Mrs. Wharton built The Mount, her mansion in Lenox, Massachusetts.

To a rather impertinent Frenchman who asked to see The Mount and who said somewhat patronizingly as he departed that he approved of it all except a bas-relief in the entrance-hall, she replied, "I assure you that you will never see it here again."

—Lubbock.

Apparently a few were allowed to become familiar.

. . . when she arrived unannounced at the villa in Sanary, [Aldous] Huxley escorted her into the drawing room by pressing gently against her behind with his cupped hand. The other guests were struck dumb by the performance, but Edith, glancing back at her host, gave him a quick sweet smile.

—R. W. B. Lewis, *Edith Wharton*, 1975.

With some of her acquaintance, the strain was not only fierce but mutual.

Once, when a winter holiday party at Ste. Claire was breaking up, [Kenneth] Clark walked out with [Bernard] Berenson to B. B.'s car. Sitting back in the "panting Lancia," Berenson uttered a sigh of relief and observed that he felt exactly as though he had just been let out of school. The car drove off, and Clark made his way back to the terrace, where Edith stood waving good-bye. "Now," she remarked, turning to the house. "I can take off my stays."

—Lewis.

She was fond of Henry James, whom she drove about in her motorcar. On occasion, the subject of money made their friendship precarious. Wharton was born to money, married it, inherited it, and made a great deal of it from her novels. She was also generous—but generosity required that she be devious.

Very often indeed it was Henry who sat with her to watch, what he adored, the large unfolding of the country-side as they swept across it. She mentioned once that the car in which they were riding had been bought with the proceeds of her last novel. "With the proceeds of *my* last novel," said Henry meditatively, "I purchased a small go-cart, or hand-barrow, on which my guests' luggage is wheeled from the station to my house. It needs a coat of paint. With the proceeds of my next novel I shall have it painted."

—Lubbock.

[Wharton] organized an appeal for funds with which to present James five thousand dollars on his seventieth birthday, "for the purchase of a gift, the choice of which will be left to him." Apprised of the scheme, James was offended. "A more reckless and indiscrete undertaking," he wrote in a letter, "with no ghost of a preliminary leave asked, no hint of a sounding taken, I cannot possibly conceive—and am still rubbing my eyes for incredulity." He wrote Wharton a letter which "completely poisoned" her plans for a trip to Italy. It was the only true break in their friendship—a break repaired in time.

. . . with a greater success, she plotted in secret. Both novelists published with Scribner's. Wharton arranged with Scribner's that they offer James an eight thousand dollar advance on his novel *The Ivory Tower,* half on signing and half on delivery; secretly, Scribner's was to take the eight thousand dollars from Edith

Wharton's own royalties. James accepted the three thousand six hundred dollars—his agent took ten percent—with the greatest joy, and without suspicion.

—Lewis.

W. S. Porter (O. Henry) 1862–1910

W. S. Porter, who published fiction as O. Henry, was born and briefly educated in North Carolina. Seeking his fortune in Texas he worked as a teller in a bank, was convicted of embezzlement, and spent three years in prison, where he began to write his stories.

In prison, he

. . . and three convict friends formed the Recluse Club, with a secret meeting place that included a kitchen with silverware, napkins, and an excellent cupboard, and if not a wine cellar at least a weekly supply of liquor. Sunday nights they met for dinner, wearing white shirts, and ate soup, a roast, vegetable, mince pie, and bread pudding. A placecard indicated seating for each of the four members. That their trousers still carried prison stripes was matter for weekly regret.

—[Editor's paraphrase].

George Santayana 1863–1952

The philosopher Santayana was also poet and novelist. Late in his life he disclosed this surmise to his biographer.

"I suppose Housman was really what people nowadays call 'homosexual.' "

"Why do you say that?" I protested at once.

"Oh, the sentiment of his poems is unmistakable," Santayana replied.

There was a pause, and then he added, as if he were primarily speaking to himself:

"I think I must have been that way in my Harvard days—although I was unconscious of it at the time."

—Daniel Webster Cory, *Santayana: The Later Years,* 1963.

When he was a professor at Harvard, Max Eastman's mother found him "dangerously fascinating. . . . He looks like Milton's Satan. . . "

He wrote his biographer an intemperate letter.

"For heaven's sake, dear Cory, do stop Ezra Pound from sending me his book. Tell him that I have no sense for truc poetry, admire (and wretchedly imitate) only the putrid Petrarch and the miserable Milton; that I don't care for books, hardly have any, and would immediately send off his precious volume to the Harvard Library or to some other cesspool of infamy. That is, if he made me a present of it. If he sent it only for me to look at and return, I would return it unopened, because I abhor all connection with important and distinguished people."

—Cory.

Cory returned to his hotel, from an evening with Santayana, and wrote down the old man's words.

"For the first time in my life I am in mortal danger of being bored. I have been thinking about my predicament—a not unusual one for a man of nearly eighty-eight—and if I go completely blind, I shall try to entertain myself as best I can by translating Latin or French or Spanish poems I have known for years by heart."

—Cory.

The mind endured the body's frailties. Cory wrote:

How vividly I recall today, after some ten years, that frail shell of a body, wrapped in an old brown dressing gown and hunched up in an armchair with a rug across his knees. In one hand he held a volume of the Triton edition of his works (the print is larger in this de luxe edition) and in the other the magnifying glass to assist the sight of one tired eye. There on the desk the red crayon was handy the moment he decided that an amputation was necessary in the body of reason.

—Cory.

Lincoln Steffens 1866–1936

A muckraker early in the century, author of a famous Autobiography, *Steffens remains in the popular consciousness especially for one piece of phrasemaking. Having returned from a trip to Russia with William Bullitt in 1919, he met with the financier Bernard Baruch.*

Baruch, sitting for a portrait bust, said, "So you've been over into Russia." And not for the first time, far from the last, Steffens replied, "I have been over into the future, and it works," by which he meant, in part, that the Bolsheviks were not a bad dream but real and there to stay. According to Bullitt, it was on the train to Stockholm, days before they even made their first contacts with Bolshevik agents and set out for the Russian frontier, that Steffens had begun to rehearse his celebrated mantra. In its perfected form—"I have seen the future, and it works"—it would ring in Western ears for the next two decades.

—Justin Kaplan, *Lincoln Steffens,* 1974.

Edwin Arlington Robinson 1869–1935

In 1905, E. A. Robinson was unknown, had not sold a poem for five years, and lived in New York almost penniless, occasionally helped out by a part-time job. In March of that year, he received a letter from a man with whom he was unacquainted and from whom he had no reason to expect any communication. It came from the White House and read:

Dear Mr. Robinson:
I have enjoyed your poems, especially "The Children of the Night," so much that I must write to tell you so. Will you permit me to ask what you are doing and how you are getting along? I wish I could see you.

Sincerely yours,
Theodore Roosevelt

—*The Letters of Theodore Roosevelt, IV, The Square Deal 1903-1905,* ed. Elting E. Morison, 1951.

Later, Robinson discovered that one of Roosevelt's sons had read his poems at the urging of a prep school teacher, who happened to own a volume Robinson had published at his own expense.

After hearing from Robinson in reply to his letter, President Roosevelt bullied his own publisher into taking Robinson on, reviewed the book from the White House when it appeared, and created a sinecure for Robinson at the Custom House in New York. (The poet received two thousand dollars a year for opening his rolltop desk each morning, reading the morning paper, closing the rolltop, leaving the newspaper on his chair as evidence that he had put in an appearance, and going home.) When President Taft took office, Robinson was informed he would be required to put in a day's work. He resigned, but in the meantime he had been recognized as a poet.

He was a shy man, especially among women. He spent every summer at the MacDowell Colony outside Peterborough, New Hampshire. His biographer tells about a conversation with Esther Bates as they walked from the Colony into the village and back again.

"I'm afraid I'm not going to be able to say anything," he remarked uneasily. She made some reply and they walked on. After ten minutes—"I'm not saying anything," he stammered, in evident distress. At last, on their silent return, they approached the [Colony]. "Well," he murmured, "I don't seem to have said anything."

—Chard Powers Smith, *Where the Light Falls,* 1965.

He was gifted, however, with a laconic pungency, especially if he discovered affectation in another writer.

And there was the young poet who, distracted by the horror of life, frequently remarked that he was going to shoot himself. One evening, having remained silent through dinner, he left the dining room early and presently was discovered in front of Colony Hall, face down in the grass in the center of the circular drive. One after another, the writers went out to him, offered solacing wisdom, elicited no stir from the prostrate one, and ended standing around him in a circle of concern. Presently E.A. joined it, and for a long time he considered the unhappy form. At last he spoke—"The ants will get him."

—Smith.

In a relatively lengthy speech he responded to reckless prolixity.

It was a different young writer, a bouncing lady novelist, who made a daily practice of joining E.A.'s table at dinner, beaming at him, and announcing her achievement of the day—never less than five thousand words. Finally, following one of the silences her proclamations always caused, E.A. creased his brow in his scowl of excruciating precision, pursed his lips and said: "This morning I deleted the hyphen from 'hell-hound' and made it one word; this afternoon I redivided it and restored the hyphen."

—Smith.

He liked to tell about a misprint.

Nancy Byrd Turner told me of E.A.'s recounting at dinner the misadventure of the sonnet "Reuben Bright." Reuben was a worthy butcher who greatly loved his wife, so when she died

He packed a lot of things that she had made
Most mournfully away in an old chest
Of hers, and put some chopped-up cedar boughs
In with them, and tore down the slaughter house.

E.A. said that an "inspired printer" set it that when Reuben had put her things in the chest he

. . . put some chopped up cedar boughs
In with them and tore down to the slaughter house.

—Smith.

Robinson had a phrase that he applied, without censure or approbation but with awe, to people who seemed audacious or even gaudy in personal style. He called Amy Lowell a "high roller," and Lucius Beebe the same. The highest of all the rollers, perhaps, was Isadora Duncan. When someone suggested that Miss Duncan was partial to oysters and champagne, Robinson paused and added, "Well, she didn't refuse whiskey."

He did not add that Miss Duncan entertained designs on his chastity. The poet Percy MacKaye brought William Vaughn Moody, Ridgely Torrence, and Robinson to meet Miss Duncan at her studio in Carnegie Hall in 1908.

As the elevator landed them on her floor, a door burst open at the farther end of the corridor, and the vibrant Isadora, in Greek costume, swept forward like a maenad, with a rout of revellers at her heels. Immediately behind her, clutching her hand, was a white-bearded old man in full evening dress with coat-tails flying and spectacles turned up over his brow, John Butler Yeats, father of the poet; and behind him, hand in hand, wildly dancing, a roomful of other guests.

"Take hold, take hold!" The four poets joined the gay "Snap-the-whip," as the Duncan led it back into the studio; Torrence noted Robinson's faint, somewhat dazed smile.

There were introductions. Thereupon, the dancer picked up a Greek wine jar and paid tribute to each of the poets in a dance which was all his own. "You know," she exclaimed, "dancers were made for poets." She had known only MacKaye, but she seemed, as she danced, to know the others almost as they knew each other. For Moody, her dance was like the awakening of the figures on a Grecian urn, classic and ritualistic; but for Robinson, it was ironic, a little mocking and full of subtle humor . . .

Robinson allured her. There was another occasion in her studio when she danced before him flicking a lighted cigarette mischievously under his nose. MacKaye, watching, was amused how stiff and troubled Robinson seemed. Yet he liked her, for she had imagination and intellect.

Then, on Christmas Eve, she came with a motor-car full of friends to the Judson and sent word that she wished to see Robinson, and Torrence, too. . . . She kept Robinson at her side and pushed the others into an adjoining room, accompanied by a half dozen bottles of champagne.

Alone with Robinson, she told him what she wanted of him. He was not sober, but his head had the clarity which alcohol seemed never to dispel. He had one love, the Muse, he said, and that was all he could manage. Venus was persuasive and engaging, Tannhäuser, sympathetic but not interested. She told of her art, of her struggles, of fame and its evanescence. "You have one of the enduring arts. Mine perishes with me. These two pitiful legs are all I have to demonstrate my art with. Only through the love of a poet can I be touched by the enduring flame."

Tannhäuser proved impregnable. Torrence noted how relieved Robinson looked when Venus, resigned and relaxed, finally opened the door to her other friends.

—Hermann Hagedorn, *E. A. Robinson: A Biography,* 1938.

Even in the familiar MacDowell Colony, Robinson's eminence could become a problem for him.

One morning Nancy Byrd Turner was early to breakfast, she and a new colonist, female, being the first at E.A.'s table. Presently he came downstairs, looked dubious, and advanced. Nancy introduced him—"This is Mr. Robinson." The stranger exploded: "Robinson!—not E.A. Robinson!—not *the* Mr. Robinson?"

Long, bleak silence. E.A. spoke—"A Mr. Robinson."

—Smith.

Frank Norris 1870–1902

*The young realistic novelist (*McTeague *1899,* Thc Pit, *1903), Norris cared enough for fame to mock it. Once he conspired with friends: they were to enter a restaurant where he was already seated, point, and whisper loudly,* "That's him!"

Stephen Crane 1871–1900

As a young man, on a camping trip with friends, Crane practiced courage.

. . . He had reached through the cracks of the floor of their cabin to retrieve a mirror when suddenly he uttered a horrifying yell: "A snake bit me on the hand!" They laid him on a cot, cauterized his wound with a hot poker, and plied him with the cure-all for snake-bite: whiskey. "It was of no avail. The patient was failing rapidly, as in faltering tones he gave them the last messages to his family. His friends stood around him gloomily; then one spoke up, 'Well, as we can't do anything more for poor old ------, I, for one, want a wack at that snake.' 'Me, too!' chorused the others, their pale faces flushing with resolution. Arming themselves with suitable weapons, they lowered a lantern under the cabin and all gazed intently down the opening, clutching their weapons. Then one gave a yell. 'B'Gosh, it's a setting hen!' The others gave a look and then began to laugh hysterically. The pallid youth upon the couch, who had been giving a noble exhibition of how a brave man can die, suddenly became very drunk."

—R. W. Stallman, *Stephen Crane,* 1968.

After his success with The Red Badge of Courage *(1895), Crane went to live in England. He attended a dinner party where he met a distinguished writer under unusual circumstances.*

A nobleman and his mistress, Madame Zipango, were guests of Griswold's supper party, and Henry James arrived to pay his compatriots a call. Madame Zipango, whose lover had by then passed out from too much imbibing, poured champagne into James' top hat. . . . James just then was cross-questioning Crane about literary style.

—Stallman.

From England Crane shipped out to cover the Spanish-American War.

A friend of Van Wyck Brooks recalls Crane's bravery at Guantánamo when our troops were huddled against an earthwork at which the Spaniards directed an unusually vicious fire. "Suddenly Crane, who was incapable of bravado, let himself quietly over the redoubt, lighted a cigarette, stood for a few moments with his arms at his sides, while the bullets hissed past him into the mud, then as quietly climbed back over the redoubt and strolled away. It was impossible . . . to question the insouciance of this act: Crane's bearing was that of a somnambulist. He appeared to be, as it were, detached from himself, possessed by an irresistible impulse to register, in his body, and without regard to the safety of his body, certain sensations."

—Stallman.

When the Americans invaded Puerto Rico, Harding Davis and Crane were with them. While Harding Davis slept—Crane was supposed to awaken him—Crane coolly crept forward of the advance posts into the town of Juana Díaz. As he ambled into the first street he came to, smoking a cigarette, his khaki suit, slouched hat, and leggings were all that were needed to drive the first man who saw him into retreating to arouse the garrison. Within ten minutes, Harding Davis later reported, the *alcalde* surrendered the town to its lone occupier. "Crane told me that no general in the moment of victory had ever acted in a more generous manner. He shot no one against a wall, looted no churches, levied no forced loans. Instead he lined up the male members of the community in the Plaza, and organized a joint celebration of the conquerors and conquered . . . that overflowed from the Plaza into the by-streets and lashed itself into a frenzied carnival of rejoicing."

—Stanley Weintraub, *The London Yankees*, 1979.

Versions of this story vary. Richard Harding Davis's featured a literary Colonel.

"He knew that it did not fall to the lot of every Colonel to have his victories immortalized by the genius who wrote *The Red Badge of Courage.* 'I am glad to see you,' he cried eagerly. 'Have you been marching with my men?' Crane shook his head. 'I am sorry,' said the Colonel. 'I should like you to have seen us take this town.' 'THIS town!' cried Crane in polite embarrassment. 'I'm really very sorry, Colonel, but I took this town myself before breakfast yesterday morning.' "

—Stallman.

Returned to England, the young novelist reverted to his spendthrift and madcap life—which soon would end. (Wallace Stevens, employed briefly as a reporter for the New York Tribune, *was to cover Crane's funeral in 1900.) He and Henry James attended the annual mud-bowl regatta in Rye—James the referee wearing knickerbockers, ghillies, and a homburg; Crane content to wear breeches and puttees.*

"Baron Crane" would dress for dinner in formal attire like a proper English gentleman. If he could not boast of titles and heraldry, he could brag about the captured Spanish flag he had brought back from Cuba to hang in the entrance chamber of the Manor. Nothing pleased him better than his role as Lord of Brede Manor, says Ford Hueffer [Ford Madox Ford]. "He strewed his floors with rushes; a vast pack of dogs clustered around his hearth . . . and every passing tramp was welcome to a cut of beef and a draught of ale. Yet, curiously enough, when the fit took him, he would assume the dress and speech of an American plainsman and pace the sunk lanes of his demesne, a picturesque figure with his shock of hair, piercing eyes and rather weak mouth, his rough attire of shirt and breeches, with revolver swinging at his hip."

—Stallman.

Theodore Dreiser 1871–1945

Dreiser was another author noted for appreciation of himself. Once he confided to his literary executor H. L. Mencken that after years of thought he had decided on his own last words: "Shakespeare, I come!" He found it annoying that the Swedes never gave him a Nobel Prize.

Early in 1921, Dreiser urged Mencken to advance him for the "Noble" prize, calling it "a nice piece of change" and offering a bribe. "Start the ball," he wrote, "and if I snake the forty thousand—isn't that what the lucky mutt is supposed to draw?—you get five thousand."

—W. A. Swanberg, *Dreiser,* 1965.

Mencken told him how to spell Nobel.

Waldo Frank noted another sort of greed.

Once Frank and a few others were his evening guests. There was a cake, and Frank observed with fascination his host's insensate lust to get at that cake: "Dreiser licked his lips. . . . Dreiser's eyes bulged, his hands thrummed. She cut a slice. Dreiser tipped his chair, sprawled forward. . . . Then, the lady noticed his behavior. Swiftly, as if working against a possible crisis, the good lady put a piece of cake on the plate and handed it to Dreiser. He fell to, rolling his eyes. The lady proceeded to serve Theodore Dreiser's guests.

—Swanberg.

He was known for his parties.

To this stag gathering in St. Luke's Place came Mencken, Sherwood Anderson, Van Vechten, Llewelyn Powys, Boyd, Burton Rascoe and others. Powys did not know some of the guests, and others were also meeting for the first time. Dreiser did not trouble to introduce them. . . .

He served only beer to this hundred-proof group. They sat around the bare, rugless room in disconsolate, desultory conversation until the door opened and a handsome young man staggered in, bearing a bottle of champagne. He was Scott Fitzgerald, already famous for *This Side of Paradise* and *The Beautiful and*

Damned. An admirer of Dreiser, whom he had never met, he teetered from one guest to another, then located Dreiser and gave him the bottle.

"Mr. Dreiser," he said, "I get a great kick out of your books."

—Swanberg.

Dreiser's guests watched in dismay as he put the champagne in the icebox. Fitzgerald removed a flask from a coat pocket and got drunker.

Bennett Cerf remembered an incident between Dreiser and his publisher Horace Liveright.

Horace said, "I'll make a deal with you, Dreiser. The first fifty thousand dollars I get for your book in Hollywood, you get complete. After that, we go fifty-fifty."

Dreiser said, "You won't get a dollar for it. Nobody will make that picture, Horace."

Horace said, "Watch me!"

So they shook hands. In those days fifty thousand dollars was a lot of money for movie rights. But Horace sold *American Tragedy* for eighty-five thousand dollars! When he came back, of course, Horace had to boast about his triumphs, and I was a very good person to tell, because I was always appreciative. So he called me up and said, "What do you think I got for *American Tragedy?* Eighty-five thousand dollars! Wait till I tell Dreiser!"

I said, "Gee, I'd like to be there."

He said, "I'm taking him to lunch next Thursday at the Ritz, and I'd like you to come and watch Dreiser when I tell him."

So the three of us went to the Ritz. The main dining room had a balcony all the way around it, a few steps above the main part of the restaurant, and we had a table on the balcony right next to the railing.

Dreiser said, "What do you want with me, Liveright?"

Horace was very coy. He said, "Now, now, we'll have our lunch."

Dreiser was getting grumpier. "What have you got to tell me?"

Finally after we had finished our meal, before the coffee came, Horace said, "Dreiser, I sold *American Tragedy.*"

Dreiser said, "Oh, come on."

Horace said, "I did."

Finally Dreiser said, "Well, what did you get for it?"

Horace said, "Eighty-five thousand dollars."

It took a few moments for this to sink in, and then Dreiser let out a cry of triumph. He exulted, "What I'm going to do with that money!" He took a pencil out of his pocket and began writing on the tablecloth. He said, "I'm going to pay off the mortgage on my place up in Croton and I'm going to get an automobile," and so on.

Horace listened for a minute, then reminded Dreiser, "You know, you're not getting the whole eighty-five thousand. Remember our deal? You get fifty and then we split the thirty-five. You're going to get sixty-seven thousand, five hundred."

Dreiser put down his pencil and looked at Liveright. He said, "Do you mean to tell me you're going to take seventeen thousand, five hundred dollars of *my* money?"

Horace said, "Dreiser, that was the deal we made. You didn't think I'd sell your book at all."

Just at this moment the waiter brought the coffee in. Suddenly Dreiser seized his cup and threw the steaming coffee in Liveright's face. It was shocking. Horace jumped up, coffee streaming down his shirt front. Luckily it didn't hit him in the eyes. Dreiser got up from the table without a word and marched out of the restaurant. Horace, always the showman, always gallant, stood there mopping himself up, and retained enough of his equilibrium to say, "Bennett, let this be a lesson to you. Every author is a son of a bitch."

—*At Random*, 1977.

When Dreiser's book about Russia plagiarized passages written by Sinclair Lewis's wife Dorothy Thompson—an astonishing event, perhaps explained by Dreiser's use of amateur editorial assistance—the rival novelists became enemies. Shortly afterward, in 1930, Lewis instead of Dreiser became the first American to win the Nobel Prize for literature, which did not make Dreiser more fond of Lewis.

In March 1931 the two novelists met at a dinner for a visiting Russian novelist, and Lewis was drunk. Dreiser congratulated him, probably without sincere affection, and in response Lewis blew a raspberry. After dinner, Lewis declined to address the Russian visitor, declaring that he did not want to speak in front of the man who had "plagiarized three thousand words from my wife's book." When Lewis refused Dreiser's demand for an apology, Dreiser slapped him across the face.

Lewis thereupon addressed him: "Theodore, you are a liar and a thief."

James Weldon Johnson 1871–1938

On a trip to Japan, the author of God's Trombones *(1927) was tested for inspiration.*

Before I finished with my luggage, three reporters came into my stateroom; three of the same who had been interviewing and photographing me. One of them asked, "Mr. Johnson, did you see Fujiyama this morning?" I answered that I had. "Mr. Johnson," he continued, "the people of Japan would be greatly honored to have from you a poem on Fujiyama." With that, he planked a pad down in front of me and offered me a pencil. I was never so taken unawares in my life. I lamely explained that with so inspiring a subject together with the Japanese language, a fitting poem would come spontaneously, but such a thing was impossible to a poet working in the barbarous English tongue. They went away quite disappointed.

—James Weldon Johnson, *Along This Way,* 1933.

Willa Cather 1873–1947

Willa Cather grew up in Nebraska, which became the setting for most of her fiction. After graduating from the University of Nebraska in 1895, she worked as a journalist and published poems and short stories. From 1906 to 1912 she helped to edit McClure's *magazine in New York. Witter Bynner worked there as a young man, after her resignation, and remembered*

. . . Miss Cather's cold harshness in refusing to let us withdraw from publication, in *McClure's* magazine, "The Birthmark" which friends of hers assured us at a tense session with her in Mr. McClure's office might ruin the life, even by suicide as in the story, of another friend of hers and theirs upon whose disfigurement and dilemma it was based. I can hear her now, saying briskly: "My art is more important than my friend."

—*Prose Pieces,* 1979.

The friend survived.

The wife of the editor of the Saturday Review of Literature *made the mistake of invading Cather's hours of writing.*

Mrs. Canby, who lived not far from her, tells how, in her naïveté, before she had ever met Miss Cather, she once made her way to Bank Street, Number Five, in the sacred hours of the morning, though probably near noon, rang the bell in the vestibule: with the purpose of inviting the author of *A Lost Lady* to dinner.

After considerable delay, the buzzer buzzed; Marian Canby, walking into the dark lower hall of the small apartment house and looking skyward, saw no angel but a very dark, dour face, peering formidably over the banisters.

"Who are you, what do you want?"

The editor's wife blushed and stammered out her invitation, whereupon the face above grew kind, warm and ruddy. But the evening was hazardous. Willa Cather, disliking on sight the young English journalist who made up the foursome, retired into one of her dudgeons, and when she found herself alone with her hosts explicitly requested that she might come alone to dine henceforth, unless there were someone who could be guaranteed to her liking.

—Elizabeth Shepley Sergeant, *Willa Cather: A Memoir,* 1953.

Ellen Glasgow 1874–1945

Born to an aristocratic family in Richmond, Virginia, Ellen Glasgow wrote novels that rebelled against the tradition of gentility in Southern fiction. Barren Ground *(1925) is best known of her works. She was fond of her dogs.*

She arrived in London and spent some time with her brother at Moncorvo House. And she mailed picture postcards to "Mr. Billy Bennett" and "Mr. Jeremy Glasgow" at One West Main Street, Richmond, Virginia. She sent Billy a picture of a landscape where she thought he would like to run and said that she hoped that he and "precious Jeremy" had had their drive today. On other cards, she sent Billy a picture of a Skye Terrier, which she thought he might like to have for a playmate; and she sent Jeremy a picture of a Sealyham so that he could see the stock from which he had sprung. And finally she sent "Mr. William Bennett" a postcard picture of the first Girls' Sunday School in Gloucester with the note on the back: "A Sunday

School for darling Billy to chew." Ellen not only wrote cards to Jeremy and Billy, she also had clothes and collars especially made for them in London.

Ellen was in Maine resting from the completion of her novel and trying to escape from the strain of Jeremy's long illness when she was suddenly called home. She rushed back to Richmond in order to be with Jeremy in his last hours. She found him in the final stages of pneumonia, but she believed that he recognized her before his death. Jeremy had been ill for almost a year. In December, 1928, he had had a gall bladder operation but had partially recovered. In July, 1929, his condition worsened and it became necessary for him to have a second operation. The operation was performed not by a veterinarian, but by a famous surgeon in Richmond. Specialists from New York and Philadelphia were consulted by telephone, and everything known to medicine was tried in an effort to save his life. When it seemed as if he would recover, Ellen went to Maine on her doctor's recommendation to try to prevent a nervous breakdown.

Her nerves were not helped much when she received the doctor's bill some weeks after Jeremy's death. She was incensed, not because of the amount, but because it read: "Services for dog." She thought it should have read: "Services for Mr. Jeremy Glasgow."

—E. Stanley Godbold, *Ellen Glasgow and the Woman Within,* 1972.

Amy Lowell 1874–1925

From the same family as the poets James Russell (see p. 102) and Robert (see p. 324), sister to Abbott Lawrence who was president of Harvard, Amy Lowell was short, rotund, energetic, and—especially for a Bostonian of family—eccentric. On the boat back from a trip to Europe, Lowell first tried to conceal one of her famous habits.

Usually, in the small hours, when the dancing and the blaring band had stopped, Amy would go up on deck to smoke her cigars in the cool air when no one was around to stare at her. She had stopped trying to deceive her sister-in-law. Anne knew Amy smoked, and it seemed hypocritical not to light up a cigar in front of her. But, out of respect for the Lowell family's reputation, Amy still did not smoke in public places. However, on one of her night promenades on deck someone saw her bulky figure pacing the deck, the glowing cigar like a rosy beacon revealing her face every time she took a puff. This bit of shipboard gossip was noised around the floating community, and when the ship docked, she was met by newspaper reporters clamoring for the facts. Amy, thoroughly exasperated by this time, admitted angrily that she smoked cigars—and what of it?

In these times it seems incredible, but the news made headlines the next morning in the *New York Tribune* and other dailies. Amy would not have minded the publicity if it had only been about herself, but the news value of the story seemed to be largely based on the fact that she was Harvard President Abbott L. Lowell's sister. She decided to make the most of it, however, partly because of the pleasure she took in defying the shibboleth that made a sin of women's smoking, partly because of her desire to shock people, and finally because her sense of showmanship told her it could be a means of getting notice for her next volume. . . .

—Jean Gould, *Amy: The World of Amy Lowell and the Imagist Movement,* 1975.

She had a genius for publicity and organization. She stole Ezra Pound's Imagism away from him—and Pound relabeled the movement Amygism.

She was in London in 1914 when the war started, an event which she regarded as a personal affront.

In London Miss Lowell immediately arranged to have her automobile crated and shipped home, to prevent it from being commandeered, and set about finding passage for herself. That night people marched down Piccadilly waving flags and shouting support for the Belgians and French, singing the *Marseillaise* and shouting, "We want war! We want war!" It sounded, she wrote Harriet Monroe, "savage, abominable." And there was no passage to be had to America. She was in a panic. Feeling trapped, she raged at a bobby on his beat and at the crowds massed in the streets, indignant that the police had done nothing to help her make her way to her hotel. "Don't they know I'm Amy Lowell?" she screamed, and when back inside the safety of the Berkeley she lit one of her long cigars and paced up and down her suite. "And it was this month that my book of poems was coming out here!" she claimed erroneously to herself and Ada Russell. "What attention will it get with this going on? What has happened to England? Why don't they stop the war?"

—Stanley Weintraub, *The London Yankees,* 1979.

Back home in Massachusetts she generally commanded more respect. And if she could not at first make her identity known, she would find a way to do so.

One incident that became legendary occurred around this time (1915–16) when her car broke down in the country and had to be repaired in a local garage. When the proprietor presented his bill, she told him to charge it, and started to leave. "Just a minute, ma'am; how do I know your credit is any good?" he asked suspiciously. Her answer was simply to repeat her name, but he looked so doubtful that she told him, "My brother is president of Harvard University," adding, as a challenge, "Call Harvard and ask him if you don't believe me!" And she walked out of the garage. Calling Kirkland 7600, the man got Abbott Lawrence Lowell on the phone and explained skeptically, "Some big fat dame whose engine broke down wants to charge her bill—claims she's your sister."

"What is she doing now?" asked the president of Harvard.

"She's across the road . . . sittin' on a stone wall, smoking a cigar!"

Lawrence, who was resigned to Amy's habits, assured him, "That's my sister, all right!"

—Gould.

Stirred perhaps by her notoriety as much as by "Patterns," crowds came to hear her read. There were a few bad moments.

Miss Lowell was once lecturing before an audience in some eastern city, reading her own poems. She started to read a poem, but at a certain spot the audience tittered. She stopped, eyed them sternly, and waited for silence. When it came, she began again; but again they tittered in the same place. This time she stopped longer and looked at them even more sternly. Finally, when she reached the passage a third time and they once more tittered, she closed the book with a snap, said savagely but very precisely to them, "You unregenerate sons of bitches!" and walked off the platform.

—Eunice Tietjens, *The World at My Shoulder,* 1938.

Quite by accident at Wellesley she had hit upon a trick that never failed to win her listeners. After hearing the first poem, the students couldn't seem to make up their minds whether to applaud then or wait till the end—or perhaps they were puzzled by the poetry itself—Amy couldn't tell. At last she demanded impatiently: "Well?—Clap or hiss, I don't care which, but for Christ's sake, do something!" The result of course was a burst of laughter and applause; from then on, she had the listeners in the palm of her hand.

—Gould.

Her manners did not endear her to Willa Cather, who visited Lowell's Victorian mansion, Sevenels, in company with the literary scholar and Columbia professor George Edward Woodberry. Lowell sent her limousine to fetch them—as a friend of Cather remembers Cather telling it.

By the time they reached Sevenels, with its mansard roofs, lawns, shrubberies, and gardens Professor Woodberry had told Willa Cather about the Keats manuscripts, letters and books that Miss Lowell was indefatigable in collecting: Miss Lowell had discovered, she claimed, a good deal that was fresh. He itched to see for himself.

But after they were introduced into the waxed, baronial spaces that one might well expect of a Boston Lowell, a considerable delay set in. Miss Lowell was still dictating—in bed, of course—to her secretary aloft. Mrs. Ada Russell, her devoted ex-actress friend and lady-in-waiting, offered them tea and a dozen amenities and explanations. But currents of impatience had set in, and the bulky, dynamic Poetess-Imagist rushing upon them, at last—full of casual bonhommie and friendliness, in her long, plain, rich silk, buttoned, Quaker-like, from collar to toes—perhaps found them a bit stiff: if Amy Lowell wanted the esteem and sought the friendship of a noted scholar, this was hardly the way to behave, Willa thought.

Of course, her opinion was not important to Amy. Willa Sibert Cather was just a Houghton Mifflin author whom the Imagist *might* get around to reading in due course. Though, she preferred detective stories to novels of the prairie!

Well, they were eventually led, as I recall, fairly fuming, to the Sacred Precinct; the safe where Amy kept her treasures; or else, perhaps, the Keats material was unlocked and brought by the Priestess-Imagist to her library table. In any event, the Professor, so modest and so learned, eventually extended his eager right hand.

But the owner stepped forward touchily, seized the "item," set her thumbs and fists firmly on the two edges like a monk with a missal and held it herself under the Professor's nose. He must not *touch* it—nobody might *touch* her rarities. It was clear that they were so much a part of her person that a violation would occur if the most revered scholar so much as turned a page. She, Amy, would do the turning.

Willa, at this point in her story, stifled with fury, just blew up. Her sentences, always broken, emphatic, and colloquial but ordered, exploded like fireworks. Woodberry, the great Woodberry, revered of students and scholars was at Sevenels but a slum child with dirty hands!

—Elizabeth Shepley Sergeant, *Willa Cather: A Memoir,* 1953.

Gertrude Stein 1874–1946

Gertrude Stein attended Radcliffe where she studied psychology under William James and later undertook experiments in brain anatomy at Johns Hopkins University. In 1902 she forsook science, moved herself to Europe, and became a writer. In Paris she collected paintings and befriended artists of all sorts. Three Lives *(1909),* Tender Buttons *(1914), and* The Making of Americans *(1925) are some of her works.*

She was notoriously fond of Ford cars.

Gertrude ordered a new Ford, a two-seater, which arrived in early December, 1920, stripped of all the amenities. Riding in the car for the first time, Alice remarked that it was nude. "There was nothing on her dashboard, neither clock nor ashbox nor cigarette lighter." Gertrude answered, "Godiva," and that became the name of the car. It was in Godiva, parked at the curbside, that Gertrude often scribbled at her poems on odd scraps of paper. She had discovered, while waiting for Alice to attend to errands, that her lofty position in the driver's seat was an inspiring spot in which to write.

—James K. Mellow, *Charmed Circle*, 1974.

Everyone who came to Paris met Gertrude Stein and felt initially in awe. Eventually almost everyone quarreled with her. When she met Robert McAlmon's bride Winifred Bryher, the young writers were still at the stage of awe.

. . . spotting the couple as she rode along, she pulled over to the curb and lumbered down from the vehicle. Bryher recalled the meeting vividly: "Two penetrating eyes in a square impassive face seemed to be absorbing every detail of my appearance. 'Why McAlmon,' a puzzled voice remarked, 'you did not tell me that you had married an ethical Jewess. It's rather a rare type.' " Bryher's ancestors had all been English Protestants and German Lutherans, but as she observed, "You did not argue with Gertrude Stein. . . ."

—Mellow.

William Carlos Williams remembered his first encounter.

But the highlight was tea at Gertrude Stein's. I had looked forward to this with great expectation. A small place to which we were admitted by someone, probably Miss Toklas, to find that two or three others had preceded us, Miss Stein herself coming forward to greet us and find chairs for us beneath that astonishing wall of Picasso's paintings, largely of the "blue period," in three tiers above us. It was a good-sized, very high room more or less cubical in shape—the lot of us sitting around, where we could, facing a small cabinet at the end wall with doors that opened right and left.

There was some little difficulty about the chairs which opened the conversation upon the mention of a visit there only a few months earlier by Ezra Pound. One chair in particular, an antique, one which Miss Stein especially treasured, was offered him with the warning that it was not very strong and would he be a little careful how he used it. With which he sprawled in it in his usual fashion and broke one of the back legs. She never forgave him. That was a good start.

We looked at the paintings. Who could not have done so? It was one of the sights of Paris. Tea was served, after or during which Miss Stein went to the small cabinet, opened it and began to take out her manuscripts, one at a time, telling us the titles and saying that she hoped some day to see them printed. I can't remember the exact sequence of what followed, but one way or another she asked me what I would do were the unpublished books mine and I were faced with the difficulty she was experiencing.

It must have been that I was in one of my more candid moods or that the cynical opinion of Pound and others of my friends about Miss Stein's work was uppermost in my mind, for my reply was, "If they were mine, having so many, I should probably select what I thought were the best and throw the rest into the fire."

The result of my remark was instantaneous. There was a shocked silence out of which I heard Miss Stein say, "No doubt. But then writing is not, of course, your *métier*."

That closed the subject and we left soon after.

—*The Autobiography of William Carlos Williams,* 1951.

And there was Hemingway.

Alice was in the habit of telling Gertrude, when she went out on her afternoon walks, "Don't you come home with Hemingway on your arm," and, of course, one day she did. They had had a long discussion, and Gertrude finally said, "Hemingway, after all you are ninety percent Rotarian."

"Can't you make it eighty percent?" Hemingway asked.

"No," Gertrude answered, "I can't."

—Mellow.

Martha Foley started to interview Stein for the Paris Herald, *but fell afoul of Alice B. ("Pussy") Toklas.*

I did not enjoy Miss Stein's arrogant, rude way of answering my questions, and Pussy's constant interjection of her own comments confused me. Thinking I might get a better interview if Pussy were absent, I whispered to Miss Stein, "I would like to see you alone sometime." I had heard the expression "bum's rush." Pussy made its meaning clear. I was out of there, the street door slammed behind me, before I could say good-bye.

—Martha Foley, *The Story of Story Magazine: A Memoir,* 1980.

Stein's conceit was undeniable.

Lipchitz asked Gertrude to come to his studio and pose for him, and she agreed. Lipchitz found her an interesting subject, and her egotism memorable. He recalled Gertrude's telling him, once, very solemnly, "Jacques, of course you don't know too much about English literature, but besides Shakespeare and me, who do you think there is?"

—Mellow.

With her brother Leo she was an early admirer of Picasso, who painted her portrait. ("It doesn't look like her," someone complained to Picasso. "It will," said Picasso.) Apparently she approached Picasso more even-handedly than she had Lipchitz. "There are two geniuses in art today," she told him, "you in painting and I in literature." Picasso, who read no English, reportedly asked her brother, "What does she write?"

She had a talent for friendship, certainly, and a loyalty to friends who remained loyal to her. The photographer Cecil Beaton remembered a story from 1939.

On his last evening at Bilignin, Beaton had felt oppressed by the atmosphere and decided to take a walk before dinner: "I'd been closeted in this small house, or in the small car overrun with dogs, all day." When darkness came, and with it the drenching rains of a mountain squall, and Beaton had not returned, the two women and Rose became frightened. A neighbor stopped to ask Gertrude if she had heard the latest war news. "War?" Gertrude answered. "Who cares about war? We've lost Cecil Beaton!"

—Mellow.

Her autobiography, which she called The Autobiography of Alice B. Toklas, *was a considerable success. News magazines made much of her when Paris was liberated, and she was a public figure. Her publisher Bennett Cerf interviewed her on radio.*

I started the radio interview by remarking, "Gertrude Stein, here you are on a coast-to-coast hookup. This is going to be your chance to explain to the American public what you mean by these writings of yours." I added, "I'm very proud to be your publisher, Miss Stein, but as I've always told you, I don't understand very much of what you're saying."

She replied promptly, "Well, I've always told you, Bennett, you're a very nice boy but you're rather stupid."

—*At Random,* 1977.

One of her GI friends was Leon Gordon Miller.

Frequently the two of them took walks around Paris. On one of these occasions, Miller accompanied Gertrude to the butcher shop. Everywhere in Paris, after the war, there were long lines waiting in front of the shops. Food was scarce and people had to wait hours to fill their meager ration allowances. Gertrude, with perfect aplomb, simply walked to the head of the line, expecting service. There were catcalls from the angry housewives. The butcher explained, *"Elle est écrivaine" ["She is a writer"]*—and the catcalls grew louder. One irate woman turned and spat. Miller was so embarrassed he left the store. When Gertrude came out, she lashed into him, calling him a "chicken coward." In France, she insisted, writers and creative people were privileged because they had "less time to spare on routine."

—Cerf.

Her last words were worthy of her.

The operation was scheduled for the afternoon of July 27. Alice waited anxiously beside Gertrude's bed—Gertrude was already under heavy sedation. She turned to Alice and murmured, "What is the answer?" Alice, unable to answer, remained silent. Gertrude said, "In that case, what is the question?" . . . At about 5:30 in the evening, she lapsed into a coma. Doctors worked on her for an hour. At 6:30, she was pronounced dead.

—Mellow.

Robert Frost 1874–1963

When Frost journeyed to England in 1912 he was unknown and virtually unpublished in America. He assembled the poems of A Boy's Will, *submitted them to the publishing firm of David Nutt on a casual recommendation, and the book was accepted. While the book was in production, he received a communication from another American resident in England.*

It was a calling card bearing Pound's address—10 Church Walk, Kensington—beneath which Pound had written and initialed a curt message: "At home—sometimes. . . ." Pound answered his knock through the closed door, asking who it was and ordering him to wait. Frost had interrupted him in the process of taking a "bird-bath," and the greatest surprise occurred when the door was finally opened by a young man—with a tousle of red hair and a neatly trimmed red beard, blue-gray eyes and a nervous manner—wrapped in an Oriental dressing gown.

. . . he hoped Frost had a copy of the book with him. No, he had not yet seen a copy of the book; he supposed it must be bound and ready to be sent to reviewers. Then, said Pound, he and Frost would make the brief trip over to the office of David Nutt and demand a copy. They did, with Pound taking charge, so that when Frost saw the first bound copy of *A Boy's Will,* with its attractive pebble-grained and copper-colored cloth binding, the thin volume was being placed in Pound's hands, not Frost's. Back they went to 10 Church Walk and Pound immediately sat down to read, directing Frost to find a magazine and keep himself busy for a while. Before long, the silence of the room was broken by Pound's chuckling just before he said, in a pompous tone which amused Frost, "You don't mind our liking this?"

"Oh, no," Frost answered, "go right ahead!"

—Lawrance Thompson, *Robert Frost, the Early Years 1874–1916,* 1966.

Frost was the first to admit that he was jealous of other poets. When he resided in Cambridge, fall and spring, he sometimes accepted an invitation to talk with Harvard undergraduates.

Here sits Robert Frost in a corner, his eyes scanning the room for approaching enemies. Undergraduates ask questions about

Yeats, Eliot, Pound. The corpses of Yeats, Eliot, and Pound litter the floor of the housemaster's living room. Someone mentions Robert Lowell's name. Frost says he guesses Lowell is pretty good. Of course he's a *convert,* he says, he lays the word out like a frog in a biology lab. Frost remembers a story. Because he smiles when he remembers it, his audience understands that it is a malicious story. Frost tells us that Allen Tate's a convert too; once he saw Tate at a party standing next to a Jesuit, and he walked over to them; he asked the Jesuit, "Are you a *convert?*" "No," says the Jesuit; "Well, neither am I," says Frost, and walks away.

—Donald Hall, *Remembering Poets,* 1978.

When he talked with other poets he made it a contest.

Frost and Stevens traded literary gossip before resuming the playful teasing of each other they had started in 1935.

"The trouble with you, Robert, is that you're too academic," said Stevens.

"The trouble with you, Wallace, is that you're too executive," retorted Frost.

"The trouble with you, Robert, is that you write about—subjects."

"The trouble with you, Wallace, is that you write about—bric-a-brac."

. . . in May 1960, Frost returned to Washington for the first series of lectures in his new role of Honorary Consultant in the Humanities to the Library of Congress. The first of several official functions arranged to hail his arrival was a luncheon in the Whittall Pavilion on May second, attended by several members of the Library staff and other invited guests. One outsider who was brought in by Roy P. Basler, chief of the Library's Manuscript Division and Frost's personal link with the Library staff, was someone Frost had no great desire to see. Carl Sandburg was in town to receive the "Great Living Americans" award from the U.S. Chamber of Commerce later in the day. Basler had had some difficulty persuading Sandburg to come to the luncheon honoring Frost, but Sandburg had agreed, and now appeared at the Pavilion wearing a wool scarf about his neck and a black fedora on his head. When Basler saw him at the door, he turned to Frost and announced, "Robert, here's Carl Sandburg come to lunch." As Basler later recorded it, Frost turned, grinned without moving or offering his hand, and said, "Don't you know enough to take off your hat when you come in the house?" Sandburg gave a throaty chuckle, and removed his fedora with an exaggerated flourish. As he did so, a lock of his silvery hair fell forward and covered his eye. "Don't you ever comb your hair?" Frost baited. Sandburg chuckled again, and without saying a word, took a comb from his coat pocket, lifted the silver forelock back into place, and offered the comb to Frost. "You could use a comb yourself," he laughingly retorted. The guests who were observing the interchange laughed, as Frost took out an ancient comb of his own and ran it through his tousled white hair with little effect. Then, to more laughter, the two poetic rivals shook hands and parted to mix with the crowd, but not before Frost reminded Sandburg, "I'd as soon play tennis with the net down as write free verse." During the luncheon, Frost aimed several more barbs in the direction of Sandburg, who did not seem to take offense at any of Frost's only half-good-natured "jokes." After lunch had been cleared, Mumford rose to invite either of the two distinguished guests to speak if he desired to do so. "Let Carl pay a tribute to me," said Frost quickly. "He oughta praise me, my poetry." Sandburg declined with another throaty guffaw, and the lunch was immediately adjourned. "Was I really bad?" Frost asked Basler later. . . .

T. S. Eliot, sitting in the third-row-center beside his wife and Frank Flint, was the object of Frost's gaze and the butt of some of his more pointed remarks. "I can understand," said Frost, "how someone of another nationality might wish to become an American. But I could never see how an American chose to become, for instance—a Canadian."

The occasion was a lecture and poetry reading by Archibald MacLeish, who had just arrived at Bread Loaf for a brief visit, and Frost, for the first time in the Conference, found himself sharing the limelight with a poet whose reputation rivaled his own. Wallace Stegner, one of the younger members of the Bread Loaf staff, has described what happened:

"Early in the proceedings [Frost] found some mimeographed notices on a nearby chair and sat rolling and folding them in his hands. Now and again he raised the roll of paper, or an eyebrow, calling the attention of his seat mates to some phrase of image. He seemed to listen with an impartial, if skeptical, judiciousness. About halfway through the reading he leaned over and said in a carrying whisper, 'Archie's poems all have the same *tune.*' As the reading went on, to the obvious pleasure of the audience, he grew restive. The fumbling and rustling of the papers in his hands became disturbing. Finally MacLeish announced 'You, Andrew Marvell,' a tour de force that makes a complete thirty-six-line poem out of a single sentence. It was a favorite. Murmurs of approval, intent receptive faces. The poet began. Then an exclamation, a flurry in the rear of the hall. The reading paused, heads turned. Robert Frost, playing around like an idle, inattentive schoolboy in a classroom, had somehow contrived to strike a match and set fire to his handful of papers and was busy beating them out and waving away the smoke."

—Lawrance Thompson and R. H. Winnick, *Robert Frost, the Later Years, 1938–43*, 1976.

On at least one occasion, Frost's enviousness was used to manipulate him. One of his famous services was to lobby for Ezra Pound's release from St. Elizabeth's, where Pound had been incarcerated after broadcasting to American troops on the Italian radio. Archibald MacLeish was the manipulator.

I asked MacLeish how he planned to persuade Frost to intervene. Oh, he said, he would just tell Robert that Ezra was getting *too much attention,* locked up down there; if we get him out, people won't notice him so much.

So Frost talked to the Attorney General on a couple of occasions, he called on some legislators, he talked with Sherman Adams, and his opinions were accepted in the newspapers as benign and fair-minded. MacLeish started the campaign, but once he was committed to help, Frost worked hard, making special trips to Washington, trying with his charm to influence the influential. Gradually Washington's attitudes toward Pound altered and the Justice Department was able to release him in 1958. Four years later, when I saw Frost next, I asked him how he had happened to work for Pound's release. He looked cunning, amused, and pleased with himself as he told me that Ezra was getting *too much attention,* being locked up down there; we got him out, now people don't notice him so much. . . .

—Hall.

Some observers have speculated that Frost required an apparently wicked motive before he could manage to do a good deed.

At other times he was just jealous.

Well in advance of the last day of 1946, Kay Morrison let Frost know that she and her husband planned to spend New Year's Eve with some Cambridge friends whom Frost did not know well. Though she invited the poet to join them, she was not surprised when he declined to do so. A few years before, when he had gone with them to a similar gathering, he had been too ill at ease to enjoy himself, so much so, in fact, that Kay had afterward suggested to Frost that henceforth he get up his own New Year's celebration, inviting friends of his own choosing.

Arriving for work at 35 Brewster Street on the afternoon of New Year's Day, 1947, it appeared to Kay that this year Frost had followed her advice. The shades were still drawn. The house was suffused with the stale reek of cigar smoke. The chairs in the living room were out of their usual position and the table in the dining room was wet with spilt whiskey. There was broken glass on the carpet and a plate held the crumbled remains of crackers and cheese.

She found Frost upstairs in his study. He greeted her cheerfully.

"I see you had a party," she said.

"Yup."

"Who was here?"

"People from Chicago," Frost said. "A couple of old friends who happened to be in town. I had them over."

"Your friends smoked a lot of cigars."

"Yup."

"And cigarettes."

Frost nodded.

"And spilled so much liquor on the table that it's spoiled the finish."

"Guess we got a little careless," Frost said.

Kay searched his eyes, and shook her head. "Robert," she said at last. "You know perfectly well there was no one here last night but you. You made all this mess just so I wouldn't know you spent New Year's Eve alone."

Frost chuckled and, after some hesitation, admitted the party had indeed been a hoax. He told how he had stood over the gas stove holding cigars and cigarettes in pincers until they were reduced to ashes, how he had filled the ashtrays, broken the glass on the floor, and poured whiskey onto the table top.

—Thompson and Winnick.

When he taught a poetry workshop at Bread Loaf, he pulled no punches.

Then he said, "Who *wrote* this poem?," his voice heavy with disgust. The young woman—I remember that she was small, attractive in a Cambridge manner, married to a Harvard graduate student—acknowledged authorship, looking deliberately stalwart. "No," said Frost, "I mean, who *really* wrote it?" There was silence, bewilderment. After a long pause, while Frost held to the sides of the podium with evident anger, and stared at the audience as if he dared anyone to speak, the woman spoke again. "I wrote it," she said, "and I don't know what you're talking about."

"*You* didn't write it," Frost said, and waved the typed page in the air. "You know who wrote it?"—his voice pronounced the name with the heaviest sarcasm he could summon, and he could summon sarcasm as well as anyone: *"T. S. Eliot!"*

—Hall.

As a young man in Derry, New Hampshire, before he went to England, he had tried chicken farming. He was never much of a farmer—he liked to say that once a man had known the pleasure of making a metaphor, it unfitted him for ordinary work—but he retained an affection for chickens. Kathleen Morrison remembered leaving him at his last farmhouse, in Vermont in the forties, then returning to find the house be-chickened.

I had earlier, at his request, ordered one hundred "unsexed-linked pullorum-free" baby chicks to be delivered to Ripton. . . . After a week or so in Cambridge . . . I arrived at the farmhouse to discover the kitchen completely taken over by brooders. A powerful smell pervaded the house, and a very happy Robert Frost sat in the living room in front of the large potbellied stove, papers all around him on the linoleum-covered floor, on all available space on the reed organ, while the backless and armless sofa was occupied by government bulletins on the care of poultry.

—*Robert Frost: A Pictorial Chronicle,* 1974.

Frost's family life was tragic: a first son died in infancy, a daughter went insane, another daughter died in childbirth, a son killed himself. A younger American poet recalled a conversation.

Robert Frost at midnight, the audience gone
to vapor, the great act laid on the shelf in mothballs,
his voice is musical and raw—he writes in the flyleaf:
For Robert from Robert, his friend in the art.
"Sometimes I feel too full of myself," I say.
And he, misunderstanding, "When I am low,
I stray away. My son wasn't your kind. The night
we told him Merrill Moore would come to treat him,
he said, 'I'll kill him first.' One of my daughters thought things,
thought every male she met was out to make her;
the way she dressed, she couldn't make a whorehouse."
And I, "Sometimes I'm so happy I can't stand myself."
And he, "When I am too full of joy, I think
how little good my health did anyone near me."

—Robert Lowell, *Histories,* 1973.

As an occasional college teacher, in residence mostly at Amherst and Dartmouth, Frost bothered little with the conventions of the classroom. He taught anxiety at Harvard.

He then issued a directive that confused a few of [his students] as much as they had been on the first day of class: "Now the modern psychiatrist would try to do something for you by saying, 'Don't worry: work.' But I'm going to treat you like normal healthy Harvard boys. I'm going to leave you with the motto: 'Don't work; worry.' " After the class had broken up, Frost was walking along the street toward the subway when one of the boys overtook him. "Mr. Frost," he said, with a troubled look, "I don't quite understand the assignment." "About worry?"

"Yes, what should I worry about? You see, I'm a senior and I need to get a B in this course if I'm to graduate so—"

"All right," said Frost. "Worry about that."

—Thompson and Winnick.

Two years before he died, Frost read a poem at President Kennedy's inauguration. In the glare of sun and snow, the old man was unable to read the doggerel poem he had written for the occasion, although Vice-President Johnson attempted to provide shade with his hat. Instead Frost said his old poem about this country's growth into nationhood, "The Gift Outright"—changing the last line from "Such as she was, such as she would become," to "Such as she was, such as she will become."

He had grown to a great age. In the dining car of a train, someone called out to him, "Congratulations on your longevity." "To hell with my longevity," he called back, "read my books."

Ill at eighty-eight, he was not ready to die, as Kathleen Morrison noted.

I tried again, telling him that if he were in the hospital, it would be much easier for Dr. Harrison to make the necessary tests. That remark sparked the explosion. Robert rose, drawing his red silk wrapper about him like a Roman senator, stood glaring at us both, and announced, "This is when I walk out of your lives—all of you." And with the steely-cold look that he could bring to his eyes, he marched upstairs. Dr. Jackson, somewhat taken aback, quickly explained that from his observation of symptoms and recognition of the pills already prescribed, he considered Robert to be in serious condition and in dire need of hospitalization. This opinion hardly came as a surprise, for I had been warned even before Robert's Russian visit that an emergency might occur at any time, caused by prostate trouble and a possible growth.

"What shall I do?" Dr. Jackson asked, adding, "I'd like to say goodbye to him before I leave." I told him that he would find Robert in the bedroom directly overhead. Dr. Jackson had hardly gone up the stairs before he was down again. Robert had refused to acknowledge his presence. "Was he lying face down or face up?" I asked. "Face down." "In that case," I said, "it will be three hours before I can get him to the hospital. I wish it had been the other way."

—Morrison.

He found a mocking symbol of resurrection in a flower.

Crises were few, but each with its own distinction. On one occasion when his daughter Lesley was visiting, I arrived triumphant with a very special lily I had found to cheer him. "Take it away! Don't mock me!" he shouted. I left the room.

—Morrison.

Sherwood Anderson 1876–1941

Winesburg, Ohio *(1919) was a shocking book, as Anderson recollected.*

Item . . . A letter from a woman, the wife of an acquaintance. Her husband was a banker. I had once sat at her table and she wrote to tell me that, having sat next to me at the table and, having read my book, she felt that she could never, while she lived, be clean again.

Item . . . There was a man friend who was spending some weeks in a New England town. He was leaving the town one morning on an early train and, as he walked to the railroad station, he passed a small park.

In the park, in the early morning, there was a little group of people, two men, he said, and three women, and they were bending over a small bonfire. He said that his curiosity was aroused and that he approached.

"There were three copies of your book," he said. The little group of New Englanders, men and women . . . he thought they must all have been past fifty . . . he spoke of the thin sharp Calvin Coolidge faces . . . "they were the town library board."

—*Sherwood Anderson's Memoirs: A Critical Edition,* ed. Ray Lewis White, 1969.

Anderson was himself shocking, as Ben Hecht told in a series of anecdotes.

Sherwood and I became friends. I learned that his nickname was Swatty, that he had run away from a schoolteacher wife and two children in Ohio, that he had owned a factory there which had burned down, bankrupting all who had invested in it, and that he had wandered for several months through cornfields and prairies, a victim of amnesia. He had arrived on foot in Chicago wearing a shaggy beard and still uncertain of his identity, but nevertheless landed a job immediately as a copy writer for Taylor-Critchfield & Co., where his inability to remember his name or where he came from stamped him as a genius in his employer's mind and resulted in his getting a bigger salary than anybody else writing copy for the firm.

I learned also that he had never been to any school, but that his wife, Cornelia (abandoned in Ohio), had taught him spelling and punctuation after their marriage. She had induced him to read a few books, over which they had quarreled violently because she liked them and he did not. He had left her because he considered reading a dangerous thing and books a corrupting power; and he had read no books since, nor was he ever going to.

Of these and a hundred other tales Sherwood told about himself, I believed almost nothing.

My first novel, *Erik Dorn,* had just come off the presses. I had received three advance paper-backed copies. I gave one immediately to Sherwood. My friend Swatty was now a literary force in the Republic. Prizes had fallen to him, and his name was almost as big as Dreiser's in the world of writing.

I had written reams of copy about the art of Sherwood Anderson, before and after his fame. I felt happy joining him for lunch, for I had heard he had read and liked my book. So had Mencken. But I was more eager to have my friend Swatty in my corner. Mencken wrote only for the *Smart Set.* Sherwood would be able to whoop it up for me in a half-dozen periodicals which had come to consider his word as artistic law.

Flushed with these visions of logrolling, I sat down opposite Sherwood in our favorite restaurant—a noisy place full of shirt-sleeved working people. Sherwood handed me back the white-and-purple-striped copy of my novel and laughed at my eagerness.

"It's all right," he said, "not bad at all. I read it with real interest."

"Thanks," I said.

"But I've got something important to tell you," Sherwood said. "It's a big idea that came to me last night about you and me. We've been friends now for seven years. That's a long time to be friends. It kind of wears off and loses its point, friendship does. My idea is that we become enemies from now on. Real enemies. You do everything you can to injure me. Attack me, denounce me, try to steal my girls, ravish my wife—anything you want. And I'll do the same to you. That way we can have a lot of fun—instead of just piddling along as a couple of fellows getting more and more bored with each other."

And Sherwood looked at me with a chuckle.

"I'll begin with your book, *Erik Dorn,*" he said.

—Ben Hecht, *A Child of the Century,* 1954.

Morley Callaghan also underwent the Anderson experience.

The night my wife and I went to dine with Anderson in the Washington Mews, where he was staying, we all sat around a long table after dinner, drinking and talking till two in the morning. We talked about many things. Hemingway's name came into the conversation. Next day I was meeting Max Perkins. As soon as he saw me he said, "I hear you had an interesting evening with Sherwood last night. I hear you made a splendid defense of Hemingway's Catholicism." Defend it! A look of indignant consternation must have come on my face. "Why, I never mentioned it. Why—" Taking my arm, Perkins said urgently, "Now just a minute. Before you go any further, please let me explain something to you. Don't let this spoil Sherwood for you. It's happened with others. You must understand Sherwood wasn't really lying. . . ."

—Morley Callaghan, *That Summer in Paris,* 1963.

Jack London 1876–1916

After years of waterfront life, as a sailor at sea and a would-be gold miner in Alaska, Jack London became one of the most prolific of our writers. A newspaper reporter observed the production line. Manyoungi was London's Korean houseboy, Charmian his second wife—

Here is a complete day with Jack: Up betimes. Breakfast, with Manyoungi serving. About eleven o'clock Jack calls. I go up one flight of stairs. He is still in bed; large pillows at his back; pages of manuscript on a quilt in front of him. He has just finished a story. There is a puddle of cigarette butts in a saucer on the table near his bed. Also a reading lamp with a green shade and a decanter surrounded by glasses. The bed is one of those black walnut four-posters affected by captains of windjammers. While we are drinking a Scotch, Charmian comes in and says, "Good morning." She's a crisp echo of one of those efficient young ladies you see in the Metropolitan Life Insurance Company when you go in to talk about an annuity. She picks up the manuscript pages from the quilt and steps out just as quietly and as quickly as the best-trained girl high up in the tower at Twenty-third Street and Madison Avenue. I drink a second drink. So does Jack. Manyoungi comes in with two cups of coffee. Manyoungi is an obsequious mind reader. Before you know it he has everything you want at your elbow. He drops two lumps in my coffee. "Why the syrup?" Jack asks. Manyoungi is stingy with the sugar for the master's cup and stands anxiously by while he samples it. "Right as rain," the master says. There is no change in the look in Manyoungi's eyes. He gathers up the pages of notes that are scattered on the floor where Jack has tossed them. These consist of pencil scribblings torn from notebooks, pages ripped from magazines, columns from newspapers.

Between sips of the coffee Jack asks his bodyservant for a certain portfolio. The boy brings it, opens it, and places the bundle of new notes on the quilt in front of the master. Then he brings some old-fashioned clothes pins which he places on the table. When he has these arranged so the master will not waste any motion in reaching for them, he picks up the discarded pages of notes and goes into the next room. When he opens the door, I hear the steady click of a typewriter touched by expert fingers. "That would be Charmian typing off the morning's work," I say. Jack nods. He is busy with his new notes. There are pages from a book in the litter. Having arranged them to his satisfaction, he reaches up and, with the old-fashioned wooden clothes pins, fastens them in little bundles to a double clothes line strung across the bed. The clothes line operates on two brass pulleys fastened in diagonal corners of the room and are as silent and efficient as everything else in the house. The notes dangle a few inches from Jack's nose when he leans back against the pillows.

Charmian comes in again. Altogether it is hardly ten minutes since she picked up the last page of Jack's longhand script from the bed. She is back with the whole thing finished. She has an original and one carbon copy. These she places on the bed near Jack's hand.

"If we do as well tomorrow with this story as we did today, we'll have something great," she says with quiet enthusiasm. You feel the enthusiasm.

"What do you mean by that we?" Jack snaps. The enthusiasm evaporates.

"Well, I just mean . . ."

"Don't mean it. Get busy with these."

He gives her a sheaf of notes scribbled with a pencil. She leaves to copy them off. For a moment her eyes differ but slightly from Manyoungi's. There is a beaten look in them.

While we are having a drink downstairs, she comes in. She is cheerful, almost spontaneous.

"A thousand and twenty-one words today, Mate," she says.

"Good."

Barely eleven o'clock and Jack has finished a thousand and twenty-one words. It is bookkeeping in Paradise. A thousand and twenty-one words!

—Joseph Noel, *Footloose in Arcadia,* 1940.

The same observer noted a conflation of creators.

As I appraised the humble eyes and slightly bowed head of the Korean boy when he approached his master, a thought flashed through my mind that a few million Manyoungis in our country would create a despotism in a generation. Toward the end of his tenure the boy fell into the habit of calling London "Mr. God." Jack liked it.

—Noel.

The young Sinclair Lewis supplied London with plots for magazine stories. Visiting London at his establishment in Carmel, California, Lewis recalled "the literary high point" of his visit.

At a neighboring cabin Jack picked up James's *The Wings of the Dove* and, standing there, short, burly, in soft shirt and black tie, the Master read aloud in a bewildered way while Henry James's sliding, slithering, gliding verbiage unwound itself on and on. Jack banged the book down and wailed, "Do any of you know what all this junk is about?"

—Richard O'Connor, *Jack London: A Biography,* 1964.

Upton Sinclair 1878–1968

Precocious and prolific, Sinclair began his literary career at fifteen, writing dime novels. A biographer wrote of his output in his twentieth year.

. . . he turned out eight thousand words every day including Sunday. To do this required two stenographers working full time, taking dictation for some three hours one afternoon and then transcribing it for the next day and a half. In the evening Upton revised manuscript and afterward, during a long walk, invented adventures for the next day's dictation. Every morning he taught himself to play the violin or attended classes at Columbia.

It is not possible to know precisely how much and what he wrote in this period. Years later he was himself unable to identify whether many of the works written under his various pseudonyms were in fact his, but during the eighteen-month period from June 1897 to November 1898—most of it coinciding with his full-time graduate study at Columbia University—Sinclair turned out magazine material totalling approximately 1,275,000 words. . . .

—Leon Harris, *Upton Sinclair: American Rebel,* 1975.

As he grew older, his fiction concerned itself with social issues. He intended The Jungle *(1906) as socialist ideology—but for most readers it remained the exposé of an industry and a source of nausea.*

At the utopian community of Arden in Edgemoor, Delaware, founded to support Henry George's single-tax, Sinclair was first among equals.

Upton was not universally popular at Arden, his vanity about his career and his assumption of moral leadership causing both some amusement and some resentment. The children of the community were much given to mimicking the high voice in which he slowly dictated to his secretary in his open writing tent and his at least daily questions, "Any reporters to see me? Anybody looking for me?"

Scott Nearing sixty years later remembered too the little children beating their chests ostentatiously and shouting, "Sinclair! Sinclair!" And later, when he visited Upton in Pasadena, the old muckraker whom he hadn't seen for years met him at the door with no greeting, but instead with the question, "Have you seen the bust?" Without another word he led the confused Nearing to his office where placed opposite his desk so he could see it was a just finished bust of himself.

—Harris.

Sinclair was almost elected governor of California in 1926. He had a way of staying in the public eye.

He failed to convince the authorities to let him take the place of the book clerk, John Gritz, who for selling a copy of *Oil!* was found guilty and fined one hundred dollars. Sinclair also failed in his attempt to get himself arrested for selling a copy of his banned book to a policeman. When he revealed that the copy of *Oil!* he had sold to the officer was in fact a copy of the Bible inside a cover of his book in order to draw attention to the fact that on a number of his offending pages he was quoting from the Songs of Solomon, the charges against him were dropped.

—Harris.

Carl Sandburg 1878–1967

People who knew both Frost and Sandburg have argued late into the night: which poet was the more difficult? Bruce Weireck recalled Sandburg's performance at Cornell College, in Mt. Vernon, Iowa. Most of it took place before the poetry reading.

"He refused, though he had already consented to the arrangement, to dine with the large group of ladies who were sponsoring him, and who had charged the guests a nice sum for the privilege. We hastily arranged, at his suggestion, a table for six at the Faculty Club. Then he relented, and consented just to appear at the banquet and greet the ladies. Once there, he liked them and told them all with dubious diplomacy that but for our 'dragging him off to the club,' he would have been charmed to dine with them. A remark, needless to say, that put those of us who were trying to look after him right behind the eight ball. . . . This was bad enough, but more was to follow. We were late getting to the club and Carl was sulky. Didn't like the excellent dinner that was ready, insisting on only a large bowl of breakfast food. Conversation was desultory, and he snubbed Garreta Busey when she ventured some literary query as to the relative difficulty of writing prose and poetry. At seven-fifteen, with the lecture forty-five minutes away, he went upstairs for a nap with instructions to wake him in half an hour. I did so, finding him cozy in long red underwear. About eight, he discovered that he had none of his books to read from. He doesn't remember his own poems as he does the ballads. I made a dash home for my copies, and at eight-thirty he began the eight-o'clock reading and song fest and quite charmed everybody."

—North Callahan, *Carl Sandburg, Lincoln of Our Literature,* 1970.

He liked goats, and being photographed.

Bernard Hoffman, who was a photographer for *Life Magazine* for some years, called on Sandburg at his Michigan home in order to do a story. The weather was so cold that even the goats were virtually freezing outside, recalls Hoffman. Whereupon, Sandburg called them into the house and about fifteen of the shivering animals crowded into one of the rooms. Sandburg did not stop with this hospitality. He took up his guitar and played for the visiting goats. "They listened politely," said Hoffman.

—Callahan.

For many years Sandburg worked the bulk of his time on his popular biography of Abraham Lincoln.

He lived on the shore of Lake Michigan, and every morning he would put his mind in rhythm and discipline for the day's work. He walked on the sand at the edge of the lake, head down, mop-hair flying. His hand gestured privately and his lips moved, trying on the words for size and stability. The time never varied;

it was the hour after sunrise, whether the sun rose or not. People who lived on the bluff behind the beach would see Carl far below, shambling along the water's edge, and they said you could set your watch by him. No one ever did, but you could. Those same people on the bluff knew all about Carl and how he was writing *The War Years.* The two volumes of *The Prairie Years* were already published and nearly everyone had read it, and besides, Carl was not a secret man; if you asked what he was working on, he would tell you.

Once the great joke was hatched, it had to be carried out. Quite a few people living nearby were involved in the arrangements and a good many more wanted to see it work out. The plan was simple, clean, and inexpensive. A committee went into Chicago and hired a long, lean actor for a one-day stand. They bought a beard for him and costumed him in a frock coat, a stovepipe hat, and a shawl.

Then one morning, the jokers and their friends gathered at the top of a bluff to see it work. You could set your watch by Carl, and from the top of the bluff, you could see him a long way off, loose-jointed, shambling, keeping to the water's edge where the footing was firm.

When Carl was about a quarter of a mile away, the tall, top-hatted actor was signaled to walk toward him. He had been instructed to meet Carl just below the place where the gallery had settled to watch. The tall, black figure was made enormous by the two feet of hat on top of him. The beard was a masterpiece and the shawl flapped in the wind.

Carl, as always, wore his disreputable hat which framed rather than covered his light-colored hair. As usual, his head was down, studying on the unmarked wetness of the beach the cadences of the words which he would write that day. The figures drew slowly together and then the jokers saw them pass. Carl looked up for a moment and then his head was down again as he moved on, studying the sand.

The majestic, tall dark actor, on the other hand, looked over his shoulder, and then he broke and ran up the steep path to the bluff. He was winded and his beard had slipped by the time he made it. The gallery of onlookers quickly surrounded him.

"What did he do?"

"Nothing. He just looked at me for a moment."

"Didn't he do anything?"

"Yes, he bowed."

"Well—didn't he say anything?"

The actor was still getting his breath and his eyes were a little crazy.

"He said . . . and that's all he said."

"Said what?"

"It was just after he bowed. He said, 'Good morning, Mr. President.' "

—Callahan.

Vachel Lindsay 1879–1931

Lindsay told about being a student at the Chicago Art Institute when Vice-President Theodore Roosevelt came visiting.

". . . So I walked up to the man, and since he looked like his picture, I said, 'Isn't this the Vice President?'

"He said, 'I am,' and we shook hands with mutual pleasure. Then we had a flow of mutual soulful smiles for several seconds. He wanted to know my line. I told him I was just a student learning to draw. I said, 'You don't want somebody to walk around here with you or anything like that, do you?' I was keeping step with him. We walked abreast in sooth.

"But the V.P. answered with his blandest tone that he preferred to enjoy the works in solitude."

—Dale Kramer, *Chicago Renaissance,* 1966.

Lindsay was a prodigious speaker of his own poems, and knew them all by heart. (He claimed that his voice never tired because his ancestors had called hogs for generations.) Another poet envied him.

Once when he and I both were reading in Madison, Wisconsin, he offered, during a period of several days, to perform gratis in any schools roundabout which wanted him. I asked him about his strength to carry such giving. He answered with a swaying shrug of his shoulders and a characteristic wave of his hand, as though to say, "Ask a river about its strength."

—Witter Bynner, *Prose Pieces,* 1979.

Alfred Kreymborg, who calls himself "Krimmie" in his autobiography, witnessed a performance before a women's club in Los Angeles.

Vachel began harmlessly enough with a group of his dulcet moon poems delivered *pianissimo.* Some of the ladies looked relieved; the rest seemed disappointed. Presently the poet announced The Santa Fé Trail as his next number, and Krimmie leaned forward. Vachel carried his innocent *pianissimo* up to the point in which the first brazen motor-car, racing along from the East, makes its appearance on the old Indian trail. Then he dropped his piccolos and flutes, sounded the deeper instruments in his lungs and the quick beat in his hands and feet and chanted and stamped with abandonment. Suddenly, more autos raced past on their roaring way westward, and Vachel bellowed names like an announcer in a Union Depot—

> "Cars from Concord, Niagara, Boston,
> Cars from Topeka, Emporia, and Austin—"

and marching up and down like a negro preacher in a cakewalk trance, shouted exultantly—

> "While I sit by the milestone
> And watch the sky,
> The United States
> Goes by."

Then followed the "snapping explosiveness" of the auto-horns—

> "Here comes the *dice*-horn, here comes the *vice*-horn,
> Here comes the *snarl*-horn, *brawl*-horn, *lewd*-horn,"

only to be interrupted by the song of the Rachel-Jane, the *pianissimo* refrain—

> "Not defeated by the horns
> Sings amid a hedge of thorns:—
> Love and life,
> Eternal youth—
> Sweet, sweet, sweet, sweet."

The women had turned to a congregation swaying to the beat of the chant and the step on the stage, and no matter how syncopated the rhythm or how sudden the changes in pitch, mimicked the poet rapturously. The close, with its whispered cadence, was greeted with an awe-struck silence and then an explosive pandemonium. Knitting, gossiping and kindred concerns had been forgotten, and Krimmie got up and, tempted to jump on the chair, applauded the audience as well as the miracle-man. . . .

—*Troubadour: An Autobiography*, 1925.

Wallace Stevens 1879–1955

When he was almost forty, after Harvard, after a job as a reporter in New York, after law school and practice, Stevens took a job in the legal department of an insurance company in Hartford, Connecticut. ("Money is a kind of poetry," he said in one of his aphorisms.) He was a private man, as his daughter remembered him.

She talks about coming upon her father in a dark part of the house sitting in a chair in silence, a habit which mystified and frightened her. On this occasion, she watched him for some time, and finally approached his chair, cautiously touched his knee, and asked what he was doing. "Thinking," he answered gruffly.

—Michael Ryan, *Poetry*, Sept. 1979.

Brendan Gill grew up a generation younger in the same Hartford and remembered the poet walking to work.

It was the custom in Hartford in those days for people driving to work to offer rides to people walking to work; the offer was made almost as readily to strangers as to friends. My father, for example, often set out on foot for his office, several miles distant from his house, knowing that someone was sure to stop and give him a lift; in his case, being a prominent figure in the community, he was likely to be greeted by name. Stevens, though not a prominent figure in the community, certainly gave the impression of being one; he was a tall, good-looking, well-tailored man, with white hair neatly parted and powerful shoulders. Morning and evening, he walked the mile or so between his house and his office and even in rain or snow would never accept a ride; people learned to leave the forbidding pedestrian alone. His solitary walking had a purpose: he composed as he walked. *Ursa faber* poised on a curb waiting for a light to change was trying out on his inward ear sweet sounds—"the emperor of ice cream," perhaps, or "the auroras of autumn." Rocking slightly from side to side as he lumbered forward, Stevens was as obviously engaged in putting one foot of verse in front of the other as he was in putting one physical foot in front of the other. Once, my sister, glancing out of a window, saw Stevens going by her house. As she watched, he slowed down, came to a stop, rocked in place for a moment or two, took a step backward, hesitated, then strode confidently forward—left, right, left, right—on his way to work. It was obvious to her that Stevens had gone back over a phrase, dropped an unsatisfactory word, inserted a superior one, and proceeded to the next line of the poem he was making.

—*Here at the New Yorker*, 1975.

Like many Connecticut executives, Stevens liked to go south in the winter; images of Florida color his poetry. Gill told a Florida story.

In my memory is an episode the leading figures of which are Frost and Stevens. I was told it by Stevens and I often play it over in my mind, like a short home movie, for the pleasure it gives me. The time is late at night and the place is Florida. Frost and Stevens, who are staying at the same resort hotel, have been out drinking at a bar somewhere along the beach. Tipsily, in perfect contentment, they are making their way back to the hotel on a boardwalk that runs a foot or so above the sand. They are holding fast to each other, and each is sure that it is he who is supporting his companion. Frost staggers, catches his heel on the edge of the boardwalk, and starts to fall. Stevens strengthens his hold on him, but in vain—over Frost goes, with Stevens on top of him. The two bulky old poets fall in a single knot onto the sand and start rolling over and over in the moonlight down the long slope of the beach to the edge of the sea.

—Gill.

Frost told another.

At Key West Stevens had come to call with an associate lawyer from the South, both men well along in their cups. "Frosh never fayshed life," said Stevens to the Southerner. "Tell him the story about the woman with the wooden leg in the sleeping car." The story was told, and then later told again after the two drinkers had forgotten their telling, but neither time could Frost get the point. . . .

—Robert Francis, *A Time To Talk: Conversations and Indiscretions,* 1972.

Louise Bogan told yet another, in a letter to Morton D. Zabel.

. . . I will tell you a funny story, as a New Year's present. —It seems that Wallace Stevens invaded the little private literary colony inhabited by Hemingway and Dos Passos, and wives, in Key West. He was very drunk (I am telling this to you from Dos Passos' version of it, told to Edmund [Wilson]), and he barged in on Hemingway and began to lay him out. "You're a cad," he said to H., "and all your heroes are cads and you are all your heroes, so you must be a cad!" H. took this very meekly, they say, replying, "Come now, Stevens, I'm really not so bad as all that, am I?" "Yes," said Stevens, and stormed out. He then turned his steps toward the home of Dos Passos, and he found the Dos Passos ménage listening to the phonograph and having a cocktail before dinner. "So you're Dos Passos," said S., "and here I find you, playing cheap things on the phonograph and surrounded by women in pajamas. I thought you were a cripple and a man of culture! Women in pajamas!" and he stormed out of there. Now, Dos Passos' comment on all this is, that Stevens is a disappointed man, who doesn't dare to live the life of an artist, preferring the existence of an insurance broker, so that he tends to idealize men of letters, very probably, under the influence of liquor. —But as I see it, Stevens was quite right: the sight of the Dos Passos ménage, being O so liberated and free and emancipated and pajamaish was enough to give anyone a turn.

—*What The Woman Lived: Selected Letters of Louise Bogan, 1920–1970,* ed. Ruth Limmer, 1973.

Seldom did he approach literary folk under other circumstances. During a rare poetry reading, he is reported to have dropped the aside: "If the boys in the office could see me now. . . ."

Once Allen Tate, the distinguished poet and man of letters, was at a gathering with Stevens, and he asked if he might drop by for a brief chat when he next came to Hartford. Stevens answered, "No."

—Suzi Mee, "The Double Life of Wallace Stevens," *Harvard Magazine,* Sept.–Oct. 1979.

Carl Van Vechten 1880–1964

Djuna Barnes, author of Nightwood, *told Edmund Wilson this story about Carl Van Vechten—critic, novelist, friend of Gertrude Stein.*

He had gone into a bookstore in some provincial city and put on a name-spending act: "I read this book of Cabell's in manuscript"; "Conrad told me that he was not really satisfied with this novel," etc. At last, the bedazzled bookseller said: "May I ask who you are, sir?"

"Oh, I," said Van Vechten in a camping manner, "am Edna St. Vincent Millay!"

—Edmund Wilson, *The Twenties,* 1975.

H. L. Mencken 1880–1956

The editor of the American Mercury, *champion of Theodore Dreiser and Sinclair Lewis, Mencken did not welcome every new writer. When Thomas Wolfe's agent*

next sent a batch of Wolfe's short stories to the magazine's New York Office, the Sage took one look at the dirty, dogeared, greasy manuscripts, partially written on butcher's paper, turned to Angoff, and howled, "Take them out! They're not even sanitary."

—Sara Mayfield, *The Constant Circle,* 1968.

He and Dreiser corresponded with ponderous whimsy.

"The other day a dog peed on me," Mencken wrote. "A bad sign." Possibly Dreiser recognized this as a subtle reference to his own weakness for omens. He recalled Mencken's custom, after a beerfest, of taking friends to Poe's grave and urinating on it as a mark of respect. "A spirit message informs me," he replied, "that the dog who so offended you now houses the migrated soul of Edgar Allen Poe, who thus retaliates."

—W. A. Swanberg, *Dreiser,* 1965.

Mencken made an unusual contract with a Canadian film producer.

In exchange for the rights to Mencken's *A Neglected Anniversary,* a deadpan hoax on the origin of the bathtub, written for the New York *Evening Mail* some thirty years before, the Canadian producer agreed to furnish Mencken *with two cases of Labatt's ale a month for the rest of his life.*

—Mayfield.

A stroke in 1948 disabled much of his mind. Although he worked hard in therapy, he was unable to read or write.

August brought in foaming steins of the Canadian ale still sent to Mencken in return for the rights to the story of the bathtub hoax. With a long Havana cigar in one hand and a tall drink in the other, the Maestro's spirits began to revive and his wit flashed as of old. Then the visitor asked about Edgar Lee Masters: "I believe he died in 1948, didn't he?"

"Yeah." Mencken's grin faded. "I believe he died the same year I did."

—Mayfield.

Witter Bynner 1881–1968

With his friend Arthur Davison Ficke, Bynner perpetrated one of the more successful hoaxes in the history of American poetry. It was 1914, and the friends were stimulated by the recent rage for poetic movements—Ezra Pound's "Imagism" in particular.

The method of composition was simple. Sometimes we would start with an idea, sometimes with only a phrase, but the procedure was to let all reins go, to give the idea or the phrase complete head, to take whatever road or field or fence it chose. In other words it was a sort of runaway poetry, the poet seated in the wagon but the reins flung aside. Some of the results seemed so good to us that Ficke and I signed, sealed, and filed a solemn document swearing that the whole performance had been done as a joke.

—*Prose Pieces,* 1979.

When the two poets published their hoax as a book called Spectra, *Bynner himself reviewed it in the* New Republic.

There is a new school of poets, a new term to reckon with, a new theory to comprehend, a new manner to notice, a new humor to enjoy. It is the Spectric School; composed, as far as the present publication goes, of a man, the cornerstone, and a woman, the keystone—Emanuel Morgan and Anne Knish. In the preface to the volume just issued under the title *Spectra,* Anne Knish refers to "our group"; so that I suppose we shall soon be hearing the names of other members of the spectric edifice. Meantime we must be content with the rhymes of a "founder" and the free verse of an "interpreter."

—Bynner.

He included as a sample Emanuel Morgan's "Opus 104."

How terrible to entertain a lunatic!
To keep his earnestness from coming close!

A Madagascar land-crab once
Lifted blue claws at me
And rattled long black eyes
That would have got me
Had I not been gay.

—Bynner.

The results were gratifying.

With few exceptions, critics and reviewers took the book seriously, many more of them praising than damning it. Poetry followers all over the country responded to it with zeal. Magazine editors accepted Spectric poems. Ardent enthusiasts bought many copies for voluntary distribution, and the Spectric School had become an established institution alongside the schools it secretly parodied.

—Bynner.

A well-known poet and editor sat Bynner down.

Alfred Kreymborg told me one day at lunch in New York that he had persuaded the Spectrists to compile an issue of his magazine *Others*. Illuminating my vague knowledge of the group, he told me of friends of his who knew both of the founders, and assured me with a real gleam in his eye that Anne Knish was a great beauty.

—Bynner.

Many years later, Bynner could wonder if the hoaxers were the hoaxed.

Many a discerning critic of poetry is convinced to this day that, liberated by our pseudonyms and by complete freedom of manner, Ficke and I wrote better as Knish and Morgan than we have written in our persons. Once in a while we think so ourselves.

—Bynner.

Ludwig Lewisohn 1882–1955

Morley Callaghan met Lewisohn in Paris and a third person sat in on a conversation.

Ludwig Lewisohn came over to me. It was time we knew each other, he said. We should have a talk. A great idea, I agreed. I would be sitting at the Coupole at two the following afternoon. And indeed, I was there.

Before Lewisohn's arrival, the young American named Whidney, from Chicago, who lived with his wife in an opulent apartment a few blocks away from the café, came and sat down beside me. "Do you mind if I sit in on this?" he asked. "I heard you and Lewisohn talking last night. I've read his book *Upstream*. I'd like to listen in on your conversation, if you don't mind. I promise I'll just sit here and listen."

Then Lewisohn came slowly along the street, looking very dignified, very professional, his hat severely straight on his head. When I waved to him, he came and sat down with us. The conversation went like this: "Well, now, how is your book doing, Mr. Callaghan?"

"All right, I think," I said.

"How long has it been out?"

"Just a few months."

"Don't they let you know how it's doing?"

"It's had a good reception. But it's a book of stories, you know. With some luck, I think it'll reach five thousand."

"Five thousand," he said, looking distressed. "With all the publicity you've had? Five thousand?"

"It's a book of stories. How's your novel doing?"

"Why, it's already done thirty thousand."

"Splendid," I said, feeling like a nobody.

"But I expect to do much better than thirty thousand," he said importantly. We began an earnest discussion about sales promotion, and kept it up till my friend Whidney suddenly cut in. "Excuse me. Will you excuse me?" he asked firmly. "I have something to say."

"Go ahead."

"I was present when you two met last night. Well, I was a businessman, myself. I wanted to be here when you great artists talked. I thought it would be intellectually stimulating. You know what you sound like? A couple of businessmen."

Giving Whidney one long appraising glance, Mr. Lewisohn then finished his drink.

—Morley Callaghan, *That Summer in Paris,* 1963.

William Carlos Williams 1883–1963

When Williams was a young man studying at the University of Pennsylvania Medical School, he showed a poem to a professor of English.

The professor put it down, thought a while, and delivered an opinion: "I can see that you have a sensitive appreciation of the work of John Keats' line and form. You have done some creditable imitations of his work. Not bad. Perhaps in twenty years, yes, in perhaps twenty years you may succeed in attracting some attention to yourself. Perhaps! Meanwhile, go on with your medical studies."

Then, as professors are likely to do, he opened a desk drawer and showed the young man some pages of his own. "I, too, write poems. And when I have written them I place them here—and—then I close the drawer."

—Louis Simpson, *Three on the Tower,* 1975.

Williams wrote and published many books over a long life, but never departed from his medical practice. Jean Starr Untermeyer asked him a favor.

I wrote to Dr. William Carlos Williams, then traveling in the West, and asked (with apologies) if he would consent to read for us for fifty dollars, which was all we could promise him at that time. . . . His answer to my inquiry was so characteristic that I must record it here: "Hell, yes," ran his short note. "I used to deliver babies for half that sum."

—*Private Collection,* 1965.

On a trip to Paris he met expatriate writers.

Went to Hemingways' at 10:30 to see the baby. Found him to be two pounds underweight, otherwise well. Retracted his foreskin. He naturally cried, to his parents' chagrin.

—*The Autobiography of William Carlos Williams,* 1951.

Apparently there was time for other matters besides poetry and obstetrics. He met the baroness Elsa von Freytag Loringhoven, a handsome and eccentric woman who advised him that what he "needed to make [him] great was to contract syphilis from her. . . ."

Wallace Stevens at one time was afraid to come below Fourteenth Street when he was in the city because of her. And there was a Russian painter who on turning in one night in his small room had her crawl out naked from under his bed. He ran, ducked in at a neighbor's across the hall. She refused to leave the premises until he agreed to follow her to her own apartment.

—Williams.

She followed Williams out to his home in Rutherford, New Jersey.

Bob McAlmon was here at supper one night when I received a call to see a sick baby at Union Avenue. I took my bag and went out to my car which was standing at the curb. But as I went to get into it a hand grabbed my left wrist. It was she.

"You must come with me," she said in her strong German accent. I was taken aback, as may easily be imagined, and nonplussed besides, because—well, she was a woman.

It ended as she hauled off and hit me alongside the neck with all her strength. She had had some little squirt of a male accomplice call me from supper for this. I just stood there thinking. But at that moment a cop happened to walk by.

"What's the matter, Doc, this woman annoying you?"

"No," I said, and she lit out down the street. "Let her go."

I bought a small punching bag after that to take it out on in the cellar, and the next time she attacked me, about six o'clock one evening on Park Avenue a few months later, I flattened her with a stiff punch to the mouth. I thought she was going to stick a knife in me. I had her arrested, she shouting, "What are you in this town? Napoleon?"

—Williams.

Brendan Gill accompanied Williams on his housecalls when Williams was no longer a young man.

Williams and I would pull up in his car in front of some not very savory-looking bungalow, and Williams would slap my knee and say, "Wait till you get a look at this one!" We would ring the bell, and the door would be opened by some slatternly woman in her late twenties or early thirties, wearing a soiled rayon dressing gown and with her dyed hair done up in a dozen or so pink plastic curlers. She would have an infant in her arms, purple-faced from screaming and with diapers unpleasantly tapestried, and the odds were that however sick the infant was, the mother was suffering from something equally unpleasant—at the very least, so I seem to remember, a severe case of post-nasal drip. Williams wouldn't be daunted. He would examine the baby, write out a prescription, and then spend five or ten minutes in happy banter with the dull, distracted, and wholly undesirable mother. Back in the car, he would be breathing hard and radiant. "What a girl!"

One day his wife, Floss, to whom Williams was devoted, asked him with understandable impatience, "Bill, tell me the truth.

Do you want to make love with every single woman you meet?"

Williams took the question seriously, and after a minute or two of grave thought he replied, "Yes. I do."

—*Here at the New Yorker,* 1975.

Maxwell Perkins 1884–1947

Perkins was the great Scribner's editor whose authors included Fitzgerald, Hemingway, and Wolfe. He suffered from the quotidian inconsistency of the writing profession.

"Hold up galley forty for big change," cabled Scott Fitzgerald from somewhere in Europe while *The Great Gatsby* was in hand. "The correction," he wrote in his following letter, "—and God! it's important— . . . is enclosed herewith." But as a postscript to this same letter he added with characteristic inco-ordination of the constants of time, space and type-metal, "I hope you're setting publication date at earliest possible moment."

—Roger Burlingame, *Of Making Many Books,* 1946.

Perkins was given, understandably, to moments of eccentricity.

Once, when an author stood in Perkin's office pouring out his unhappiness, Perkins went to the window as if overcome by the burden of his sympathy. After a while, however, he said, without turning:

"You know I can't understand why all these busy people move so slowly. The only ones who move fast are the boys on roller skates who have nothing to do. Why don't we—why doesn't everybody—wear skates?"

—Burlingame.

The best-known Perkins story has many variants. Edmund Wilson wrote this version in a letter to Burton Rascoe in 1929. (It was some decades before other anecdotalists could commit the proper words to print.) The novel was A Farewell to Arms.

It seems that Hemingway's novel, in its serial form, had to be expurgated for the readers of *Scribner's Magazine.* And when Maxwell Perkins came to go through the manuscript, he found three words which he was doubtful about printing even in the book.

The words were *balls, shit,* and *cocksucker.* So he had a solemn conference on the subject with old Mr. Charles Scribner. The first two words were discussed, and it was decided to suppress them, but when Perkins came to the third—which he thought Mr. Scribner had probably never heard—he couldn't get it out, and wrote it down on a piece of paper. Old Mr. Scribner put on his pince-nez and considered it with serious attention—then said, "Perkins, do you think that Hemingway would respect you, if he knew that you were unable to say that word, but had to write it out?" Perkins was so flustered by the incident that he forgot and left the memorandum pad with *cocksucker* on it on a bracket in his office, where it was just on the level of the eyes of anybody who came in. He didn't discover it until just before he left in the afternoon—by which time it had thrown the whole Scribner's office into a state of acute embarrassment, deep mental and moral distress, and troubling mystification.

—Edmund Wilson, *Letters on Literature and Politics,* 1977.

In another telling, the words were "shit, piss, fuck," and Perkins had noted them on his calendar under the legend, "Things To Do Today."

Erskine Caldwell was another of Perkins's discoveries. He wrote his recollections of an early dialogue.

PERKINS: By the way, I've read all your stories on hand now, including the new ones you brought yesterday, and I don't think I need to see any more for a while.

CALDWELL: (Silence)

PERKINS: I think I wrote you some time ago that we want to publish one of your stories in *Scribner's Magazine.*

CALDWELL: I received the letter. You haven't changed your mind, have you? I mean about taking a story?

PERKINS: Changed my mind? No, Not at all. The fact is, we're all in agreement here at the office about things. I guess so much so that we've decided now to take two stories, instead of one, and run them both in the magazines at the same time. We'd like to schedule them for the June issue. One of them is called "The Mating of Marjorie" and the other one is "A Very Late Spring." They're both good northern New England stories. There's a good feeling about them. It's something I like to find in fiction. So many writers master form and technique, but get so little feeling into their work. I think that's important.

CALDWELL: I'm sure glad you like them—both of them.

PERKINS: Now about these two stories. As I said, we want to buy them both. How much do you want for the two together? We always have to talk about money sooner or later. There's no way of getting around that, is there?

CALDWELL: Well, I don't know exactly. I mean about the money. I haven't thought much about it.

PERKINS: Would two-fifty be all right? For both of them. . . .

CALDWELL: Two-fifty? I don't know. I thought maybe I'd receive a little more than that.

PERKINS: You did? Well, what would you say to three-fifty then. That's about as much as we can pay, for both of them. In these times magazine circulation is not climbing the way it was, and we have to watch our costs. I don't think times will get any better soon, and maybe worse yet. Economic life isn't very healthy now. That's why we have to figure our costs so closely at a time like this.

CALDWELL: I guess that'll be all right. I'd thought I'd get a little more than three dollars and a half, though, for both of them.

—A. Scott Berg, *Max Perkins, Editor of Genius,* 1978.

Ring Lardner 1885–1933

Ring Lardner was known to drink. An acquaintance recorded a story that Lardner told after he had been drinking for some time.

"Once there were two foxes in the bathtub together, Pat and Mike. They took turns sponging each other off. Finally, one said to the other, 'Here,' he said, 'here, you've been sponging off me long enough!'—so he kicked out the stopper. And, what do you think? the next morning they woke up in the same street."

—Edmund Wilson, *The Twenties,* 1975.

Lardner frequented the Friar's Club in New York City.

Ring went there one night after the theater and sat drinking and listening to various people play the piano. With the excuse that he did not want to go home in evening clothes he stayed through the next day, sometimes talking to whoever came along, but mostly sitting alone in a melancholy mood. The second day passed the same way. At the end of the third day someone approached him and said, "Have you heard the one about the—" Ring got up abruptly and left. A few minutes later an actor came in and said, "My God, the statue's gone!"

—Donald Elder, *Ring Lardner: A Biography,* 1956.

And the Lambs Club.

Ring was sitting with Paul Lannin, a composer and musical director, in the Lambs club one evening when a Shakespearean actor with a head of wild, unruly hair passed by to the bar. When he came by a second time, Ring stopped him and asked, "How do you look when I'm sober?"

One time Ring and Arthur Jacks made a trip to South Bend to visit Ring's sister, who was ill in the hospital there. At their hotel they had a stock of liquor which included some good Canadian whiskey and some raw Midwestern corn moonshine of very recent date. After a heavy night Jacks awoke first, in need of a drink. He tried some of the Canadian whiskey, but it promptly came up. Undaunted, he tried again, with the same result. After he had made three or four unsuccessful attempts, Ring opened one eye and said:

"Arthur, if you're just practicing, would you mind using the corn?"

—Elder.

Sinclair Lewis 1885–1951

In 1920, the young novelist would publish Main Street. *Shortly before publication, he met a writer whose work had helped to model his. George Jean Nathan wrote about the time he and H. L. Mencken first met Lewis.*

". . . strangling us and putting resistance out of the question, and yelling at the top of his lungs, [he] began: 'So you guys are critics, are you? Well, let me tell you something. I'm the best writer in this here gottdamn country and if you, Georgie, and you, Hank, don't know it now, you'll know it gottdamn soon. Say, I've just finished a book that'll be published in a week or two and it's the gottdamn best book of its kind that this here gottdamn country has had and don't you guys forget it! . . .'

"Projected from Smith's flat by the self-endorsing uproar—it kept up for fully half an hour longer—Mencken and I jumped into a taxicab, directed the driver to speed us posthaste to a tavern where we might in some peace recover our equilibrium and our ear-drums, and looked at each other. 'Of all the idiots I've ever laid eyes on, that fellow is the worst!' groaned Mencken, gasping for breath. . . .

"Three days later I got the following letter from Mencken, who had returned to Baltimore:

"Dear George: Grab hold of the bar-rail, steady yourself, and prepare yourself for a terrible shock! I've just read the advance sheets of the book of that Lump we met at Schmidt's and, by God, he has done the job! It's a genuinely excellent piece of work. Get it as soon as you can and take a look. I begin to believe that perhaps there isn't a God after all."

—Sara Mayfield, *The Constant Circle,* 1968.

Even as writers go, Lewis was competitive. Burton Rascoe told of an encounter with Sherwood Anderson.

"That evening we called upon Sherwood to tell his famous Mama Geighen story—his best unpublished story and his most hilarious story, published or unpublished. He was in top form about this fantastic binge he went on with George Wharton and about their encounter with the massive and marvelous woman who ran a saloon on the side of the road in Wisconsin, far from town or village. He sent us into gales of laughter, and he smiled modestly in satisfaction that his performance had been good. Lewis left the room. He came back after a minute or so. He had turned his collar and his vest hindpart before, parted his hair severely, powdered his face white. He held his hands before him, tips of fingers to tips of fingers. There was a look of severe piety on his face. He delivered an extempore sermon on the evils of drink and on the evil that women like Mama Geighen do in this world, so realistically that had he delivered it in precisely the same way in a Protestant church where he was not known I am sure it would have been accepted as a very elevating and ennobling sermon indeed. We all paid this manifest genius as an actor, improvisor, orator as well as great novelist the tribute of complete silence until he had concluded. Then there was an uproar of laughter and acclaim. Lewis went into a bedroom to remove the powder and change his collar and vest. Sherwood was sitting beside me on a piano bench. Sherwood was jealous and mad as a wet hen because his performance had been capped. He turned to me and said, 'It's a pity. He wants it so bad, and he will never have it.' I did not ask Sherwood what he meant by 'it.' I knew. He meant 'genius.' "

—Mark Schorer, *Sinclair Lewis: An American Life,* 1961.

Lewis was given to practical jokes involving intricate disguises. On this occasion, he was to be interviewed by a French journalist named André Siegfried.

The day came and Lewis spent the morning and early afternoon in bars. When he came to his hotel he summoned a friend to come to his assistance, and when the friend arrived, he found Lewis teetering in the middle of the room, telephone still in hand. Announcing that he would be all right after a half hour's nap, he retired to his bedroom and left his friend to receive the French delegation. When it arrived, the friend said that the novelist was resting after a day of arduous artistic labor but would appear very soon. Time passed, Siegfried grew restive; the friend entered the bedroom; Lewis was still sleeping soundly. Further apologies, increasing restiveness, awkwardness, until suddenly the bedroom door opened. Then an old man with a white beard, side whiskers, metal-rimmed spectacles, and a cane, tottered into the room and introduced himself in quavering nasal tones as Dr. E. J. Lewis, who had come to Paris to visit his son.

—Schorer.

It took some time for the device to be discovered.

When Lewis married the journalist Dorothy Thompson, he met his match.

Then he telephoned his wife. "Dorothy," he said, breathing heavily, still dazed, "Oh Dorothy!"

She thought that he was ill and asked in quick alarm, "What's the matter?"

"Dorothy, I've got the Nobel prize."

"Oh, have you!" she said briskly. "How nice for you! Well, I have the Order of the Garter!"

—Schorer.

He went to Stockholm to receive the prize.

It was the season of the festival of Santa Lucia, when lovely girls crown their heads with seven burning candles and wander about offering coffee to strangers, and it is said in Stockholm still that on the first night that Lewis was in his hotel, such a creature appeared in his room and, with her mythological appearance, terrified him into screaming.

—Schorer.

In London he met Thomas Wolfe.

. . . one night after he and Lewis had been dining and Wolfe had returned to his lodgings several hours after midnight and was on his way to bed, Lewis telephoned to say that he must return to Bury Street immediately, it was a matter of the greatest urgency. Wolfe pulled his clothes back on and returned to find Lewis in the company of another man. When he entered, Lewis cried in triumph, "You see! Didn't I tell you he was a big bastard?"

—Schorer.

Bennett Cerf recalled an occasion on which Lewis avoided meeting another novelist.

That fall, before he left for Italy, Red [Lewis] spent his last night before sailing at our house. Just as the three of us were finishing a quiet dinner at home, Bob Haas phoned to say that Bill Faulkner was with them for the evening and asked if we'd like to join them. I was so sure Red would be delighted that I said yes without even asking him. But Red said, "No, Bennett. This is *my* night. Haven't you been a publisher long enough to understand I don't want to share it with some other author?" So I had to call Bob back and decline.

We sat and talked for a while; then Red, who had to get up at the crack of dawn, said goodnight and went upstairs to our guest room on the fourth floor. Since it was very early, Phyllis and I were still sitting in the living room, two floors below, when suddenly Red shouted down the stairwell, "Bennett! Bennett!" We were afraid something awful had happened, so I rushed to the stairs and called, "Red. What is it?" And he said, "I just wanted to be sure you hadn't slipped out to see Faulkner."

—*At Random*, 1977.

Ezra Pound 1885–1972

When William Carlos Williams attended the University of Pennsylvania, where Ezra Pound was another student, ". . . I met Ezra Pound in my room in the dormitory." Williams provides quick glimpses: "Ez meanwhile had quit fencing and joined the lacrosse squad." The friends visited each other at home during vacation.

He could never learn to play the piano, though his mother tried to teach him. But he "played" for all that. At home, I remember my mother's astonishment when he sat down at the keyboard and let fly for us—seriously. Everything, you might say, resulted except music. He took mastership at one leap; played Liszt, Chopin—or anyone else you could name—up and down the scales, coherently to his own mind, any old sequence. It was part of his confidence in himself. My sister-in-law was a concert pianist. Ez never liked her.

—*The Autobiography of William Carlos Williams*, 1951.

That confidence never left him, and doubtless derived from his upbringing; when his father visited Pound in London years later, he would brag to Ezra's English acquaintances, "That kid knows everything!"

Once Pound and Williams took a walk in New Jersey.

As we went along Union avenue, Ez walking with his usual swagger, I said to him, "Look, Ez, there's the winter wheat (it was three or four inches high) coming up to greet you."

"It's the first intelligent wheat I've ever seen," was his reply.

—Williams.

Before he left the United States for Europe, Pound tried teaching at Wabash College in Crawfordsville, Indiana—an endeavor which ended in a small disaster.

The story, soap-operatic as it now appears, is that he had fed and lodged a penniless young girl from a stranded burlesque show, whom he had found in a blizzard. The Misses Hall, from whom he had rented the rooms, went up—after his departure the next morning—for the usual cleaning and discovered the sleeping girl. They were maiden ladies in a small Midwestern town and had let the quarters before only to an elderly professor. They telephoned the president of the college and several trustees; the affair became public; only one outcome was possible.

—C. David Heymann, *Ezra Pound: The Last Rower,* 1976.

*He sailed to Italy, published his first book of poems—*A Lume Spento *(1908)—and wended his way to London where he made a spectacle of himself. Ford Madox Ford is not always a reliable reporter, but there is evidence to support his description of the young Pound, whom he would see advancing*

. . . with the step of a dancer, making passes with a cane at an imaginary opponent. He would wear trousers made of green billiard cloth, a pink coat, a blue shirt, a tie hand-painted by a Japanese friend, an immense sombrero, a flaming beard cut to a point, and a single, large blue earring.

—*Return to Yesterday,* 1932.

It was Ford, Pound later noted, who helped him "to get toward a natural way of writing . . . by rolling on the floor undecorously and holding his head in his hands, and groaning" over Pound's poetic archaisms.

But it was Yeats whose presence brought Pound to London, and to whom Pound—recovered from lacrosse—gave fencing lessons. "He would thrash around with the foils like a whale," said Pound of Yeats.

At least on one occasion Pound felt overlooked.

A group went to the Old Cheshire Cheese, where Yeats held forth at length on the ways of bringing music and poetry together. Pound sought attention by eating two red tulips.

—William Van O'Connor, *Ezra Pound,* 1963.

In his pursuit of the new, Pound struggled with the English. Once he challenged the Georgian poet Lascelles Abercrombie.

Abercrombie—small, shy, and bespectacled—had written in one of the literary weeklies that young poets should abandon barren realism and study Wordsworth. Long an admirer of *The Gentle Art of Making Enemies,* Pound composed a response which lacked only the signature of the barbed butterfly to be Whistlerian.

> Dear Mr. Abercrombie:
>
> Stupidity carried beyond a certain point becomes a public menace. I hereby challenge you to a duel, to be fought at the earliest moment that is suited to your convenience. My seconds will wait upon you in due course.
>
> Yours sincerely,
> Ezra Pound

When a friend told him that Pound was an expert fencer, the mild Abercrombie was terrified. Then, realizing that the challenged party had the privilege of choosing the weapons, he accepted, and proposed that they bombard each other with unsold copies of their own books.

—Stanley Weintraub, *The London Yankees,* 1979.

Pound's discovery of T. S. Eliot, like his recognition of Joyce, Frost, and others, was a triumph of taste and generosity. His help to Eliot included the famous revision of Eliot's The Waste Land. *On another occasion, reading ill-tempered commentary by the usually moderate Eliot, Pound told him:*

"That's not your style at all. You let *me* throw the bricks through the front window. You go in at the back door and take out the swag."

—Louis Simpson, *Three on the Tower,* 1975.

Pound moved to France. (Gertrude Stein called him a "village explainer, excellent if you were a village, if you were not, not.") In 1925 he took up residence in Rapallo, Italy. He became obsessed with the economic theory of Social Credit, and an admirer of the Italian dictator Mussolini.

He had a new reputation, for needless irascibility. On a visit to Paris in 1929 he came upon Joyce holding court and was enraged by what he took to be a climate of sychophancy. Of one slim youth he enquired, in withering tones, whether he might be writing an *Iliad,* or would it be a *Divina Commedia.* One should not say such a humiliating thing to anyone, certainly not to anyone who has done no harm, but it is especially regrettable that he should have said it to Sam Beckett.

—Hugh Kenner, *The Pound Era,* 1971.

In the 1930s Pound's paranoia embraced anti-Semitism, and during the war he remained in Italy, broadcasting to American troops on the Italian radio. His old friend Williams heard about it from his wife, who heard about it from a bankteller.

Then one day Floss came home to tell me that one of the tellers at the bank had asked her if I knew a person in Italy called Ezra Pound.

"He was talking about something on the radio last night."

"Ezra Pound?" said Floss.

"Something about ol' Doc Williams of Rutherford, New Jersey, would understand. Something like that—but I couldn't get the rest of it."

—Williams.

After the war, when American authorities brought Pound from Italy to Washington to stand trial for treason, he was judged mentally unfit for trial. Robert Lowell visited him at St. Elizabeth's where he was incarcerated. "Possum" was Pound's affectionate nickname for T. S. Eliot.

Horizontal on a deckchair in the ward
of the criminal mad. . . . A man without shoestrings clawing
the Social Credit broadside from your table, you saying,
". . . here with a black suit and black briefcase; in the brief,
an abomination, Possum's *hommage* to Milton."
Then sprung; Rapallo, and the decade gone;
and three years later, Eliot dead, you saying,
"Who's left alive to understand my jokes?
My old Brother in the arts . . . besides, he was a smash of a poet."
You showed me your blotched, bent hands, saying, "Worms.
When I talked that nonsense about Jews on the Rome

wireless, Olga knew it was shit, and still loved me."
And I, "Who else has been in Purgatory?"
You, "I began with a swelled head and end with swelled feet."

—Robert Lowell, *History,* 1967.

In 1958, Pound was released from St. Elizabeth's on condition that he return to Italy. He lived for a time in the hills of the Italian Tirol, which reminded him of America's sugarbush country.

Pound thought the castle might be self-sufficient if it had maple syrup for sale, but the maple trees he ordered from America, like the vinestocks Jefferson brought to Virginia from France, refused to survive (but are said to have brought poison ivy into Italy).

—Kenner.

Nothing had worked out as he wished. When he spoke, in later years, it was to retract what he had earlier said or done. In 1960 a visitor remembered listening to a poem, on a disc in Harvard's Poetry Room, which Pound had recorded in 1939.

On the label of a huge 33 r.p.m. disc, a note insisted, "Do Not Play Band Six." Naturally enough, when I first played these records as an undergraduate I immediately played Band Six. It was a marvelous reading of "Sestina: Altaforte," also known as the Bloody Sestina, where Pound in the mask of Bertrans de Born praises war. . . .

Innocently that morning, forgetting that I had defied a handwritten prohibition, I filled a pause by praising his reading of the poem. Pound interrupted his silence with a black look. "So they're letting them listen, are they?"

I remembered my lawlessness then, and confessed it. He muttered again about Harvard's promises. I asked him the obvious question: why had he demanded that the poem be proscribed?

He paused a while, I suppose, to find the phrase.

"War," he said, "—is no longer—amusing."

—Donald Hall, *Remembering Poets,* 1978.

In the last years he lived almost completely in a silence of his own choosing. A young poet knocked at his door in Venice, never expecting Pound to answer it himself.

To his astonishment, the door opened to reveal Ezra Pound in bathrobe and slippers. In his confusion, the young man burbled, "How are you, Mr. Pound?"

Pound looked down at him for a moment, out of the *hauteur* of his silence, and then uttered a single word, in the melody which sometimes resembled W. C. Fields.

"Senile," he said.

—Hall.

Elinor Wylie 1885–1928

Poet and novelist, Wylie wrote verses distinguished by their high polish, and a novel about the poet Shelley. Her biographer describes her on a fluttering visit to England.

Her ridiculous side galloped gaily forth next day when she was very late for lunch, so late that the dining-room was about to close. She dashed in, pale, preoccupied, her mouth pinched to the size of a threepenny bit, her eyes large and brooding. She asked us in tones of deep tragedy if there were any of the little lobsters left, the tiny Swanage lobsters she was so fond of, and if the best of the veal and ham pie had been consumed. Luckily there was a lobster left and plenty of pie, though not perhaps quite the best bits. But what, we queried, could have detained her fifty minutes past lunch time in a familiar and humdrum seaside town? Well, apparently the explanation was that some friend or companion of Mr. Shelley had snatched some relic, bit of bone or odd portion from his funeral pyre on the beach, and it was buried in the graveyard of St. Thingumy's church. So she had sat on a near-by grave and wept for an hour. . . . She relished the half-sized lobster none the less.

—Nancy Hoyt, *The Portrait of an Unknown Lady*, 1935.

By all accounts she was a frail and volatile creature, sometimes aided by steady if impatient friends.

Katherine Anne Porter was routed from her bed when the doorbell was rung at 4 A.M. by the wealthy and beautiful Elinor Wylie (Mrs. William Rose Benét), who seemingly had all of the material advantages that Miss Porter lacked then. "Katherine

Anne," Miss Wylie began, "I have stood the crassness of this world as long as I can and I am going to kill myself. You are the only person in the world to whom I wish to say good-by."

Miss Porter reportedly looked Miss Wylie dispassionately in the eye and responded: "Elinor, it was good of you to think of me. Good-by."

—Virginia Spencer Carr, *The Lonely Hunter: A Biography of Carson McCullers,* 1975.

Hilda Doolittle (H.D.) 1886–1961

Doolittle published her poetry under her initials—from her early Imagist poems, which are brief and brilliant, through the long meditative poems of her later years. William Carlos Williams remembered her as a young woman at the University of Pennsylvania, when Ezra Pound was in love with her.

There was about her that which is found in wild animals at times, a breathless impatience, almost a silly unwillingness to come to the point. She had a young girl's giggle and shrug which somehow in one so tall and angular seemed a little absurd. She fascinated me, not for her beauty, which was unquestioned if bizarre to my sense, but for a provocative indifference to rule and order which I liked. She dressed indifferently, almost sloppily and looked to a young man, not inviting—she had nothing of that—but irritating, with a smile.

Ezra was wonderfully in love with her and I thought exaggerated her beauty ridiculously. To me she was just a good guy and I enjoyed, uncomfortably, being with her. For sometimes I called at the observatory alone and even stayed the night there—to my embarrassment on one occasion. I took Hilda to a Mask and Wig tryout and dance one night and even got some dirty looks from Ezra over it.

She asked me if when I started to write I had to have my desk neat and everything in its place, if I had to prepare the paraphernalia, or if I just sat down and wrote.

I said I liked to have things neat.

Ha, ha!

She said that when she wrote it was a great help, she thought and practiced it, if taking some ink on her pen, she'd splash it on her clothes to give her a feeling of freedom and indifference toward the mere means of the writing.

—*The Autobiography of William Carlos Williams,* 1951.

Alexander Woollcott 1887–1943

During the years when he was drama critic for The New Yorker, *Woollcott attended a dinner party at which the Prince of Wales was guest of honor.*

After the ladies had been excused and the gentlemen were about to start on their port and cigars, the Prince begged those present to retire as he wished a private conversation with Mr. Woollcott. The gentlemen bowed out as requested, leaving his Royal highness and a Woollcott whose imagination caught fire with probabilities: matters of state, perhaps, a speech to the Empire, or even an introduction by Woollcott to a volume of letters by Edward.

When the doors were closed, the Prince looked squarely at him and began with "Woollcott . . . ?"

"Sir," came the anticipatory reply. At that precise moment he might gladly have been willing to lay down his life for the Crown.

"You've something to do with that magazine from the States, *The New Yorker,* don't you?"

Woollcott's outthrust chest began to deflate and his spine sagged against the back of his chair.

"Yes, sir, I do."

"Then why the devil don't I get it more regularly? Do look into it, will you?"

—Howard Teichmann, *Smart Aleck,* 1976.

The playwright Charles MacArthur arrived at Woollcott's house in Vermont and discovered that Woollcott had left. "Junior" Treadwell, who was Woollcott's servant, told him

"Mr. Woollcott said you were late and that he considered it a broken engagement."

"Five minutes late for dinner and the theater and he says it's a broken engagement?"

"Yes, sir."

"I'll be right back, Junior," Charles MacArthur promised. Hurrying to the nearest grocery store, MacArthur bought dozens of packages of raspberry Jell-O and then returned to Wit's End.

Junior met him at the door.

"Yes, Mr. MacArthur?"

"Junior, I've got to go to the bathroom. Do you mind?"

"No, sir. You know where it's at."

Of course he did. Once inside, MacArthur locked the door, peeled off his overcoat, closed the drain to the bathtub, tore open package after package of raspberry Jell-O, and emptied them into the bottom of the tub. This done, he gleefully ran three or four inches of hot water, following with an equal amount of cold water. Then he opened the window, permitting the wintry winds to fill the small bathroom. When he had finished, Charlie picked up his coat, stuffed his pockets with empty Jell-O packages, unlocked the door, and let himself out, closing the bathroom door behind him.

"Everything all right, Mr. MacArthur?" Junior asked.

"Thank you. I feel much better," the playwright answered.

"I'll tell Mr. Woollcott you were here."

"You do that, Junior."

Six hours later an infuriated Woollcott stood in his bathroom looking down at a tubful of quivering Jell-O.

"MacArthur and his practical jokes," he fumed. "Son of a bitch had to make it red. Lime would have gone much better with this room."

—Teichmann.

Others played tricks as well.

Someone had told Woollcott of a poor poet living in the woods an hour's drive from the island.

"You know poets, Jo," Woollcott told him, "they're always on the brink of starvation. Pile up the car with everything we have—hams, bacon, eggs, bread, a few bottles of wine. We are nothing if not generous."

Hennessey did as he was asked, and together he and Woollcott set off in search of the impoverished maker of verses. They found the cottage without much trouble. It was a bit larger than they had anticipated. They were stunned, however, when they rang the doorbell and were greeted by a French maid in an afternoon uniform.

"Archibald MacLeish's country home was almost as beautiful as his wife," Hennessey said gallantly. "What neither Aleck nor I knew was that MacLeish's father owned Carson, Pirie, Scott, the second largest department store in Chicago. MacLeish was very polite in accepting the food. He thanked us properly and we stayed a moderate amount of time and then went back to the island."

—Teichmann.

On the whole one understands their provocation. Woollcott visited the playwright Moss Hart at his house in Bucks County.

Immediately upon entering the Hart household, Woollcott took to insulting his host, his host's guests, and his host's taste in architecture, household furnishings, and social acquaintances. He then demanded and was shown the master bedroom, where he disrobed, got into bed, ordered the heat turned off throughout the entire house, asked for and received a frosted milk shake and a large chocolate cake. Next he embarked upon a loud and unprintable discourse on the dishonesty of the Hart servants.

Woollcott retired for the night, but not before he wrote in the guest book, "I wish to say that on my first visit to Moss Hart's house, I had one of the most unpleasant evenings I can ever recall having spent."

—Teichmann.

When Hart told Kaufman the story, he finished by saying

"But suppose he'd broken his leg on the way out," Moss suggested, "and I had to keep him there?"

Kaufman peered over the rims of his glasses staring at Hart. Then he took off his medium-distance glasses and put on the pair he wore for typing. Whipping a single sheet of paper into the machine, he rolled it through. His long fingers suddenly flashed across the keyboard of the typewriter.

"Act One, Scene One," he wrote.

—Teichmann.

So started The Man Who Came to Dinner.

Marianne Moore 1887–1972

William Carlos Williams remembered Moore young: ". . . a rafter holding up the superstructure of our uncompleted building, a caryatid, her red hair plaited and wound twice around the fine skull. . ." She was editor of The Dial *and friend of the poets who gathered in New York: Wallace Stevens, Alfred Kreymborg, William Carlos Williams, Hart Crane, Mina Loy. In an autobiography Kreymborg remembered an excursion to watch Christy Mathewson pitch.*

Never having found her at a loss on any topic whatsoever, I wanted to give myself the pleasure at least once of hearing her stumped about something. Certain that only an experience completely strange to her would be the thing, I invited her to a ball game at the Polo Grounds. This descent into the world of the low-brow started beautifully. It was a Saturday afternoon and the Cubs and Giants were scheduled for one of their ancient frays. The "L" was jammed with fans and we had to stand all the way uptown and hang on to straps. Marianne was totally oblivious to the discomfiture anyone else would have felt and, in answer to a question of mine, paraded whole battalions of perfectly marshalled ideas in long columns of balanced periods which no lurching on the part of the train or pushing on the part of the crowd disturbed. Wait till we reach the grounds, I promised myself, and Matty winds up, tosses a perfect fadeway, the batter misses it, and Marianne goes on talking.

Well, I got her safely to her seat and sat down beside her. Without so much as a glance toward the players at practice grabbing grounders and chasing fungos, she went on giving me her impression of the respective technical achievements of Mr. Pound and Mr. Aldington without missing a turn in the rhythm of her speech, until I, a little impatient, touched her arm and, indicating a man in the pitcher's box winding up with the movement Matty's so famous for, interrupted: "But Marianne, wait a moment, the game's about to begin. Don't you want to watch the first ball?" "Yes indeed," she said, stopped, blushed and leaned forward. The old blond boy delivered a tantalizing fadeaway which hovered in the air and then, just as it reached the batter, Shorty Slagle, shot from his shoulders to his knees and across the plate. "Strike!" bawled Umpire Emslie. "Excellent," said Marianne.

Delighted, I quickly turned to her with: "Do you happen to know the gentleman who threw that strike?"

"I've never seen him before," she admitted, "but I take it it must be Mr. Mathewson."

I could only gasp, "Why?"

"I've read his instructive book on the art of pitching—"

"Strike two!" interrupted Bob Emslie.

"And it's a pleasure," she continued imperturbably, "to note how unerringly his execution supports his theories—"

—*Troubadour: An Autobiography,* 1925.

Her eccentricities became more pronounced in later years. While she still lived in Brooklyn, she kept a bowl of subway tokens in her living room, by way of apology for the distance her visitors had to travel to see her. It was not possible to depart without taking a token. Normally she treated her guests to lunch at a nearby restaurant, but occasionally she found herself stymied.

An acquaintance invited to lunch at Marianne Moore's was met at the door by the lady herself, in anguish. "Mr. Wilson," she said, "I am in despair." She had telephoned her favorite neighborhood restaurant for reservations, and discovered that it was closed. "I'm afraid we'll have to make do," she said, "with what I can find in the refrigerator."

After disappearing into the kitchen for a few minutes, Miss Moore reappeared with two trays identically outfitted for lunch. Each contained half a small glass of tomato juice which she had heated to resemble tomato soup, half an apple, two triangles of cheese wrapped in foil, a tuna salad sandwich, a dish of nuts, a dish of canned pears, an elderly nectarine, and two chocolate petits fours. Between the two trays she placed a large bowl of Fritos, which she recommended as "nutritional."

When Mr. Wilson departed, Miss Moore pressed into his hand a paper bag, apparently a snack for the journey home; it contained two taffy pecan bars and a tube of anchovy paste.

A young man came to Marianne Moore's Brooklyn apartment with books for her to sign. As she meticulously corrected small errors in each of the printed editions, he let his eyes wander over her furnishings, finally resting on a door frame, from which was hanging on two chains something that looked like a trapeze. Miss Moore was seventy-two years old. When he could contain himself no longer, her visitor asked Miss Moore, "Miss Moore, what is that up there in the doorway?"

She did not look up. "Oh," she said, "that's my trapeze."

—[Editor's paraphrase].

George Plimpton took her to Yankee Stadium where she watched a pitcher named Bill Monbouquette.

Marianne Moore peered out over the railing of the second-tier box and noticed that Monbouquette had a most disturbing habit at the end of his delivery, which was to cup his groin at the jockstrap and give it a little heft, as if to rearrange what was within. "That is interesting, what he does at the completion of his toss," she had said, and our little group stared transfixed as, sure enough, he did it every time. It was an integral part of his pitching motion, surely quite unconscious since it was hardly a gesture one would think of oneself doing in front of twenty thousand or so people, time after time. We discussed whether he should be told, whether an umpire should come out and say, "Hey, don't do that, please . . . our sensibilities!" or whether the television cameras ever lingered below his waist when he was pitching, and if he *was* told, what it would do to his pitching abilities . . . to realize suddenly that for the fifteen years or so of his career he had been displaying across the country this faintly obscene peculiarity of his—like being told one's fly had been open for *years.* It might have kept Monbouquette from ever picking up a baseball again without blushing and having to drop it. Miss Moore was quite serene about what she had discovered. "There is an insouciance in that gesture which is appealing," she said. "He should not be told. We should keep mum." She wrote his name down in her little book. "Monbouquette," she said, barely audibly. " 'My little bouquet.' Absolutely correct."

—George Plimpton, *Shadow Box,* 1977.

It was Plimpton who arranged the meeting of poets—Moore had tea with Muhammad Ali.

Some weeks later I was able to arrange our tea with Ali. . . . For reasons I have forgotten, we had it at Toots Shor's establishment, in mid-Manhattan. The place was almost empty when Miss Moore and I arrived—a slack time in the place, about four in the afternoon. . . .

Presently Muhammad Ali arrived with Hal Conrad. He slid in behind the table and arranged himself next to Miss Moore. He gazed at her hat, which was the . . . tricorne. Almost immediately, as if she had yet to arrive, he turned to Hal and me and asked who she was and what he was expected to do. Had a photographer arrived?

Miss Moore listened attentively to what Conrad and I had to say about her—a great sports fan, one of the most distinguished poets in the country. . . .

"Mrs. Moore," said Ali, turning and looking at her, "a grandmother going to the fights? How old is she?" he suddenly asked, turning toward me and whispering loudly. I was taken aback.

"Oh, forty," I said idiotically, producing the first number that came to mind.

"Is that so?" commented the champion. "The way you settled her down in here so careful I reckon she's got to be a grandmother, seventy-nine going on eighty, or maybe ninety-six." He inspected her. "They have these women up in Pakistan," he confided in me loudly, "who live to be one hundred and *sixty.* They haul pianos up and down these hills. They eat a lot of yogurt."

Miss Moore sat patiently through this, smiling faintly. The fighter turned to her suddenly and asked, "Mrs. Moore, what have you been doing lately?"

"I have been subduing my apartment," she said in her high, thin voice. "I have just moved in from Brooklyn to a new apartment which is strange to me and needs taming."

"Is that so?" The champion ordered a glass of water. "Yes," he said to the waiter. "We is tiptop at Toots." He turned back to Miss Moore."Well, I am considering farming, myself," he said. "I'd like to sit and look across the fence at the biggest bull in the world—jes' sit and rock back and forth and look at him out there in the middle of the field, feeding."

"Oh yes," Miss Moore said. She was quite shy with him, ducking her head and peeking at him. "Can we come and look with you?"

"You can sit on the porch with me, Mrs. Moore," Ali said.

She made a confused, pleased gesture and then had a sip of her tea. He ordered a bowl of beef soup and a phone. He announced that if she was the greatest poetess in the country, the two of them should produce something together—"I am a poet, too," he said—a joint-effort sonnet, it was to be, with each of them doing aternate lines. Miss Moore nodded vaguely. Ali was very much the more decisive of the pair, picking not only the form but also the topic: "Mrs. Moore and I are going to write a sonnet about my upcoming fight in Houston with Ernie Terrell," he proclaimed to the table. "Mrs. Moore and I will show the world with this great poem who is who and what is what and who is going to win."

"We will call it 'A Poem on the Annihilation of Ernie Terrell,' " Miss Moore announced. "Let us be serious but not grim."

"She's cute," Ali commented.

A pen was produced. Ali was given a menu on which to write. He started off with half the first line—"After we defeat"—and asked Miss Moore to write in Ernie Terrell (which she misspelled "Ernie Tyrell" in her spidery script) just to get her "warmed up." He wrote most of the second line—"He will catch nothing"—handing the pen over and expecting Miss Moore to fill in the obvious rhyme, and he was quite surprised when she did not. She made some scratchy squiggles on the paper to get the ink flowing properly. The fighter peered over her shoulder.

"What's that say?" he asked.

"It doesn't say anything. You could call them 'preliminaries.' Terrell should rhyme nicely with 'bell,' " Miss Moore said tentatively. I could see her lips move as she fussed with possibilities. Finally, Ali leaned over and whispered to her, " 'but hell,' Mrs. Moore."

"Oh, yes," she said. She wrote down "but hell," but then she wrestled with it some more, clucking gently, and murmuring about the rhythm of the line, and she crossed it out and substituted, "he will get nothing, nothing but hell."

Ali took over and produced his next line in jig time: "Terrell was big and ugly and tall." He pushed the menu over to her. His soup arrived. He leaned low over it, spooning it in, and glancing over to see how she was coming along. While he waited, he told Conrad and me that he was going to try to get the poem out over the Associated Press wire that afternoon. Miss Moore's eyes widened, perhaps at the irony of all those years struggling with *Broom* and the other literary magazines, and now to be with a fighter who promised instant publication over a ticker machine. It did not help the flow of inspiration. She was doubtless intimidated by the presence next to her, especially at his obvious concern that she, a distinguished poet, was having such a hard time holding up her side: speed of delivery was very much a qualification of a professional poet in his mind. He finished his soup and ordered another. The phone arrived and was plugged in behind the banquette. He began dialing a series of numbers—hotels, most of them—but the room numbers he requested never seemed to respond.

Finally, seeing that she had not got anywhere at all, he took the poem from her and completed it. It was not done in a patronizing way at all but more out of consideration, presumably that every poet, however distinguished, is bound to have a bad day and should be helped through it. He tried some lines aloud which he eventually discarded: "When I hit him with my right/ He'll become a colored satellite. . . .

"Now, let's see," he said as he began to write. He had moved close to her, so that she appeared to be looking down the long length of his arm to watch the poem emerge. "Yes," she said. "Why not?" as he produced a last couplet. The whole composition, once he had taken over, took about a minute. With the spelling corrected, it read as follows:

After we defeat Ernie Terrell
He will get nothing, nothing but hell,

Terrell was big and ugly and tall
But when he fights me he is sure to fall.
If he criticize this poem by me and Miss Moore
To prove he is not the champ she will stop him in four,
He is claiming to be the real heavyweight champ
But when the fight starts he will look like a tramp
He has been talking too much about me and making me sore
After I am through with him he will not be able to challenge Mrs. Moore.

The stratagem of involving her in the poem, particularly as a pugilist herself, was clever: Miss Moore nodded in delight, despite its being a truncated sonnet. She made a tiny fist. "Yes, he has been making me sore," she said.

A photographer arrived—something of a surprise. He was from one of the wire services. I suspect that Muhammad Ali, knowing that he was meeting someone of distinction, if not quite sure *whom,* had arranged for the photographer so that the event could be recorded. Miss Moore did not seem to mind. She allowed Ali, who continued to dominate the afternoon, to dictate the poses. His idea was to have the photograph show the two of them working on the poem. "We've got to show you *thinking,* Mrs. Moore," he said. "How you show you're thinking hard is to point your finger into the middle of your head." He illustrated, jabbing his forefinger at his forehead, closing his eyes to indicate concentration. She complied, pursing her lips in feigned concern as she pondered the poem. The photographer clicked away happily.

Miss Moore then expressed a wish to see the Ali shuffle—a foot maneuver Ali occasionally did in mid-fight which looked like a man's trying to stay upright on a carpet being pulled out from underneath him. Ali said he would be delighted to show her the shuffle. He thought it would be best to do it out in the street where he had room to do her a really *good* shuffle. But when we walked outdoors, a crowd immediately collected—I think the word was around the neighborhood that the fighter was in Toots Shor's—so we came back through the revolving door and he did the shuffle right there in the foyer. Miss Moore was delighted. She asked him to do it again, and when he went out and did the shuffle for the people in the street, she watched him through the revolving door.

"Well," she said when he had left, "he had every excuse for avoiding a performance. But he festooned out in as enticing a bit of shuffling as you would ever wish to see."

"He 'festooned'?" I asked.

"He certainly did. . . ."

—Plimpton.

Robinson Jeffers 1887–1962

When the poet Robinson Jeffers settled in Carmel, California, he stayed put. Refusing to go east to see his publisher, he quoted Thomas Carlyle: "Any the smallest alteration of my silent daily habits produces anarchy to me. . . ." In another letter he repeated something he had heard told about himself.

Somebody has a nice story about passing along the road below here, an evening in 1921 or so. They looked up in the twilight and saw a stump of a tower, and me on top rolling a stone into place. They went to China, returned to America, went to Italy, returned. In 1924 they were here again and looked up from the sea-road in the twilight to the same stump of a tower, hardly any higher, and me on top carefully rolling a stone into place.

—*Selected Letters of Robinson Jeffers,* ed. Ann M. Ridgeway, 1968.

Raymond Chandler 1888–1959

Chandler wanted to withdraw from writing the filmscript of The Blue Dahlia, *but did not want to disappoint his producer, John Houseman. He came up with a proposal.*

. . . he said that he might be able to finish the script if he wrote it while drunk. Alcohol would calm his nerves and give him the confidence to continue in the face of the mistrust and insults he had received.

Houseman was dismayed by the proposal, because Chandler was not a young man and he knew that work of this kind might endanger his health. But Chandler began to produce a series of conditions that seemed to lessen the risk. The idea was that

Paramount would provide two limousines to stand by day and night outside of Chandler's house. They would fetch the doctor for Cissy, who was recovering from an operation on her foot, take the maid to do the shopping, and deliver the script to the studio. In addition, there had to be round-the-clock nurses and a doctor available to give Chandler vitamin shots, since he never ate while drinking. Further, a direct telephone line had to be installed between the house and the producer's office at Paramount, and secretaries were to be on hand at all hours for dictation, typing, and other necessities.

Houseman hesitated, since the responsibility would be his if anything went wrong; but in the end he agreed to the terms and the arrangements were made. He and Chandler went out to Perino's Restaurant, and there Chandler had three double martinis before lunch and three stingers afterward. Houseman drove him home to Drexel Avenue, and Chandler went inside to lie down on the couch. The limousines, the secretaries were all in place. For the next week or so Chandler worked intermittently. He was never out of control; he was just in another realm. Houseman recalls seeing him slumped over the dining room table, taking a nap. He wouldn't sleep for long, but would wake up and continue, glass in hand. In the evenings he would sit with Cissy and listen to the gas company's radio program of classical music that ran from eight to ten. Then he would go to his study and try a few more lines before he dozed off again. In this way, the screenplay was finished. . . .

The most famous incident linking Chandler to the film of *The Big Sleep* is his reply to a telegram sent by Hawks asking who killed Owen Taylor, the Sternwood chauffeur who ends up in the family limousine under ten feet of water at the end of a pier. Chandler checked the text, thought about it, and wired back: "I don't know."

—Frank MacShane, *The Life of Raymond Chandler,* 1976.

T. S. Eliot 1888–1965

Born in St. Louis, educated at Harvard, Eliot lived most of his life in England. Pound had arrived first, and heard of Eliot from Conrad Aiken, who said "there was a guy at Harvard doing funny stuff. Mr. Eliot turned up a year or so later." Pound told a story out of their early friendship.

"So Mr. Eliot came to London, with all the disadvantages of a . . . sym*me*trical education . . . and dutifully joined the Aristotelian Society. . . . And he took me to a meeting. And a man with a beard down to here . . . spoke for twenty minutes on a point in Aris*tot*le; and another with a beard down to *here* rose up and refuted him. . . . And I wanted *air.* So we were on the portico when old G. R. S. Mead came up, and catching sight of me said 'I didn't expect to see *you* here'; whereat Eliot with perfect decorum and suavity said,

" 'Oh, he's not here as a phil-*os*-opher;
He's here as an an-thro-pologist.' "

—Hugh Kenner, *The Pound Era,* 1971.

Eliot's humor, constant but often covert, did not form part of his public costume. When he was editing for The Egoist, *the magazine decided to inaugurate a column of letters from readers.*

In order to get the correspondence off to a good start, Eliot invested himself with no less than five pseudonyms. It was typical of the ingenious playfulness with which he treated many things, and not least himself. He was Charles Augustus Conybeare of the Carlton Club, Liverpool, asking where the writers of philosophical articles in *The Egoist* obtained their ideas. He was the Rev. Charles James Grimble of the Vicarage, Leays, who thought it a sensible policy to let people know about foreign ways and to keep their minds open. He was J. A. D. Spence, a master at Thridlingston Grammar School, deploring the way in which Ezra Pound had rehabilitated Ovid, and praising Ezra's enemy Gosse. He was Muriel A. Schwarz of 60 Alexandra Gardens, Hampstead, N.W. who thought that an article written by Wyndham Lewis had cast a slur on "the cheery philosophy of our brave boys in the trenches" (this was a touch of satire to please Bertrand Russell); finally, he was Helen B. Trundlett of Batton, Kent, who saw the War as a "Great Ordeal which is proving the well-spring of a Renaissance of English poetry"—a satirical reference to Rupert Brooke.

—Robert Sencourt, *T. S. Eliot: A Memoir,* 1971.

After he became famous and turned publisher with Faber and Faber, Eliot was generous to younger poets, sought them out and invited them to tea. William Empson told a story from an early encounter.

"Do you really think it necessary, Mr. Eliot," I broke out, "as you said in the preface to the Pound anthology, for a poet to write verse at least every week?" He was preparing to cross into Russell Square, eyeing the traffic both ways, and we were dodging it as his slow reply proceeded. "I had in mind Pound when I wrote that passage," began the deep sad voice, and there was a considerable pause. "Taking the question in general, I should say, in the case of many poets, that the most important thing for them to do . . . is to write as little as possible."

—*T. S. Eliot: A Symposium,* compiled by Richard March and Tambimuttu, 1949.

He read his poems aloud; he entertained questions.

In 1929, there was a meeting of the Oxford Poetry Club at which he was the guest of honor. . . . An undergraduate asked Eliot: "Please, sir, what do you mean by the line: *'Lady, three white leopards sat under a juniper-tree?'*" Eliot looked at him and said: "I mean, *'Lady, three white leopards sat under a juniper-tree.'* "

—*T. S. Eliot, the Man and His Work,* ed. Allen Tate, 1967.

Eliot suffered for many years from a bad marriage with his unstable first wife Vivien. When they separated, it was Eliot's decision.

If he could have forgotten Vivien, she could not forget him. She would return to his office in Russell Square and try to waylay him on the stairs. . . . There are stories of her coming to his lectures wearing a placard bearing the words "I am the wife he abandoned. . . ."

—Sencourt.

After his separation from Vivien, Eliot for many years shared an apartment with John Hayward, scholar and critic who was confined to a wheelchair. Vivien Eliot died in 1947. To the astonishment of everyone who knew him, Eliot then married the young woman who had been his secretary at Faber and Faber.

. . . the second marriage was "prepared as secretly as if it had been a conspiracy." In one account, Eliot did not inform John Hayward of his plans in advance, he waited until after they were married. "Why didn't you tell me before?" Hayward is reported to have asked. To which Eliot replied, "Well, John, I thought you would be so cross." The official version, however, "vouched for by the present Mrs. Eliot," has Eliot telling Hayward about it two days before the wedding. Hayward takes the news of Eliot's leaving "extremely well." Eliot promises to pay three hundred pounds a year of the four hundred and seventy pounds' yearly rent for the next four years, and keeps his promise.

As time went by Hayward told resentful stories about Eliot's leaving to get married. John Hayward has been called "the most malicious gossip in London." There have been as many claimants to this as to the title of the wickedest woman in London, but if Hayward told the stories attributed to him he was surely a contender. In one account Eliot handed him a letter breaking the news and hovered around while he read it. Hayward said, "Sit down, my dear Tom, and let's talk about it." Eliot replied, "Oh, no, no, I can't, the taxi is waiting." Hayward is also reported to have said that Eliot had been removing his clothes by stealth from the flat for weeks before his departure, and that he telephoned to say he was married and not coming back. "Think of the treacherousness of a man taking all his shirts and all his ties, little by little!"

—Louis Simpson, *Three on the Tower,* 1975.

Although he became an English citizen Eliot never denied his American origins. If he had tried to forget, people would have reminded him.

To some graduate students at the University of Iowa who sent him a phonograph record, "You've Come a Long Way from St. Louis," Eliot replied that he particularly liked the last line: "But, baby, you've still got a long way to go!"

—T. S. Matthews, *Great Tom: Notes Toward the Definition of T. S. Eliot,* 1974.

Hugh Kenner told about lunch with Eliot, speaking of himself as "the guest."

After jugged hare at the Club ("Now there is jugged hare. That is a very English dish. Do you want to be English; or do you want to be safe?"); after the jugged hare and the evasions, he addressed his mind to the next theme. "Now; will you have a sweet; or . . . *cheese*?" Even one not conversant with his letter to the *Times* on the declining estate of Stilton [Nov. 29, 1935, p. 15] would have understood that the countersign was *cheese.* "Why, cheese," said his guest too lightly; one does not crash in upon the mysteries. There was a touch of reproof in his solicitude: "Are you sure? You can have ice cream, you know." (At the Garrick!)

No, cheese. To which, "Very well. I fancy . . . a fine Stilton." And as the waiter left for the Stilton, Eliot imparted the day's most momentous confidence: "Never commit yourself to a cheese without having first . . . *examined* it."

The Stilton stood encumbered with a swaddling band, girded about with a cincture, scooped out on top like a crater of the moon. It was placed in front of the Critic. ("Analysis and comparison," he had written some 40 years earlier, "Analysis and comparison, methodically, with sensitiveness, intelligence, curiosity, intensity of passion and infinite knowledge: all these are necessary to the great critic.") With the side of his knife blade he commenced tapping the circumference of the cheese, rotating it, his head cocked in a listening posture. It is not possible to swear that he was listening. He then tapped the inner walls of the crater. He then dug about with the point of his knife amid the fragments contained by the crater. He then said, "Rather past its prime. I am afraid I cannot recommend it."

He was not always so. That was one of his Garrick personae. An acquaintance reports that at dinner in Eliot's home "an ordinary Cheddar" was "served without ceremony."

The Stilton vanished. After awing silence the cheese board arrived, an assortment of some half-dozen, a few of them identifiably cheeses only in context. One resembled sponge cake spattered with chocolate sauce. Another, a pockmarked toadstool-yellow, exuded green flecks. Analysis and comparison: he took up again his knife, and each of these candidates he tapped, he prodded, he sounded. At length he segregated a ruddy specimen. "That is a rather fine Red Cheshire . . . which you might enjoy." It was accepted; the decision was not enquired into, nor the intonation of *you* assessed.

His attention was now bent on the toadstool-yellow specimen.

This he tapped. This he prodded. This he poked. This he scraped. He then summoned the waiter.

"What is that?"

Apologetic ignorance of the waiter.

"Could we find out?"

Disappearance of the waiter. Two other waiters appear.

"?"

"——."

He assumed, at this silence, a mask of Holmesian exaltation:

"Aha! An Anonymous Cheese!"

He then took the Anonymous Cheese beneath his left hand, and the knife in his right hand, the thumb along the back of the blade as though to pare an apple. He then achieved with aplomb the impossible feat of peeling off a long slice. He ate this, attentively. He then transferred the Anonymous Cheese to the plate before him, and with no further memorable words proceeded without assistance to consume the entire Anonymous Cheese.

—Kenner.

Later that same day, Kenner told Wyndham Lewis the story of the Anonymous Cheese. "Oh, never mind him," *said Lewis. "But he doesn't come* in here *dressed as Westminister Abbey."*

In 1951 a twenty-two-year-old American poet, recently graduated from Harvard and on his way to a fellowship at Oxford, called on Eliot at Faber and Faber, at Eliot's invitation.

Then it was four o'clock, or nearly; it was time for Eliot to conclude our interview, and take tea with his colleagues. He stood up, slowly enough to give me time to stand upright before he did, granting me the face of knowing when to leave. When this tall, pale, dark-suited figure struggled successfully to its feet, and I had leapt to mine, we lingered a moment in the doorway, while I sputtered ponderous thanks, and he nodded smiling to acknowledge them. Then Eliot appeared to search for the right phrase with which to send me off. He looked at me in the eyes, and set off into a slow, meandering sentence. "Let me see," said T. S. Eliot, "forty years ago I went from Harvard to Oxford. Now you are going from Harvard to Oxford. What advice can I give you?" He paused delicately, shrewdly, while I waited with greed for the words which I would repeat for the rest of my life, the advice from elder to younger, setting me on the road of emulation. When he had ticked off the comedian's exact milliseconds of pause, he said, "Have you any long underwear?"

—Donald Hall, *Remembering Poets,* 1978.

Igor Stravinsky told about having dinner with the Eliots in a restaurant in New York, in the last year of Eliot's life.

At the end of dinner Eliot asked Stravinsky to drink a toast "To another ten years for both of us." Stravinsky, who was then eighty-one (but who was to outlive Eliot by six years), thought the chances "so improbable that the clink of our glasses rang hollow, and the words sounded more like a farewell." As they left the restaurant "we could not help overhearing the *maître d'hôtel* say to the *vestiaire* that 'There you see the greatest living poet and the greatest living composer together.' But my wife saved the day by saying in just the right tone, 'Well, they do their best.' "

—Matthews.

Eugene O'Neill 1888–1953

Son of a theatrical family, O'Neill worked at a variety of jobs before he began writing for the theater in 1913. Like many another American writer, he suffered from a frailty.

O'Neill's drinking often led to blackouts; in fact, in 1909 his first marriage had resulted from one. He woke up in some flophouse with a girl in bed next to him, and he said, "Who the hell are you?" and she said, "You married me last night."

—Bennett Cerf, *At Random,* 1977.

Edmund Wilson encouraged him to depart the wagon, and paid for his indiscretion.

He was then completely on the wagon, and you were cautioned not to offer him anything to drink. But I got so bored with his nonresponsive silence that one night, having dinner with him in a Greenwich Village restaurant, I decided to prime him with some wine, which with no hesitation he accepted. . . .

After dinner, we went on to my apartment at 3 Washington

Square North, and, once started talking, it seemed O'Neill could never stop. What was striking was that he quite lost connection with anything that was said by me or Mary. He did not answer questions or seem to recognize that we were there at all. He disregarded all our hints. We got up and crossed the room; we made remarks which with anyone else would have brought the session to a close. But his talk was an unbroken monologue. And he drank up everything we had in the house: when a bottle was set before him, he simply poured out drinks for himself, not suggesting that we might care for any. If we said we ought to go to bed, he paid no attention to this. He told us at length about a rich man who lived near him in Connecticut. . . .

—Edmund Wilson, *The Twenties*, 1975.

In 1936 O'Neill won the Nobel Prize. He did not enjoy his celebrity. He would not travel to Stockholm to receive his prize, and he refused to be photographed for the newsreels, as a friend recalled.

They wanted him to pose for a faked scene of his getting the news. A telegraph boy was to be shown approaching their door, O'Neill answers the bell, with [his wife] at his side, and then a big grin as he shows her the telegram. When I told Gene about it, his only comment was, 'To hell with them!' "

—Louis Sheaffer, *O'Neill: Son and Artist*, 1973.

Newspaper columnist Sidney Skolsky told about his one visit to a nightclub.

Went to a nightclub only once in his life. . . . He said it would be the last time. That evening, during a lull in the entertainment, the owner of the club made an announcement to the effect that America's greatest playwright was among those present. The spotlight soon found O'Neill and he was forced to stand and take a bow. Later, when ready to leave, he was presented with a bill for sixty dollars. He looked at the check for a moment, took out a pencil, and wrote across it: 'One bow—sixty dollars." He walked out."

—Croswell Bowen, *The Curse of the Misbegotten: A Tale of the House of O'Neill*, 1959.

He would not write for the movies, even though the star of Hell's Angels *requested him.*

. . . while in Europe, O'Neill . . . received a cable on behalf of Jean Harlow, explaining that Miss Harlow wanted the best available American dramatist to write a screen-play for her. Would O'Neill please cable back, collect, confining his answer to twenty words. O'Neill cabled: "No No No No No No No No No No No No No No No No No No No O'Neill."

—Bowen.

On his tombstone he requested this inscription:

EUGENE O'NEILL
THERE IS SOMETHING
TO BE SAID
FOR BEING DEAD.

—Sheaffer.

Robert Benchley 1889–1945

He was writer, comedian, newspaper man, and frequenter of the Round Table at the Algonquin. His friend Donald Ogden Stewart wrote The Parody Outline of History.

One day he and Mr. Stewart emerged from Tony's to find it raining. A pedestrian carrying an umbrella came past Tony's doorway, and Mr. Stewart ducked under the man's umbrella, gripped him by the arm, said, "Yale Club, please," and steered his startled victim down the street, leaving Mr. Benchley gaping after him, lost in admiration.

"If drinking can do that for a man," Mr. Benchley mused, "there must be something in it after all."

—John Keats, *You Might As Well Live: The Life and Times of Dorothy Parker,* 1970.

Benchley died of drink. (Someone once warned him that something he was drinking was "slow poison." "So who's in a hurry?" said Benchley.) His satire typically mocked its author.

"It took me fifteen years to discover that I had no talent for writing, but I couldn't give it up because by that time I was too famous."

—*Dictionary of Biographical Quotation,* eds. Richard Kenin and Justin Wintle, 1978.

He conquered writer's block.

Once, he had been trying to start a piece but couldn't get it under way, so he went down the corridor to where a poker game was in progress, just to jolt his mind into starting up. Some time later, he returned to his room, sat down to the clean sheet of paper in the typewriter, and pecked out the words "The." This, he reasoned, was as safe a start as any, and might possibly break the block. But nothing else came, so he went downstairs and ran into a group of Round Table people, with whom he passed a cheerful hour or so. Then, protesting that he had to work, he went back upstairs, where the small, bleak "The" was looking at him out of the expanse of yellow paper. He sat down and stared at it for several minutes, then a sudden idea came to him, and he finished the sentence, making it read "The hell with it," and got up and went happily out for the evening.

—Nathaniel Benchley, *Robert Benchley,* 1955.

He collected books.

. . . over the desk was a five-foot shelf of books that were collected for their titles alone. Over the years, he acquired such items as *Forty Thousand Sublime and Beautiful Thoughts, Success with Small Fruits, Talks on Manure, Keeping a Single Cow, Bicycling for Ladies, The Culture and Diseases of the Sweet Potato, Ailments of the Leg, In and Out with Mary Ann, Perverse Pussys. . . .*

—Benchley.

His drinking became visionary, or he feared that it did.

Late one winter evening, he and a friend were leaving Tony's, and when they got outside a soft, silent snow was falling. Then suddenly, under the Sixth Avenue Elevated, they saw a line of elephants, trunk in tail, padding through the snow, and on the tail of the last elephant hung a red light. Quietly, Robert and his friend turned and went back inside, clutched the edge of the bar, and ordered two double brandies. For a while, neither of them spoke. Then Robert cleared his throat.

"Did you—ah—see anything?" he asked. "Anything out of the ordinary?"

"You mean outside?" his friend said, hopefully.

"Yes," said Robert. "Over toward Sixth Avenue, sort of."

It turned out that what they had seen were the Hippodrome elephants, on their way downtown for a new show. . . .

—Benchley.

His son Nathaniel remembered eating out with his father in Hollywood.

We went to the Trocadero, and he kept looking at himself in every available mirror. When, in the course of events, we left to go home, he went to a uniformed man at the door and said, "Would you get us a taxi, please?"

The man turned, and regarded him icily. "I'm very sorry," he said. "I happen to be a rear admiral in the United States Navy."

"All right, then," said my father. "Get us a battleship."

—Benchley.

George S. Kaufman 1889–1961

Kaufman's one-liners were almost as famous as the plays on which he collaborated, including Of Thee I Sing *(1931),* You Can't Take It with You *(1936), and* The Man Who Came to Dinner *(1939). One story took place in Hollywood.*

On one Sunday evening Kaufman attended a farewell party for Behrman, who was supposedly leaving the next day for New York. At the last minute, Behrman was asked by the studio to do some rewriting, and Kaufman encountered him on the lot. "Ah," said Kaufman, "forgotten but not gone."

—S. N. Behrman, "They Left 'em Laughing," *The New York Times,* Nov. 21, 1965.

Another occurred during a game of cards.

To a partner . . . who asked to be excused to visit the men's room, he replied, "Gladly. For the first time today I'll know what you have in your hand."

—Malcolm Goldstein, *George S. Kaufman,* 1978.

Kaufman wrote plays and later filmscripts for the Marx Brothers. On the stage, they never stuck to their lines. During a tryout in Philadelphia, with Kaufman out of town, his producer attempted to discipline the actors.

Sam Harris came to inspect the proceedings at a matinee and, provoked to irritation by what he witnessed, went backstage to complain to his stars in Groucho's dressing room. Pretending to be irritated in turn, they opened his fly, exposed his male member, and pushed him through the door before he quite knew what had happened.

In New York the brothers continued to take liberties with the script, though there they ran the risk of doing so in front of Kaufman, who made it a practice to drop in on his plays. After one matinee performance at which they had departed from the script, he went backstage to protest. Groucho countered with, "Well, they laughed at Edison, didn't they?" Replied Kaufman, "Not at the Wednesday matinee, they didn't."

—Joe Adamson, *Groucho, Harpo, Chico and Sometimes Zeppo,* 1973.

Kaufman did not espouse the Stanislavsky method.

When the actor, puzzled about a movement recommended to him by Kaufman, asked what should be his motivation for carrying it out, the terse reply was, "Your job."

—Goldstein.

Harold Ross 1892–1951

The founder and editor of The New Yorker *had a long history of association with the man who came to dinner.*

I was in Harold Ross's office one hot day in the middle of August, 1928, when the phone rang, and he turned to it impatiently and said, sourly, to the transmitter, "Yeah? Hi, Aleck. Just a second." He cupped the transmitter with his hand and said, "It's Woollcott. He wants to tell me about the wedding of Charlie MacArthur and Helen Hayes . . . O.K., Aleck, go ahead."

Alexander Woollcott . . . began talking in the fluent, practiced, almost compulsive way he had of telling a story. Ross promptly put the receiver down, gently, on the top of his desk, got up, walked across the room, and began alternately staring out the window and scowling at the jabbering receiver. An unintelligible babble came out of it, a little like the sound track of a Donald Duck animated cartoon. Against this dim and distant monologue, wasted on the office air, Ross set up a counterpoint of disdainful comment. "Listen to that glib son-of-a-bitch," he said. "He thinks he's holding me spellbound. . . ."

—James Thurber, *The Years with Ross,* 1959.

Ross was known for pronouncements.

He said once to a secretary of his, "Never leave me alone with poets."

—Thurber.

Some of his insults were apparently inadvertent.

One afternoon Sherwood Anderson was brought into Ross's office and introduced to the editor. On such occasions, when there was time, Ross was briefed by one of us as to the nature and stature of a visiting author's work—not that it ever did much good. Ross stood in awe and reverence of no writer. He had been through too much with too many of them. I am sure that, after the introduction, he said, "Hi, Anderson," in his large freewheeling way, and then launched into whatever came into his mind. This meeting was notable for one of his reckless literary pronouncements: "There hasn't been a good short story writer in America, Anderson, since O. Henry died."

—Thurber.

His friends were astounded at his gullibility.

Ross had a deep affection for Lardner, as well as great admiration. He once told me, "I asked Lardner the other day how he writes his short stories, and he said he wrote a few widely separated words or phrases on a piece of paper and then went back and filled in the spaces."

—Thurber.

Even his friends never knew quite how to take him.

There were times when it was hard to tell whether Ross was acting on a generous impulse or being defensive. Archibald MacLeish wrote a long poem entitled "The Hamlet of A. MacLeish," and Edmund Wilson wrote a cruel, witty parody of it for *The New Yorker,* which he called "The Omelet of A. MacLeish." Immediately after the parody appeared, MacLeish happened to be having lunch in the Oak Room of the Algonquin. Ross was also in the room, and on leaving it he found that he had to walk past MacLeish's table. Making a curious protective gesture with one arm, he stopped, leaned over MacLeish, and said in a loud voice, "That must have hurt! That must have *hurt*!" To this day, MacLeish is puzzled as to whether Ross, fearing that MacLeish might swing at him, spoke the words out of fear or out of sympathy.

—Brendan Gill, *Here at the New Yorker,* 1975.

Elmer Rice 1892–1967

The playwright recalled making acquaintance with Hollywood.

Several months after the sale of the motion picture rights to *On Trial,* the movie's director, James Young, husband of the famous silent-picture star Clara Kimball Young, called me up. He wanted my opinion of the scenario he had written. Flattered to be consulted by this august personage, for I was still a little in awe of actors, writers and producers, I went to see Young in his room at the Lambs Club—my first visit to that celebrated gathering place of male actors. I listened to his reading in utter astonishment: he had made the crucial revelatory scene of the play into a prologue! When he asked me, with obvious self-satisfaction, what I thought of the scenario, I hardly knew how to answer. I asked if he had seen the play and was not surprised when he said no. Not wanting to come right out and say that he had completely destroyed the suspense, I discoursed, as tactfully as I could, upon the importance of the play's structure. He followed my exposition in sheer amazement. At its conclusion he crossed the room, put his hand on my shoulder and said,

"Say, kid, you had a great idea there!" It was my first contact with the motion picture industry.

—Elmer Rice, *Minority Report*, 1963.

Edna St. Vincent Millay 1892–1950

John Peale Bishop and Edmund Wilson, friends from their Princeton days, shared love for the author of "Renascence."

. . . After dinner, sitting on her day bed, John and I held Edna in our arms—according to an arrangement insisted upon by herself—I her lower half and John her upper—with a polite exchange of pleasantries as to which had the better share.

She referred to us, I was told, as "the choir boys of Hell," and complained that our both being in love with her had not even broken up our friendship.

—Edmund Wilson, *The Twenties*, 1975.

She had perhaps burned her candle at both ends. The last years of her brief life were difficult.

. . . wretched as Edna felt, she made several reading tours, one in California during the summer of 1940. Some of her old friends there got in touch with her, among them Upton Sinclair, who came to the Community Theater at Pasadena when she was scheduled to read. She had known "Uppy" years before, but had seen little of him since her Village days, and greeted him warmly when he came to the dressing room. Eugen [Boissevain, her husband] was with her of course, and the three visited briefly. When it was time for her to go onstage, Sinclair was astonished to see Eugen draw a flask out of his hip pocket and hand it to Edna. She took "a heavy swig" and handed it back. . . . Then she left the dressing room to go into the wings, and "Uppy" went out front to hear her read her poetry. After the performance he returned backstage, and when Edna came off following numerous bows and repeated applause, Eugen brought out the flask again without a word and she drained it.

—Jean Gould, *Edna St. Vincent Millay: The Poet and Her Book*, 1969.

Dorothy Parker 1893–1967

Parker's short stories and poems brought her considerable fame, but her public witticisms—or the insults and wisecracks attributed to her—brought her more.

There was a feud with Clare Boothe Luce, playwright of The Women *(1936) who married* Time's *founder and was elected as a congresswoman from Connecticut. Meeting Parker in a doorway, Luce deferred: "Age before beauty," said she. "Pearls before swine," said Parker as she walked through.*

Edmund Wilson in his book The Twenties *collected a paragraph of Parkerisms.*

When I told her once—what she didn't know—that a former lover of hers had died, a young, good-looking and well-to-do fellow who had suffered from tuberculosis, she said crisply, "I don't see what else he could have done." On one occasion, after the *Vanity Fair* crisis, we ran into Condé Nast in the lobby of the Algonquin. He said that he was going on a cruise: "And, Dorothy, I wish you would come with me." "Oh, I wish I could!"—immediately followed, as soon as Nast had gone on, by "Oh, God, make that ship sink!" She was beglamoured by the idea of Scott Fitzgerald, and I arranged to have her meet him and Zelda. We sat at one of those Algonquin tables, too narrow to have anyone across from you, so that one sat on a bench with one's back to the wall: "This looks like a road company of the Last Supper."

—1975.

George Oppenheimer wrote a successful play featuring a character based on Parker; then Ruth Gordon wrote yet another.

All of which left Dorothy Parker muttering darkly that she wanted to write her autobiography, but was afraid that if she did, "George Oppenheimer and Ruth Gordon would sue me for plagiarism."

—John Keats, *You Might As Well Live: The Life and Times of Dorothy Parker,* 1970.

Maybe her most famous single remark rose to the occasion of the Yale prom: "If all these sweet young things were laid end to end, I wouldn't be the slightest bit surprised."

Many of her wisecracks derived from similar insights. Her biographer recorded her contributions to a conversation.

Dorothy listened, wide-eyed, and at last joined the conversation.

"You know," she murmured, in accents that seemed to breathe nothing but the most worshipful admiration, "that woman speaks eighteen languages? And she can't say 'No' in any of them."

And when the table gossip turned to an actress who had fallen and broken a leg in London, Mrs. Parker seemed distraught.

"Oh, how terrible," she muttered to her neighbor at the table. "She must have done it sliding down a barrister."

At a Hallowe'en party given by newspaper editor Herbert Bayard Swope, she saw people gathered around a washtub, and asked what in the world they were doing.

"They're ducking for apples," someone explained.

She sighed. "There," she murmured, "but for a typographical error, is the story of my life."

—Keats.

For a time she shared a small office with Robert Benchley.

It was said that after Mr. Benchley left she was so lonely (and so desirous of companionship that would give her an excuse not to work) that she had another sign lettered on the door: MEN.

—Keats.

Her husband Alan Campbell died of a drug overdose. A novelist friend remembered Parker as she waited for the coroner. Lillian Hellman told the story.

[Peter] Feibleman was with her when Alan Campbell's body was taken to the coroner's car. (No charge of suicide was ever made.) Among the friends who stood with Dottie on those California steps was Mrs. Jones, a woman who had liked Alan, had pretended to like Dottie, and who had always loved all forms of meddling in other people's troubles. Mrs. Jones said, "Dottie, tell me, dear, what I can do for you."

Dottie said, "Get me a new husband."

There was a silence, but before those who would have laughed could laugh, Mrs. Jones said, "I think that is the most callous and disgusting remark I ever heard in my life."

Dottie turned to look at her, sighed, and said gently, "So sorry. Then run down to the corner and get me a ham and cheese on rye and tell them to hold the mayo."

—*An Unfinished Woman,* 1969.

John P. Marquand 1893–1960

He was Margaret Fuller's great-nephew.

Lacking money in Brahmin Boston, yet married to a Sedgewick, he suffered a social dilemma. He satirized a club he could not afford to join—and when he made money writing fiction joined it.

On one of his early visits to his new club, John Marquand commented to an elderly member that he had heard that old Mr. Sears—whose town residence the gray brick mansion that houses the club had originally been—had required his daughters, when he received them in the drawing room, to walk backward from Mr. Sears' presence when it was time for them to depart. The older member's comment was, "Times have changed since then."

—Stephen Birmingham, *The Late John Marquand,* 1972.

At his estate in the Bahamas Marquand was anecdotal.

John would tell his famous stories seated in a chair beneath an ancient wooden sign which proclaimed, "I am Monarch of All I Survey." Some of John's favorite stories were about his friend Gene Tunney who, for all the roughness of his trade as a prize fighter, had an elegant, almost mincing speaking style of which John was an excellent mimic. "Charming" was a word Tunney used frequently, and John loved to tell of Tunney's account of lunching in Havana one day with Ernest Hemingway, whom Tunney pronounced as "perfectly charming." Hemingway had served, according to Tunney, some "charming martinis," and then, after a "charming" lunch, a great many more "charming martinis" which, as Hemingway downed them, had the effect of making the author somewhat less charming. He became, in fact, quite belligerent. John's version of what happened then went like this:

"Gene told me that Hemingway had these Siamese cats, and that even the cats were drinking martinis. Hemingway would kick off his slippers and scratch the cats' backs, and then he began talking about foul blows in boxing and began to demonstrate them on Gene. Gene said, 'Ernest knows a lot about boxing, but perhaps I know a bit more about it than Ernest. Ed Fink, who was Al Capone's bodyguard, was my teacher. And all of a sudden Ernest came at me and started swinging. He came up and cut me across the lips, and there was blood, and then he jabbed me in the left elbow, I said to Ernest, "Do stop it, please, Ernest," but he kept right on punching. I didn't want to get on the outside—I really pride myself on my in-fighting—and I thought to myself: what Ernest needs is a good little liver punch. There's a little liver punch, and it has to be timed exactly, and when I saw the moment I let him have it. I was a little alarmed, if I do say so! His knees buckled, his face went gray, and I thought he was going to go down. But he didn't, and for the next few hours Ernest was perfectly charming.' "

—Birmingham.

Marquand had a heart attack, then returned to the world he wrote about and lived in.

John was back in his old form, swinging his glass in his hand as he entertained his audience, holding forth on what he called "the lack of taste and reticence" in younger American writers. A few minutes later, he was talking about his weeks in the Newburyport hospital and how, as part of his therapy, an abdominal massage had been prescribed. His nurse, John confided, had whispered to him during the procedure, "How lucky I am to be able to manipulate the lower abdominal muscles of a man like you!"

—Birmingham.

E. E. Cummings 1894–1962

When Cummings was a young man he borrowed his father's car and parked it illegally and indiscreetly. His father was a minister.

One night Cummings was taken by Arthur Wilson down to the area around Scollay Square to visit one Marie Hayes, whose bad reputation was apparently known to the police. Wilson became very drunk, and Cummings departed in search of some oranges to help his friend sober up. While he was gone, the police came upon the Cummings automobile with its clergyman's license plates parked outside Miss Hayes's apartment. They blew its horn to summon the owner, and getting no response, "had it towed away," so the notes read, "to a garage (from which I subsequently got it: cynical remarks, grins, at me, by cops the next morning).". . . The clerk said something to the Judge "about my being young 'we all of us make mistakes' . . . [Judge:] WHAT WERE YOU DOING AT THAT HOUR OF THE MORNING IN THAT APARTMENT (address?)—; answer: 'Why to tell you the truth I was stopping with a sick friend' . . ."

—Richard S. Kennedy, *Dreams in a Mirror,* 1979.

The judge at home was less lenient.

On that night, Marie Hayes, having been told by the police the name of the owner of the automobile that was being towed away, telephoned Edward Cummings at 3 A.M. "Eddie?" she inquired in a somewhat drunken voice and then reported what had happened. When Estlin arrived home, he was met by Edward Cummings standing on the stairs in his pajamas and bathrobe, denouncing him for his keeping such low company. . . . Estlin countered with the argument that Jesus was no snob toward sinners—prostitutes and other unfortunates. He would not submit to being the subject of a sermon. Later in the argument, Edward threatened to throw him out of the house. When Estlin replied, "Go ahead," Edward burst into tears, and in his disillusionment about his son, cried, "I thought I'd given birth to a god!"

—Kennedy.

In Paris with Gilbert Seldes and John Dos Passos, Cummings again fell foul of the law.

Cummings asked the gendarme why he was being arrested, and the gendarme replied, "For pissing on Paris." Cummings pointed out that he had merely pissed on the fiacre. "Le fiacre—

c'est Paris!" exclaimed the gendarme, and took him along—Seldes and Dos Passos following. . . . Seldes overheard this colloquy between the arresting gendarme and the officer behind the desk:

"Un Américain qui pisse."

"Quoi—encore un pisseur Américain?"

Cummings told me the dialogue that took place inside.

"Would you do that in your own country?" asked the officer behind the desk.

"Yes," replied Cummings.

"Menteur!" screamed the sergeant of police.

"Why do you call me a liar?" asked Cummings.

"Because I know about America—I have a relative there."

"Where?"

"In Brook-leen."

Cummings was asked where he lived, and a gendarme went outside to check with Seldes and Dos Passos. When it was found that he had told the truth, he was permitted to leave, but with orders to report to a magistrate the next morning. . . . When Cummings showed up, he was greeted by several hastily drawn posters announcing, "Reprieve Pisseur Américain!"

—Charles Norman, *The Magic Maker, E. E. Cummings,* 1958.

Cummings continued, however, to urinate in public.

. . . Dos Passos and Cummings came down from Paris. With Aragon we went to a restaurant and had a gay dinner with several bottles of wine; then we returned to my studio over the blacksmith shop. I [Malcolm Cowley] made a speech against book fetishism. The burden of it was that wherever I lived books seemed to accumulate; some were bought, some were gifts, some came by mail and others appeared one didn't know how; they moved in like relatives and soon the house was crowded. . . . I went over to the shelves and pulled down an assortment of bad review books and French university texts that I wouldn't need again. After tearing some of them apart I piled them all on the asbestos mat in front of the stove; then I put a match to the pile. It was a gesture in the Dada manner, but not a successful one, for the books merely smoldered. We talked about bad writers while the smoke grew thicker; then Cummings proved that he was a better Dadaist—at least in someone else's studio—by walking over and urinating on the fire.

—Malcolm Cowley, *Exile's Return,* 1934.

Charles Norman visited Cummings in New Hampshire in 1957.

On one of my visits to his farm he suddenly appeared in the doorway of my room, where I was reading by the light of a kerosene lamp. It was two o'clock in the morning; I had retired perhaps an hour before. He said quietly: "Would you like to see a flying saucer?" I leaped up and in pajamas and flopping sandals followed him to the roof.

It was a flat roof with a railing around it, like a captain's walk. Mrs. Cummings was peering through a telescope. Cummings pointed to a bright point in the sky and handed me a pair of binoculars. Another pair was in his hands, and for several minutes we all stood in silence while the dews of the night and the fog that comes on little cat feet crept over my sandals.

It took me some time to adjust the binoculars and find the object at which I was to peer. I saw in the sky, perhaps five or fifteen miles distant, a bright light cradled in a shallow arc shaped like a cigar-end. In the August night thronged with stars the light blazed like a planet; from time to time it whipped downwards a few feet, then soared to its former position. It not only whipped to the right, but sometimes to the left, and this gave me the idea it was some kind of balloon, perhaps a meteorological balloon. I was foolish enough to suggest this, and received for my pains incredulous, star-lit looks from both Cummings and his wife, who thereupon returned to their saucer-gazing, disregarding me. After a while, the dews and the damp had gone above my sandals, and I decided to call it a night.

I did not know until the next morning that I had gone to bed disgraced. The subject came up at breakfast, and I stuck to my view: it was a meteorological balloon.

Did I agree it did not look like any balloon I had hitherto seen?

Yes—I had to agree to that.

"There you are," Cummings said.

I had the feeling that he and his wife were seeing me in a new light—Charles obtuse, Charles a little slow on the uptake.

And this unnerved me. I said: "What do *you* think it was, if not meteorological instruments?"

Cummings replied: "Little men from another planet."

—Charles Norman, *Poets & People,* 1972.

Dashiell Hammett 1894–1961

Lillian Hellman wrote of Hammett

I remember: Hammett and I are having breakfast with friends in the country, served on one of those ugly bar arrangements with high stools. Hammett is teasing me. He tells about a hunting trip when, in an attempt to aim at a high-flying duck, I had hit a wild lilac bush. He is saying that I have no sense of direction about anything.

I say, "Don't count on it. I could spit in your eye if I wanted to. How much says I can't do it?"

"The Jap prints," he says, meaning a rare set of Japanese art books he has just bought and loves, "fifty dollars, and anything you want to say to me for a whole week."

I spit directly into his eye and the daughter of the family screams. Hammett had a quiet laugh that began slowly and then creased his face for a long time. It begins now and is increased by the perplexed, unhappy looks of the others at the table. He says, proudly, "That's my girl. Some of the time the kid kicks through."

Many years later, unhappy about his drinking, his ladies, my life with him, I remember an angry speech I made one night: it had to do with injustice, his carelessness, his insistence that he get his way, his sharpness with me but not with himself. I was drunk, but he was drunker, and when my strides around the room carried me close to the chair where he was sitting, I stared in disbelief at what I saw. He was grinding a burning cigarette into his cheek.

I said, "What are you doing?"

"Keeping myself from doing it to you," he said.

—*An Unfinished Woman,* 1969.

He gave up drinking but not stubbornness.

In 1951 he went to jail because he and two other trustees of the bail bond fund of the Civil Rights Congress refused to reveal the names of the contributors to the fund. The truth was that Hammett had never been in the office of the Congress, did not know the name of a single contributor.

The night before he was to appear in court, I said, "Why don't you say that you don't know the names?"

"No," he said, "I can't say that."

—Hellman.

James Thurber 1894–1961

Thurber worked in Paris for the local edition of the Chicago Tribune. *His editor asked him to supply small items to fill blanks at the ends of columns.*

The only one I remember went like this, with a Washington date line: " 'A man who does not pray is not a praying man,' President Coolidge today told the annual convention of the Protestant Churches of America."

—Burton Bernstein, *Thurber,* 1975.

Working for an American paper on the Riviera, he invented social notes from all over.

. . . a gay and romantic cavalcade, indeed, infested the littoral of our imagination. "Lieutenant General and Mrs. Pendleton Gray Winslow," we would write, "have arrived at their villa, Heart's Desire, on Cap d'Antibes; bringing with them their prize Burmese monkey, Thibault." Or "The Hon. Mr. Stephen H. L. Atterbury, Chargé-d'Affaires of the American Legation in Peru, and Mrs. Atterbury, the former Princess Ti Ling of Thibet, are motoring to Monte Carlo from Aix-en-Provence, where they have been visiting Mr. Atterbury's father, Rear Admiral A. Watson Atterbury, U.S.N., retired. Mr. Stephen Atterbury is the breeder of the famous Schnauzer-Pincher, Champion Adelbert von Weigengrosse of Tamerlane, said to be valued at $15,000."

—Bernstein.

Even when old and blind he stuck to his habits.

He had an affair with a *New Yorker* secretary, but his blindness made for tactical problems. He had to rely on one of the magazine's office boys to lead him about; as his run of bad luck would have it, the office boy assigned to him was eighteen-year-old Truman Capote. "I worked as a boy in the Art Department then," Capote recalled, "and one of my jobs was to take Thurber to his girlfriend's apartment. She was as ugly as sin, so it served him right. I would have to wait for him at the apartment till he was finished, and then I'd dress him. He could undress by himself but he couldn't dress by himself, couldn't even cross the street by himself. Now since Helen Thurber would dress him in the morning, she knew how he looked. Well, one time I put his socks on the wrong side out, and when he got home, I gather Helen asked him a lot of questions. The next day, Thurber was furious at me—he said I did it on purpose. . . ."

—Bernstein.

Ben Hecht 1894–1964

Working for the Chicago Daily Journal, *Hecht was told to "go out and pick up a story."*

I recall also the story of the Runaway Streetcar. A motorman had fainted at his controls, and his streetcar, filled with screaming passengers, had hurtled wildly through the streets. I remember Gene [Cour's] photograph of terrified pedestrians waving their arms at a passing streetcar, and I remember the "staging" of the picture. It had involved an outlay of five dollars. I am unable either to recall or to figure out now in what manner I made this fantastic lie sound plausible enough to be accepted as news, how or with what data and witnesses I could have backed it up. But I remember it in print on the front page. And I remember Mr. Hutchens, ever loyal to his staff, defending me a little incoherently against an outraged representative of the traction company, come to demand apologies and denials:

"Your organization, sir, is already in sufficiently bad odor with its grafted franchises and boodle politics." Mr. Hutchens' bloodshot eyes flashed at the traction mogul. "I advise you not to add to your crimes that of libel against the press. And in conclusion I can tell you, I would rather take the word of any of my reporters than the sworn testimony of all the millionaires of Chicago."

—Ben Hecht, *A Child of the Century,* 1954.

He made up everything.

Another of my stories was flashed on the city in a seven-column front-page headline: "Earthquake Rips Chicago." A four-column cut of a great fissure opened by the quake on the Lincoln Park beach accompanied the story. Gene and I had spent two hours digging the fissure. There was other corroboration—housewives who reported dishes spilled from pantry shelves and broken, stenographers who reported the top of the Masonic Temple to have swayed dangerously, and several male citizens who had been thrown to the ground by the impact of the quake while at work in their shops. These were, of course, all my relatives, this time with their true names and addresses attached. For several days, during which an angry rival press sought to belittle the *Journal*'s great scoop of the earth's upheaval, my aunts, uncles and cousins stood firm in their memories of terror and shock.

—Hecht.

In Hollywood Hecht wrote a movie for Howard Hughes.

The work I did for Hughes was a movie called *Scarface.* News that it was a biographical study of Al Capone brought two Capone henchmen to Hollywood to make certain that nothing derogatory about the great gangster reached the screen. The two henchmen called on me at my hotel. It was after midnight. They entered the room as ominously as any pair of movie gangsters, their faces set in scowls and guns bulging their coats. They had a copy of my *Scarface* script in their hands. Their dialogue belonged in it.

"You the guy who wrote this?" I said I was.

"We read it." I inquired how they had liked it.

"We wanna ask you some questions." I invited them to go ahead.

"Is this stuff about Al Capone?"

"God, no," I said. "I don't even know Al."

"Never met him, huh?"

I pointed out I had left Chicago just as Al was coming into prominence.

"I knew Jim Colisimo pretty well," I said.

"That so?"

"I also knew Mossy Enright and Pete Gentleman."

"That so? Did you know Deanie?"

"Deanie O'Banion? Sure. I used to ride around with him in his flivver. I also knew Barney."

"Which Barney?"

"Barney Grogan—Eighteenth Ward," I said.

A pause.

"O.K., then. We'll tell Al this stuff you wrote is about them other guys."

They started out and halted in the doorway, worried again.

"If this stuff ain't about Al Capone, why are you callin' it *Scarface?* Everybody'll think it's him."

"That's the reason," I said. "Al is one of the most famous and fascinating men of our time. If we call the movie *Scarface,* everybody will want to see it, figuring it's about Al. That's part of the racket we call showmanship."

My visitors pondered this, and one of them finally said, "I'll tell Al." A pause. "Who's this fella Howard Hughes?"

"He's got nothing to do with anything," I said, speaking truthfully at last. "He's the sucker with the money."

—Hecht.

He also worked with David Selznick.

After three weeks' shooting of *Gone With the Wind,* David had decided his script was no good and that he needed a new story and a new director. The shooting had been stopped and the million-dollar cast was now sitting by collecting its wages in idleness.

The three of us arrived at the Selznick studio a little after sunrise. We had settled on my wages on the way over. I was to receive fifteen thousand dollars for the week's work, and no matter what happened I was not to work longer than a week. I knew in advance that two weeks of such toil as lay ahead might be fatal.

Four Selznick secretaries who had not yet been to sleep that night staggered in with typewriters, paper and a gross of pencils. Twenty-four-hour work shifts were quite common under David's baton. David himself sometimes failed to go to bed for several nights in a row. He preferred to wait till he collapsed on his office couch. Medication was often necessary to revive him.

David was outraged to learn I had not read *Gone With the Wind,* but decided there was no time for me to read the long novel. The Selznick overhead on the idle *Wind* stages was around fifty thousand dollars a day. David announced that he knew the book by heart and that he would brief me on it. For the next hour I listened to David recite its story. I had seldom heard a more involved plot. My verdict was that nobody could make a remotely sensible movie out of it. Fleming, who was reputed to be part Indian, sat brooding at his own council fires. I asked him if he had been able to follow the story David had told. He said no. I suggested then that we make up a new story, to which David replied with violence that every literate human in the United States except me had read Miss Mitchell's book, and we would have to stick to it. I argued that surely in two years of preparation someone must have wangled a workable plot out of Miss Mitchell's Ouïdalike flight into the Civil War. David suddenly remembered the first "treatment," discarded three years before. It had been written by Sidney Howard, since dead. After an hour of searching, a lone copy of Howard's work was run down in an old safe. David read it aloud. We listened to a precise and telling narrative of *Gone With the Wind.*

We toasted the dead craftsman and fell to work. Being privy to the book, Selznick and Fleming discussed each of Howard's scenes and informed me of the habits and general psychology of the characters. They also acted out the scenes, David specializing in the parts of Scarlet and her drunken father and Vic playing Rhett Butler and a curious fellow I could never understand called Ashley. He was always forgiving his beloved Scarlet for betraying him with another of his rivals. David insisted that he was a typical Southern gentleman and refused flatly to drop him out of the movie.

After each scene had been discussed and performed, I sat down at the typewriter and wrote it out. Selznick and Fleming, eager to continue with their acting, kept hurrying me. We worked in this fashion for seven days, putting in eighteen to twenty hours a day. Selznick refused to let us eat lunch, arguing that food would slow us up. He provided bananas and salted peanuts. On the fourth day a blood vessel in Fleming's right eye broke, giving him more of an Indian look than ever. On the fifth day Selznick toppled into a torpor while chewing on a banana. The wear and tear on me was less, for I had been able to lie on the couch and half doze while the two darted about acting. Thus on the seventh day I had completed, unscathed, the first nine reels of the Civil War epic.

—Hecht.

Hecht was available as a consultant to Hollywood, supplying advice on the mores of the American natives.

I remember a phone call to Nyack from the M-G-M Studio in Hollywood. Bernie Hyman, then the studio head, wished my help on a plot problem that had arisen in a two-million-dollar movie being prepared for shooting.

"I won't tell you the plot," he said. "I'll just give you what we're up against. The hero and heroine fall madly in love with each other—as soon as they meet. What we need is some gimmick that keeps them from going to bed right away. Not a physical gimmick like arrest or getting run over and having to go to the hospital. But a purely psychological one. Now what reasons do you know that would keep a healthy pair of lovers from hitting the hay in Reel Two?"

I answered that frequently a girl has moral concepts that keep her virtuous until after a trip to the altar. And that there are men also who prefer to wait for coitus until they have married the girl they adore.

"Wonderful!" said the Metro head of production. "We'll try it."

—Hecht.

Edmund Wilson 1895–1972

Wilson was a man of letters who published poetry, fiction, and drama as well as essays on history, society, language, and literature. A forbidding figure to many, his nickname, "Bunny," seemed to hint at another side.

"Dos Passos had a vivid memory of first meeting Edmund in 1922 in the offices of *Vanity Fair*, 'a slight sandy-haired young man with a handsome clear profile. He wore a formal dark business suit.' While waiting for the elevator, 'Bunny gave an accent to the occasion by turning, with a perfectly straight face, a neat somersault.' "

—Edmund Wilson, *The Twenties*, 1975.

In order to make quick work of his mail, he printed a card on which he could check the appropriate category.

Edmund Wilson regrets that it is impossible for him to:

READ MANUSCRIPTS,

WRITE ARTICLES OR BOOKS TO ORDER,

WRITE FOREWORDS OR INTRODUCTIONS,

MAKE STATEMENTS FOR PUBLICITY PURPOSES,

DO ANY KIND OF EDITORIAL WORK,

JUDGE LITERARY CONTESTS,

GIVE INTERVIEWS,

CONDUCT EDUCATIONAL COURSES,

DELIVER LECTURES,

GIVE TALKS OR MAKE SPEECHES,

BROADCAST OR APPEAR ON TELEVISION,

TAKE PART IN WRITERS' CONGRESSES,

ANSWER QUESTIONNAIRES,

CONTRIBUTE TO OR TAKE PART IN SYMPOSIUMS OR "PANELS" OF ANY KIND,

CONTRIBUTE MANUSCRIPTS FOR SALES,

DONATE COPIES OF HIS BOOKS TO LIBRARIES,

AUTOGRAPH BOOKS FOR STRANGERS,

ALLOW HIS NAME TO BE USED ON LETTERHEADS,

SUPPLY PERSONAL INFORMATION ABOUT HIMSELF,

SUPPLY PHOTOGRAPHS OF HIMSELF,

SUPPLY OPINIONS ON LITERARY OR OTHER SUBJECTS.

—Brendan Gill, *Here at the New Yorker*, 1975.

Wilson had no use for small talk. Harvard friends gave a party for him when he wintered in Cambridge the first time; when they asked if he had enjoyed it, he answered, "Yes. Never do it again."

Alfred Kazin described him at Cape Cod.

Wilson's arrival on the Wellfleet beach regularly caused a stir. . . . He sat without ease; he scooped up a handful of sand and let it drift slowly through his half-clenched fist as people running out of the water gathered around him only to run back into the water. So many staring, giggling, and deadly scrutinizers, guessing that he was "someone," made him nervous, but he unhappily sat on, unable to make his escape. So he talked. He talked as if he were reluctant to talk but too stubborn to stop. He talked as if talking were a physical difficulty forced upon him by a disagreeable world. . . .

"My dear boy," he had greeted me on the beach the week before, "have I given you my lecture on Hungarian? No? Then sit down and listen." There was also this new book on magic. He was very proud of his magician's lore and often set out to do tricks that did not always succeed. He was too distracted. At Rachel's birthday party one summer, he came with his equipment and disappeared into the lean-to searching for newspapers he said he needed for his act. Time passed, no Edmund. We looked in and found him absorbedly reading one of the newspapers.

—Alfred Kazin, *New York Jew,* 1978.

His friendship with Vladimir Nabokov disintegrated in a public battle of letters to the New York Review of Books *after Wilson had corrected Nabokov's Russian in his review of Nabokov's translation and edition of Pushkin's* Eugene Onegin.

In their relationship Wilson seems often to have chosen to play the Russian; Nabokov, the American. When Nabokov visited Wilson at Stamford, Connecticut, in 1942 . . . they went for a long stroll during which Wilson initiated the conversation by asking whether or not Nabokov believed in God. "Do you?" Nabokov replied. "What a strange question!" muttered Wilson.

—Andrew Field, *Nabokov: His Life in Part,* 1977.

John Dos Passos 1896–1970

In his journal, Edmund Wilson remembered Dos Passos.

Cummings and Dos Passos. They had once taken a trip to Spain together. When we got to a town, Cummings said, I'd want to go out to the square or somewhere to see if I could find something [he meant a girl]. Dos would never go with me—he'd say, "I'll just stay here in the hotel, I think." One day I said to him. "Dos: don't you ever think about women?" No. "Don't you ever dream about sex?" No. What I went through with that man! He'd wake me up in the night groaning and throwing himself around in his sleep. I'd say, "What's the matter, Dos?" He'd say, "Why, I thought there were some beautiful wild swans flying overhead." One day I said, "You know, sometimes sex appears in dreams in very much disguised forms. You may be dreaming about sex without knowing it. Tell me one of your dreams—what did you dream about last night, for example?" He said, "Why, I dweamed I had a bunch of aspawagus and I was twying to give it to you." This had evidently stopped Cummings in his tracks.

—*The Twenties,* 1975.

F. Scott Fitzgerald 1896–1940

Fitzgerald and Edmund Wilson were classmates at Princeton.

After the success of This Side of Paradise *(1920), and his marriage to Zelda, Fitzgerald lived a continual party.*

In April they went to Princeton to "chaperon" houseparties. "We were there three days," Fitzgerald wrote a friend. "Zelda and five men in Harvey Firestone's car and not one of us drew a sober breath. . . . It was the damndest party ever held in Princeton & every one in the University will agree." Zelda, whom Fitzgerald introduced all around as his mistress, turned cartwheels down Prospect Street and came to breakfast at Cottage with a demi-john of applejack, which she poured over the omelets to make *omelettes flambées.* . . .

Around New York he remained the incorrigible undergraduate. He and Zelda surrendered to impulses which wouldn't even have occurred to more prosaic souls. The two of them taking hands after a Carnegie Hall concert and running like the wind—like two young hawks—down crowded 57th Street, in and out of traffic. Scott doing handstands in the Biltmore lobby because he hadn't been in the news that week, and, as Oscar Wilde said, the only thing worse than being talked about is being forgotten. Scott and Zelda at the theater sitting quietly during the funny parts and roaring when the house was still. Scott whimsically divesting himself of coat, vest and shirt in the sixth row of the *Scandals,* and being helped out by a posse of ushers. Scott and Zelda going to a party, one of them on the roof of the taxi and the other on the hood.

After one of their brawls they framed a set of house rules which were only partly facetious. Item: "Visitors are requested not to break down doors in search of liquor, even when authorized to do so by the host and hostess." Item: "Week-end guests are respectfully notified that invitations to stay over Monday, issued by the host and hostess during the small hours of Sunday morning, must not be taken seriously."

—Andrew Turnbull, *F. Scott Fitzgerald, a Biography,* 1962.

Van Wyck Brooks attended a dinner party.

". . . Fitzgerald and Zelda, his wife, arriving an hour late when the others had finished, sitting at table fell asleep over the soup that was brought in, for they had spent the two previous nights at parties. So Scott Fitzgerald said as he awoke for a moment, while someone gathered Zelda up, with her bright cropped hair and diaphanous gown, and dropped her on a bed in a room near by. There she lay curled and asleep like a silky kitten. Scott slumbered in the living-room waking up suddenly again to telephone an order for two cases of champagne, together with a fleet of taxis to take us to a nightclub. That moment and scene bring back now a curious note of the twenties that one did not connect with insanity and tragedy then, while I was drawn to the Scott Fitzgeralds, whom I never really knew but who seemed to me, so obviously, romantic lovers."

—Turnbull.

In France they were friends with Sara and Gerald Murphy, whom Fitzgerald later used as models for characters in Tender Is the Night.

Once when the four of them were driving to Les Halles, Fitzgerald, who didn't much care for the color of the old market, created a little color of his own by chewing hundred franc notes (the equivalent of twenty-dollar bills) and spitting them out the taxi window. "Oh Scott, they're so dirty!" Sara protested, but Fitzgerald went right on. Finally the driver could stand it no longer. Stopping the cab, he ran back to retrieve some of the money. Fitzgerald jumped into the driver's seat and headed for the Seine, saying he was going to plunge them into it. As he came to one of the ramps, they managed to get the wheel away from him and return it to the terrified driver who came flapping up behind them in his long coat.

Another time Fitzgerald stole a *tri-porteur*—a three-wheeled delivery wagonette—and scooted crazily around the Place de la Concorde while policemen whistled and motorists swore. If anyone could control him, it was Murphy, for Scott stood in awe of Gerald's unfailing propriety. Once when they were leaving a nightclub, Scott slipped to the floor and pretended to pass out. "Scott," said Gerald, "this is *not* Princeton and I am *not* your roommate. Get up!" Fitzgerald obeyed.

—Turnbull.

Morley Callaghan and his wife visited Fitzgerald in Paris, and Fitzgerald read aloud to them a passage from Hemingway's A Farewell to Arms. *Callaghan expressed reservations. "If you're not impressed, it's all right, Morley," said Fitzgerald looking injured.*

Then I became aware that he was nodding to himself, as if agreeing with himself, not with me. Leaning forward, his face suddenly pale, he said, "Let's have lunch tomorrow, Morley."

"I'd be glad to have lunch," I said. Perhaps I should have expressed more warmth and enthusiasm, but his tone and his pallor now worried me. The way he watched me began to make me feel unhappy.

"Whom would you like to have lunch with us?" he asked mildly, his head on one side.

"It doesn't matter, Scott."

"Clive Bell, the art critic, is in town. Do you know his work?"

"I've read his book."

"No," he said, pondering and still watching me intently. "No, I don't think he impresses you enough."

"I'd like to meet him, if you'd like to have him along," I said, laughing awkwardly. In a swift glance at my wife I saw she was as uneasy as I was. In our hurt embarrassment we both waited. Though Scott had an awful pallor, and I knew he was getting drunk, he smiled sweetly, his head on one side again, as he considered some grave problem. "No, I don't think Clive Bell impresses you, Morley," he said, with his deceptive smile. Then half to himself, "Who does impress you, Morley?"

My face began to burn, and my wife, stiffening, sat helplessly on the edge of her chair, no doubt remembering all I had told her about Scott. With her eyes she was pleading with me to go. But before I could speak, stand up, make the necessary polite little remarks, Scott himself stood up slowly. "Would this impress you, Morley?" he asked sweetly.

Suddenly he got down on his knees, put his head on the floor and tried to stand on his head.

—Morley Callaghan, *That Summer in Paris,* 1963.

It was Fitzgerald who had Hemingway brought to the attention of his editor, at Scribner's, Max Perkins.

Hemingway told this story in his posthumous memoir, A Moveable Feast.

Much later, in the time after Zelda had what had then called her first nervous breakdown and we happened to be in Paris at the same time, Scott asked me to have lunch with him at Michaud's restaurant on the corner of the rue Jacob and the rue des Saints-Pères. He said he had something very important to ask me that meant more than anything in the world to him and that I must answer absolutely truly. . . .

Finally when we were eating the cherry tart and had a last carafe of wine he said, "You know I never slept with anyone except Zelda."

"No, I didn't."

"I thought I had told you."

"No. You told me a lot of things but not that."

"That is what I have to ask you about."

"Good. Go on."

"Zelda said that the way I was built I could never make any woman happy and that was what upset her originally. She said it was a matter of measurements. I have never felt the same since she said that and I have to know truly."

"Come out to the office," I said.

"Where is the office?"

"Le water," I said.

We came back into the room and sat down at the table.

"You're perfectly fine," I said. "You are O.K. There's nothing wrong with you. You look at yourself from above and you look foreshortened. Go over to the Louvre and look at the people in the statues and then go home and look at yourself in the mirror in profile."

"Those statues may not be accurate."

"They are pretty good. Most people would settle for them"

"But why would she say it?"

"To put you out of business. That's the oldest way in the world of putting people out of business. Scott, you asked me to tell you the truth and I can tell you a lot more but this is the absolute truth and all you need. You could have gone to see a doctor."

"I didn't want to. I wanted you to tell me truly."

"Now do you believe me?"

"I don't know," he said.

"Come on over to the Louvre," I said. "It's just down the street and across the river."

We went over to the Louvre and he looked at the statues but still he was doubtful about himself.

"It is not basically a question of the size in repose," I said. "It is the size that it becomes. It is also a question of angle." I explained to him about using a pillow and a few other things that might be useful for him to know.

"There is one girl," he said, "who has been very nice to me. But after what Zelda said—"

"Forget what Zelda said," I told him. "Zelda is crazy. There's nothing wrong with you. Just have confidence and do what the girl wants. Zelda just wants to destroy you."

"You don't know anything about Zelda."

—Ernest Hemingway, *A Moveable Feast,* 1964.

With their money gone, and the Depression at its height, the Fitzgeralds returned to the United States where Zelda spent most of her time in a series of insane asylums. Malcolm Cowley visited them while Zelda was home with a nurse.

Her face was emaciated and twitched as she talked. Her mouth, with deep lines above it, fell into unhappy shapes. Her skin in the lamplight looked brown and weatherbeaten, except that on the left cheek there were four parallel red streaks where she had raked it with her fingernails, so that she made me think of a starved Indian in war paint.

After we said good night to her, Scott installed me in a worn green armchair, the only one in the living room. On the table beside me he put a pint of whiskey from his bootlegger. It was all mine, he said, since he wasn't drinking. He went out to the kitchen for a glass of water. . . .

He stood in front of me holding his glass. "That girl had everything," he said. "She was the belle of Montgomery, the daughter of the chief justice of the Alabama Supreme Court. We met at the governor's ball. Everybody in Alabama and Georgia knew about her, everybody that counted. She had beauty, talent, family, she could do anything she wanted to, and she's thrown it all away."

"That sounds like something from one of your own stories," I said.

"Sometimes I don't know whether Zelda isn't a character that I created myself. And you know, she's cuckoo, she's crazy as a loon. I'm madly in love with her. Excuse me for a moment, I'm thirsty tonight."

Scott disappeared again; I heard the door slam and the faucet squeak. When he came back he started talking about himself and his family background. "I have a streak of pure vulgarity that I like to cultivate. One side of me is peasant and one aristocratic. My mother was a rich peasant, Molly McQuillan. She kept telling me, 'All this family is a lot of shit. You have to know where the money is coming from.' She was as realistic as Karl Marx. I've been reading him; Bunny Wilson made me do it. My father belonged to the same Baltimore family as Francis Scott Key. What if they tore down the monument to the author of 'The Star Spangled Banner' and instead built one for me because I died for communism—a monument to the author of *The Great Gatsby?*" He looked down at me in the armchair and said almost shyly, "What did you think of *Gatsby?*"

I hadn't read *Gatsby* at the time, although I had admired Fitzgerald's stories in *The Saturday Evening Post,* which most of my literary friends regarded as beneath their notice. He didn't want to talk about the stories, except to boast of how much he was paid for them—$4000 each, at his best rate. "I'm a professional," he said. "I know when to write and when to stop writing. But wait till you read my new novel." . . .

We went back to the living room. Some time later his mood changed, I suspect because he had been brooding over my confession that I hadn't read *The Great Gatsby.* "I tell you Max Perkins of Scribner's is a real man," he said truculently. "You don't know he's a real man. If you don't know that, you don't know anything." Sitting on a stool he leaned forward, bringing his face close to mine, so that I felt like a criminal being examined by the district attorney. "What do you know anyway?" he asked as if for the benefit of a jury. "What do you know about people? What do you know about writing? Did you ever write a book half as good as *The Great Gatsby?* I tell you that's a book you can't touch." He paused, and a moment later his face broke into a bad-boyish smile. "You know this water I've been drinking?" he said, raising the glass. "It's only half water. The other half is grain alcohol."

I wanted to say "Surprise!"

—Malcolm Cowley, *The Dream of the Golden Mountains,* 1979.

In Hollywood at a party one night Scott and Zelda collected all the women's purses and boiled them. Later that same night, with Reginald Simpson and James Montgomery Flagg, they went looking for a writer named John Monk Saunders, whom Zelda considered too popular with women. Flagg told about it.

At last we stopped at the foot of a tall hill and Reg and I decided to let the Fitzgeralds get out and climb up to see if it really happened to be the right place. We thought we'd prefer having the pants bitten off the Fitzgeralds by a possible bulldog. They found Saunders in and called down to us. It was okay and we climbed up through the Jap garden to the house where

Saunders was in his pajamas and a Sulka dressing robe and sandals; smiling imperturbably and getting drinks as if nothing surprised him. He turned on his phonograph and we set about chatting, with the exception of Mrs. F., who in prowling around found a pair of editor's shears and then sat down next to Saunders on a lounge, pulled open his robe and took a deep inhalation, then called:

"Scott, come here. John smells lovely!"

Scott went over and sat on the other side of Saunders and they buried their noses in his manly chest. They sighed luxuriously. Nothing fazed Saunders. Then Mrs. F. remembered the shears and began gently urging her host to let her perform a quick operation on him, explaining with quiet eloquence that his earthly troubles would be over if he would submit. Saunders "firmly but politely" declined emasculation.

—Aaron Lathem, *Crazy Sundays,* 1971.

In 1936 Hemingway published "The Snows of Kilimanjaro," in which a dying novelist remembered an old friend:

> *The rich were dull and they drank too much, or they played too much backgammon. They were dull and they were repetitious. He remembered poor Scott Fitzgerald and his romantic awe of them and how he had started a story once that began, "The very rich are different from you and me." And how someone had said to Scott, Yes, they have more money. But that was not humorous to Scott. He thought they were a special glamorous race and when he found they weren't it wrecked him just as much as any other thing that wrecked him.*

When Fitzgerald read the story he wrote Hemingway in protest. In later printings of the story "Scott Fitzgerald" became "Julian."

In 1938 Fitzgerald went to the house of Frederick and Florence March for a special showing of Hemingway's film, The Spanish Earth. *Lillian Hellman told the story.*

When we left the Marches, Dorothy Parker asked a few of us to her house for a nightcap. (She had known Ernest for many years, and while they didn't like each other, the night was pleasant enough to make both of them affectionate.) I had met Scott Fitzgerald years before in Paris, but I had not seen him again until that night and I was shocked by the change in his face and manner. He hadn't seemed to recognize me and so I was surprised and pleased when he asked if I would ride with him to Dottie's. My admiration for Fitzgerald's work was very great, and I looked forward to talking to him alone. But we didn't talk: he was occupied with driving at ten or twelve miles an hour down Sunset Boulevard, a dangerous speed in most places, certainly in Beverly Hills. Fitzgerald crouched over the wheel when cars honked at us, we jerked to the right and then to the left, and passing drivers leaned out to shout at us. I could not bring myself to speak, or even to look at Fitzgerald, but when I saw that his hands were trembling on the wheel, all my rides from Metro came rushing back, and I put my hand over his hand. He brought the car to the side of the road and I told him about my old job at Metro, the awful rides home, my fears of California drivers, until he patted my arm several times and then I knew he hadn't been listening and had different troubles.

He said, "You see, I'm on the wagon. I'll take you to Dottie's but I don't want to go in."

When we finally got to Dottie's, he came around to open the door for me. He said softly, "It's a long story, Ernest and me.". . .

I said, "But Dottie wants to see you. Everybody in that room wants to meet you."

He shook his head and smiled. "No, I'm riding low now."

"Not for writers, nor will you ever. *The Great Gatsby* is the best. . . ."

He smiled and touched my shoulder. "I'm afraid of Ernest, I guess, scared of being sober when. . . ."

I said, "Don't be. He could never like a good writer, certainly not a better one. Come. You'll have a nice time."

I put out my hand and, after a second, he smiled and took it. We went into the hall and turned left to the living room. Nobody saw us come in because the four or five people in the room were all turned toward Ernest, who stood with his back to the door, facing the fireplace. I don't know why he did it, or what had gone on before, but as we started into the room, Hemingway threw his highball glass against the stone fireplace. Fitzgerald and I stopped dead at the sound of the smashing glass: he stepped back into the hall and turned to leave, but I held his arm and he followed me through a swinging door as if he didn't know or care where he was going. Dottie and Hammett were in the kitchen. . . .

I said, "Ernest just threw a glass."

Dottie said, "Certainly," as she kissed Fitzgerald.

—*An Unfinished Woman,* 1969.

Fitzgerald lived with Sheilah Graham in Hollywood where he was an unsuccessful screenwriter.

One night Fitzgerald came home to Sheilah as happy as if he had been drinking, but he hadn't. He had seen an advertisement in the *Los Angeles Times:* The Pasadena Playhouse was going to première a new play based on F. Scott Fitzgerald's "A Diamond as Big as the Ritz." He called the Playhouse and asked them to reserve two seats "somewhere near the back." Then he ordered a limousine and chauffeur; this event was too showy for his bouncy Ford. Sheilah wore a gray and crimson evening gown; Scott had on his tuxedo. They could have been on their way to one of the debutante parties which the younger Fitzgerald immortalized.

When they reached the Playhouse, there were no crowds in front of the theatre. Fitzgerald wondered if it could be the wrong night and went off to find out. When he returned, he said, "It's the students—they're giving the play in the upstairs hall." The two first-nighters, dressed for box seats and velvet chairs, sat on wooden benches at the back of the hall, once again alone. Just before curtain time about a dozen students wandered in, the girls in skirts and slacks, the boys without ties.

Scott laughed all through the play and at the end decided, "I'm going backstage. It might encourage them to know the author came to see them." The young actors could not hide the fact that they were surprised to see Fitzgerald—they had assumed that he was dead.

—Lathem.

Louise Bogan 1897–1970

Bogan was born in Maine and spent most of her life in New York City, writing elegantly formed lyrics and reviewing poetry for The New Yorker.

In a letter to Edmund Wilson, Bogan at thirty-eight wrote about a love affair with a young poet.

I, myself, have been made to bloom like a Persian rose-bush, by the enormous love-making of a cross between a Brandenburger and a Pomeranian, one Theodore Roethke by name. He is very, very large (6 ft. 2 and weighing 218 lbs) and he writes very very small lyrics. 26 years old and a frightful tank. We have poured rivers of liquor down our throats, these last three days, and, in between, have indulged in such bearish and St. Bernardish antics as I have never before experienced. . . . Well! Such goings on! A woman of my age! He is amusing, when not too far gone in liquor; he once won a ΦBK and he has just been kicked out of Lafayette, from his position of instructor in English. He is just a ripple on time's stream, really, because he is soon going to Michigan . . . —I hope that one or two immortal lyrics will come out of all this tumbling about.

—*What the Woman Lived: Selected Letters of Louise Bogan, 1920–1970*, ed. Ruth Limmer, 1973.

William Faulkner 1897–1962

When William Faulkner was a special student at Ole Miss, he was loathe to speak in class. A Professor in an English class therefore asked him directly: "Mr. Faulkner, what did Shakespeare have in mind when he put those words in the mouth of Othello?"

"How should I know?" said Faulkner.

In 1921 he accepted employment as postmaster at the University of Mississippi post office. He was perhaps the worst postmaster in the history of the profession. He sat writing at the back of the post office, as far from the service windows as he could station himself. While customers waited to buy stamps, he continued to write, striving to withhold attention. Sometimes if they rapped loudly on the window with a coin he would arise and serve them grumpily. When he was not writing, he was entertaining. His friends were welcomed to the post office for coffee and games of bridge and to read the boxholders' magazines which Faulkner kept on a table in what he called the Reading Room.

On December 2, 1924, a postal inspector from Corinth, Mississippi, forwarded a series of "charges" including "neglects official duties," "mistreatment of mail," and "indifferent to interests of patrons." It was alleged in support of these charges that "you mistreat mail of all classes, including registered mail; that you have thrown mail with return postage guaranteed and all other classes into the garbage can by the side entrance . . ."; and, "some patrons have gone to this garbage can to get their magazines. . . ."

In 1929 he married Estelle, an old sweetheart, after she divorced her first husband; in 1936 he ran a classified ad disclaiming responsibility for any debts she had incurred. Money and drinking were continual family problems. When his daughter Jill begged him not to get drunk, he asked her who ever heard of Shakespeare's child.

He wrote Hollywood scripts to improve his finances and kept on drinking.

One category of stories concerns Faulkner's drinking, and these are told with some awe and implied admiration:

—the time he attended a polo match, drank too much, borrowed a polo pony and rode it onto the field, fell off, and woke up "starin' right into Darryl Zanuck's teeth bendin' over me" (so he is quoted). "It was such a feelin' of horror that I became instantly sober."

—The time they cleaned out his office after he had left Warner Brothers, and in his desk found only an empty bottle and a sheet of yellow foolscap on which he had written, five hundred times, "Boy meets girl."

—The time he hired a male nurse, whose duties were to follow at three paces with a small black bag containing a bottle, to be produced as needed, and to make sure that Faulkner reached the studio on time the next morning. . . .

Another variety of story revolves around Faulkner's refusal to become involved in Hollywood's social life:

—The time, for example, when (it is alleged) he was at last prevailed upon to attend a party at the house of his current employer, found himself increasingly bored but, not wanting to seem rude by excusing himself publicly, went to the second floor, opened a window, and escaped by climbing down a trellis.

—The time he accepted an invitation to a party at Marc Connelly's house and his friends, thinking that attractive feminine companionship might make him more responsive to the occasion, got him a "date." After picking her up Faulkner spent the evening sitting in a chair, puffing his pipe and sipping a drink. At last the girl went to Connelly and said, "I don't think

Mr. Faulkner likes me. He hasn't said a word to me all evening. I'm going home." Connelly hurried to Faulkner and asked, "Don't you like your date?" Faulkner puffed his pipe, looked up, and said, "Which one is she?" . . .

Another kind of story hinges on Faulkner's impermeable Mississippi mannerisms and outlook: . . .

—And the time (probably the most famous of the Faulkner Hollywood stories) when he grew tired of reporting to the little office assigned to him and asked his superiors if they would allow him to write "at home." The permission was given: some weeks later his employers were horrified to receive a post card postmarked "Oxford, Mississippi"—the place *he* had meant.

—Robert Coughlin, *The Private World of William Faulkner,* 1954.

When Faulkner became a celebrated novelist, he visited New York, to the consternation of his publisher Bennett Cerf.

And as for Faulkner—well, I couldn't stand the pace. I went home, first saying to Bill, "Remember, there'll be a fellow from the *Times* at the office at ten o'clock in the morning." That was the last we saw of him until I got a call from the Algonquin Hotel several days later; Bill had gone into the bathroom, slipped down against the steam radiator and was badly burned. We rushed him to the hospital, where he spent a good part of his vacation. The day before he went home, I said, "Bill, aren't you ashamed of yourself? You come up here for your first vacation in five years and you spend the whole time in the hospital." Very quietly—he was always very quiet—Bill said, "Bennett, it was *my* vacation."

—*At Random,* 1977.

Late in life he taught at the University of Virginia.

A young woman came to Charlottesville to do graduate work on his novels. She was bright, intense, shy, dedicated, and humorless. The academic year was almost done, and Faulkner was planning to return to Mississippi, when she gathered enough courage to make an appointment with him. She told her friends that when she met him she would reveal the extent to which she had read him—she had read *A Fable* only two times; she had read every other book more than *four times*—and then she would tell him that his work had changed her life.

When she sat in the chair opposite him, she placed her purse on a radiator. The purse hurled itself to the floor, debouching its multiform contents, and she spent the first minutes of her appointment on hands and knees beside William Faulkner, gathering together the debris of her universe.

When she assumed her chair, neither spoke. Then she told Mr. Faulkner that she had read all his books many times; she had read *A Fable* only two times, she told Mr. Faulkner, and she had read all his other books *four times;* . . . then she told him that his books had changed her life.

William Faulkner replied, "Last Saturday I fell off a horse and broke my collar bone."

—Nancy Heffernan, in a letter to editor.

Thornton Wilder 1897–1976

In 1927 Wilder found himself in Miami Beach at the same time as Gene Tunney, who had recently beaten Jack Dempsey to become heavyweight champion of the world. Tunney had revealed himself, in newspaper interviews, as a student of serious literature.

Wilder . . . paid his respects to the world's outstanding athlete by sending a note to Tunney's hotel. After consulting with Billy Powell, a public relations man, Tunney responded to Wilder's note with an invitation to breakfast. Learning that Wilder was interested in serious music, Tunney arranged that the waiter serving breakfast be a singer, so that midway through their scrambled eggs Wilder's ears were assailed by a rendition of the toreador song. But Tunney was genuinely charmed by Wilder who, unlike other men of letters in Tunney's acquaintance, was still a young man—about the same age as Tunney, in fact. Having discovered a good companion, Tunney invited Wilder to play some golf, an invitation Wilder had to decline, never having held a club in his hands.

Later Wilder and Tunney planned a celebrated excursion.

News of their projected "walking tour" of Europe achieved for Wilder a kind of exposure that not even *The Bridge* could achieve for him. . . . The *New York Times* and newspapers all over America displayed considerable breathlessness over the Tunney-Wilder tour, and British papers such as the *London Daily Chronicle* and the *London Daily Mail* heralded the imminent arrival of the two celebrities with uncontained excitement. . . . In actuality, Wilder, together with his mother and sisters Isabel and Janet, sailed for England on July 7, 1928, and upon arrival settled down in a house in Surrey. Tunney defeated Heeney on July 26 and forthwith retired from the ring and sailed for Ireland on August 16. About ten days later, Tunney and Wilder met and proceeded to make final plans for their tour of the continent; whenever the two men emerged out of doors, English villagers and members of the working press followed them. . . .

Tunney arranged for Wilder to call upon Mr. and Mrs. Bernard Shaw; at his behest Mrs. Shaw arranged a lunch. The meeting between Shaw and Wilder was not a success; the two men disliked each other on sight. . . . On the third of September, Tunney and his entourage checked into the newly opened Hotel George V [in Paris]—along with such distinguished fellow guests as Zelda and Scott Fitzgerald. Wilder arrived shortly afterward, but characteristically headed for a more modest hostelry on the left bank. For Tunney, a highlight of the Paris visit was a gathering Wilder arranged with a number of his friends. Converging at the Ritz Bar were Wilder and Tunney; three friends of Tunney's (Leonard Hanna, Billy Powell, and Bill McGeehan); Robert Maynard Hutchins, then dean of the Yale Law School, and his wife Maude; and Scott Fitzgerald. Maude Hutchins, a young, strikingly attractive brunette, was not then (and as it turned out subsequently never was) content to be a mere adjunct to her handsome, brilliant husband. Intelligent, perceptive, and gifted, she wanted more than anything to be taken very seriously. Scott Fitzgerald, who, ironically, was married to a woman of similar disposition, utterly failed to assess Mrs. Hutchins properly. Not entirely sober, Fitzgerald was able to see in her only a good-looking young bride; to his eyes, her attractive femininity was all that distinguished her in this gathering of successful and celebrated men. He chose to flatter, fulsomely and patronizingly, this very self-contained woman, and after a few minutes, she proceeded to lay him out with a number of well-chosen phrases. Tunney was so shocked at the spectacle that he left, together with his friends, Hanna and Powell, in a taxi; Hutchins, wholly composed, calmly gathered up his wife and serenely departed. Wilder, in a state of excruciating embarrassment, disappeared while Fitzgerald, unnerved and bewildered, remained at the bar . . .

—Richard Goldstone, *Thornton Wilder, an Intimate Portrait,* 1975.

Wilder and Tunney walked to Chamounix, ascended Mont Blanc by lift, visited Arles and Nimes, went on to Marseilles, and finally to Rome where Tunney married his fiancée. Wilder declined to be best man.

John Wheelwright 1897–1940

John Wheelwright, poet and Boston Brahmin, was expelled from Harvard for a multitude of sins. One of them was a misspelling, giving rise to the oversimplified story that he was dismissed from the university for his eccentric orthography. On probation, Wheelwright was required to submit a written explanation when he missed a class. One day he wrote that, when he had witnessed Miss Lillian Gish floating on a block of ice toward a high dam, in a film called Way Down East, *he had become "afflicted with naushaw."*

His mind had to an extreme a literal quality. For example, take the occasion when he insulted Amy Lowell. At a reading and discussion she conducted before the Harvard Poetry Society, Wheelwright, aged nineteen, asked, "How do you write, Miss Lowell, when you have nothing to say?" Years afterward he delighted to tell or hear anyone else tell that story, and he used it in one of his most ingratiating poems; but the point was he hadn't the slightest intention of insulting Miss Lowell. He was inquiring for information. He wanted to know how one might write poetry out of mere impulse.

—Winfield Townley Scott, *Exiles and Fabrications,* 1961.

He attended Communist Party cell meetings wearing a full-length fur coat; he lent color to numerous gatherings in Cambridge and Boston.

At a reception given by Theodore Spencer for Allen Tate, neither host nor guest of honor was overly astounded when Wheelwright made from one end to the other of the room a slow progress underneath the huge floor rug; nor was Wheelwright perturbed when he emerged, dusted his clothes lightly, and opened conversation with a group of speechless undergraduates. This may have been about the time he was tossed out of Yaddo, the literary colony. His offense there was pre-empting a bathroom all day during which, comfortable in the tub, he had eaten bananas while contemplating a little Buddha or, possibly, billikin. Banana skins all over the place.

—Scott.

Harry Crosby 1898–1929

Crosby has been noted mainly not for his poems and journals but for his suicide in 1929; to some writers he symbolized the end of an era.

Crosby and his wife Caresse came from rich families; J. P. Morgan was Harry's uncle. In 1928 the couple met a wise man in Egypt who said: "My wealth I measure by the things I do without." Harry decided that his library was too large.

. . . it became Harry's purpose to dispose of his books once he had read them. He decided to reduce his library from ten thousand volumes to one thousand to one hundred to ten to one, the one true book containing one true word. . . . So he commenced to give away the books. . . . He pressed first editions of Baudelaire on anyone he met and liked, and finally commenced a pretty trick, smuggling rare volumes into Seine-side bookstalls, marking them with absurdly low prices, and leaving them among odds and ends, laughing to imagine with what amazement they would be discovered by browsers, and with what confusion the bookstall owners would respond to Harry's mischief.

—Geoffrey Wolff, *Black Sun: The Brief Transit and Violent Eclipse of Harry Crosby,* 1976.

Yet he continued to acquire things.

Excess was the only measure he knew. When he ate, he ate oysters, and when he drank, he drank champagne, and too much of both, yet he paid no price, laid on no fat and managed not to appear foolish. If he saw something he wished to have, he had it: "Went out this morning to buy silk pyjamas but came back with a 1st edition of Les Illuminations very rare as there were only 200 copies edited by Verlaine." Another day, going to look for zebra skins, he returned home with the skeleton of a girl wrapped in a yellow raincoat, her feet hitting the stairs of 19 rue de Lille as he carried her to his library, where he hung her from a bookcase. . . .

—Wolff.

When he started to publish books, Crosby solicited a manuscript from D. H. Lawrence, promising to pay in gold pieces. When the manuscript arrived, Crosby was in France and Lawrence in Italy. It took some time to acquire the gold, which could not be exported from the United States and which was illegal in France.

Harry wanted to get the gold to him as quickly as possible, but no one we knew was going to Italy. In his desk he found a small square Cartier box that had held rue de Lille notepaper, and he was busy wrapping each disk in cotton.

"The Rome Express leaves tonight at eight," he said, "what time is it now?" (He had no clock there to watch over him.) It was nearing seven. "I'll take the package to the train myself and ask some passenger to mail it in Florence"—the free circulation of gold was forbidden then as now.

"But it might fall into the hands of a crook," Armand protested. "It's too dangerous."

"If I can't tell an honest man when I see one then I deserve a crook." Harry crossed himself and went on preparing the package. He rang and ordered the car for 7.30.

Bill Sykes went off with him and he told us later that he and Harry arrived at the Gare de l'Est a few minutes before train time, Harry in his oversized mink-lined greatcoat that had been Cousin Walter's, the undeviating dark blue suit and grey spats, bareheaded as always. He hurried along the station beside the *wagons lits* through the confusion of a transcontinental *départ,* searching for his "honest man," but he hadn't found him when the guard called *en voiture.* At the final moment a distinguished Englishman with a schoolboy of about twelve at his side pulled down the window of one of the compartments on the Florence sleeper, and leaned out. Immediately Harry spotted him and called up through the din, "Would you help me out, sir, by mailing this in Florence when you arrive?"

"Glad to—not a bomb, I trust," as he reached down a friendly hand.

"No, it's gold," shouted back Harry as the train began to move.

"Then we'd better introduce ourselves. My name's Argyll," called back the man.

"Crosby," shouted Harry, "it's gold for a poet." They both waved a salute.

In a day or two Lawrence wrote us that the gold had been delivered in person by the Duke of Argyll.

—Caresse Crosby, *The Passionate Years,* 1979.

Vladimir Nabokov 1899–1977

After years of exile from Russia in Berlin and Paris, Nabokov emigrated to the United States in 1940.

. . . Five years later—by then he was living in Massachusetts—when Nabokov and his wife went to receive their citizenship papers, they took with them, as the two sponsors, Miss Amy Kelly, a very charming older woman and estimable scholar who taught English at Wellesley College, and Professor [Michael] Karpovich [who taught Russian history at Harvard]. Just before the examination time Karpovich said to Nabokov:—**Now look here, I want to ask you something. Don't joke, please don't joke with them. This is quite serious, you know. Don't joke. —O.K.,** Nabokov agreed, but it was not to be. The examiner **(—of Italian origin apparently, judging by his slight accent)** gave Nabokov a phrase to read, *The child is bald,* which seemed a little silly to Nabokov, but he read it. The examiner corrected him and said:—**No, it is not bald. It is bold.** Nabokov replied that babies don't have very much hair. The examiner acknowledged the fact with mock interest and next asked Nabokov a question on American history. Nabokov didn't even understand the question, but within a moment the two men were kidding each other and roaring with laughter, while the apprehensive Karpovich stood looking at them as if they were both madmen.—**You passed, you passed,** the examiner gasped at last. Nabokov remembers the day with great affection: **—I had a wonderful time becoming an American citizen. That was an absolutely wonderful day.** He cites this incident as an illustration of the Russian lack of a sense of humour and also, by implication, of his own innate Americanness.**—That's very characteristic, you know. This rather prim Russian who wants to be very serious, and this easygoing American way of settling things. He saw at once that I could read English. It was very soothing, very soothing.**

—Andrew Field, *Nabokov: His Life in Part,* 1977.

Nabokov chased butterflies and lectured on literature.

He prepared lectures for about one hundred teaching hours, and, working on a calculation of approximately twenty typed pages for a fifty-minute lecture, he wrote nearly two thousand pages. He would read his lectures at a slightly subdued pace, and he developed early on an extremely subtle way of glancing up and down, though he is sure that his more alert students were never in doubt of the fact that he was reading, not speaking from notes, including even the bits of local colour (these alone were changed from place to place over the years) and dramatic improvisations (Gogol pleading with his doctors to have the leeches removed from his nose) with which he conservatively spiced his hours. It was wise preparation for his two decades in America:**—The labour was tremendous, but I had no labour after that, thinking about them, I could think about something totally different while I was delivering my lecture. . . .** On odd occasions Nabokov had a little joke by which he gave himself empirical proof of the inadequacies of the classroom situation. After reaching some point in his lecture at which he thought it would be nice to stop, he would, and he would begin to read again from the beginning of that same lecture. He found that for as long as two minutes absolutely no one would notice anything. All heads would be bowed and a roomful of pencils would continue to perform industrious exercises in place. Then, gradually, heads would rise.**—And not only that, some people would giggle, but you would hear other people say: "What's so funny?"**

—Field.

Someone once asked him to list scenes from the historical past which he would like to have witnessed on film.

Shakespeare in the part of the King's Ghost.

The beheading of Louis the Sixteenth, the drums drowning his speech on the scaffold.

Herman Melville at breakfast, feeding a sardine to his cat.

Poe's wedding. Lewis Carroll's picnics.

The Russians leaving Alaska, delighted with the deal. Shot of a seal applauding.

—Vladimir Nabokov, *Strong Opinions,* 1973.

Ernest Hemingway 1899–1961

Young Hemingway wrote many stories, and all but two were lost.

Everything I had written was stolen in Hadley's suitcase that time at the Gare de Lyon when she was bringing the manuscripts down to me to Lausanne as a surprise, so I could work on them on our holidays in the mountains. She had put in the originals, the typescripts and the carbons, all in manila folders. . . . I had never seen anyone hurt by a thing other than death or unbearable suffering except Hadley when she told me about the things being gone. She had cried and cried and could not tell me. I told her that no matter what the dreadful thing was that had happened nothing could be that bad, and whatever it was, it was all right and not to worry. We would work it out. Then, finally, she told me. I was sure she could not have brought the carbons too and I hired someone to cover for me on my newspaper job. I was making good money then at journalism, and took the train for Paris. It was true all right and I remember what I did in the night after I let myself into the flat and found it was true.

—*A Moveable Feast,* 1964.

Hemingway was determined to go to any length to be a writer; possibly he was equally determined to annoy his friends, like Robert McAlmon.

The next day, on the way to Madrid, our train stopped at a wayside station for a time. On the track beside us was a flatcar, upon which lay the maggot-eaten corpse of a dog. I, feeling none too hale and hearty, looked away, but Hemingway gave a dissertation on facing reality. It seemed that he had seen in the war the stacked corpses of men, maggot-eaten in a similar way. He advised a detached and scientific attitude toward the corpse of the dog. He tenderly explained that we of our generation must inure ourselves to the sight of grim reality. I recalled that Ezra Pound had talked once of Hemingway's "self-hardening process." At last he said, "Hell, Mac, you write like a realist. Are you going to go romantic on us?"

I spurted forth some oath and went to the dining car to order whisky.

—Robert McAlmon, *Being Geniuses Together,* 1970.

Hemingway loved to box. So did Morley Callaghan, who recalled this story.

On the way to the American Club in the taxi, it seemed to me that Scott and Ernest were at ease with each other. There was no sense of strain and Scott looked alert and happy. We joked a bit. At the club—I remember the scene so vividly—I remember how Scott, there for the first time, looked around in surprise. The floor had no mat. Through the doorway opening into the next room, he could see two young fellows playing billiards. Scott sat down on the bench by the wall, while Ernest and I stripped. Then Ernest had him take out his watch and gave him his instructions. A round was to be three minutes, then a minute for a rest. As he took these instructions, listening carefully, Scott had none of Miró's air of high professionalism. He was too enchanted at being there with us. Moving off the bench, he squatted down, a little smile on his face. "Time," he called.

Our first round was like most of the rounds we had fought that summer, with me shuffling around, and Ernest, familiar with my style, leading and chasing after me. No longer did he rush in with his old brisk confidence. Now he kept an eye on my left and he was harder to hit. As I shuffled around I could hear the sound of clicking billiard balls from the adjoining room.

"Time," Scott called promptly. When we sat down beside him, he was rather quiet, meditative, and I could tell by the expression on his face that he was mystified. He must have come there with some kind of a picture of Ernest, the fighter, in his head. For Ernest and me it was just like any other day. We chatted and laughed. And it didn't seem to be important to us that Scott was there. He had made no comment that could bother us. He seemed to be content that he was there concentrating on the minute hand of his watch. "Time," he called.

Right at the beginning of that round Ernest got careless; he came in too fast, his left down, and he got smacked on the mouth. His lip began to bleed. It had often happened. It should have meant nothing to him. Hadn't he joked with Jimmy, the bartender, about always having me for a friend while I could make his lip bleed? Out of the corner of his eye he may have seen the shocked expression on Scott's face. Or the taste of blood in his mouth may have made him want to fight more savagely. He came lunging in, swinging more recklessly. As I circled around him, I kept jabbing at his bleeding mouth. I had to forget all about Scott, for Ernest had become rougher, his punching a little wilder than usual. His heavy punches, if they had landed, would have stunned me. I had to punch faster and harder myself to keep away from him. It bothered me that he was taking the punches on the face like a man telling himself he only needed to land one big punch himself.

Out of the corner of my eye, as I bobbed and weaved, I could see one of the young fellows who had been playing billiards come to the door and stand there, watching. He was in his shirt sleeves, but he was wearing a vest. He held his cue in his hand like a staff. I could see Scott on the bench. I was wondering why I was tiring, for I hadn't been hit solidly. Then Ernest, wiping the blood from his mouth with his glove, and probably made careless with exasperation and embarrassment from having Scott there, came leaping in at me. Stepping in, I beat him to the punch. The timing must have been just right. I caught him on the jaw; spinning around he went down, sprawled out on his back.

If Ernest and I had been there alone I would have laughed. I was sure of my boxing friendship with him; in a sense I was sure of him, too. Ridiculous things had happened in that room. Hadn't he spat in my face? And I felt no surprise seeing him flat on his back. Shaking his head a little to clear it, he rested a moment on his back. As he rose slowly, I expected him to curse, then laugh.

"Oh, my God!" Scott cried suddenly. When I looked at him, alarmed, he was shaking his head helplessly. "I let the round go four minutes," he said.

"Christ!" Ernest yelled. He got up. He was silent for a few seconds. Scott, staring at his watch, was mute and wondering. I wished I were miles away. "All right, Scott," Ernest said savagely. "If you want to see me getting the shit knocked out of me, just say so. Only don't say you made a mistake," and he stomped off to the shower room to wipe the blood from his mouth.

—Morley Callaghan, *That Summer in Paris,* 1963.

Hemingway was fearless. The former heavyweight champion of the world, Thornton Wilder's friend Gene Tunney, visited him in Cuba.

The thought of fooling with Hemingway always made Tunney wince. Sure enough, on this occasion at the *finca,* the two began shuffling around the big living room, and Hemingway did what Tunney half expected: he threw a low punch, perhaps out of clumsiness, but it hurt. It outraged Tunney. He feinted his opponent's guard down, and then threw a whistling punch, bringing it up just a millimeter short of Hemingway's face, so that the fist and the ridge of bare knuckles completely filled the other's field of vision, the punch arriving there almost instantaneously, so that immutable evidence was provided that if Tunney had let it continue its course, Hemingway's facial structure—nose, cheekbones, front teeth, and the rest—would have snapped and collapsed inwardly, and Tunney looked down the length of his arm into Hemingway's eyes and said, *"Don't you ever do that again!"*

—George Plimpton, *Shadow Box,* 1977.

As Hemingway grew older he continued to annoy his friends, possibly with even more assiduousness. Often these scenes included tests of strength and skill. Lillian Hellman wrote about a confrontation at the Stork Club between Ernest Hemingway and Dashiell Hammett.

The Spanish War was just ended and many Republicans and their supporters had been caught in France, or in northern Spain, and had to be bailed or bought out. We had all given money to make that possible, but Ernest was in a bad humor that Stork

Club night and gave small jab lectures about safe people in New York. People began to leave our table . . . by that time Dash had had as much to drink as Ernest, and had grown too quiet. Now he put his head in his hands as Ernest spoke again of the friends who must be saved.

Ernest said, "What's the matter with you, Hammett?"

"I don't always like lectures."

I remember an angry silence, and then suddenly Ernest seemed in a good humor and Dash in a bad humor as they talked of saving intellectuals or saving ordinary people, and when Regler or I tried to speak neither of them cared. When I came back from a trip to the ladies' room, Ernest had a tablespoon between the muscles of his upper and lower arm and was pressing it hard. Hammett was staring down at the tablecloth. Just as I settled myself the spoon crumpled and Ernest threw it down with a happy grin.

He turned to Hammett, "All right, kid, let's see you do that."

Kid looked up, stared at Ernest, returned his head in his hands, and I knew there was going to be trouble. I tinkled and giggled and chatted and chittered, but nobody paid any attention. I didn't hear anything for a few minutes until Ernest said, "So you're against saving the intellectuals?"

Hammett spoke through his hands. "I didn't say that. I said there were other people in the world." He turned to me, "Come on. Let's go."

He half rose. Ernest's hand shot out and held him down. Ernest was grinning. "No. Let's see you do the spoon trick first."

Dash stared at Ernest's hand, settled in his chair again, put his head back in his hands. . . . Ernest was holding out another tablespoon as he whispered to Dash.

Dash said, "Why don't you go back to bullying Fitzgerald? Too bad he doesn't know how good he is. The best."

The hand on Dash's arm came away and the fingers spread open as the grin disappeared. Ernest said, very sharply, "Let's see you bend the spoon."

Dash got up. He was drunk now and the rise was unsteady. He said, very softly, "I don't think I could bend the spoon. But when I did things like that I did them for Pinkerton money. Why don't you go roll a hoop in the park."

—*An Unfinished Woman,* 1969.

Hemingway's book on bullfighting, Death in the Afternoon *(1932), occasioned Max Eastman's article, "Bull in the Afternoon," in which he described Hemingway's style as "wearing false hair on the chest." Several years later, the two men met by accident in the office of Max Perkins.*

Hemingway shook hands with Eastman and they swapped amenities. Then Ernest, with a broad smile, ripped open his shirt and exposed a chest which Perkins thought was hirsute enough to impress any man. Eastman laughed, and Ernest good-naturedly reached over and unbuttoned Eastman's shirt, revealing a chest as bare as a bald man's head. Everyone laughed at the contrast. Perkins got ready to expose his chest, sure that he could place second, when Hemingway truculently demanded of Eastman, "What do you mean [by] accusing me of impotence?"

Eastman denied that he had, and there were sharp words back and forth. Eastman said, "Ernest, you don't know what you are talking about. Here, read what I said." He picked up a copy of *Art and the Life of Action* on Perkins's desk, which the editor had there for some other reason, not even remembering that it contained "Bull in the Afternoon." But instead of reading the passage Eastman pointed out, Ernest began part of another paragraph, and trailed off into muttered profanity. "Read all of it, Ernest," Eastman urged him. "You don't understand it. . . . Here, let Max read it."

Perkins saw that things were getting serious. He started to read, thinking that would somehow calm things down. But Ernest snatched the book from him and said, "No, I am going to do the reading." As he started again, his face flushed, and he turned and smacked Eastman with the open book. Eastman rushed at him. Perkins, fearful that Ernest would kill Eastman, ran around his desk to grab Hemingway from behind. As the two authors grappled, all the precariously balanced books and papers on Perkins's desk toppled off, and both men fell to the floor. Thinking he was restraining Hemingway, Perkins grabbed the man on top. But when Max looked down, there was Ernest on his back, gazing up at him, his broken glasses dangling and a naughty grin from ear to ear.

—A. Scott Berg, *Max Perkins, Editor of Genius,* 1978.

Eastman and Hemingway each issued bulletins describing the engagement from notably different perspectives.

When he was a correspondent in the Second World War, Hemingway with a coterie of journalist friends determined to liberate Paris—or at least important portions of it. Sylvia Beach, bookseller and Joyce's publisher, remembered an occasion.

There was still a lot of shooting going on in the rue de l'Odéon, and we were getting tired of it, when one day a string of jeeps came up the street and stopped in front of my house. I heard a deep voice calling: "Sylvia!" And everybody in the street took up the cry of "Sylvia!"

"It's Hemingway! It's Hemingway!" cried Adrienne. I flew downstairs; we met with a crash; he picked me up and swung me around and kissed me while people on the street and in the windows cheered.

We went up to Adrienne's apartment and sat Hemingway down. He was in battle dress, grimy and bloody. A machine gun clunked on the floor. He asked Adrienne for a piece of soap, and she gave him her last cake.

He wanted to know if there was anything he could do for us. We asked him if he could do something about the Nazi snipers on the roof tops in our street, particularly on Adrienne's roof top. He got his company out of the jeeps and took them up to the roof. We heard firing for the last time in the rue de l'Odéon. Hemingway and his men came down again and rode off in their jeeps—"to liberate," according to Hemingway, "the cellar at the Ritz."

—*Shakespeare and Co.*, 1959.

According to the Hemingway tradition, the next great step in the liberation of Paris took place at the Hôtel Ritz in the Place Vendôme. Bruce, Hemingway, Pelkey, and several of the irregulars made another dash through small-arms fire from the Travellers Club to the Café de la Paix. They found the Place de l'Opéra filled with "a solid mass of cheering people." The Bruce-Hemingway party lost a carbine by theft and were roundly kissed by what seemed thousands of men, women, and babies. When they could move their vehicles again, they escaped to the Ritz, which had been open and doing business throughout the German occupation. They found the hotel completely undamaged and entirely deserted "except for the manager, the imperturbable Ausiello," who gravely welcomed the wayfarers at the door. They requested and were given lodging in the hotel, and quarters were found nearby for the "Private Army." When asked what else they needed, they answered that they would like to have fifty martini cocktails. The bartender could not be found and the cocktails were mediocre. But Ernest was finally in nominal possession of the Ritz.

He made no attempt to cover the formal surrender of Dietrich von Choltitz, the German commandant of Paris, to General Leclerc near train gate 33 at the Gare Montparnasse, though he magnanimously lent his typewriter to Joe Driscoll of *The New York Times* so that he could write a liberation story. Alan Moorehead, the British historian, found Ernest and his cronies drinking Perrier-Jouet in the Ritz Bar on the rue Cambon side, and later in the evening there was a dinner at which Ernest entertained seven uniformed American officers. Besides Colonels Bruce and Marshall and Lieutenant Westover, these included Comm. Lester Armour of the OSS, Bruce's assistant G. W. Graveson, Brig. Gen. Edwin L. Sibert, J. F. Haskell, and Capt. Paul Sapiebra. Sapiebra had been present at the ceremonial of surrender across the river. The diners exchanged signatures on the Ritz menus as souvenirs. "None of us," said Ernest, "will ever write a line about these last twenty-four hours in delirium. Whoever tries it is a chump." He continued his entertaining on Saturday with a lunch at the Ritz for Helen Kirkpatrick, Ira Wolfert, John Reinhart, Charles Wertenbaker, and Irwin Shaw. Over the brandy Helen said that she and Reinhart were going to see the victory parade in its march towards Notre Dame. Ernest tried to argue her out of it. "Daughter," said he, "sit still and drink this good brandy. You can always watch parades but you'll never again celebrate the liberation of Paris at the Ritz."

—Carlos Baker, *Hemingway: A Life Story,* 1969.

Hart Crane 1899–1932

Greenwich Village in the twenties was the scene of lively controversy. At a meeting to make peace in the war between the literary magazines Broom *and* Secession, *Malcolm Cowley read aloud a letter from Gorham Munson, an editor of* Secession, *in the presence of Hart Crane, Glenway Wescott, and others.*

. . . the meeting got underway with his reading of an angry letter from Munson, much of it a diatribe against Matthew Josephson. Halfway through his reading, Cowley saw comic possibilities in the letter: "I began to read it seriously to my audience, but . . . I was overcome by a sense of absurdity and began to declaim it like a blue-jawed actor reciting Hamlet's soliloquy."

It was at this point that the battle began to rage. Crane, as he had predicted, was Munson's chief advocate. Soon everybody was shouting—or else preparing, like Glenway Wescott, to beat a dignified retreat. "Glenway Wescott rose from the table," Cowley recollected, "very pale and stern. 'How can you people expect to accomplish anything,' he said precisely, 'when you can't even preserve ordinary parlor decorum?' He swept out of the restaurant with the air of one gathering an invisible cloak about him. . . .

"Hart Crane, with red face and bristling hair, stamped up and down the room, repeating 'Parlor, hell, parlor.". . .

—John Unterecker, *Voyager: A Life of Hart Crane,* 1969.

At times Crane tried to support himself by writing advertising copy. These jobs tended to be brief.

. . . He was assigned to writing the literature of cosmetics. Thinking to inspire him, his superiors placed on his desk numerous vials of strong perfume, whose odor he was supposed to capture in words. But the perfumes nauseated him and so one day, when he had come to work with a bad hang-over, he snatched up the whole collection and threw them out of his office window.

—Matthew Josephson, *Life Among the Surrealists,* 1962.

His friend Malcolm Cowley remembers Crane writing poetry on a country weekend.

We would play croquet, wrangling, laughing, shouting over every wicket, with a pitcher of cider half hidden in the tall grass beside the court; or else we would sit beside the fireplace in the big, low-ceilinged kitchen, while a spring rain soaped the windowpanes. Hart—we sometimes called him the Roaring Boy—would laugh twice as hard as the rest of us and drink at least twice as much hard cider, while contributing more than his share of the crazy metaphors and overblown epithets. Gradually he would fall silent, and a little later he disappeared. In lulls that began to interrupt the laughter, now Hart was gone, we would hear a new hubbub through the walls of his room—the phonograph playing a Cuban rumba, the typewriter clacking simultaneously; then the phonograph would run down and the typewriter stop while Hart changed the record, perhaps to a torch song, perhaps to Ravel's *Bolero.* Sometimes he stamped across the room, declaiming to the four walls and the slow spring rain.

An hour later, after the rain had stopped, he would appear in the kitchen or on the croquet court, his face brick-red, his eyes burning, his already iron-gray hair bristling straight up from his skull. He would be chewing a five-cent cigar which he had forgotten to light. In his hands would be two or three sheets of typewritten manuscript, with words crossed out and new lines scrawled in. "R-read that," he would say. "Isn't that the greatest poem ever written?"

—*Exile's Return,* 1934.

Cowley would realize later that Crane had worked on the poem for months, sometimes years before that evening. Afterward Crane would continue to work on it.

Painfully, persistently—and dead sober—Hart would revise his new poem, clarifying the images, correcting the meter and searching for the right word hour after hour. "The seal's wide spindrift gaze toward paradise," in the second of his "Voyages," was the result of a search that lasted for several days. At first he had written, "The seal's *findrinny* gaze toward paradise," but someone had objected that he was using a non-existent word. Hart and I worked in the same office that year, and I remember his frantic searches through *Webster's Unabridged* and the big *Standard,* his trips to the library—on office time—and his reports of consultations with old sailors in South Street speakeasies. "Findrinny" he could never find, but after paging through the dictionary again he decided that "spindrift" was almost as good and he declaimed the new line exultantly.

—Cowley.

After Crane's death, a friend found "findrinny" in Moby-Dick. *For that matter, William Butler Yeats used it twice in* Wanderings of Oisin.

Crane was an enthusiastic and loyal companion, but sometimes difficult. He visited Harry and Caresse Crosby in France.

We were aware of Hart's midnight prowlings and also aware, to our dismay, of his nocturnal pick-ups. He said he'd go out for a nightcap so it was with great relief that I heard him come in about two A.M. and softly close the stairway door. Then all was quiet. But in the morning, what a hideous awakening! Marcelle brought my morning coffee to me in hands that trembled with shock. "Oh, Madame," she said, "*quel malheur, quel malheur.*" I jumped from my bed and followed her downstairs to see what was the matter. By that time it was ten o'clock and Hart had already departed, probably as silently as he had entered, but he had left behind him traces of great activity. On the wallpaper and across the pale pink spread, up and down the curtains and over the white chenille rug were the blackest footprints and handprints I have ever seen, hundreds of them. No wonder, for I heard to my fury that he had brought a chimney-sweep home for the night.

—Caresse Crosby, *The Passionate Years,* 1979.

When he became drunk he lost his temper. Once in the country he tried to walk out on his hosts.

There was, for example, his quarrel with Bill and Sue Brown, when he swept out of their house at midnight, vowing never to come back. But the Browns lived alone on a hillside, and the path to Mrs. Addie Turner's gaunt barn of a house, where Hart was living, twisted through a second-growth woodland in which even a sober man might have lost his way. About three o'clock the Browns were wakened by the noise of Hart crashing through the bushes and then stamping on their front porch. Soon they heard him mutter, "Brrowns, Brrowns, you can't get away from them," as if he were penned and circumscribed by Browns.

—Cowley.

In the city Crane would turn sullen, leave the party, and head for the waterfront. Kenneth Burke told Malcolm Cowley about a party at the Slater Browns' in New York, when Burke tried to turn away Crane's wrath.

"Party had got to humming, and Hart had got to the stage where he felt it was time for him to become angry. I happened to be near the door when I saw him stamping across the room, all ready to leave in a huff.

"I said, 'What's the matter, Hart?' He began muttering about how awful 'all these people' were. Whereat I, being in a good-naturedly impish stage, decided to spoil his rhythm. I pointed out that he had no reason to be indignant. Everybody here was his friend, we all thought him a great poet, nobody's fighting—so what more did he want? He turned back, muttering, and got lost in the general turmoil.

"A little later, the same pattern, Hart storming toward the door in a mighty rage. So I went through my part of the routine again. I said I simply could not understand why he felt so resentful when everybody thought so highly of him, etc. Why 'these awful people'? Hart went back a second time.

"Of course there was a third time too, with Hart storming out and my plaintive, mollifying interruption, 'Now wait a minute, Hart, what's the matter now?'

"Hart turned, pointed, and shouted at the top of his voice, 'I can't stand that damned dog!' "

—Malcolm Cowley, *A Second Flowering*, 1956.

In at least half of the stories told about Hart Crane, he throws something out a window.

It all started, Slater Brown recalled, after everyone had gone off to sample some of Bina Flynn's wine. Hart, who more than sampled, eventually made everyone promise to write to Mexico's President Calles, whom he admired. Since he and Brown had been studying Spanish together, Hart reasoned, each of them should be able to produce a masterful document. And Hart dashed home to begin work on his. But, alas, the Spanish wouldn't flow; Hart, furious, tossed his typewriter out the window. After he'd dashed down, rescued it, and returned to his second-floor study, he discovered that it still wouldn't write Spanish and he tossed it out the window again.

—Unterecker.

His biographer recounted a dream.

. . . he had the feeling, long after he was awake, that it was something he had actually experienced. He had gone to bed exhausted, and when he woke up, he was in his old room on 115th Street. He got up, remembering that he had to hunt for something in the attic, and as he stumbled through the dusty attic—half awake—he kept trying to remember what he was looking for. Whatever it was, it was in a trunk. He was sure of that. It was very dark in the attic, but when he found the trunk, there was enough light for him to see that it was full of his mother's clothes. He started rummaging through them, looking for whatever it was he was looking for, pulling out dresses, shoes, stockings, underclothing. But the trunk was so full, it seemed he would never find what he was after. There was so much to look at that when he found the hand, he hardly realized it was a human hand; but when he found another hand and a piece of an arm, he knew there was a body in the trunk. He kept pulling out piece after piece of it, all mixed in with the clothing. The clothing was covered with blood. It was not until he had almost emptied the trunk that he realized he was unpacking the dismembered body of his mother.

—Unterecker.

Pursued by such horrors, Crane went to Mexico on a Guggenheim Fellowship in 1931; Katherine Anne Porter kept notes of their conversations.

". . . he would talk slowly in an ordinary voice, saying he knew he was destroying himself as poet, he did not know why, and he asked himself why, constantly. He said once that the life he lived was blunting his sensibilities, that he was no longer capable of feeling anything except under the most violent and brutal shocks: 'and I can't even then deceive myself that I really feel anything,' he said. He talked about Baudelaire and Marlowe, and Whitman and Melville and Blake—all the consoling examples he could call to mind of artists who had lived excessively in one way or another. Later, drunk, he would weep and shout, shaking his fist, 'I am Baudelaire, I am Whitman, I am Christopher Marlowe, I am Christ' but never once did I hear him say he was Hart Crane. . . . He talked of suicide almost every day. Whenever he read of a suicide in the newspapers, he approved and praised the act. . . . He described the suicide of Harry Crosby as 'imaginative; the act of a poet.' Once while he was still stopping at my house he ran out of his room—it was night, and the moon seems to have been shining, again—rushed up to the roof which was only one story high, and shouted that he was going to throw himself off. . . . I called out to him, 'Oh don't. It's not high enough and you'll only hurt yourself.' He began to laugh immediately, a curiously fresh sober humor in the laughter, and came down by way of an apricot tree with branches spreading over the roof. He sat and talked a little while, went in and began to play the piano loudly and incoherently—it was very old and out of tune—and after about an hour of this he left the house, and did not return. He had got into difficulties in town and spent the night in jail. . . ."

—Philip Horton, *Hart Crane, the Life of an American Poet,* 1937.

Finally, as if he were perfume or a typewriter, he threw himself into the sea from the ship returning from Mexico to the United States. A passenger remembered the end.

"On that ill-fated morning, one of the ship's officers told us that Crane had been in the sailors' quarters the previous night, trying to make one of the men, and had been badly beaten. Just before noon, a number of us were gathered on deck, waiting to hear the results of the ship's pool—always announced at noon. Just then we saw Crane come on deck, dressed . . . in pajamas and topcoat; he had a black eye and looked generally battered. He walked to the railing, took off his coat, folded it neatly over the railing (not dropping it on deck), placed both hands on the railing, raised himself on his toes, and then dropped back again. We all fell silent and watched him, wondering what in the world he was up to. Then, suddenly, he vaulted over the railing and jumped into the sea. For what seemed five minutes, but was more like five seconds, no one was able to move; then cries of 'man overboard' went up. Just once I [Gertrude Vogt] saw Crane, swimming strongly, but never again."

—Unterecker [notes].

Allen Tate 1899–1978

Tate soldiered in the literary wars for more than fifty years. When he and Yvor Winters were both advising the magazine Hound and Horn, *they fought continually. Winters liked to say that Tate once boarded a train in Tennessee and bought a ticket to California where he intended to confront Winters, bringing with him in his suitcase only a brace of dueling pistols and two bottles of sourmash; the whiskey ran out in Texas, Winters said, and Tate turned around.*

Malcolm Cowley remembered a meeting.

When he made his first trip to New York in June 1924, there was nothing cosmopolitan in his appearance except possibly the cane he carried. Hart Crane, with whom he had corresponded, introduced him to a Greenwich Village party, and it was there I met him. He was a slight young man with delicate features and an enormous forehead. Later I heard that when Allen was a boy, he was thought to have water on the brain. His mother once said, "Son, put that book down and go out and play with Henry. You are straining your mind and you know your mind isn't very strong." Was it as a delayed rejoinder that he wore a Phi Beta Kappa key conspicuously on his vest? I liked him at first glance, but I said severely, "We don't wear our Phi Beta Kappa keys any longer."

—"Remembering Allen Tate," *The Georgia Review,* Spring 1980.

Thomas Wolfe 1900–1938

In his autobiographical work, Look Homeward, Angel, *the stonecutter W. O. Gant is Wolfe's father. When the book was published, Wolfe's hometown of Asheville, North Carolina, was aghast at his indiscretions. But Wolfe's mother laughed as she read the book, rocking on her porch, and was heard to cry out: "It's the God's truth! It's the God's truth!"*

When Wolfe first met his editor, Max Perkins of Scribner's, he was prepared to sacrifice some of God's truth.

Visibly trembling, Wolfe took off his coat and sat down as this mild-mannered, New England-looking gentleman, with almost no preliminaries, began discussing the scene in *O Lost* where the madam buys a stone angel from Gant for the grave of one of her "girls."

"I know you can't print that," Wolfe broke in. "I'll take it out at once, Mr. Perkins."

"Take it out?" The blue eyes looked offended. "Why, it's one of the greatest short stories I've ever read!"

—Andrew Turnbull, *Thomas Wolfe: A Biography,* 1967.

It was not until his second meeting with Perkins that Wolfe found out for certain that his novel would be published.

On his way out of the office Wolfe ran into John Hall Wheelock, the poet who was also a Scribner editor; Wheelock said he hoped Wolfe had a good place to work—"you've got a big job ahead"—and Wolfe reeled out of the building in a drunken glory, knowing that his book would indeed be published. Scribners is at Forty-eighth Street, and when Wolfe came to his senses, he was on One hundred and tenth with no memory of how he had gotten there.

—Turnbull.

In 1929 he met F. Scott Fitzgerald, and the two men enjoyed a conversation. Late in the evening, however, Wolfe left Fitzgerald behind in the Ritz Bar

"surrounded by Princeton boys, all nineteen, all drunk, and all half-raw. He was carrying on a spirited conversation with them about why Joe Zinzendorff did not get taken into the Triple-Gazzazza Club: I heard one of the lads say, 'Joe's a good boy, Scotty, but you know he's a fellow that ain't got much background.'—I thought it was time for Wolfe to depart, and I did."

—Turnbull.

When his first novel was successful Wolfe became famous as a curiosity as well as an author.

A well-known figure around New York, he was quickly recognizable because of his size and impact, and he wouldn't have been in a night club very long before the grinning bandleader struck up "Who's Afraid of the Big Bad Wolf?" That fall a cartoon in *The New Yorker* showed a disheveled giant berating a mild runt at a cocktail party while one woman said to another, "He looks a little like Thomas Wolfe, and he certainly makes the most of it." A subsequent item in that magazine's "Talk of the Town" told of Wolfe being joined in the elevator of his apartment house by a lady with a police dog that began jumping all over him. When he pushed the dog away, the lady said, "Wolfe! you great, obnoxious beast!" Wounded, the author had "spent the rest of the day wandering along the waterfront in the rain, bumping into warehouses and brooding like a character in one of his novels." The matter was cleared up when the elevator man told him the police dog's name was Wolf. . . .

—Turnbull.

Andrew Turnbull told about Wolfe's way of writing; after a day behind the pencil, he endured an editorial conference.

He was slow to begin . . . but once under way he was indestructible. He would draw up a chair to his heavy oaken writing table, light yet another cigarette, choose a stub pencil from the coffee can in which he kept them, purse his mouth for concentration, and then for several hours, almost without pause, the unnumbered manila sheets covered with his onrushing scrawl would fall to the floor as if blown by a fan, while the typist scurried to and fro to gather them up, not daring to ask about words she couldn't read since Wolfe grew annoyed at the slightest interruption. There were moments when he puffed at the cigarette stuck to his lower lip and squinted at the ceiling through the spiralling smoke, the pencil poised over the yellow sheet looking like a jackstraw in his giant hand. Sometimes, after brief reflection, he would crumple up the page and begin anew, but this was rare. The copy he would take to Scribners at the end of the afternoon was largely first draft, with only an occasional word crossed out or changed. . . .

His conference with Perkins was scheduled for 4:30. . . . Perkins would read the fresh material, seldom taking issue with a word or a sentence. Wolfe's style was Wolfe's style, his unique way of saying things, and not to be tampered with. Instead, Perkins bent his energies . . . on getting Wolfe to eliminate certain paragraphs, scenes, or chapters. "Tom, this is good," he would say, "this is excellent, but in view of your over-all plan, don't you think it would be better if you cut from here to there?" Twisting and agonizing in his chair as in the days of the 47 Workshop, Wolfe would say, "No, Goddamn it!" and "To hell with it!" and finally agree, perhaps with the provision that he be allowed to write a transitional sentence—whereupon he would go into the next office and toss off a transitional sentence of several thousand words. . . .

—Turnbull.

Margaret Mitchell 1900–1949

"I hoped to study medicine," she said, "but while I was at Smith College my mother died and I had to come home to keep house." She worked on a newspaper, married, and when an accident limited her activities, read books until she was driven to write one.

Although she wrote copiously she had small thought of publishing Gone With the Wind. *Publication was almost an accident, when a Macmillan editor named H. S. Latham visited Atlanta.*

Just about a year ago I went to Atlanta looking for possible new authors. One of the first things that was said to me on the occasion of this visit was to the effect that probably the most important novel being written at that time in that locality was Peggy Mitchell's. No one seemed to know what the book was about, but a great many people knew apparently that "Peggy" was at work on something and that was enough to bring cordial, even insistent, recommendation to their lips.

Finally it was my good fortune to meet Peggy Mitchell. She proved to be a diminutive person with a very lively sense of humor and a proficiency in the art of conversation rarely encountered these days. We talked about a good many things at this first meeting, and more particularly about Southern literature, about which I found she had, as indeed about many things, positive ideas. Finally after my circumlocutions I swung the conversation around to her own work. Imagine my surprise and disappointment when she informed me, very pleasantly but with firmness, that while she might have been playing around with the idea of doing a novel some time or other, she had nothing to show me. . . .

A few hours before I left Atlanta, the telephone in my hotel room rang and Miss Mitchell's voice came to me over it informing me that she was downstairs in the lobby and would like to see me. I went down, and I shall never forget the picture I have of Margaret Mitchell as I then saw her—a tiny woman sitting on a divan, and beside her the biggest manuscript I have ever seen, towering in two stacks almost up to her shoulders.

—*Margaret Mitchell and Her Novel* Gone With the Wind, 1936 [no author given].

Years later, Mitchell told the story from her side.

He'd asked for it, and I'd felt very flattered that he even considered me. But I'd refused, knowing in what poor shape the thing was. And that day he was here, I'd called up various and sundry hopeful authors and would-be authors and jackassed them (that is a friend's phrase) about in the car and gotten them to the tea where they could actually meet a live publisher in the flesh.

One of them was a child who had nearly driven me crazy about her book. I'd no more than get settled at my own work than here she was, bellowing that she had gone stale or that she couldn't write love scenes and couldn't I write them for her? Or she was on the phone picking my brains for historical facts that had taken me weeks to run down. As twilight eve was drawing on and I was riding her and some of her adoring girl friends home from the tea, somebody asked me when I expected to get my book finished and why hadn't I given it to Mr. Latham.

Then this child cried, "Why, are you writing a book, Peggy. How strange you've never said anything about it. Why didn't you give it to Mr. Latham?" I said I hadn't because it was so lousy I was ashamed of it. To which she remarked—and did not mean it cattily—"Well, I daresay. Really, I wouldn't take you for the type who would write a successful book. You know you don't take life seriously enough to be a novelist. And you've never even had it refused by a publisher? How strange! *I've* been refused by the very best publishers. But my book is grand. Everybody says it will win the Pulitzer Prize. But, Peggy, I think you are wasting your time trying. You really aren't the type."

Well, suddenly, I got so mad that I began to laugh, and I had to stop the car because I laughed so hard. And that confirmed their opinion of my lack of seriousness. And when I got home I was so mad still that I grabbed up what manuscript I could lay hands on. . . .

—*Margaret Mitchell's* Gone With the Wind *Letters,* ed. Richard Harwell, 1976.

The extraordinary success of Gone With the Wind *(1936), as we read of it in her letters, sounds almost depressing. She wrote no other novels.*

I'm awfully ignorant about authors. I've known so few and so few of them intimately. Do all of them have to go through this? If so, how do they ever have the courage to write a second book? Are all of them put in such positions that they cannot go out of their houses? When they go to parties (I ventured to one tea) are their veils jerked off, their sashes torn loose, the seams of their skirts parted from their waists? Do people scream at them and poke them with their long fingernails?

—Harwell.

As David Selznick made the film, Mitchell heard that F. Scott Fitzgerald had been assigned to work on the script. (Nothing came of it.)

I dearly loved his books and still do and re-read them ever so often. "This Side of Paradise" is the most perfect crystallization of an era in all American fiction. It makes me feel sad when I think how utterly past that era is now. I'm sure Mother and I picked him up in our car one day when he was at Camp Gordon during the war. The streetcar tracks had not been laid that far at that time and we usually hauled twelve soldiers to town every time we went out to see Stephens [her brother]. After he got famous and I saw his picture I remembered him.

—Harwell.

Langston Hughes 1902–1967

Principally a poet, the greatest innovator among black American writers, Hughes also wrote novels, short stories, autobiography, non-fiction, and drama.

When he was a child his mother used him as a prop for her own dramatic reading.

Once she chose a poem about a Roman mother with two sons. She was to play the mother, and Langston and another little boy would be her children. She made herself and the two boys Roman-style garments, and together they presented a fine sight. But Langston was not at all happy about being on stage playing a Roman boy. Right in the middle of the reading he began to roll his eyes around and around. The audience twittered. Fearing that she was boring them, Carrie became more intense in her dramatic reading. Langston, his face otherwise expressionless, opened his eyes wider and rolled them faster. Unable to control themselves any longer, some members of the audience burst out laughing, and in seconds the entire auditorium was in an uproar. Later, Langston got a spanking he would never forget.

—James S. Haskins, *Always Movin' On: The Life of Langston Hughes,* 1976.

His breakthrough as a poet began when he was a busboy in a Washington hotel; Vachel Lindsay dined at the hotel before performing his own poems.

That evening, as Lindsay dined in the hotel restaurant, Langston laid the poems next to his plate, saying he liked Lindsay's poems and here were some of his. Embarrassed, he hurried away before Lindsay could respond.

In the next morning's paper, Langston was surprised to read that Vachel Lindsay had "discovered" a young black poet, who was working as a busboy, and had read some of the young man's poems to the hotel audience the previous night. When he reported for work, he was met by a crowd of reporters and photographers. A picture of Langston dressed in his busboy uniform and carrying a tray of dishes appeared in most of the Washington newspapers.

—Haskins.

He traveled in his own country and among his own people.

Leaving New Orleans at the end of one summer, Langston Hughes stopped on the way north to visit old blacks with stories to tell about their time in slavery. He talked to one old man who owned a hat that absolutely fascinated Hughes. The hat had become its own patches—patches of miscellaneous pieces of cloth, of leather and even of linoleum. He felt that the hat summed up and symbolized the difficult endurance of the black in America, surviving through slavery into the present day. Langston Hughes traded the old man his new hat for the old one. Getting back to New York, the hat was a prized possession, and so Hughes took it to his bank on Fifth Avenue, and placed it in a suitcase inside his safe-deposit box along with his grandmother's shawl and some of his manuscripts. Six months later, returning to the bank to take something out of his safe-deposit box on a Saturday morning, Hughes opened the box, and to his astonishment a huge swarm of moths whirled out of it, flying all over the room and lighting on the crowds of rich Fifth Avenue people. Hughes closed the suitcase as quickly as he could and ran out of the bank. He went to Central Park, opened the suitcase to air the moths out of it, and found that nothing remained of the old hat except some colorful dust—and presumably a piece or two of linoleum.

—[Editor's paraphrase].

When Hughes traveled abroad he brought American music with him for company, which in Russia earned him the companionship of Arthur Koestler.

Koestler arrived in Ashkhabad a few days after Langston and checked in at the same hotel. Hearing the sounds of American jazz, he knocked on the door and introduced himself—in English! . . . The two traveled together from then on.

—Haskins.

He planned his last appearance with care. He even made sure that humor—his tried and true weapon against sadness—played a part in his memorial service by arranging for someone to read his poem "Wake":

Tell all my mourners
To mourn in red—
Cause there ain't no sense
In my bein' dead.

—*Selected Poems of Langston Hughes,* 1973.

And at the end of the service, a request he had made before he died was carried out. As a parting joke to his friends, a jazz trio played the old tune, "Do Nothing Till You Hear from Me."

John Steinbeck 1902–1968

Steinbeck grew up in California and often used that state as the scene of his fiction: Tortilla Flat *(1935),* In Dubious Battle *(1936),* Of Mice and Men *(1938).* The Grapes of Wrath *(1939) followed a family to California from the dust bowl of Oklahoma.*

In 1956, Steinbeck read an interview Faulkner had given after receiving the Nobel Prize in 1950.

When those old writing boys get to talking about The Artist, meaning themselves, I want to leave the profession. I don't know whether the Nobel Prize does it or not, but if it does, thank God I have not been so honored. They really get to living up to themselves, wrapped and shellacked. Apparently they can't have any human intercourse again. Bill said he only read Homer and Cervantes, never his contemporaries, and then, by God, in answer to the next question he stole a paragraph from an article I wrote for the Saturday Review eight months ago.

—*Steinbeck: A Life in Letters,* eds. Elaine Steinbeck and Robert Wallsten, 1975.

Steinbeck traveled to Russia several times, but never mastered the language. In 1947 he wrote dispatches for the Herald Tribune, *traveling with the photographer Robert Capa.*

. . . I admit our Russian is limited, but we can say hello, come in, you are beautiful, oh no you don't, and one which charms us but seems to have an application rarely needed: "The thumb is second cousin to the left foot." We don't use that one much. So in our pride we ordered for breakfast, an omelet, toast and coffee and what has just arrived is a tomato salad with onions, a dish of pickles, a big slice of water melon and two bottles of cream soda.

—Steinbeck and Wallsten.

When Steinbeck himself won the Nobel Prize in 1962, the year of Travels with Charley, *he feared the consequences.*

I've always been afraid of it because of what it does to people. For one thing I don't remember anyone doing any work after getting it save maybe Shaw. This last book of Faulkner's was written long ago. Hemingway went into a kind of hysterical haze. Red Lewis just collapsed into alcoholism and angers. It has in effect amounted to an epitaph. Maybe I'm being over-optimistic but I wouldn't have accepted it if I hadn't thought I could beat the rap.

—Steinbeck and Wallsten.

He had published nothing further when he died six years later.

Nathanael West 1903–1940

In Miss Lonelyhearts *(1933), West's hero writes a column of advice for the lovelorn in response to letters from readers. He held the mirror up to nature.*

. . . late in April, less than a month after the book's publication, West answered a phone call and heard a voice say: "This is Mrs. ______, and I'm suing you for using a letter in your book which I wrote to a woman who runs an advice-to-the-lovelorn column in a Trenton, N.J., paper." She hung up, leaving West bewildered. Then he called his publisher and discovered that another woman had threatened to institute an action based on the same letter, which, she said, she had written to a New York newspaper.

—Jay Martin, *Nathanael West: The Art of His Life,* 1970.

West's brief life ended in a car accident. His friends were not wholly surprised.

Once, when driving with Schrank into New York to consult with Mayer about some changes, he went through eleven consecutive stop lights after leaving the Lincoln Tunnel, once swerving around a trolley, and finally hit a taxi that was just starting across an intersection. He settled on the spot for the slight damages, but Schrank, convinced that West was trying to kill both of them, walked the rest of the way. . . .

—Martin.

His producer at Republic Studios, for whom West wrote screenplays, remembered an earlier adventure.

"We were coming home late . . . in a light rain, and we had to cross a main irrigation ditch. It was about 40 or 50 feet deep, with sullen, black, cold water, and it was about 50 feet wide and had no regular bridge, only a series of pine planks laid across—no guardrail, no nothing. In this sleety rain we could hardly see, and suddenly he realized he's passing the so-called bridge—so he swings the car abruptly onto the bridge . . . and the momentum . . . tips the car and with the slippery wood we tilted over on our side and started to fall . . . and then stopped . . . at a slight angle. Now, I'm sitting in Nate's lap . . . and we're both sitting there looking down into this jet black water . . . scared to death. We're afraid that the car is going to topple at any moment, and we don't know what the devil is holding us up.

"Now, Nate had great physical and personal courage . . . and he sat there very quietly. I was so scared I *couldn't* talk, frankly, I had no muscular reaction at all, and I was afraid to move out of his lap.

"Then Nate says: 'Well, now what do we do?—let's think about it.' He steadied me because he was so cool and unhurried. *This* was a West gesture: the world's worst driver, when he got into a jam, he thought coolly and properly. He finally said: 'Look, Lennie, *slowly* try to crawl over your way, and maybe your weight will counterbalance the car. If *not,* and we go over, try to throw that door open. . . . When you start moving, think of only one thing: if the car starts to fall, you reach for that door handle and throw it—get it open no matter what else you do . . . because we can get out of the car through that door, even if we go into the drink.'

"So I started to inch my way over. And in those days we

had the gear shift between us; that was a problem because in some weird manner I had vaulted over it completely. . . . Now it stood in my way. Nate said, 'Take your time, don't rush it. It'll be all right—so we'll get wet.'

"I slowly crawled over that way. For some reason the car trembled but didn't fall. I got more and more courage the further I got because finally I was in reach of that door. So I slowly opened the door—I didn't push it open very far, but just enough to get one leg out of the car—and then slowly wormed my body out of it. Then . . . I opened it more and held onto the car and said, 'You try the same thing.'. . . . For an apparently ungainly man, he's pretty agile—well built and in good condition. He gets out of the car and nothing happens. So we back up a way from the car and look. In constructing this pine bridge, they left a beam extending up about six to eight inches . . . the door handle had caught on this 2 x 2 and the car was joggling and teetering on it. *That's* Nate West."

—Martin.

Louis Zukofsky 1904–1978

Zukofsky was an Objectivist Poet, a friend of Ezra Pound. His fellow Objectivist George Oppen, upon finishing a collection of poems, spoke of it to Zukofsky.

Walking with Louis when *Discrete Series* was in manuscript, George was discussing it with him before showing it to anyone else. Louis turned and with a quizzical expression asked George, "Do you prefer your poetry to mine?"

"Yes," answered George, and the friendship was at a breaking point.

—Mary Oppen, *Meaning: A Life,* 1978.

John O'Hara 1905–1970

John O'Hara was a newspaperman who turned to fiction, becoming a prolific author of short stories and novels. In 1935, he published his second novel, Butterfield 8. *It was a lively number for those days, which made it amusing when the bindery mistakenly bound several hundred copies in the covers of a life of John Wesley, founder of Methodism.*

Some O'Hara stories, in various versions, became notorious.

The 9 February 1942 "Entertainment Week" column included the first appearance in print of the now-famous anecdote of the time when Hemingway, James Lardner and Vincent Sheean were pooling their funds during the Spanish Civil War and trying to figure out what to do with the extra money. Hemingway said, "Let's take the bloody money and start a bloody fund to send John O'Hara to Yale."

—Matthew J. Bruccoli, *The O'Hara Concern: A Biography of John O'Hara,* 1975.

With a friend like Hemingway, John O'Hara (not to mention F. Scott Fitzgerald, Gertrude Stein, Morley Callaghan . . .) had no need for an enemy.

One night in spring 1944 the John Herseys, the Vincent Sheeans, Joel Sayre, Paul de Kruif and Ernest Hemingway and Martha Gellhorn were in the back room at Tim Costello's bar on Third Avenue. The Hemingways left early. When the others left, O'Hara was standing on the sidewalk, very drunk, and he said to them, "Nice people!" Hersey learned that while he had been with the group in the back room, O'Hara had come into the bar. Costello told him who was there. Muttering angrily that he hadn't been invited, O'Hara hooked his blackthorn walking stick on the bar and began drinking. Some time later, Hemingway, on his way out, spotted O'Hara and pounded him hard on the back, with which he had been having trouble, and said, "When did you start carrying a walking stick?"

"That's the best piece of blackthorn in New York City."

"It is, is it? I'm going to break it with my bare hands."

"Fifty says you can't."

Hemingway took the bet and said, "Not only that, but I'm going to break it over my own head." He did.

—Bruccoli.

Bennett Cerf was his publisher, and a source of O'Hara stories.

He came to see me one day and said he thought he'd like to call the book *A Small Hotel,* for one of Dick Rodgers' songs.

He said, "Do you think Dick will mind?" Dick and John were great friends from *Pal Joey,* the musical they had written together, but I said that John should at least ask, so he went to see Dick.

He came back about a half-hour later, black with rage, as only John O'Hara could get in those days. He said, "I'm calling it *The Farmers Hotel,*" and stamped out.

As soon as he was out of sight, I called Dick Rodgers at his office. Dick said, "He came in here and said he wanted to name his book *A Small Hotel,* after one of my songs. I said, 'That's great, John, but to be exact, the name of the song is "*There's* a Small Hotel." ' O'Hara said, 'When I need you to name my books, I'll tell you,' and left without another word."

During the time Cardinal Spellman was my neighbor, he complained to me several times about John O'Hara's books. John was really way out ahead in writing sex scenes and using four-letter words and whatnot. Now his books are mild in comparison with the stuff that's coming out, but then they were quite daring. *A Rage to Live* was considered very gamy because it had a detailed episode of a seduction, described rather graphically. Finally I said to Spellman, "He's one of your boys. Why don't you talk to him? I'd like to bring John to lunch. Would you like to have him?" The Cardinal said, "I'd love to meet him." I told this to John, wondering how he'd react. He was delighted. He drove up in his brand-new Rolls-Royce and parked it in the courtyard, where elaborate arrangements had been made to reserve a parking space for him—a ritual that was repeated many times over the years. I said, "Now, John, please don't go off the handle or something." I remember John's reply: "Which one of us is the Catholic? You don't have to tell me how to behave."

Usually, whenever I went over to the Cardinal's house, one of the maids would open the door and I'd wait for him to come downstairs to the little reception room. This time the Cardinal came to meet us in our courtyard. He was a little nervous about the meeting, too. I said, "Your Eminence, this is Mr. John O'Hara." John bent over and kissed the Cardinal's ring; then took an envelope out of his pocket and said, "My mother was always very much interested in your favorite charity, the Foundling Home, and I'd like to give you a donation for it." The

Cardinal's face was a study—he hadn't expected this to happen at all, and neither did I. He was astounded.

The three of us walked over to lunch, and they took to each other at once. We had a wonderful time. They forgot I was there. After lunch the Cardinal insisted on showing us his coin collection in the Archbishopric.

In December, 1950, Bill Faulkner was passing through New York on his way to Stockholm to receive the Nobel Prize, so Phyllis and I gave a small dinner party for him the night before he left and invited Belle and John, who had never met Faulkner. The Nobel Prize was probably the one thing on earth that John yearned for most, and he was quite an authority on the subject; so within a few minutes of being introduced, he informed Bill that the Nobel money he was about to receive would be tax-free—a fact that none of the rest of us was aware of. Then after dinner when Bill needed a light, John leaned across the table and handed him a cigarette lighter that had been given to John, which had an inscription from his old friend, the playright Philip Barry. When Bill admired it, John said he'd like Bill to keep it to mark the big event. Bill merely said thank you and put the lighter in his pocket, not rising to the occasion. It was easy to see that John was deeply offended. . . .

—*At Random,* 1977.

Clifford Odets 1906–1963

The young playwright opened Waiting for Lefty *in New York, a city looking for social answers, in 1935 at the height of the Depression. The play set corrupt union bosses in conflict with labor rank and file; the question was whether to strike or not.*

When the audience at the end of the play responded to the militant question from the stage: "Well, what's the answer?" with a spontaneous roar of "Strike! Strike!" it was something more than a tribute to the play's effectiveness, more even than a testimony of the audience's hunger for constructive social action. It was the birth cry of the thirties.

—Harold Clurman, *The Fervent Years,* 1945.

Later Odets wrote some bland plays—George S. Kaufman asked, "Odets, where is thy sting?"—and went to Hollywood. Alfred Kazin visited him there.

I sat with Clifford Odets and the Irish actor Barry Fitzgerald one Sunday afternoon on the patio of Odet's splendid rented house overlooking a splendid Hollywood chasm between two mounds of desert, listening to the Brahms First on his splendid Capehart—a "miracle of modern music making" *that turned records over.* Barry Fitzgerald, looking as peaceful and funny as he did in his movies, was contentedly smoking his pipe, an Irish shepherd nodding over invisible sheep. Odets's face always tried to be a mask—he *had* begun as an actor—but relapsed into a battlefield; in the white beams of California sunshine burning down on us that afternoon, every feature was spotlighted; every facet of skin worked against every other facet of skin. There was no rest in that face. There would be no rest for Clifford Odets in this life, not even in Hollywood. But meanwhile there was Brahms on an old-fashioned Sunday afternoon of listening to the phonograph. Odets pointed a finger to the sky and said in hushed tones, "It comes from there." He was invaded by Brahms all over his body, possessed by Brahms. He shook in public rapture, gratitude, and exaltation. He blew a kiss to the music. His glasses, swinging carelessly from his hand as he vibrated prayerfully in his chair, fell and shattered on the flagstones. As I looked down at the pieces in some concern, he haughtily explained that he had half a dozen pairs in his study.

—*New York Jew,* 1978.

W. H. Auden 1907–1973

Neville Coghill remembered a turning point in the young poet's life.

"One morning Mr Wystan Auden, then an undergraduate at Christ Church, blew in to Exeter College for his tutorial hour with me, saying, 'I have torn up all my poems.'

" 'Indeed! Why?'

" 'Because they were no good. Based on Wordsworth. No good nowadays.'

" 'Oh. . . ?'

" 'You ought to read Eliot. I've been reading Eliot. I now see the way I want to write. I've written two new poems this week. Listen!' "

—*T. S. Eliot: A Symposium,* compiled by Richard March and Tambimuttu, 1949.

Auden married not for love but out of compassion.

He also, very suddenly, married. Christopher Isherwood, temporarily living in Amsterdam, had met Erika Mann, the eldest daughter of Thomas Mann. Branded as a public enemy of the Third Reich, she was threatened with the loss of her German citizenship, and hoped to find an Englishman she could marry so that she could become a British subject. She asked Isherwood if he would be willing to marry her, but he refused and instead suggested that she write to his friend Wystan Auden, explaining the situation. She did so. Auden wired back "Delighted.". . .

—Charles Osborne, *W. H. Auden: The Life of a Poet,* 1979.

He tried to arrange other such marriages of convenience. "After all," he asked E. M. Forster, "what are buggers for?"

After he emigrated to the United States in 1939, Auden lived in Brooklyn Heights in a house that sheltered, from time to time, Carson McCullers, Paul and Jane Bowles, Richard Wright, Louis MacNeice, as well as Benjamin Britten and Peter Pears, Marc Blitzstein, Salvador and Magda Dali, Pavel Tschelitchev, and Gypsy Rose Lee—who was taking time off from stripteasing in order to write The G-String Murders. *Paul Bowles described how the arrangement worked.*

"Auden ran it: he was exceptionally adept at getting the necessary money out of us when it was due. We had a good cook and an impossible maid (except that I doubt that any maid could ever have kept that house completely clean and neat), and we ate steaming meals that were served regularly and punctually in the dim, street-floor dining room, with Auden sitting at the head of the table. He would preface a meal by announcing, 'We've got a roast and two veg, salad and savoury, and there will be no political discussion.' "

—*Without Stopping,* 1972.

He taught at the University of Michigan, then lectured at Barnard at Ursula Niebuhr's suggestion.

"One afternoon before he started his lecture, he looked around in his short-sighted way, and held out his hand. I got up and provided him with some chalk, as he often had written words or names on the blackboard. "No,' he said, with that wonderful smile, 'Smackers! What about the smackers?' At that time, I had not the foggiest idea what smackers were, but my colleagues soon enlightened me. After the lecture I arranged for the bursar to send him his modest stipend at once."

—*W. H. Auden, a Tribute,* ed. Stephen Spender, 1975.

Auden lectured everywhere, and left people talking.

The lecture he gave at Harvard in 1947 on *Don Quixote* as part of a series commemorating the quatercentenary of the birth of Cervantes, is still talked of, for he had consumed a few too many martinis before lecturing, began by apologizing for his new set of dentures, and then launched upon *Don Quixote* by admitting that he'd never managed to read that novel through to the end, and doubting whether anyone in his audience had.

—Osborne.

In New York Auden read in the newspaper that Dorothy Day, founder of the Catholic Worker Movement and editor of the Catholic Worker, *had been fined $250 because her hostel for derelicts was not up to code. As Miss Day left for court the next day—the* New York Times *reported—she walked past a gathering of bums looking for handouts.*

"From their midst a man, who looked much like the rest, stepped out and pressed a piece of paper into her hand. 'I just read about your trouble,' the man said. 'I want to help out a little bit toward the fine. Here's two-fifty.' Miss Day, elated over having, as she thought, $2.50, thanked her benefactor and hurried on. In the subway on her way to Upper Manhattan Court, she looked at the cheque. It was for the full amount of the fine, $250. And it was signed by W. H. Auden. Miss Day was apologetic for not having recognized him. 'Poets do look a bit unpressed, don't they?' she said."

—Spender.

Auden aged rapidly. His face became so lined, Stravinsky remarked, "Soon we shall have to smooth him out to see who he is." James Stern remembered a competition.

"He and I used to have a race as to which of us would be the first to lose all his teeth. I forget who won, but it was a near thing. He had just acquired his first set [of dentures] . . . when—at a Boston tea-party given in his honour by a group of elderly ladies—the hostess asked him to extinguish the flame under the silver kettle. Wystan, now forty-five and far from thin, filled his lungs to capacity. And blew! 'My dear, the *din!* My uppers went crashing into my neighbour's empty teacup!' "

—Spender.

At a Stravinsky dinner party—Auden allegedly drank a jug of Gibsons before it, a bottle of champagne during it, and a bottle of Cherry Heering after it—he rose to form.

He trotted out several of his party pieces, among them his view that the time had not yet come to admit that "Shakespeare was in the homintern, or, for that matter, that Beethoven was queer"; and his descriptions of Rilke as "the greatest Lesbian poet since Sappho" and of Yevtushenko as "the poor man's *Howl.*" Before leaving, he forbade his hosts to attend a poetry reading he was soon to give: "I never allow anyone I know to come to those things. First of all, I want to keep my tricks to myself, and second, I'm always afraid someone in the back of the hall is going to shout something like 'We've heard all that before' or 'Get her!' "

—Osborne.

He rose to many occasions.

In the autumn of 1962, traveling from New York to New Haven by train to lecture at Yale University, he sat in the club car and was eyed furtively for some time by two Yale students who finally sent a note to him which read, "We can't stand it a minute longer: Are you Carl Sandburg?"

Auden sent a note in reply: "You have spoiled mother's day."

—Osborne.

Theodore Roethke 1908–1963

Roethke grew up in Saginaw, Michigan, and attended the University of Michigan in Ann Arbor. He was a large man and affected toughness, but the mask sometimes slipped, revealing his sensitivity; then he would cover himself again. When he was a young teacher a colleague could not identify a bird call.

"It's a vireo," Ted said at once and went on with great earnestness talking about birds, all kinds of birds, for maybe fifteen minutes but he broke off, saying, "Aw, shit, who wants to know about birds anyhow?"

—Allen Seager, *The Glass House,* 1968.

He was manic depressive, and his manic periods announced themselves in memorable fashion.

The day of his first class was October 2. The students gathered in the classroom but Ted was not there. At this period he was at the height of his power and reputation as a teacher. His students had the air of disciples; they waited half an hour. Suddenly the door burst open and Ted appeared, panting with exhaustion, his face grey and wet with sweat, his damp trousers clinging to his legs. He had walked or run all the way from downtown Seattle, a distance not less than five miles. He flung himself against the blackboard in a kind of crucified pose, muttering incoherently. His students knew that he was subject to such attacks and one of them ran to the English Department office and got the Secretary, Mrs. Dorothy Bowie. . . . When a man as big as Ted goes off the rails, it is a frightening spectacle. . . . Mrs. Bowie . . . called the city police and said, "This is a very distinguished man and he is ill. All we want you to do is take him to a sanitarium. No rough stuff."

Ted feared and hated cops. When he saw them, he made one lunge at them but they seized him and smoothly handcuffed his hands behind his back. There wasn't any rough stuff. They were gentle but firm. And they led old Ted, the distinguished man, the poet and friend of poets everywhere through the corridors of Parrington Hall just as classes were changing, with his head bent nearly to his knees and the cops sedately around him. David Wagoner said, "The tears ran down my face and everybody who saw it felt soiled, a little ashamed."

—Seager.

He was assiduous in controlling his literary career, but he could not always control himself. John Berryman told Roethke's biographer about the confrontation between Roethke and Edmund Wilson.

Berryman was living in Princeton then and one day, meeting Wilson on the street, Wilson said, "This man Roethke—is he any good?"

"He's brilliant," Berryman said.

Wilson, whose enthusiasm for new poets has been less than tepid, said, "Humph."

"You asked me. I told you," Berryman said.

Out of this encounter apparently, Ted received an invitation from the Wilsons to a Christmas party. Berryman says that when he and his wife arrived, one wall of the Wilson's living room was a bank of flowers, dozens of them, bearing the card of "Theodore Roethke." It was a characteristic gesture. (When he was in New York Ted was always sending masses of flowers to his friends and running up big bills at Max Schling's which Doubleday would have to vouch for.) Mrs. Wilson was delighted and eagerly awaited Ted's arrival.

Around nine o'clock in the evening, Ted came in "aggressively sober," Berryman asserts. He paid his devoirs to his hostess and went at once into the dining room where a large collation lay ready. He was offered a drink but called instead for tomato juice. He took a large piece of cheese and a bunch of hothouse grapes in one hand and with his tomato juice in the other, went in to join the gathering. He found a chair next to a very handsome woman of about thirty-five and at once began a lively conversation. In one of those inexplicable lulls that sometimes comes over a party, Berryman heard Ted say vehemently, "But it only costs a hundred bucks to go to the Caribbean. Come on. Let's go."

This offer seems to have been promptly rejected and Ted got up, still carrying the cheese and grapes, and wedged himself in next to Wilson, who was sitting on a sofa. Ted said to him, "Come on. Let's blow this and go upstairs and I'll show you some of my stuff."

"I can't do that. I'm the host," Wilson very properly replied.

Ted glowered at him. "You hate all contemporary poets, don't you?"

Wilson began to protest angrily and Ted reached over, seized Wilson's cheek, and said, "Why, you're all blubber."

"Get out of here, you half-baked Bacchus!" Wilson cried.

Ted got out.

—Seager.

When at parties he assumed he should proposition all women.

And there was the pretty young faculty wife whom Ted was groping on the dance floor who said, "There's a bedroom right over there, Ted. Come on, let's go."

Ted blanched and drew back.

—Seager.

Like many authors, he felt perfectly objective about deserving the Nobel Prize. He wrote his editor at Doubleday suggesting that they manipulate Stockholm.

"Why shouldn't we begin mending and weaving and doing whatever is necessary to bring the Nobel in poetry to America? Certainly I'm a vastly better poet than Quasimodo, and this last French man is good but does the same thing over and over. I think Wystan Auden should be next, then Pablo Neruda, then me and that's a cold, considered objective judgment."

—Seager.

It is widely assumed, by people who have never met one, that poets are dreamy and uncompetitive, as given to flower-sniffing as Ferdinand. Here is some evidence to the contrary.

Theodore Roethke read his poems in Boston and Robert Lowell gave a party for him afterwards. The living room was full of poets. When everyone had gathered, Lowell suggested that Roethke should read one more poem. Roethke agreed, but asked

Lowell to read one also. Lowell agreed, but suggested that I. A. Richards, the venerable critic who had recently taken up poetry, read a poem also. Richards was agreeable, but suggested that all the other poets present be asked to read one too.

Lowell retreated to his bookshelves and returned with copies of everyone's books. John Holmes read first. Philip Booth and others followed, ending with Roethke, Lowell and Richards. When the last poet had read the last poem, the evening had gone late, and many bottles were empty. Just as people began to gather themselves to leave, Roethke asked if he might say one more, a piece about Richard Nixon which he had just composed on his journey east. All heard him with deference, and when he finished he remarked that he was *glad* he had written that poem, it was a *good* one. Thereupon I. A. Richards decided that he should like to read one more poem also—his *best* poem, he said. Now let's see, where was it? He looked through his first volume and couldn't find it. While everyone waited, he paged carefully through his second book. When he did not find it, he said, "Well, perhaps I have not yet published it." After a pause, he continued, "No, actually I think I have not *written* it yet!"

Roethke stood up and bellowed, "All right, you old bastard. You win! You win!"

—[Editor's paraphrase].

When Roethke's mind was afflicted, a number of topics obsessed him. Shortly before his death, in the company of the bewildered Irish poet Thomas Kinsella, he exercised his old obsession about gangsters or The Mob.

Early one evening, Ted was driving Kinsella down a long straight road on Bainbridge Island. Half a mile ahead they saw a car standing crossways in the road. Ted stopped his car at once.

"That's how they come to get you," he said.

"Who?" Kinsella asked innocently.

"Ah, the Mob," Ted snarled, and turned his car around and started back the way they had come. They found a filling station and Ted got on the phone to the Bainbridge police, a force of only two or three men. He said, "The Mob's got a road-block down here. You better pick me up. You need someone who knows how to use a Tommy gun," and he gave his name and the address of the filling station. The police must have thought someone was kidding them, for they did not show up.

—Seager.

Richard Wright 1908–1960

Wright was born in Mississippi and grew up in Tennessee. He published Native Son *in 1940, when he was thirty-two. The road to literature had been indirect.*

Every morning before work, Wright would stop at the American Bank to see his friend the elevator operator and read the *Memphis Commercial Appeal.* It was probably in May, 1927, that he read an editorial in that paper lambasting H. L. Mencken, who was then editor-in-chief of *The American Mercury.* Although Richard had never heard of Mencken, he was immediately intrigued by him for the simple reason that the South seemed so hostile to him. . . . An Irish Catholic . . . lent Richard his library card so that he could pretend to borrow books in his name. He must have handed this carefully forged note with a pounding heart to the librarian, who read, "Dear Madam: Will you please let this nigger boy have some books by H. L. Mencken?" This was how Wright obtained *A Book of Prefaces* and one volume of *Prejudices.*

—Michel Fabre, *The Unfinished Quest of Richard Wright,* 1973.

He knew how to protect himself by using the prejudice of others.

In Mexico, John Steinbeck and Herbert Kline drove Richard to the train depot and the three men discussed the South and its prejudices. The moustached, craggily handsome Steinbeck turned his eyes from the road and asked Richard: "Have you got any subversive literature in your baggage?" "Yes," Richard answered, "I've got Lenin's *What Is to Be Done,* Karl Marx's *Das Kapital. . . .*" Steinbeck looked concerned. "Don't take such stuff; they'll grab you at the border for a Red," he warned Richard. "Ship your baggage and travel by air," Kline admonished. But Richard smiled to reassure the two men and said, "I'll risk it." He thought it was possible to enter the South, act as he knew whites wanted Negroes to act, and not have any trouble, even though his baggage contained books which advocated "dangerous thoughts."

Richard took a sleeper from Mexico City and rode with American whites, Mexicans, Germans, English and Spaniards, but when the train reached the Texas border, the races were separated. The white people were put into one coach and the black man, Richard, was put into another coach. A queer kind of segregation occurred in his coach; he sat at one end and the white American conductor motioned the Mexicans to the opposite end.

Soon the customs official came through the train; he examined the baggage of the Mexicans and then approached Richard. When he saw the official start to walk in his direction he washed all expression from his face, widened his eyes slightly and tried to look stupid. He was trying desperately to recall how he had acted when he was a child in the South and resolved to act that way again, for he wanted no trouble. If he gave any offense, there was no one to help him; the only other brown-skinned people were Mexicans and he knew that the state of Texas despised them equally, if not more, than they did a black man.

"What you got here, boy?" the inspector drawled.

"Just baggage."

"Well, open up," he said.

Richard opened a suitcase which contained clothing.

"All right. What's in there?" the man asked, pointing to Richard's typewriter.

"My typewriter."

The air around the two men seemed to change abruptly. It seemed to Richard that soundless bells were clanging like the far-off yet approaching sirens of fire engines as the man stared first at the large standard typewriter in a custom-designed case and then into his face.

"Is it yours, boy?" the official asked.

"Oh, yes, sir," Richard answered.

There was another silence while the man stared at Richard suspiciously. Finally, he made up his mind: "What do you do? Teach school?"

"No, sir; I write," Richard said.

"You're a preacher?" the official half asked and half declared, as if he had not heard Richard's answer.

"No, sir; I'm a writer," Richard told him again.

"What's in there?" the man asked, pointing to the case containing Richard's books.

"Books."

By this time the customs official was genuinely puzzled and he bent over the box to glance at the rows of books.

"What are these books?"

"Just books," Richard told him.

"You teach school, don't you?" the man asked.

"No, sir; I'm a writer."

"You're a preacher," the official insisted.

"I'm a writer," Richard said once again.

He knew that the man had never in his life met any black men who, if they were not laborers, were not schoolteachers or preachers, and he was puzzled because he could not fit Richard into a familiar category.

A sense of chill, of hair lifting slightly out of the pores on the back of his neck entered Richard's body when the man bent over, picked up *Das Kapital,* glanced at the title and asked: "Boy, these books ain't Communistic, are they?"

"Oh, no, sir," Richard lied. "They are books dealing with writing."

"Dealing with writing," the inspector repeated slowly, uncomprehendingly. He had been so conditioned that he could not actually recognize words he had not been conditioned to hear. "All right, you can pack up now," he said uneasily.

Richard quickly locked his baggage with nervous fingers, expecting at any moment to be told to open his cases again and spread out all his books and papers. What would happen if the man saw the new novel he was working on? A thin line of perspiration formed along his upper lip; in the story was a girl who married a white man and then murdered him. Ah, God! the man was still standing by his seat. Now, what? Richard wondered.

"Where were you born, boy?" the man asked.

"Mississippi, sir," Richard said.

At last the official had one familiar fact to which he could cling and his face changed entirely.

"I knew you was a Southern nigger," he said, smiling happily. "You niggers can travel all over the world, but when I meet a Southern nigger, I know it.

"O.K., boy," the man said, still affable, as he walked away down the aisle.

—Constance Webb, *Richard Wright: A Biography,* 1968.

James Agee 1909–1955

Agee published first as a poet, later wrote stories and articles for magazines, and was posthumously recognized as a novelist, especially for A Death in the Family *(1957).*

Robert Sandek was his friend when Agee was an undergraduate at Harvard.

Jim did not especially love Harvard as he loved Exeter, but he did appreciate its people and its atmosphere of personal freedom. He could come and go at will. . . . But it was his comprehension of human behavior and a great fear of his own behavior that set him apart. For it was Jim who, coming back weak and sick from Stillman Infirmary to the Yard one midwinter's night, could smash his fist into the glass door of a moving streetcar on the Mt. Auburn Street line when the conductor closed the door in his face; who could rise at 4:30 on Sunday mornings to walk up the river and help the Cowley fathers serve communion at their Episcopal monastery; who would proudly struggle into white tie and tails in order to sing Bach in the Glee Club; who so adored Helen Hayes in *Coquette* that he saw it seven times in a week; who would spend a whole New York weekend in an all-night movie; who would mimic Lee and Grant at Appomattox ("Mah sword, Suh!" with an elaborate bow. "Drink to that!" replies General Grant sliding out of his chair onto the floor); who could sit up all night writing a poem or talking and smoking so that his fingers were stained to the color of a horse chestnut.

—*Remembering James Agee,* ed. David Madden, 1974.

Agee knew Whittaker Chambers when they both worked at Time*—before Chambers testified against Alger Hiss. Chambers recalled his last meeting with Agee.*

. . . life had separated us. I was engaged in certain well-known events. Later, I was confined about two years, writing a book.

Jim was in Hollywood, working with John Huston. Then came two heart attacks in quick succession. From his sick room came, too, seven- and eight-page letters, penciled in the minute, slantwise, beautiful script which was a personal cipher that took hours to decode. In the spring of 1952, we both happened into New York. Jim came unexpectedly to my hotel, and we walked down Fifth Avenue together—very slowly, he could only inch along now, so that I saw that he was taking his last walks.

He stopped before a show window in which cruelly elegant mannequins in exaggerated posture swam in a sickly lavender light. He stared at them for awhile. Then, "It's a pansy's world," he said, looking at them and at the city around us. We laughed. It was a summing up. Later, I bought two chocolate Easter eggs for his little girls.

—Madden.

Charles Olson 1910–1970

At Black Mountain College, the innovative school in North Carolina where he was rector, Olson was not only administrator and teacher but universal student. Six and a half feet tall, not meager, he was an ungainly and engaging dancer to his instructor Merce Cunningham.

He was "marvelous," Cunningham told me: "He came regularly, worked hard" and underwent considerable physical risk. Olson told Cunningham that he didn't have to look at him if he didn't feel like it. But "I *enjoyed* him," Cunningham told me; "it wasn't unhappy to watch him—he was something like a light walrus."

—Martin Duberman, *Black Mountain: An Exploration in Community,* 1972.

By taking part in everything, he annoyed some of his admirers.

Another student recalls the time Natasha Goldowski gave a "non-credit" seminar on cybernetics from the galley proofs of Norbert Wiener's first book. A lot of people sat in, including Olson, who was particularly fascinated by the fact that Wiener had worked with a team of specialists from a variety of fields. According to the student, Olson "blathered on at some length" about how "beautiful" that kind of team effort was; there was only one thing wrong with it—they should have had a poet. "I thought Natasha would clobber him," the student recalls. And in a similar vein, Jonathan Williams remembers that when David Tudor played Boulez's Second Sonata during the summer of 1951, Olson "made some remark like, 'It's the only piece of music since Bach.' He's only heard *three* pieces since Bach," Williams commented. . . .

—Duberman.

Black Mountain, which sheltered its share of eccentrics, occasionally aroused suspicion among the surrounding hillfolk.

Olson himself set the pattern. The hill people had made up tales about "the giant that walks the roads at night," and one of them decided to see whether the giant was really so tough. The man came onto the campus, sought Olson out and baited him. Olson, who'd never hit anybody and despite his size seemed more awkward than strong, finally lost his temper and socked the guy—and apparently was elated when it turned out he'd broken the man's jaw.

—Duberman.

Delmore Schwartz 1913–1966

It was Delmore Schwartz who first announced that "even paranoiacs have enemies." He knew as well as anyone; when his first book was published (In Dreams Begin Responsibilities, *1938*), *he sent a copy to his brother Kenneth, who replied that he had*

"liked the book very much except for the fact that I don't like poetry as I can't understand it. I showed it to a few people and they were very much impressed except for the fact that they didn't have $2.50 they would have bought the book."

—Russell Fraser, "Delmore Schwartz and the Death of the Artist," *Michigan Quarterly Review,* Fall 1979.

Surely the most relentless enemy was nearer to hand. Once in Princeton, R. P. Blackmur came to bail him out of the drunk tank. "Punish me," said Schwartz.

Sometimes a terrible lethargy afflicted him, like that of Goncharov's Oblomov.

Living in Cambridge, he recited Valéry to get himself up in the morning, never mind the hangover or the depression that was more cause than effect. "Il faut tenter de vivre." This sounded stoical-romantic, and he modified it later. It "has now become—il faut get out of the pajamas every other day." He hated to travel, and he died without having been to Europe. "How could I go to Europe," he said, "when I can't even shave at home?"

—Fraser.

Robert Lowell wrote about Schwartz in Life Studies.

To Delmore Schwartz
(Cambridge 1946)

We couldn't even keep the furnace lit!
Even when we had disconnected it,
the antiquated
refrigerator gurgled mustard gas
through your mustard-yellow house,
and spoiled our long maneuvred visit
from T. S. Eliot's brother, Henry Ware. . . .

Your stuffed duck craned toward Harvard from my trunk:
its bill was a black whistle, and its brow
was high and thinner than a baby's thumb;
its webs were tough as toenails on its bough.
It was your first kill; you had rushed it home,
pickled in a tin wastebasket of rum—
it looked through us, as if it'd died dead drunk.
You must have propped its eyelids with a nail,
and yet it lived with us and met our stare,
Rabelaisian, lubricious, drugged. And there,
perched on my trunk and typing-table,
it cooled our universal
Angst a moment, Delmore. We drank and eyed
the chicken-hearted shadows of the world.
Underseas fellows, nobly mad,
we talked away our friends. "Let Joyce and Freud,
the Masters of Joy,
be our guests here," you said. The room was filled

with cigarette smoke circling the paranoid,
inert gaze of Coleridge, back
from Malta—his eyes lost in flesh, lips baked and black.
Your tiger kitten, *Oranges,*
cartwheeled for joy in a ball of snarls.
You said:
"*We poets in our youth begin in sadness;*
thereof in the end come despondency and madness;
Stalin has had two cerebral hemorrhages!"
The Charles
River was turning silver. In the ebb-
light of morning, we stuck
the duck
-'s web-
foot, like a candle, in a quart of gin we'd killed.

—1956.

To obtain a divorce from his first wife, Gertrude Buckman, required invention.

In February, Delmore and Gertrude agreed to file for a divorce, not without some hesitation on both sides. The proceedings turned out to be a farce, since New York State laws required proof of adultery to establish sufficient grounds for divorce and Delmore was either unwilling or unable to supply such evidence. So they decided to stage their own findings of what he called "specious adultery," and rented a hotel room in New York, then summoned their friends Maurice and Charlotte Zolotow to witness the scene. The Zolotows were to enter the hotel room just in time to see a woman disappearing into the bathroom while Delmore lounged on the bed in a guilty attitude. Since no woman could be found to play the part of the adulteress, however, Gertrude herself stood in. "This was one time when he wasn't with another woman," she remarked to William Barrett.

—James Atlas, *Delmore Schwartz,* 1977.

He died in a cheap Manhattan motel, his whereabouts unknown to his friends; his body lay unclaimed at Bellevue. His last years were mean and squalid—with redeeming moments of manic monologue.

Talking for hours without a pause, gesticulating frantically, drinking shots of bourbon and paying for them with hundred-dollar bills, Delmore would elaborate on the anecdotes perfected through many years of practice: his marriages, the sex life of T. S. Eliot, his lost inheritance, and the years at George Washington High School, where he had been "the brightest person ever tested," interspersed with Hollywood gossip and Giants' batting averages. And there were some new exotic variations tailored to the demands of a college audience, including a notable account of how Queen Elizabeth had traveled to the Orient to learn secret techniques of fellatio, which involved introducing rare herbs into her mouth—and had then returned to England, where the first beneficiary of these recondite practices was none other than Danny Kaye.

—Atlas.

Randall Jarrell 1914–1965

Peter Taylor and Robert Lowell were undergraduates at Kenyon College, where John Crowe Ransom taught and was editor of the Kenyon Review, *and where Jarrell was a young instructor. Taylor told of a class with Jarrell.*

I enrolled in an eight o'clock class in American literature which he taught at Kenyon. It was held on the third floor of Ascension Hall. Since it was an eight o'clock, Randall was frequently late meeting it. We would look out the third-floor windows and see him sprinting down the Middle Path, often eating his breakfast as he ran. The rule at Kenyon was that the class had to wait on a professor only until the second bell. The boys would cup their hands and shout to Randall how many minutes or seconds he had, and he kept coming. Sometimes the bell would ring when he was already on the stairs, but regardless of that, when the bell rang, the class, most of it, would stampede down the stairs.

—*Randall Jarrell, 1914–1965,* eds. Robert Lowell, Peter Taylor, and Robert Penn Warren, 1967.

He was a man wholly committed to literature and worshipped literature's makers. His wife recollected a tentative literary identification.

"When some guests mistook our small framed picture of Chekhov for Randall's father, Randall sighed after they had gone (he was never prepared for the world's uncultivatedness), 'People, *people*! Is there no limit to what people don't know?'

"But before we went to bed that night, he took a long look at Chekhov's picture and a long look at himself in the mirror. 'You know what?' he said. 'What?' I said. 'If you blur your eyes. . . .' And I said, 'It's so, Randall. It's so.' "

—Lowell *et al.*

His friends were the best poets of his generation, and he did not hesitate to annoy his friends. John Berryman wrote about Jarrell and Lowell visiting him in Princeton.

". . . he had a hangover, and that was very amazing because Jarrell did not drink. He's the only poet that I've ever known in the universe who simply did not drink. So how did he get the hangover? Well, he'd been to a cocktail party the day before in New York and had eaten a poisoned canapé.

"So here's Jarrell walking up and down in my living room, miserable and witty. And very malicious, as he could certainly be, making up a brand-new Lowell poem full of characteristic Lowell properties, Lowell's grandfather and Charon, and the man who did not find this funny at all was Lowell."

—Lowell *et al.*

John Berryman 1914–1972

At Columbia as an undergraduate, Berryman ran for class office and the track team, until Mark Van Doren's classes turned him toward poetry. Saul Bellow remembered a later Berryman at Princeton.

He spoke in a Princeton mutter, often incomprehensible to me. His longish face with its high color and blue eyes I took to be of Irish origin. I have known blue-eyed poets apparently fresh from heaven who gazed at you like Little Lord Fauntleroy while thinking how you would look in your coffin. John was not one of these blue-eyed serpents. Had you, in a word-association test, said "Devil" to him, he would have answered "John Webster." He thought of nothing wicked. What he mainly thought about was literature. When he saw me coming, he often said, "Ah!" meaning that a literary discussion was about to begin.

—Saul Bellow, "Introduction," *Recovery*, 1973.

And in another context.

Once as we were discussing Rilke I interrupted to ask him whether he had, the other night, somewhere in the Village, pushed a lady down a flight of stairs.

"Whom?"

"Beautiful Catherine, the big girl I introduced you to."

"Did I do that? I wonder why?"

"Because she wouldn't let you into the apartment."

He took a polite interest in this information. He said, "That I was in the City at all is news to me."

We went back to Rilke. There was only one important topic. We had no small-talk.

In Minneapolis one afternoon Ralph Ross and I had to force the window of a house near Seven Corners to find out what had happened to John. No one had seen him in several days. We arrived in Ross's Jaguar, rang the bell, kicked at the door, tried to peer through the panes and then crawled in over a windowsill. We found ourselves standing on a bare gritty floor between steel bookstacks. The green steel shelves from Montgomery Ward's, meant for garages or workshops, for canned peaches in farmer's cellars, were filled with the elegant editions of Nashe and Marlowe and Beaumont and Fletcher which John was forever importing from Blackwell's. These were read, annotated, for John worked hard. We found him in the bedroom. Face down, rigid, he lay diagonally across the double bed. From this position he did not stir. But he spoke distinctly.

"These efforts are wasted. We are unregenerate."

—Bellow.

Bellow remembered their last meeting.

He had arrived during a sub-zero wave to give a reading in Chicago. High-shouldered in his thin coat and big Homburg, bearded, he coughed up phlegm. He looked decayed. He had been drinking and the reading was a disaster. His Princeton mutter, once an affectation, had become a vice. People strained to hear a word. Except when, following some arbitrary system of dynamics, he shouted loudly, we could hear nothing. We left a disappointed, bewildered, angry audience. Dignified, he entered a waiting car, sat down, and vomited. He passed out in his room at the Quadrangle Club and slept through the faculty party given in his honor. But in the morning he was full of innocent cheer. He was chirping. It had been a great evening. He recalled an immense success. His cab came, we hugged each other, and he was off for the airport under a frozen sun.

—Bellow.

Carson McCullers 1917–1967

Katherine Anne Porter, visiting the writer's colony of Yaddo, had trouble from her fellow writer and admirer McCullers. (McCullers once pointed Katherine Anne Porter out to Newton Arvin, Longfellow's biographer, as "the greatest female writer in America now—but just wait until next year.")

The day that Carson pounded on Miss Porter's door of the mansion and pleaded forlornly, "Please, Katherine Anne, let me come in and talk with you—I do love you so very much," Miss Porter demanded that Carson leave. She shouted from within that she would not come out until Carson had vacated the hall. It was 6:30 P.M., however, and time for dinner. Both women knew not to risk Mrs. Ames's displeasure by being a minute late. Soon Miss Porter heard her devotee's feet shuffling off down the corridor. After a brief interval, the elder woman cautiously opened the door and stepped out. To her astonishment, there lay Carson sprawled across the threshold. "But I had had enough," said Miss Porter. "I merely stepped over her and continued on my way to dinner. And that was the last time she ever bothered me."

—Virginia Spencer Carr, *The Lonely Hunter: A Biography of Carson McCullers*, 1975.

McCullers lived in Brooklyn Heights, in the house where Auden made the rules. Thanksgiving, 1940, was a day of discovery.

After dinner, over brandy and coffee before the fire in the great, groundfloor drawing room with Gypsy Rose Lee, Reeves, Auden, Davis, and newcomers MacNeice, Britten, and Pears, Carson heard the screaming siren of a distant fire engine drawing closer as though its destination was their street. Carson and Miss Lee, always alert to the extraordinary and exciting, rushed outside to view the spectacle. Running three or four blocks, Miss Lee's long strides leading the way, Carson suddenly caught her arm and shouted breathlessly for her to stop. Then she exclaimed: "Frankie is in love with her brother and the bride, and wants to become a member of the wedding!" Miss Lee stared at her friend as though she had suddenly lost her mind, but as the two walked silently back to the house, Carson was trembling. She was certain now of the style and theme of her book. Its focus had sharpened at last.

—Carr.

Summering in Nantucket in 1946, she leapt into another genre. Tennessee Williams had written her a fan letter and invited her to visit him.

After a discussion of the theatre one night, Williams suggested to Carson that she should try to write drama. By this time he was convinced that all of Carson's works would make "strong theatre." Encouraged by his enthusiasm, as well as goaded by Edmund Wilson's remarks that *The Member of the Wedding* was static and lacked a sense of drama, Carson decided to begin work immediately on a dramatic adaptation of the book. The next morning Williams acquired a portable typewriter for her. Then they positioned themselves at opposite ends of the long dining-room table and began to write. Sometimes they worked into the afternoon, a bottle of whiskey between them, which they passed back and forth.

—Carr.

Robert Lowell 1917–1977

His old friend John Thompson remembered the poet who stayed in bed, and the determined but hapless athlete.

Forty years ago in the carpenter's Gothic of Douglass House, demolished now, at Gambier, Ohio, in the long gabled upstairs room he shared with Peter Taylor, Robert Lowell had the intelligent habit of lying in bed all day. Around that bed like a tumbledown brick wall were his Greek Homer, his Latin Vergil, his Chaucer, letters from Boston, cast-off socks, his Dante, his Milton. Even in those days before he had published a word we knew he belonged among the peers who surrounded him.

The poems he wrote and rewrote and rewrote in bed then were as awkward as he was, the man of the Kenyon squad who plowed sideways into his own teammates, but strong as a bull, spilling them all over, who never won a game. He aspired to be a Rhodes Scholar, and thus had to be an all-around man like Whizzer White. In those days Lowell couldn't tie his own shoe laces.

—"Robert Lowell," *New York Review of Books,* Oct. 27, 1977.

He had gone to Kenyon College to work with John Crowe Ransom, and found Randall Jarrell there.

His apprenticeships were many—Ford Madox Ford and Allen Tate in this story; earlier Richard Eberhart who taught him at St. Mark's school; later Pound, Eliot, and Williams.

LOWELL: I met Ford at a cocktail party in Boston and went to dinner with him at the Athens Olympia. He was going to visit the Tates, and said, "Come and see me down there, we're all going to Tennessee." So I drove down. He hadn't arrived, so I got to know the Tates quite well before his appearance.

INTERVIEWER: Staying in a pup-tent.

LOWELL: It's a terrible piece of youthful callousness. They had one Negro woman who came in and helped, but Mrs. Tate was doing all the housekeeping. She had three guests and her own family, and was doing the cooking and writing a novel. And this young man arrived, quite ardent and eccentric. I think I suggested that maybe I'd stay with them. And they said, "We really haven't any room, you'd have to pitch a tent on the lawn." So I went to Sears, Roebuck and got a tent and rigged it on their lawn. The Tates were too polite to tell me that what they'd said had been just a figure of speech. I stayed two months in my tent and ate with the Tates.

—Frederick Seidel in *Writers at Work,* 2nd series, 1963.

There were bouts of madness, a manic depressive cycle which included delusions. Stanley Kunitz remembered one occasion.

Once, when I visited him at McLean's Hospital in Boston, he read "Lycidas" aloud to me, in his improved version, firmly convinced that he was the author of the original.

—"The Sense of a Life," *New York Times Book Review,* Oct. 16, 1977.

Active in the political sixties, Lowell refused President Johnson's invitation to the White House and marched in Washington. Norman Mailer described his encounter with Lowell, on this occasion, in The Armies of the Night.

Robert Lowell and Norman Mailer feigned deep conversation. They turned their heads to one another at the empty table, ignoring the potentially acolytic drinkers at either elbow, they projected their elbows out in fact like flying buttresses or old Republicans, they exuded waves of Interruption Repellent from the posture of their backs, and concentrated on their conversation, for indeed they were the only two men of remotely similar status in the room. . . .

Lowell, whose personal attractiveness was immense (since his features were at once virile and patrician and his characteristic manner turned up facets of the grim, the gallant, the tender and the solicitous as if he were the nicest Boston banker one had ever hoped to meet) was not concerned too much about the evening at the theater. "I'm just going to read some poems," he said, "I suppose you're going to speak, Norman."

"Well, I will."

"Yes, you're awfully good at that."

"Not really." Harumphs, modifications, protestations and denials of the virtue of the ability to speak.

"I'm no good at all at public speaking," said Lowell in the kindest voice. He had indisputably won the first round. Mailer the younger, presumptive, and self-elected prince was left to his great surprise—for he had been exercised this way many times before—with the unmistakable feeling that there was some faint strain of the second-rate in this ability to speak on your feet. . . .

A silence.

"You know, Norman," said Lowell in his fondest voice, "Elizabeth and I really think you're the finest journalist in America."

Mailer knew Lowell thought this—Lowell had even sent him a postcard once to state the enthusiasm. But the novelist had been shrewd enough to judge that Lowell sent many postcards to many people—it did not matter that Lowell was by overwhelming consensus judged to be the best, most talented, and most distinguished poet in America—it was still necessary to keep the defense lines in good working order. A good word on a card could keep many a dangerous recalcitrant in the ranks.

Therefore, this practice annoyed Mailer. The first card he'd ever received from Lowell was on a book of poems, *Deaths for the Ladies and other disasters* it had been called, and many people had thought the book a joke which whatever its endless demerits, it was not. Not to the novice poet at least. When Lowell had written that he liked the book, Mailer next waited for some word in print to canonize his thin tome; of course it never came. If Lowell were to begin to award living American poets in critical print, two hundred starving worthies could with fairness hold out their bowl before the escaped Novelist would deserve his turn. Still, Mailer was irked. He felt he had been part of a literary game. When the second card came a few years later telling him he was the best journalist in America, he did not answer. Elizabeth Hardwick, Lowell's wife, had just published a review of *An American Dream* in *Partisan Review* which had done its best to disembowel the novel. Lowell's card might have arrived with the best of motives, but its timing suggested to Mailer an exercise in neutralsmanship—neutralize the maximum of possible future risks. Mailer was not critically equipped for the task, but there was always the distant danger that some bright and not unauthoritative voice, irked at Lowell's enduring hegemony, might come along with a long lance and presume to tell America that posterity would judge Allen Ginsberg the greater poet.

This was all doubtless desperately unfair to Lowell who, on the basis of two kind cards, was now judged by Mailer to possess an undue unchristian talent for literary logrolling. But then

Mailer was prickly. Let us hope it was not because he had been beaten a little too often by book reviewers, since the fruit of specific brutality is general suspicion.

Still Lowell now made the mistake of repeating his remark. "Yes, Norman, I really think you are the best journalist in America."

The pen may be mightier than the sword, yet at their best, each belong to extravagant men. "Well, Cal," said Mailer, using Lowell's nickname for the first time, "there are days when I think of myself as being the best writer in America."

—*The Armies of the Night,* 1968.

Later, matters improved between the two writers.

Kunitz was a good friend for many years.

Everywhere Cal (as he was known to his friends) went he brought his turmoil with him, hand-in-hand with his batch of stained and crumpled manuscripts. "I am tired," he had written. "Everyone is tired of my turmoil." His blue-gray eyes behind his glasses were vague and restless, till they began to glitter. He seemed so full of self, so disconnected from his surroundings, that you could not believe he noticed anything; but somehow, indoors or out, little escaped him. On his next visit to your place he would inquire about a painting or a piece of bric-a-brac that had been moved, joke about the gain in weight of your fat cat Celia, or comment on the most trivial household acquisition. In the garden or on a country walk he would ply you with questions about the names and properties of flowers, about which he appeared to be totally ignorant; but then he would astonish you by publishing a poem full of precise horticultural detail.

His talk was expressive with gesture, the stirring of an invisible broth, interspersed with the shaping of a vase in air—or was it Lilith's archetypal curves that he was fashioning? When he slumped onto your sofa like an extended question mark, tumbler in hand, chain-smoking, dropping his ashes, spouting gossip or poetry, you knew that the moon would have to drift across the sky before he would be ready to go, leaving at least one memorial cigarette hole burnt into cushion or rug behind him. You were bleary with fatigue, but you cherished the rare electricity of his presence. And you would have been desolate if he had not returned.

—Kunitz.

Blair Clark, who had known him at St. Mark's, was his close friend for forty-five years—best man at his first two weddings. Once Clark flew to Buenos Aires to bring him home from a psychiatric clinic. There were other times.

I remember once, a dozen years before he died, bringing him back to my house in New York in one of his crazed escapes from home. Watching him breathe in heavy gasps, asleep in the taxi, the tranquillizing drugs fighting the mania, I thought that there were then two dynamos within him, spinning in opposite directions and tearing him apart, and that these forces would kill him at last. No one, strong as he was, could stand that for long. And finally, the opposing engines of creation and repression did kill him in a taxi in front of his own real home.

—Blair Clark, "On Robert Lowell," *The Harvard Advocate*, Nov. 1979.

Shirley Jackson 1919–1965

After writing "The Lottery," Jackson became obsessed with witchcraft and with her own possession of diabolical power.

Once, when for some reason she was angry with her publisher, Alfred Knopf, she learned that he was journeying up to Vermont to ski. . . . She made an image of wax and stuck a pin in one leg of the image, and, sure enough, Knopf broke a leg skiing—broke it, indeed, in three places.

—Brendan Gill, *Here at the New Yorker*, 1975.

Brendan Gill told of an encounter among Jackson, her husband the critic Stanley Edgar Hyman, and Dylan Thomas.

By this stage of his life, Thomas was no longer the promising romantic boy of the Augustus John portrait; he was a tubby little man, with thinning hair and brown teeth with holes in them. Despite his appearance, he enjoyed a considerable sexual success among suggestible college girls, whom he would approach with the honest if unappealing inquiry, "Can I jump you?" At the Hymans', a drunken Thomas put the question to a drunken Shirley, while a drunken Stanley sat contentedly in front of his TV screen, watching a night baseball game. Hearing no negative in response to his question, Thomas made a pass at Shirley, who leapt to her feet and lumbered past Stanley, with Thomas in close pursuit. She mounted the front stairs, ran along the hall, stumbled down the back stairs, and again lumbered past Stanley. Shirley and Thomas made the circuit three or four times before Stanley, irritated at having his view of the ball game repeatedly interrupted by the gross beasts jogging past him, reached out and grabbed Thomas by the belt of his trousers, causing him to fall to the floor, while the winded Shirley mounted the stairs for the last time.

—Gill.

James Jones 1921–1977

When Jones fought in the Pacific during World War II, he already knew that he would write about it.

In a costly three-day fight for a group of hills called The Galloping Horse, he was hit in the head by a fragment from a random mortar shell and spent some time in the hospital before returning up the line. He arrived at the regimental aid station with his head all covered with blood, feeling dizzy and a little hysterical, and ran into their old regimental surgeon, a light colonel, cutting strips of flesh out of a wound in the back of a boy sitting there on a table. The doctor looked up from his work and saw the new arrival.

"Hello, Jonesie," the doctor said casually. "Getting more material for that book of yours you're gonna write?"

"More than I want, Doc," he replied.

—Willie Morris, *James Jones: A Friendship,* 1978.

During the filming of From Here to Eternity, *Jones became friendly with Montgomery Clift and Frank Sinatra.*

"We talked about the injustice of life and love, . . . and then Monty and I would listen to Frank talk about Ava Gardner. We would get very, very loaded. After dinner and a lot more drinks we would weave outside into the night and all sit down on the curb next to a lamppost. It became our lamppost and we'd mumble more nonsense to each other. We felt very close." Occasionally, when they came back to the Roosevelt Hotel where they all stayed they would throw beer cans out the windows. Clift, who had learned to play the bugle, sometimes sounded it outside his window.

—Morris.

Rich and famous, Jones lived in Paris with his wife Gloria—and kept on working. He could be almost anonymous there.

He had begun *The Thin Red Line* in the small apartment on Quai aux Fleurs, the one that was situated over the *épicerie.* One day he was writing the memorable scene in which a member of the company is badly wounded and stranded in no man's land, crying out for help. . . .

While Jim was laboring on this section, there was a knock on the door of the apartment; it was the big fat wrestler who worked for the laundry coming to collect the laundry bill. The Joneses knew this fellow very well. Gloria was pregnant, and he thought they were poor struggling young Americans trying to get by in Paris. Jim answered the knock on the door with tears streaming down his face from the scene he was finishing. The laundryman thought he was crying because he did not have the money to pay the bill. The man said, "*Pas nécessaire*—It's okay. You no have to pay now."

—Morris.

Hollywood continued its patronage of Jones.

When Darryl Zanuck was preparing to film *The Longest Day,* portions of which were from Jim and Romain Gary's script of the American scenes, he telegrammed Jim in Split, Yugoslavia, where the Joneses were briefly on vacation. Zanuck's urgent wire solicited Jim to correct a small piece of American dialogue. Jim wired back, "How much for it?" and Zanuck replied, "Fifteen thousand dollars." "Okay, shoot," was the response. The wire with the line of dialogue came from Zanuck: "I can't eat that bloody old box of *tunny* fish." Jim and Gloria sat on a rock on the beach and corrected the line to read: "I can't stand this damned old tuna fish."

—Morris.

Jones added his quota to the annals of literary drunkenness; William Styron told about one occasion.

"It was my last night in Europe after a long trip—the night before we were to sail on the *United States* from Le Havre. Jim and I decided to get good and drunk, no fooling around. Jimmy Baldwin was with us. We had a few drinks before dinner, then a really fine meal, and we went out. Rose and Gloria dropped out around midnight. We were in some nightclubs, and some girls still clung around for a while. Finally even Jimmy Baldwin faded—a very good man with the bottle. He folded around four or five A.M., to give him credit maybe a little longer. The collapse of Jimmy Baldwin should've given us pause for thought, but didn't. Dawn was coming up, a beautiful late summer's morning. Jim and I decided to carry on. So we opened a little brasserie on the Left Bank and talked about life, love, literature, mortality, and sex. My wife and kids and I had to leave Paris at 7 P.M. to drive to Le Havre. All the more reason to stay up.

"At twelve noon promptly Jim and I were drinking straight-up martinis at the Ritz Bar, not an eye's-wink of sleep. We were still standing up boozing until three in the afternoon. By this time it was beginning to wear on us a little, eighteen hours straight. We poured ourselves into a taxi and went back to the Ile, with this bizarre feeling of going home drunk in the middle of the afternoon. We went in the house and the first thing I heard was a huge crash. Gloria had hurled a big teapot at both of us which missed Jim's head by an inch and shattered against the wall. Then this scream: 'If I ever lay eyes on you again may God kill me, you drunken bum!' "

—Morris.

In Paris among the literary set Jones was a ringleader for jokes.

There were also tricks. Their friend Jean Castel owned a popular bar and restaurant down a side street in St. Germain. For a long time this establishment and its owner had been terrorized by an old Romanian woman, who stood outside in a dirty flowing dress playing a squeaky mandolin, occasionally shouting obscenities through the doorway at Mr. Castel inside. Castel complained about this woman to anyone who would listen. She was ruining his business and her damnable music was driving him insane, he said, but what could he do? There were even rumors of a lawsuit. Castel announced to his friends that he was going to take a much-needed vacation in Tahiti—a long plane ride indeed from Paris. About twenty-five of his friends, led by the Joneses, put up $100 apiece and bought the Romanian woman a round-trip ticket to Tahiti the day before Castel was to leave Paris. He took his plane, and many hours later landed at the airport in Tahiti. He descended the ramp, and almost collapsed at the sight which greeted him: the Romanian woman strumming her mandolin and saying: "Welcome to Tahiti, Monsieur Castel."

—Morris.

When on Sunday afternoons French television ran dubbed American westerns, Jones dressed his son and himself in identical cowboy outfits; the two watched the films together, because Jones wanted Jamie to grow up American. "Don't ask for the fuckin' vin rouge"—he would yell at the set—"say redeye, you assholes!"

He returned to the United States in 1973, where a degenerative illness took his life. His friend Robert Alan Arthur told about Jones's last game of poker.

"Ten days before Jim went to the hospital for the last time we played what proved to be the final round. A hand of seven-card stud, and by the sixth card there are just two players left, Jim and Jamie. Both hands well disguised, both men extremely wary. The last down card. Cool and unhesitating Jim bets ten dollars. A moment passes; Jamie sees the ten, raises twenty. Jim hunches over his hand, balefully looks at his son through slitted eyes. Over the silence, in mock awe, someone says: 'The classic Freudian drama. Father and son alone in the pit, son determined to kill the father, the old man desperately struggling to hold him off.'

"Jim grins and slides in twenty dollars' worth of Hermes ivory. 'Wrong,' he says, exposing a king-high heart flush. 'Father triumphant over asshole kid.'

"Just the slightest smile from Jamie, who spread his hand

for all to see. 'Spade flush, ace high,' he says, then rakes in the nearly hundred-dollar pot. Gloria laughs, blows Jamie a kiss. The game is over. Jim looks rueful. 'Christ,' he says, 'that's not the way it's supposed to come out.'"

—Morris.

Jack Kerouac 1922–1969

Kerouac came to New York from Lowell, Massachusetts, on a football scholarship to Columbia University. Soon he quit football for literature, but perhaps not soon enough.

When Jack was on the football team at dear old Columbia, they all went down to the Village, the football team, to do the usual thing that football teams do when they aren't punishing each other. And they ran some little guy with a violin around a corner into an alley, three or four of them, and busted the violin over the guy's head. That never left Jack. It was his one guilty thing, the one thing he'd done. He went with the fullback, the left end or whatever, and cornered this poor little fag in an alley with his violin and busted it over his head. No, that never left Jack—the violence of it, against someone else. He used to get drunk and say, "We should never have hit that man with his violin."

—*Jack's Book: An Oral Biography of Jack Kerouac,* eds. Barry Gifford and Lawrence Lee, 1978.

Robert Giroux, then editor at Harcourt Brace, printed Kerouac's first novel, The Town of the City *in 1950; Kerouac dedicated it to Giroux "Since Kindness be the Venus-Star of friendship . . . To my editor, Mentor, and Friend . . ."*

Harcourt Brace policy forbade printing the dedication, which was perhaps just as well.

About a year after "The Town and the City" was published, Kerouac arrived in Giroux's office with the famous continuous roll of teletype paper on which he had written a draft of "On the Road." Kerouac announced that the book was divinely inspired, touched by the Holy Ghost. Giroux looked at the manuscript, as thick as a roll of paper towels, which had come uncorrected from the typewriter. Giroux suggested that "even after you have been inspired by the Holy Ghost, you have to sit down and read your manuscript." Then he suggested that the novel might need revision.

In an outrage Kerouac swore that nobody was going to change a single word, and, denouncing Giroux as a crass idiot, he left the office.

—Donald Hall, "A Visit with Robert Giroux," *New York Times Book Review,* Jan. 1980.

According to Gore Vidal, "Jack was bisexual, and not above using it . . . to get his way." Vidal told about an evening that began when he had dinner with William Burroughs and Kerouac.

"Then Jack decided that it was time that he and I went to bed together. As the evening waxed, it seemed to me like a less good idea, as the drink increased and the morning was near. Finally, Burroughs disappeared into the night, and Jack and I ended up at the Chelsea Hotel. . . .

"Jack was in a very cheery mood about it all, in spite of a hangover the next day. He'd run out of money, and he asked me to lend him a dollar. . . . I gave him the money and I said, 'And now you owe me a dollar.' Those were my last words to him as we parted.

"I didn't see him again until *The Dharma Bums* was published, which was '58. Meanwhile I had read *The Subterraneans,* and I said, 'Why didn't you really describe what happened that night at the Chelsea?'

He said, 'Oh, I forgot.' . . .

"Then I was doing a Studio One play for television, and a guy called Jack Barefield, . . . said that he was in the San Remo and this crazy guy suddenly got up and shouted, 'I blew Gore Vidal!' "

—Gifford and Lee.

In The Dharma Bums *(1958) Kerouac wrote about backpacking in California with his poet friend Gary Snyder, whom he called Japhy. Snyder remembered the real mountain.*

"I said to Jack, 'You know, real Buddhists are able to walk around the countryside.' So he said, 'Sure. Let's go backpacking.' . . . It was around the end of October.

"So we headed up over Sonora Pass, leaving at night in Berkeley, and went over to Bridgeport, up to Twin Lakes and went in from there, over Sonora Pass.

"It was very funny. It's very beautifully described in *The Dharma Bums,* actually. It was very cold. It was late autumn. The aspens were yellow, and it went well below freezing in the night and left frost on the little creek in the canyon we were camped at. There was a sprinkle of fresh white snow up on the ridges and peaks. We made it up to the top of the Matterhorn and came back down again. Actually, Jack didn't."

—Gifford and Lee.

Flannery O'Connor 1925–1964

Flannery O'Connor was born in Savannah, Georgia, and lived most of her life in the small town of Milledgeville, where she attended the Women's College of Georgia. A biographer recorded an instance of O'Connor's relationship with Milledgeville society.

There is, in the memory of one Milledgeville matron, the image of O'Connor at nineteen or twenty who, when invited to a wedding shower for an old family friend, remained standing, her back pressed against the wall, scowling at the group of women who had sat down to lunch. Neither the devil nor her mother could make her say yes to this fiercely gracious female society, but Flannery O'Connor could not say no even in a whisper. She could not refuse the invitation but she would not accept it either. She did not exactly "fuss" but neither did she "do pretty."

—Josephine Hendin, *The World of Flannery O'Connor,* 1970.

Frank O'Hara 1926–1966

O'Hara attended Harvard and the University of Michigan, then moved to New York for the rest of his life. The poet and editor Diane Di Prima remembered how she acquired O'Hara poems for her magazine The Floating Bear *(1961–69).*

"I would go over to Frank O'Hara's house pretty often. He used to keep a typewriter on the table in the kitchen, and he would type away, make poems all the time, when company was there and when it wasn't, when he was eating, all kinds of times. There would be an unfinished poem in his typewriter and he would do a few lines on it now and again, and he kept losing all these poems. They would wind up all over the house. . . . The poems would get into everything and I would come over and go through, like, his dresser drawers. There would be poems in with the towels, and I'd say, 'Oh, hey, I like this one,' and he'd say, 'OK, take it.' "

—Marjorie Perloff, *Frank O'Hara: A Critical Introduction*, 1977.

Joe LeSueur lived with O'Hara, and contributed to a poem's beginning.

"Sometimes . . . the details in a poem will remind me of a day I would otherwise have forgotten. Mother's Day, 1958, for example. Frank was struck by the title of a *Times* book review, 'The Arrow That Flieth by Day,' and said he'd like to appropriate it for a poem. I agreed that the phrase had a nice ring and asked him for the second time what I should do about Mother's Day, which I'd forgotten all about. 'Oh, send your mother a telegram,' he said. But I couldn't hit upon a combination of words that didn't revolt me and Western Union's prepared messages sounded too maudlin even for my mother. 'You think of a message for my mother and I'll think of one for yours,' I suggested. We then proceeded to try to top each other with apposite messages that would have made Philip Wylie applaud. Then it was time to go hear a performance of Aaron Copland's *Piano Fantasy* by Noel Lee. 'It's raining, I don't want to go.' Frank said. So he stayed home and wrote 'Ode on the Arrow That Flieth by Day,' which refers to the Fantasy, Western Union, the rain, and Mother's Day."

—Perloff.

O'Hara died after an accident on Fire Island.

A few minutes after reaching the beach, the taxi (a covered jeep) damaged a rear wheel and stopped. All the passengers descended and assembled near the left side of the taxi, away from the ocean, while the driver tried to repair the wheel. The headlights remained on because there was no other source of illumination; the beach was very dark. The driver radioed for another taxi, and the passengers milled about, waiting. O'Hara, who had been standing next to Mitchell, wandered toward the rear of the taxi. After a few minutes, another beach buggy came from the opposite direction. This buggy (an open jeep) appeared to be coming quite close to the disabled car at a speed of 15–20 m.p.h. The passengers standing in front of the taxi got out of the way, and Mitchell shouted "Frank!" At that moment, O'Hara emerged from the rear of the taxi, facing the headlights of the oncoming jeep. The young driver said he was blinded by the headlights of the stalled taxi, shining up into the air. O'Hara was struck by the right front fender, evidently in the abdomen, the jeep continued on for another ten feet or so and came to a stop.

—Perloff.

Anne Sexton 1928–1974

Anne Sexton started to write poems seriously in her thirtieth year. In 1957 she enrolled in a seminar with the poet John Holmes at the Boston Center for Adult Education. Later she took a creative writing class with Robert Lowell. The Paris Review *asked Sexton to talk about her friendship with Sylvia Plath.*

INTERVIEWER

Sylvia Plath was a member of Lowell's class [at Boston University] also, wasn't she?

SEXTON

Yes. She and George Starbuck heard that I was auditing Lowell's class. They kind of joined me there for the second term. After the class, we would pile in the front seat of my old Ford and I would drive quickly through the traffic to the Ritz. I would always park illegally in a "Loading Only Zone," telling them gaily, "It's O.K., we're only going to get loaded." Off we'd go, each on George's arm, into the Ritz to drink three or four martinis. George even has a line about this in his first book of poems, *Bone Thoughts.* After the Ritz, we would spend our last pennies at the Waldorf Cafeteria—a dinner for seventy cents—George was in no hurry. He was separated from his wife; Sylvia's Ted [Hughes] was busy with his own work, and I had to stay in the city for a seven P.M. appointment with my psychiatrist . . . a funny three. . . .

Often, very often. Sylvia and I would talk at length about our first suicide, in detail and in depth—between the free potato chips. Suicide is, after all, the opposite of the poem. Sylvia and I often talked opposites. We talked death with burned-up intensity, both of us drawn to it like moths to an electric light bulb, sucking on it. She told the story of her first suicide in sweet and loving detail, and her description in *The Bell Jar* is just that same story. It is a wonder we didn't depress George with our egocentricity; instead, I think, we three were stimulated by it—even George—as if death made each of us a little more real at the moment.

—1974.

Sylvia Plath 1932–1963

Sylvia Plath grew up in Wellesley, began writing early, and attended Smith College on a fellowship. Alfred Kazin was interviewing students for admission to a creative writing class at Smith.

The last girl in line looked like all the others. When she handed over some pages, I had grown so wary that I began to skim, then became suspicious. The writing was so coolly professional that I scented plagiarism, and said with some bitterness, "These could be published in _____ and _____." "I know," said the girl, "they've already taken them." I read them carefully and turned back to the top sheet to learn her name. "Sylvia Plath." "If you can write like this, why the dickens do you need 'creative writing'?" "I'm lonesome here, and want to talk to you."

—Alfred Kazin, *New York Jew*, 1978.

While she was a Smith student she attempted suicide for the first time. When she was released from the hospital, she was introduced to a published poet. Richard Wilbur wrote a poem about his encounter with her.

Cottage Street, 1953

Framed in her phoenix fire-screen, Edna Ward
Bends to the tray of Canton, pouring tea
For frightened Mrs. Plath; then, turning toward
The pale, slumped daughter, and my wife, and me,

Asks if we would prefer it weak or strong
Will we have milk or lemon, she enquires?
The visit seems already strained and long.
Each in his turn, we tell her our desires.

It is my office to exemplify
The published poet in his happiness.
Thus cheering Sylvia, who has wished to die;
But half-ashamed, and impotent to bless,

I am a stupid life-guard who has found,
Swept to his shallows by the tide, a girl
who, far from shore, has been immensely drowned,
And stares through water now with eyes of pearl.

How large is her refusal; and how slight
The genteel chat whereby we recommend
Life of a summer afternoon, despite
The brewing dusk which hints that it may end.

And Edna Ward shall die in fifteen years,
After her eight-and-eighty summers of
Such grace and courage as permit no tears,
The thin hand reaching out, the last word *love,*

Outliving Sylvia who, condemned to live,
Shall study for a decade, as she must,
To state at last her brilliant negative
In poems free and helpless and unjust.

—Richard Wilbur, *The Mind-Reader,* 1976.

Her college roommate recalled a visit they made to Olive Higgins Prouty, the novelist who supported Plath at Smith.

On this particular sunny afternoon with Mrs. Prouty, a pompous, obsequious butler served tea and canapés. Sitting there in her cavernous living room in our white gloves and our very best company manners, under the reproving gaze of the butler, we consumed a platter of tiny, delectable cucumber sandwiches in less than half an hour. Mrs. Prouty may or may not have been amused by our intemperance; at any rate, she instructed the astonished butler to bring another tray of sandwiches, which we obligingly devoured. Neither of us was being deliberately vulgar or gluttonous; the sandwiches were tasty and we simply didn't consider resisting them. We talked importantly with Mrs. Prouty about her literary career, about Smith, and about ourselves in the best approximation of small talk we could manage, punctuating our remarks with the incessant, audible crackle of crisp, paper-thin, sour-creamy cucumbers. We ate until we were half sick with cucumbers and suppressed glee.

—Nancy Hunter Steiner, *A Closer Look at Ariel: A Memoir of Sylvia Plath,* 1973.

She went to Cambridge University on a Fulbright, married Ted Hughes, and bore two children. The couple had separated when she called on the critic A. Alvarez.

On gloomy November afternoon she arrived at my studio greatly excited. As usual, she had been trudging the chill streets, house hunting despondently and more or less aimlessly. A block away from the square near Primrose Hill where she and Ted had lived when they first came to London, she saw a "To Let" notice up in front of a newly refurbished house. That in itself was something of a miracle in those impossible, overcrowded days. But more important, the house bore a blue plaque announcing that Yeats had once lived there. It was a sign, the confirmation she had been looking for. That summer she had visited Yeats's Tower at Ballylea and wrote to a friend that she thought it "the most beautiful and peaceful place in the world." Now there was a possibility of finding another Yeats tower in her favorite part of London which she could in some way share with the great poet. She hurried to the agent's and found, improbably, that she was the first to apply. Another sign. On the spot she took a five-year lease of the flat.

—A. Alvarez, *The Savage God,* 1972.

Plath wrote her last poems "at about four in the morning—" she said in a note written for the BBC—"that still blue, almost eternal hour before the baby's cry, before the glassy music of the milkman. . . ." She wrote great poems, and she killed herself. Her friend Alvarez concluded that she did not fully intend to die.

By these lights she seemed, in her last attempt, to be taking care not to succeed. But this time everything conspired to destroy her. An employment agency had found her an *au pair* girl to help with the children and housework while Sylvia got on with her writing. The girl, an Australian, was due to arrive at nine o'clock on the morning of Monday, February 11. Meanwhile, a recurrent trouble, her sinuses were bad; the pipes in her newly converted flat froze solid; there was still no telephone, and no word from the psychotherapist; the weather continued monstrous. Illness, loneliness, depression and cold, combined with the demands of two small children, were too much for her. So when the weekend came she went off with the babies to stay with friends in another part of London. The plan was, I think, that she would leave early enough on Monday morning to be back in time to welcome the Australian girl. Instead, she decided to go back on Sunday. The friends were against it but she was insistent, made a great show of her old competence and seemed more cheerful than she had done for some time. So they let her go. About eleven o'clock that night she knocked on the door of the elderly painter who lived below her, asking to borrow some stamps. But she lingered in the doorway, drawing out the conversation until he told her that he got up well before nine in the morning. Then she said good night and went back upstairs.

God knows what kind of a sleepless night she spent or if she wrote any poetry. . . .

Around six o'clock that morning, she went up to the children's room and left a plate of bread and butter and two mugs of milk, in case they should wake hungry before the *au pair* girl arrived. Then she went back down to the kitchen, sealed the door and window as best she could with towels, opened the oven, laid her head in it and turned on the gas.

The Australian girl arrived punctually at nine o'clock. She rang and knocked a long time but could get no answer. So she went off to search for a telephone booth in order to phone the agency and make sure she had the right address. Sylvia's name, incidentally, was not on either of the doorbells. Had everything been normal, the neighbor below would have been up by then; even if he had overslept, the girl's knocking should have aroused him. But as it happened, the neighbor was very deaf and slept without his hearing aid. More important, his bedroom was immediately below Sylvia's kitchen. The gas seeped down and knocked him out cold. So he slept on through all the noise. The girl returned and tried again, still without success. Again she went off to telephone the agency and ask what to do; they told her to go back. It was now about eleven o'clock. This time she was lucky: some builders had arrived to work in the frozen-up house, and they let her in. When she knocked on Sylvia's door there was no answer and the smell of gas was overpowering. The builders forced the lock and found Sylvia sprawled in the kitchen. She was still warm. She had left a note saying "Please call Dr. ______" and giving his telephone number. But it was too late.

Had everything worked out as it should—had the gas not drugged the man downstairs, preventing him from opening the front door to the *au pair* girl—there is little doubt she would have been saved. I think she wanted to be; why else leave her doctor's telephone number? This time, unlike the occasion ten years before, there was too much holding her to life. Above all, there were the children: she was too passionate a mother to want to lose them or them to lose her. There were also the extraordinary creative powers she now unequivocally knew she possessed: the poems came daily, unbidden and unstoppable. . . .

—Alvarez.

Her old roommate recalled an irony which Plath quoted from one of her doctors. In despair she had asked him for a lobotomy, in order to avoid or reduce her suffering. The psychiatrist laughed. "You're not going to get off that easy," he said.

Index

1. Names

Page numbers of main entries are in italic type.

Abercrombie, Lascelles, 208
Adams, Charles, 122
Adams, Clover (Mrs. Henry), 122, 123
Adams, Henry, *122–25*, 138, 143; *Democracy*, 122; *The Education of Henry Adams*, 122; *Mont-Saint-Michel and Chartres*, 122
Adams, John, 14, 24, 25, 123
Adams, John Quincy, 33
Adams, Sherman, 173
Agassiz, Louis, 103, 120
Agee, James, *315–16; A Death in the Family*, 315
Aiken, Conrad, 224–25
Alcott, Bronson, *36–40*, 94, 107
Alcott, Louisa May, 36, *107–9; Little Women*, 107, 141
Alcott, May, 108, 109
Aldington, Richard, 216
Aldrich, Lilian (Mrs. Thomas Bailey), 77, 78, 79, 80, 116, 117
Aldrich, Thomas Bailey, 116, 117, 119
Alger, Horatio, Jr., *106–7*
Ali, Muhammad, 219–23; "A Poem on the Annihilation of Ernie Terrell," 220–22
Alvarez, A., 341
Anderson, Sherwood, 156, *178–80*, 203–4, 236; *Winesburg, Ohio*, 178
Argyll, Duke of, 272, 273
Armstrong, Joseph, 95
Arnold, Matthew, 56
Arthur, Robert Alan, 333
Arvin, Newton, 323
Auchincloss, Louis, 124
Auden, W. H., *304–7*, 310, 323, 324

Bacon, Capt. Edmund, 22, 23, 24
Bakunin, Mikhail, 53
Baldwin, James, 332
Barlow, Joel, *28–29; The Columbiad*, 28; "Hasty-Pudding," 28–29
Barnes, Djuna, 192; *Nightwood*, 192
Barry, Philip, 303
Baruch, Bernard, 149
Basler, Roy P., 171, 172
Bates, Esther, 150
Baudelaire, Charles, 288
Beach, Sylvia, 141, 281
Beaton, Cecil, 168
Beaumont, Francis, 322
Beckett, Samuel, 209
Beebe, Lucius, 151
Beecher, Edward, 76
Beethoven, Ludwig von, 307
Behrman, S. N., 234
Belknap, Jeremy, 13
Bell, Clive, 258
Bell, Robert, 14
Bellew, Frank, 43
Bellow, Saul, 321, 322

Benchley, Nathaniel, 234
Benchley, Robert, *232–34*, 240
Berenson, Bernard, 145–46
Berkeley, George, 9
Berryman, John, 309, *321–23*
Bierce, Ambrose, 126
Bishop, John Peale, 238
Bishop, Joseph Bucklin, 80–81
Blackmur, R. P., 317
Blake, William, 15, 288
Blitzstein, Marc, 305
Boardman, Henry D., 95
Bogan, Louise, 191, *264–65*
Boissevain, Eugen, 238
Booth, Philip, 311
Bowen, Catherine Drinker, 127
Bowles, Jane, 305
Bowles, Paul, 305
Bowles, Samuel, 105
Bradstreet, Anne, 3; *The Tenth Muse Lately Sprung Up in America,* 3
Bremer, Fredrika, "Impressions of America" in *The Homes of the New World,* 37
Britten, Benjamin, 305, 324
Brooks, Van Wyck, 154, 256
Brown, Charles Brockden, *29–30*
Brown, Slater, 286
Browning, Elizabeth Barrett, 49, 69, 74
Browning, Robert, 49, 69
Brownson, Orestes, 40
Bryant, William Cullen, *36;* "Thanatopsis," 36
Bryher, Winifred, 166
Buckman, Gertrude, 319
Buffon, Georges, 19–20
Bullitt, William, 149
Burke, Kenneth, 286
Burnett, Whit, 141
Burns, Robert, 55
Burroughs, William, 335
Byles, Mather, *13–14*
Bynner, Witter, 133, 159, 187, *193–95*
Byrd, William, *8–9*
Byron, George Gordon, Lord, 14, 125

Cabell, James Branch, 192
Cabot, James Elliot, 45
Caldwell, Erskine, 200–201; "The Mating of Marjorie," 200; "A Very Late Spring," 200
Calhoun, John, 32
Callaghan, Morley, 180, 195–96, 257–58, 276, 301
Campbell, Alan, 240
Capa, Robert, 297
Capone, Al, 249, 250
Capote, Truman, 248
Carlyle, Jane, 101
Carlyle, Thomas, 36, 39–40, 44, 73, 223
Carpenter, Edward, 44
Carroll, Lewis, 275
Castel, Jean, 332–33
Cather, Willa, *159–60,* 164–65; *A Lost Lady,* 160
Cerf, Bennett, 157, 169, 205, 206, 301
Cervantes, Miguel de, 297, 306; *Don Quixote,* 306
Chambers, Whittaker, 315–16
Chandler, Raymond, *223–24; The Big Sleep,* 224; *The Blue Dahlia,* 223
Chanler, Gabrielle, 124
Chanler, Marjorie Terry, 123, 124
Chanler, Theodore, 123
Channing, William Ellery, 71
Chapman, John Jay, 40, 121
Chaucer, Geoffrey, 325
Chaumont, Jacques-Donatien Leray de, 12
Chekhov, Anton, 321
Chesterton, G. K., 131
Child, Francis J., 120
Childs, George W., 54
Choltitz, Dietrich von, 282
Churchill, Winston, 118, 136
Claflin, Mary, 55, 56, 57
Clark, Blair, 329
Clark, John, 107
Clark, Kenneth, 145
Clay, Henry, 32
Clemens, James Ross, 119
Clemens, Olivia (Mrs. Samuel), 115, 116, 177
Clemens, Samuel, *112–19,* 121, 126; "Fenimore Cooper's Literary Offenses," 35; *Innocents Abroad,* 118
Clemm, Maria, 69, 70
Cleveland, Grover, 68
Clift, Montgomery, 330–31

Cobbett, William, 29
Coghill, Neville, 304
Coleridge, Samuel Taylor, 14, 319
Collins, Wilkie, 53
Connelly, Marc, 266, 267
Conrad, Joseph, 192
Coolidge, Calvin, 247
Cooper, James Fenimore, *35*
Cooper, Susan (Mrs. James Fenimore), 35
Copeland, Aaron, *Piano Fantasy,* 337
Cory, Daniel Webster, 148
Cotton, John, 6
Cour, Gene, 248, 249
Cowley, Malcolm, 244, 260–61, 283, 284, 286, 289
Crane, Hart, 216, *282–89;* "Voyages," 284
Crane, Stephen, 135, *153–55; The Red Badge of Courage,* 154, 155
Crocker, Thomas, 107
Crosby, Caresse, 271, 285
Crosby, Harry, *271–73,* 285, 288
Cummings, E. E., *242–46,* 255
Cummings, Edward, 242, 243
Cunningham, Merce, 316
Curtis, George William, 52

Dali, Magda, 305
Dali, Salvador, 305
Dana, Richard Henry, Jr., 120
Dante Allegieri, 136, 325; *Divina Commedia,* 52, 209
Davis, Richard Harding, 154, 155
Day, Dorothy, 306
Degas, Edgar, 112
Dempsey, Jack, 268
Dewey, Fred, 143
Dewey, John, *143*
Di Prima, Diane, 336–37
Dickens, Charles, 33–34, 53
Dickinson, Edward, 104
Dickinson, Emily, *103–6*
Dickinson, Lavinia, 104
Dom Pedro II, 53, 56
Doolittle, Hilda, *212–13*
Dos Passos, John, 191, 243, 244, 253, *255*
Douglass, Frederick, *89–91*
Dreiser, Theodore, 121, *156–58,* 179, 192; *An American Tragedy,* 157; *Sister Carrie,* 121
Driscoll, Joe, 282
Duncan, Isadora, 151–52
Dwight, Timothy, *26–28,* 133

Eastman, Max, 148, 280; "Bull in the Afternoon," 280
Eberhart, Richard, 325
Eckert, Thomas, 63, 64
Edward, Prince of Wales, 213
Edwards, Jonathan, *9–10*
Eliot, Charles, 67
Eliot, T. S., 171, 172, 175, 208, 209, *224–30,* 305, 320, 325; *The Waste Land,* 208
Eliot, Vivien, 226
Emerson, Edward, 87, 130
Emerson, Ellen, 46, 108
Emerson, Lidian (Mrs. Ralph Waldo), 40, 82
Emerson, Ralph Waldo, 33, 36, 37, 38, 39, *40–46,* 47, 51, 53, 74, 81, 82, 85, 88, 92, 94, 102, 103, 107, 108, 113, 114, 115, 130
Empson, William, 226

Faulkner, Estelle, 266
Faulkner, Jill, 266
Faulkner, William, 205, 206, *265–68,* 297, 298, 303; *A Fable,* 267, 268
Feibleman, Peter, 240
Ficke, Arthur Davison, 193, 195
Fields, Annie, 76, 102
Fields, James T., 121
Fiske, John, 120
Fitzgerald, Barry, 304
Fitzgerald, F. Scott, 156–57, 199, *255–64,* 269–70, 276–78, 290, 301; *The Beautiful and Damned,* 156–57; "A Diamond as Big as the Ritz," 264; *The Great Gatsby,* 199, 261, 263; *Tender Is the Night,* 257; *This Side of Paradise,* 156, 255, 294
Fitzgerald, Zelda, 255, 256, 258–59, 260, 261–62, 269
Fitzhugh, William, 21, 22
Flagg, James Montgomery, 261
Fletcher, John, 322
Flint, Frank, 172
Foley, Martha, 167–68
Ford, Ford Madox, 135, 155, 207, 325

Frank, Waldo, 156
Franklin, Benjamin, *10–13*, 14, 19
Freneau, Philip, *25–26*; "The Indian Burying Ground," 25
Freud, Sigmund, 318
Freytag Loringhoven, Elsa von, 197, 198
Forster, E. M., 305
Fuller, Margaret, 40, 52, *71–76*, 241
Fuller, Timothy, 71
Fullerton, Morton, 132
Frost, Lesley, 178
Frost, Robert, *170–78*, 184, 190–91; *A Boy's Will*, 170; "The Gift Outright," 177

Gardner, Ava, 330
Gardner, Isabella, 144, 145
Gellhorn, Martha, 301
George, Henry, 183
Gill, Brendan, 189, 190, 198, 270, 329
Ginsberg, Allen, 327; *Howl*, 307
Giroux, Robert, 334–35
Glasgow, Ellen, *160–61*; *Barren Ground*, 160
Godkin, E. L., 122
Goethe, Johann Wolfgang von, 107; *Goethe's Correspondence with a Child*, 107
Gogol, Nikolai, 274
Goldsmith, Oliver, 33
Goldowski, Natasha, 316, 317
Goncharov, Ivan, 317
Gordon, Ruth, 239
Gosse, Edmund, 99–100, 125
Graham, Sheilah, 264
Grant, Ulysses S., 315
Graves, Mr., 5
Graveson, G. W., 282
Gray, Asa, 120
Greeley, Horace, *80–81*, 96
Green, Clara Bellinger, 106
Gritz, John, 184

Haas, Robert, 205
Hammett, Dashiell, *246–47*, 278–79
Hanna, Leonard, 269
Hardwick, Elizabeth, 327
Harlow, Jean, 232
Harris, Frank, *141–42*; *My Life and Loves*, 141
Harris, Sam, 235
Hart, Moss, 215; *The Man Who Came to Dinner*, 216
Harte, Bret, 118, *119–20*; "The Heathen Chinee," 119; *The Luck of Roaring Camp*, 119, 120; "Two Men of Sandy Bar," 120
Haskell, J. F., 282
Hathorne, Daniel, 50, 51
Hathorne, Maj. William, 50
Hawks, Howard, 224
Hawley, Joseph, 9, 10
Hawthorne, Julian, 49, 50, 91, 108, 109
Hawthorne, Nathaniel, 40, 41–42, *46–51*, 52, 73, 83, 92, 103; *Our Old Home*, 49; *The Scarlet Letter*, 46
Hawthorne, Sophia (Mrs. Nathaniel), 46, 49, 91
Hay, John, *The Bread-Winners*, 122
Hayes, Helen, 235, 315
Hayward, John, 226–27
Hazlitt, William, 35
H. D. *See* Doolittle, Hilda
Hecht, Ben, 178–80, *248–52*; *Erik Dorn*, 179, 180; *Gone With the Wind* (film), 250–52; *Scarface*, 249–50
Heffernan, Nancy, 267–68
Hellman, Lillian, 240, 246, 262, 278, 279
Hemings, John, 22
Hemingway, Ernest, 167, 180, 191, 197, 199, 241–42, 258, 262–64, *275–82*, 298, 301; *Death in the Afternoon*, 280; *A Farewell to Arms*, 199, 257; *A Moveable Feast*, 258; "The Snows of Kilimanjaro," 262; *The Spanish Earth* (film), 262
Hemingway, Hadley, 275
Henry, O. *See* Porter, W. S.
Herndon, William, 58
Higginson, Thomas Wentworth, 105
Hiss, Alger, 315
Hoffman, Bernard, 185
Holmes, John, 311, 338
Holmes, Oliver Wendell, 40, 45, 46, 52, 53, *67–68*, 113, 114, 115, 121
Holmes, Oliver Wendell, Jr., *126–28*
Homer, 26, 297, 325; *Iliad*, 209
Houseman, A. E., 147
Houseman, John, 223, 224

Howard, Sidney, 251
Howells, William Dean, 45, 52, 67, 115, 118, 119, *120–22*
Hoyt, Elizabeth, 125
Hueffer, Ford Madox. *See* Ford, Ford Madox
Hughes, Carrie, 295
Hughes, Howard, 249, 250
Hughes, Langston, *295–97;* "Wake," 296–97
Hughes, Ted, 338, 341
Hunt, Ebenezer, 10
Huston, John, 316
Hutchins, Maude (Mrs. Robert Maynard), 269–70
Hutchins, Robert Maynard, 269–70
Huxley, Aldous, 145
Hyman, Bernie, 252
Hyman, Stanley Edgar, 329–30

Irving, Washington, *33–35; Columbus,* 34; *Conquest of Granada,* 34; *The Sketch Book,* 33
Isherwood, Christopher, 305

Jacks, Arthur, 202
Jackson, Shirley, *329–30;* "The Lottery," 329
James, Alice, 131
James, Garth Wilkinson, 130
James, Henry, 103, 118, 120, 126, 127, 128, 129, *130–37,* 146–47, 154, 155; *The Ambassadors,* 133; *The Golden Bowl,* 133; *The Ivory Tower,* 146; *A Small Boy,* 136; *What Maisie Knew,* 132; *The Wings of the Dove,* 133, 182–83
James, Henry, Sr., 39, 47, 67, 120, 130
James, Robertson, 130
James, William, 120, 126, *128–30,* 131, 133, 165; *The Varieties of Religious Experience,* 73
Jarrell, Randall, *320–21,* 325
Jarvis, John Wesley, 16
Jeffers, Robinson, *223*
Jefferson, Martha (daughter), 18, 19
Jefferson, Martha Wayles Skelton (Mrs. Thomas), 17, 18
Jefferson, Thomas, 10, *16–25,* 210; Declaration of Independence, 10, 16
Johnson, Chapman, 23
Johnson, James Weldon, *159; God's Trombones,* 159
Johnson, Lyndon B., 177, 326
Johnson, Samuel, 48
Jones, Gloria (Mrs. James), 331, 332, 334
Jones, James, *330–34; From Here to Eternity* (film), 330; *The Longest Day* (film), 331–32; *The Thin Red Line,* 331
Jones, Jamie, 333–34
Josephson, Matthew, 283
Joyce, James, 208, 318

Karpovich, Michael, 273
Kaufman, George S., 215, *234–35,* 304; *The Man Who Came to Dinner,* 216, 234; *Of Thee I Sing,* 234; *You Can't Take It with You,* 234
Kazin, Alfred, 254, 304, 339
Keats, John, 164, 165, 196
Kelly, Amy, 273
Kennedy, John F., 20, 177
Kennedy, Sloan, 100
Kenner, Hugh, 227–29
Kerouac, Jack, *334–36; The Dharma Bums,* 335–36; *On the Road,* 334; *The Subterraneans,* 335; *The Town and the City,* 334
Kingsley, Charles, 53, 67
Kinsella, Thomas, 311
Kipling, Rudyard, 128
Kirkpatrick, Helen, 282
Kittredge, George Lyman, *144*
Kline, Herbert, 312
Knopf, Alfred, 329
Koestler, Arthur, 296
Kreymborg, Alfred, 188, 195, 216
Kruif, Paul de, 301
Kunitz, Stanley, 326, 328

Lafayette, Marquis de, 25
Lanier, Sidney, *128*
Lannin, Paul, 202
Lardner, James, 301
Lardner, Ring, *201–2,* 236
Latham, H. S., 292–93
Lawrence, D. H., 272, 273

Lee, Gypsy Rose, 305, 324; *The G-String Murders*, 305
Lee, Robert E., 315
Lenin, Vladimir, *What Is to Be Done*, 312
LeSueur, Joe, 337
Lewis, Sinclair, 158, 182, 192, *202–6*, 298; *Main Street*, 202
Lewis, Wyndham, 229
Lewisohn, Ludwig, *195–96; Upstream*, 195
Lincoln, Abraham, *57–66*, 77, 127, 185–87
Lincoln, Mary Todd (Mrs. Abraham), 66
Lindsay, Vachel, *187–89*, 295; "The Sante Fe Trail," 188–89
Lipchitz, Jacques, 168
Liveright, Horace, 157, 158
Locke, John, *Essay Concerning Human Understanding*, 9
Lodge, Henry Cabot, *138–39*
London, Charmian (Mrs. Jack), 180, 181, 182
London, Jack, *180–83*
Longfellow, Ernest, 53
Longfellow, Frances Appleton (Mrs. Henry Wadsworth), 51, 52
Longfellow, Henry Wadsworth, 46, *51–55*, 71, 102, 113, 114, 115, 120; "The Building of the Ship," 54
Louis XVI, 275
Lowell, Abbott Lawrence, 161, 162, 163
Lowell, Amy, 151, *161–65*, 270; "Patterns," 163
Lowell, James Russell, 40–41, 53, *102–3*, 120, 121, 161
Lowell, Robert, 161, 171, 209–10, 310–11, 320, 321, *324–29*, 338; *Histories*, 176; *Life Studies*, 81; "To Delmore Schwartz," 318–19
Loy, Mina, 216
Luce, Clare Boothe, 239; *The Women*, 239

McAlmon, Robert, 166, 197, 275–76
MacAlpine, William, 132
MacArthur, Charles, 213–14, 235
McCullers, Carson, 305, *323–24; The Member of the Wedding*, 324
McGeehan, Bill, 269
MacKaye, Percy, 151, 152
MacLeish, Archibald, 172–73, 215, 237; "The Hamlet of A. MacLeish," 237; "You, Andrew Marvell," 173
MacNeice, Louis, 305, 324
Mailer, Norman, 326–28; *An American Dream*, 327; *The Armies of the Night*, 326; *Deaths for the Ladies and other disasters*, 327
Manet, Edouard, 112
Mann, Erika, 305
Mann, Thomas, 305
Marlowe, Christopher, 288, 322
Marquand, John P., *241–42*
Marryatt, Frederick, *Children of the New Forest*, 126–27
Marshall, Col. S.L.A., 282
Marx, Karl, 260; *Das Kapital*, 312, 314
Marx Brothers, 235
Masters, Edgar Lee, 193
Mather, Cotton, 3, *6–8*, 9, 13; *The Wonders of the Invisible World*, 7
Mather, Increase, 4–5, 6, 13
Mather, Richard, 6
Mathewson, Christy, 216–17
Maupassant, Guy de, 131–32
Mead, G.R.S., 225
Melville, Herman, 41, *91–93*, 275, 288; *Moby-Dick*, 92, 285; *Omoo*, 92; *Typee*, 92
Mencken, H. L., 156, 179, *192–93*, 202, 203, 312; *A Book of Prefaces*, 312; *A Neglected Anniversary*, 193; *Prejudices*, 312
Millay, Edna St. Vincent, 192, *238*
Miller, Henry, 141
Miller, Joaquin, *125–26;* "Columbus," 125
Miller, Leon Gordon, 169
Milnes, Monckton, 53
Milton, John, 148, 325; "Lycidas," 326
Mitchell, Margaret, *292–94; Gone With the Wind*, 251, 292, 293, 294
Monbouquette, Bill, 218–19
Monroe, Harriet, 162
Monroe, James, 23
Montgomery, Mattie, 128
Moody, William Vaughn, 151, 152
Moore, Marianne, *216–23;* "A Poem on the Annihilation of Ernie Terrell," 220–22

Moorehead, Alan, 282
Morellet, Abbé, 12
Morgan, J. P., 271
Morrison, Kathleen, 174–75, 177, 178
Mudge, Martha, 5
Munroe, David, 133, 134
Munson, Gorham, 283
Murphy, Gerald, 257
Murphy, Sara, 257
Mussolini, Benito, 208
Myrtle, Minnie, 125

Nabokov, Vladimir, 254, *273–75;* trans. Pushkin, *Eugene Onegin,* 254
Napoleon Bonaparte, 28, 137, 198
Nashe, Thomas, 322
Nathan, George Jean, 202
Nearing, Scott, 184
Neruda, Pablo, 310
Nichols, Mrs. Gove, 69
Niebuhr, Ursula, 306
Nixon, Richard M., 311
Norman, Charles, 245, 246
Norris, Frank, *153; McTeague,* 153; *The Pit,* 153
Norton, Andrews, 53
Norton, Charles Eliot, 120
Norton, John, 3

O'Connor, Flannery, *336*
Odets, Clifford, *303–4; Waiting for Lefty,* 303
O'Hara, Frank, *336–38;* "Ode on the Arrow That Flieth by Day," 337
O'Hara, John, *300–303; Butterfield 8,* 300; *Pal Joey,* 302; *A Rage to Live,* 302
Olson, Charles, *316–17*
O'Neill, Eugene, *230–32*
Oppen, George, 300; *Discrete Series,* 300
Oppenheimer, George, 239
Osborne, Mrs. Frances Cuthbert Thomas, 92, 93
Osgood, James R., 116
Ossoli, Giovanni Angelo, Marquis, 74, 75, 76
Ossoli, Margaret Fuller. *See* Fuller, Margaret
Ossoli, Nino, 74, 75, 76

Paine, Thomas, *14–16; The Age of Reason,* 15; *Common Sense,* 14
Palfrey, John G., 120
Parker, Dorothy, *239–41,* 262, 263, 264
Parker, Theodore, 32–33
Parkman, Francis, 102, 103
Parsons, Theophilus, 120
Peabody, Andrew Preston, 120
Pears, Peter, 305, 324
Pelkey, Archie, 281
Perkins, Maxwell, 180, *199–201,* 258, 261, 280, 290, 292
Picasso, Pablo, 166, 168
Pierce, Franklin, 46, 51
Pierce, James, 120
Plath, Sylvia, 338–39, *339–43; The Bell Jar,* 339
Plimpton, George, 218
Plutarch, *Lives,* 57, 58
Poe, Edgar Allan, *68–71,* 192–93, 275; "The Raven," 71
Poe, Virginia Clemm (Mrs. Edgar Allan), 69, 70–71
Porter, Katherine Anne, 211–12, 287–88, 323
Porter, W. S., *147,* 236
Pound, Ezra, 135, 148, 162, 166, 167, 170, 171, 173–74, 193, *206–11,* 212, 216, 224, 225, 276, 300, 325; *Cantos,* 135–36; *A Lume Spento,* 207; "Sestina: Altaforte" (Bloody Sestina), 210
Pound, Homer, 206
Powell, Billy, 269
Powys, Llewelyn, 156
Prescott, William Hickling, *History of the Reign of Ferdinand and Isabella,* 34
Prouty, Olive Higgins, 340–41
Pushkin, Aleksandr, *Eugene Onegin,* 254

Quincy, Josiah, 43

Randolph, Jefferson, 17, 25
Ransom, John Crowe, 320, 325
Rascoe, Burton, 156, 199, 203
Reinhart, John, 282
Rice, Elmer, *237–38; On Trial,* 237

Richards, I. A., 311
Riley, James Whitcomb, *137–38*
Rilke, Rainer Maria, 307, 322
Robinson, Edwin Arlington, 143, *149–53;* "Reuben Bright," 151
Roche, Abbé de la, 12
Rodgers, Richard, 301, 302; *Pal Joey,* 302; "There's a Small Hotel," 302
Roethke, Theodore, 265, *308–12*
Rondel, Mary, 49, 50, 51
Roosevelt, Alice, 142–43
Roosevelt, Franklin D., 128
Roosevelt, Theodore, *142–43,* 149, 187
Ross, Harold, *235–37*
Ross, Ralph, 322
Ross, Robert, 110
Rudge, Olga, 210
Rush, Benjamin, 29
Russell, Ada, 163, 164

Sand, George, 72
Sandburg, Carl, 171–72, *184–87,* 307: *The Prairie Years,* 186; *The War Years,* 186
Sandek, Robert, 315
Santayana, George, *147–48*
Sappho, 307
Saunders, John Monk, 261–62
Sayre, Joel, 301
Scholis, Hiram, 96
Schwartz, Delmore, *317–20; In Dreams Begin Responsibilities,* 317
Schwartz, Kenneth, 317
Scott, Walter, 35
Scribner, Charles, 200
Scripps, John Locke, 57, 58
Seldes, Gilbert, 243
Selznick, David, 250–52, 294
Sewell, Samuel, *5–6*
Sexton, Anne, *338–39*
Shakespeare, William, 46, 141, 168, 265, 266, 275, 307
Shaw, George Bernard, 269, 298
Shaw, Irwin, 282
Sheean, Vincent, 301
Shelley, Percy Bysshe, 211
Sickert, Walter, 111–12
Sidney, Sir Philip, 127; "Arcadia," 50
Siegfried, André, 204
Simpson, Reginald, 261
Sinatra, Frank, 330–31
Sinclair, Upton, *183–84; The Jungle,* 183; *Oil!,* 184
Skelton, Martha Wayles. *See* Jefferson, Martha Wayles Skelton
Skolsky, Sidney, 231
Smith, Logan Pearsall, 98, 99, 100, 128
Smith, Mary, 98, 99, 100
Snyder, Gary, 335–36
Spellman, Francis, Cardinal, 302–3
Spencer, Theodore, 270
Stalin, Joseph, 319
Staples, Sam, 37
Starbuck, George, 338, 339; *Bone Thoughts,* 338
Stebbins, Thomas, 9
Steffens, Lincoln, *148–49; Autobiography,* 148
Stegner, Wallace, 172
Stein, Gertrude, *165–69,* 192, 208, 301; *The Autobiography of Alice B. Toklas,* 168; *The Making of Americans,* 165; *Tender Buttons,* 165; *Three Lives,* 165
Steinbeck, John, *297–98,* 312; *The Grapes of Wrath,* 297; *In Dubious Battle,* 297; *Of Mice and Men,* 297; *Tortilla Flat,* 297; *Travels with Charley,* 298
Stern, James, 307
Stevens, Holly, 189
Stevens, Wallace, 155, 171, *189–92,* 197, 216
Stewart, Donald Ogden, 232; *The Parody Outline of History,* 232
Stoddard, J. M., 97
Stone, William L., 36
Stowe, Calvin Ellis, 77
Stowe, Harriet Beecher, *76–80; Uncle Tom's Cabin,* 76–77
Stravinsky, Igor, 230, 307
Stuart, Dr., 21, 22
Styron, William, 332
Sullivan, Gen. John, 19
Sumner, Horace, 74, 103
Sutro, Alfred, 133
Swedenborg, Emanuel, 15
Swope, Herbert Bayard, 240
Sykes, Bill, 272

Taft, William Howard, 150
Tate, Allen, 171, 191–92, *289*, 325–26
Taylor, Edward, *5*
Taylor, Peter, 320, 325
Temple, Minnie, 126
Tennyson, Alfred, Lord, 56, 97, 103
Terrell, Ernie, 220, 221, 222
Terry, Marjorie. *See* Chanler, Marjorie Terry
Thackeray, William Makepeace, 136
Thomas, Dylan, 329–30
Thompson, Dorothy, 158, 204–5
Thompson, John, 324
Thoreau, Henry David, 36, 38–39, 40, 47, *82–88*, 94; "A Week on the Concord and Merrimack Rivers," 86
Thurber, Helen (Mrs. James), 248
Thurber, James, *247–48*
Todd, Mabel, 103
Toklas, Alice, 165, 166, 167–68, 169
Tone, Aileen, 124, 125
Torrence, Ridgely, 151, 152
Traubel, Horace, 44, 87, 100
Trollope, Anthony, 53
Tschelitchev, Pavel, 305
Tudor, David, 317
Tunney, Gene, 241–42, 268–70, 278
Turnbull, Andrew, 291
Turner, Nancy Byrd, 151, 153
Twain, Mark. *See* Clemens, Samuel
Tyndale, Mrs. Sara, 94

Untermeyer, Jean Starr, 197

Valéry, Paul, 318
Van Buren, Martin, 32
Van Doren, Mark, 321
Van Vechten, Carl, 156, 192
Vergennes, Comte de, 19
Vergil, 325
Verlaine, Paul, 272
Very, Jones, 40, *81–82*
Victoria, Queen, 53, 77
Vidal, Gore, 335
Vogt, Gertrude, 288, 289
Von Vliet, William, 96

Wagoner, David, 309
Walpole, Hugh, 132
Ward, Edna, 339, 340
Ward, Prudence, 39
Warner, Charles Dudley, 114
Washington, Booker T., *139–40*
Washington, George, 15
Webster, Daniel, 19, *30–33*
Webster, Ezekiel, 30
Webster, Noah, *29*
Weireck, Bruce, 184
Wells, H. G., 130
Wertenbaker, Charles, 282
Wescott, Glenway, 283
Wesley, John, 301
West, Nathanael, *298–300; Miss Lonelyhearts,* 298
Wharton, Edith, 134, 135, *144–47*
Wheelock, John Hall, 290
Wheelwright, John, *270–71*
Whistler, James Abbott McNeill, *109–12; The Gentle Art of Making Enemies,* 109, 208
Whitman, Eddy, 94
Whitman, Walt, 42, 43, 44, 54, 64–65, 87, *93–101,* 102, 106, 135, 288; "After All, Not to Create Only," 96; *Leaves of Grass,* 42, 43, 45, 58, 93, 94, 98, 100, 101, 102, 105, 135; "Out of the Cradle," 135; "Song of Myself," 135; "When lilacs last in the dooryard bloomed," 135
Whittier, John Greenleaf, 42, *55–57,* 112, 119; "Ichabod," 33
Wiener, Norbert, 316
Wigglesworth, Michael, *3–5,* 6; *The Day of Doom,* 3–4; *Meat out of the Eater,* 4
Wilber, Oscar F., 95
Wilbur, Richard, 339; "Cottage Street, 1953," 339–40
Wilde, Oscar, 97, 109, 110, 112, 141, 256
Wilder, Thornton, *268–70; The Bridge of San Luis Rey,* 268
William III, 5
Williams, Floss (Mrs. William Carlos), 198–99, 209
Williams, Jonathan, 317
Williams, Tennessee, 324
Williams, William Carlos, 166–67, *196–99,* 206, 209, 212, 216, 325
Willis, N. P., 34, 67
Wilson, Arthur, 243

Wilson, Edmund, 191, 192, 199, 230, 231, 238, *253–54*, 255, 260, 265, 309–10, 324; "The Omelet of A. MacLeish," 237; *The Twenties*, 239
Winters, Yvor, 289
Wister, Owen, 143
Wolfe, Thomas, 192, 199, 205, *289–92*; *Look Homeward, Angel*, 289; *O Lost*, 290
Wolfert, Ira, 282
Woodberry, George Edward, 164–65
Woodbury, Charles J., 41, 82
Woollcott, Alexander, *213–16*, 235, 236
Wordsworth, William, 304
Wright, Richard, 305, *312–15*; *Native Son*, 312
Wylie, Elinor, *211–12*

Yeats, John Butler, 151
Yeats, William Butler, 171, 207, 341; "Wanderings of Oisin," 285
Yevtushenko, Yevgeni, 307
Young, Clara Kimball, 237
Young, James, 237

Zabel, Morton D., 191
Zanuck, Darryl, 266, 331
Zukofsky, Louis, *300*

2. Topics

Abolitionism, 55
Absentmindedness, 38, 40
Accidents, 6, 51–52, 69–70, 74–76, 87, 248–49, 266, 267, 268, 298–300, 307, 329, 337–38
Acorns, 85
Acting, 71, 203–4, 235
Advertising, 283
Alcoholism. *See* Drinking
Advice, 44, 226, 229–30
Aloofness, 40, 127
American Mercury, The, 192, 312
Amherst College, 176
Amygism, 162
Aphorisms, 149
Arden, 183
Arrogance, 41, 73, 87, 162–63, 165
Arrowheads, 85
Asheville, N.C., 289
Assassination attempts, 65–66
Assassinations, 65
Atlantic Monthly, 45, 83, 85, 119, 121
Authors abroad, 28–29, 49–51, 103, 110, 118, 126, 134–35, 154, 155, 160–61, 165, 170, 207, 224–25, 227, 257, 296
Autobiography, 136, 148, 168
Autographs, 54
Automatic writing, 49–50
Backpacking, 335–36
Barnard College, 306
Baseball, 216–17, 218–19, 330
Bathing, 13, 271
Bathtubs, 193, 213–14
Bestsellers, 76, 146, 294
Bets, 246, 301
Bible, 184
Biography, 57–58
Birds, 308
Birthdays, 112–15, 119, 130
Black Mountain College, 316, 317
Blindness, 148, 248
Body, resurrection of, 6, 7
Book burning, 178, 244–45
Book reviews, 93–94, 194
Books, 22–23, 148, 208, 233, 271, 322; editions, 101; sales, 14, 25–26, 76, 86, 92, 106, 118, 146, 317
Boredom, 148
Bores, 39, 121
Boston, 42, 120
Boston Intelligencer, 93
Bowdoin College, 46
Boxing, 198, 219–23, 268, 276–78. *See also* Fights
Bragging, 138, 150–51, 195–96
Bravery, 153, 154
Bread Loaf, 172, 175
Bribery, 156
Brook Farm, 73, 87
Brooklyn Times, 93

Broom, 221, 282
Brothers, 30, 122–23, 130, 317
Buddhism, 335
Building, 38–39, 223
Business deals, 157–58, 193, 200–201

Calisthenics, 253, 258
Calvinism, 6
Cambridge University, 53, 341
Camp, 192
Cannibalism, 37–38
Card games, 234, 265, 333–34
Caricatures, 142
Cars, 121–22, 124, 134–35, 146, 163, 165–66, 242–43, 298–300, 338
Castration, 261–62
Catholic Worker, 306
Censorship, 44, 93, 102, 115, 178, 184, 290
Chameleons, 123
Charity, 38, 100–101, 146–47, 214–15, 271, 302–3, 306
Cheating, 12–13
Checklists, 253
Cheesc, 228–29
Chess, 11–13
Chicago Daily Journal, 248
Chicago Tribune, 247
Chickens, 82, 175–76
Children, 19, 48–49, 87, 88, 89–91, 92–93, 103–4, 105, 115–16, 123, 124–25, 128–30, 142–43, 184, 197, 341, 342, 343
Citizenship, 273–74
Civil War, 61, 63, 94–96, 126–27
Climate, 134
Collaboration, 38–39, 215–16
Columbia University, 183, 321, 334
Communism, 149, 270, 312, 314
Complaints, 79, 213, 265–66
Connecticut Wits, 27, 28
Contests, 69, 171, 279, 301, 307
Conversations, 20–21, 47–48, 67, 109, 118, 124–25, 130, 133, 136, 139, 150, 155, 167, 200–201, 213, 216–17, 235–36, 260–61, 287–88, 292–93, 326–27, 339
Coquette, 315
Cornell College, 184
Courtship, 17, 50–51
Creativity, 336–37, 341, 343
Criticism, 33, 35, 44–45, 51, 56, 68–69, 93, 105, 121, 122–23, 167, 182–83, 196–97
Croquet, 283

Dada, 244–45
Dancing, 88, 117, 151–52, 316
Dartmouth College, 31–32, 176
Death, 18, 25, 32, 51–52, 57, 65, 74–76, 88, 96, 118–19, 125, 136–37, 161, 169, 240–41, 275–76, 288–89, 296–97, 298, 319, 329, 337–38, 341–43
Deceptions, 227
Dentures, 306, 307
Dial, The, 216
Dictation, 27–28, 132–33, 137, 183
Diet, 26–27, 37–38, 39–40
Dining clubs, 147
Diplomats, 19, 103
Dirty words, 115, 199–200
Disputes, 6, 19–20, 58–59, 129–30, 130–31, 169, 246, 300
Divorce, 319
Dogs, 160–61, 192–93, 275–76, 286, 291
Dramatic readings, 295
Dreams, 255, 287
Dress, 30, 44, 52, 63, 65, 69–70, 79, 86, 92, 120, 125–26, 133–34, 155, 164, 207, 230, 248, 270, 296
Drinking, 79–80, 101, 153, 154, 190–91, 201–2, 223–24, 230–31, 232, 233–34, 238, 241–42, 246, 255–56, 257–58, 260–61, 262–64, 265, 266, 271, 278–79, 283, 285–86, 289, 290, 301, 307, 317, 318, 321, 322–23, 330–31, 332, 338
Duels, 208, 289

Eating, 26–27, 37–38, 39–40, 89–91, 97–98, 147, 207, 227–29, 340–41
Eccentricity, 26–27, 81–82, 87, 103–4, 110, 120, 126, 145, 160–61, 161–62, 165–66, 199, 217–18, 270–71, 271–72
Editors and editing, 11, 45, 80–81, 105, 121, 192, 199–200, 200–201, 208, 235–37, 290, 292–93, 334–35
Education, 19, 31–32, 71, 143

Egoist, The, 225
Emancipation, 139–40
Emancipation Proclamation, 63–64, 140
Emasculation, 259, 262
Embarrassments, 11, 77–80, 103, 112–15, 127, 128–30, 130–31, 167–68, 199–200, 214–15, 218–19, 269–70, 307, 325–26
Epitaphs, 13, 232
Escapes, 15, 266, 267
Excess, 271

Faber and Faber, 226, 229
Fame, 46–47, 53–54, 71, 76, 77, 109, 119, 120, 125, 138, 142, 153, 169, 230, 231, 232, 242, 254, 264, 267–68, 268–70, 291, 294, 295, 307
Family tragedy, 51–52, 176
Farming, 175–76
Fastidiousness, 17
Fathers and daughters, 19, 36, 71, 189, 266
Fathers and sons, 30, 40, 143, 206, 243, 333–34
Favors, 197, 213, 272–73
Fencing, 206, 207
Fictional characters, 33, 289
Fights, 36, 142, 242, 280, 317, 334. *See also* Boxing
Film, 157–58, 193, 223–24, 231–32, 237–38, 250–52, 275, 294, 330, 331
Fire Island, N.Y., 74, 337–38
Fish, 110–11
Flies, 18
Floating Bear, The, 336
Food, 28–29, 37–38, 39–40, 89–91, 97–98, 110–11, 119, 139, 147, 156, 169, 211, 217–18, 227–29, 297–98, 340–41
Football, 334
47 Workshop, 292
Free verse, 172, 194
French language, 11
Friends of Liberty, 14
Friendship, 82, 88, 139, 159, 168, 179–80, 225, 238, 268–70, 300, 315–16, 322, 328–29, 338–39
Fujiyama, 159
Funerals, 46, 52, 155, 296–97

Games, 11–13, 283
Gardening, 82–83
German language, 118
Gluttony, 156, 271
Goats, 185
Great Awakening, 9–10
Greed, 118, 156, 158
Green beans, 131
Grief, 18, 32–33, 52, 122, 161, 241
Grubb Street, 29
Guns, 312

Hallucinations, 81, 233–34
Hampton Institute, 139
Handwriting, illegible, 81
Harper's Weekly, 119, 121
Harvard, 5, 7, 51, 81, 82, 102, 122, 128, 138, 147, 148, 170–71, 176, 189, 224, 229, 270, 306, 315, 336
Harvard Poetry Room, 210
Haughtiness, 144, 145, 165
Health, 7, 13, 23, 133–34, 141–42
Hell's Angels, 231
Hoaxes and tricks, 10, 20–21, 108–9, 141, 153, 174–75, 186–87, 192, 193–95, 197–98, 204, 205, 271, 332–33
Hogs, 61–62, 187
Hollywood, 237, 252, 261, 266, 267, 316, 331
Homesickness, 28–29
Homonyms, 291
Homosexuality, 106–7, 132, 147, 285, 288, 305, 307, 335
Honesty, 57
Honors, 31–32, 53, 171–72. *See also* Nobel Prize
Horse trading, 59–60
Horseflies, 18
Horses, 17, 59–60, 268
Hospitality, 24, 77–80, 116–17, 215
Hound and Horn, 289
Husbands and wives, 8, 18, 46, 66, 74, 125, 204–5, 226, 240–41, 256, 258–59, 266, 319, 332
Humor, 59, 60–61, 66, 118–19, 143, 232–34, 297
Hungarian language, 254
Hygiene, 92, 192

Illness, 18, 27, 70–71, 95–96, 118–19, 131, 134, 136–37, 161, 177, 193, 198, 242, 270, 316, 322–23, 333
Imagism, 162, 164, 193, 212
Impotence, 258–59
Imprisonment, 15, 147, 247, 288
Injuries, 126–27, 153, 330
Inspiration, 30, 35, 40, 64, 76–77, 100, 159, 165–66, 185–86, 212, 215–16, 233, 265, 324, 334–35, 337
Insults, 31–32, 102–3, 142, 146, 158, 169, 171–72, 209, 236, 237, 239, 258, 280, 291, 293–94, 303, 310, 314–15
Intelligence, 30–31, 73, 74
Interior decorating, 214
Inventions, 20
Irritability, 16, 121, 158, 160, 162–63, 163–64

Jazz, 296
Jealousy, 124, 158, 170–71, 173, 174–75, 204, 205–6
Jinxes, 298
Jogging, 330
Johns Hopkins University, 165
Jokes, 5, 110–11, 116–17, 141, 186–87, 192–93, 193–95, 204, 213–14, 240, 270–71, 297, 332–33
Journalists and journalism, 80–81, 204, 247–48, 248–49

Kenyon College, 320, 325
Kenyon Review, 320
Kindly acts, 21–22, 62–63, 82–83, 100–101, 146–47, 149–50, 173–74, 306, 331
Kindness to animals, 36–37, 160–61

Lacrosse, 206–7
Last words, 57, 137, 156
Lawsuits, 298
Laziness, 30
League of Nations, 139
Lecturing, 71–72, 77, 83, 274, 306
Lethargy, 317–18
Letters and letter writing, 24, 27–28, 42, 54, 81, 149, 225, 253, 298
Libraries, 22–23, 312
Library of Congress, 22, 171
Lies, 178–79. *See also* Tall Tales
Life Magazine, 185
Literary productivity, 150–51, 181–82, 183, 336–37, 341, 343
Literary style, 132–33, 154, 208, 304–5
Loneliness, 240, 339
Longevity, 141–42
Love affairs, 50–51, 212, 238, 248, 252, 265
Lowell, Mass., 110, 334
Lust, 8–9

McClure's magazine, 159
MacDowell Colony, 150, 152
McLean's Hospital, 81, 326
Magic, 254, 329
Manners, 44–45, 130–31, 131–32, 145–46, 241, 336
Maple trees, 210
Marriage, 4–5, 8, 17, 51, 69, 74, 226–27, 230, 266, 270, 305, 341
Masculinity, 258–59, 280, 308, 316
Medicine, 21–22, 68, 197, 198
Meetings of famous people, 25, 33–34, 35, 44, 53–54, 54–55, 97, 118, 131, 135–36, 154, 170, 171–72, 195–96, 219–23, 269, 302–3, 309–10
Mental illness, 81, 102, 209–10, 260, 308–9, 311–12, 320, 326, 328, 329
Mice, 84–85
Misprints, 151, 240
Moderation, 24, 48
Money, 92–93, 146–47, 157–58, 189, 195–96, 200–201, 257, 262, 272, 301, 306, 331–32
Money-making schemes, 118, 210
Monologues, 67, 230–31, 235–36, 320
Moose, 19–20
Mosquitoes, 36
Mothers, 89–91, 100–101, 287, 295, 336
Mount Auburn Cemetery, 46, 52
Music, 185, 206–7, 268, 296, 304, 317
Myth-making, 32–33, 57–58, 85–86, 88, 103–4, 178–79

Names, 140
Natural history, 19–20
Nature, 85–86, 111
New Republic, 194
New York Review of Books, 254
New Yorker, The, 213, 235, 237, 264, 291
Nobel Prize, 20, 156, 158, 205, 231, 297, 298, 303, 310
Non sequiturs, 268
North American Review, The, 133, 139
Nursing, 94–96

Objectivism, 300
Obnoxiousness, 115–76, 160, 172–73, 184–85, 205, 206, 207, 215, 235, 256, 257–58, 261–62, 263, 270–71, 301, 323
Old age, 13, 16, 23–24, 25, 46, 53–54, 92, 101, 121, 123–24, 125, 127–28, 141–42, 148, 177–78, 230
Omens, 65–66, 192–93, 341
One-liners, 111, 112, 120, 150, 193, 202, 234–35, 239–41
Others, 195
Oxford University, 53, 229

Painters, 111–12, 166–67, 168, 187
Paradise, 123–24
Pardons, 62–63
Parody, 193–95, 237, 280, 321
Parties, 112–15, 119, 156–57, 174, 254, 255–56, 261, 266, 286, 289, 309–10, 310–11, 336
Partisan Review, 327
Patronage, 60–61, 143, 149–50
Pencil making, 83
Pets, 84–85, 123, 160–61
Phi Beta Kappa, 265, 289
Philadelphia, 29
Philosophical theories, 37
Philosophy, 128
Physical fitness, 218
Pick-ups, 9, 131–32, 255, 285, 288, 310, 329–30
Plagiarism, 71, 158, 239, 297, 298, 339
Playwriting, 215–16, 239, 324
Poetic behavior, 107–8, 128, 150, 211–12
Poetry readings, 96–97, 138, 163–64, 184–85, 187, 188–89, 191, 197, 226, 238, 270, 295, 307, 310–11, 322–23
Poetry records, 210
Poetry writing, 28–29, 94, 159, 190, 193–94, 212–13, 220–23, 226, 270, 284–85, 325, 336–37, 341, 343
Poets, 236, 307
Poison ivy, 210
Politics, 20–21, 21–22, 37, 139, 149, 183, 217, 247, 303, 312–15, 326
Polo, 266
Potato bugs, 37
Poverty, 69–70, 110–11, 214–15
Praise, 32–33, 40–41, 42, 65, 67–68, 77, 85–86, 93, 97, 121, 135, 149, 157, 170, 203, 242, 290, 323, 327
Prayer, 6, 7, 8, 42
Preaching, 9
Precosity, 7, 9, 26, 30–31, 36, 183
Prejudice, 312–15
Premonitions, 65–66
Pride, 68–69, 73, 146, 159
Prolixity, 150–51, 226
Pronunciation, 29
Prose writing, 63–64, 76–77, 132–33, 165–66, 180–82, 183, 185–86, 236, 291–92, 331
Protegés, 82, 111–12
Pseudonyms, 122–23, 193–95, 225
Public speaking, 16–17
Publicity, 43, 96–97, 162, 184
Publishers and publishing, 14, 70, 86, 101, 121, 122, 170, 199, 235–37, 272, 290
Punch, 109
Punctuality, 41, 213–14
Puns, 13–14, 304

Radcliffe College, 165
Radio broadcasts, 169, 209–10
Reading, 112, 127–28, 254, 312
Reading aloud, 58, 95–96, 135
Religion, 6, 9–10, 15–16, 22, 29, 40, 55–56, 68, 81–82, 88, 96, 104, 106, 171, 243, 254
Religious frenzy, 9–10
Retorts, 12, 16, 68, 111, 115–16, 119, 128, 132, 145, 153, 167
Revenge, 116–17, 193, 213–14
Revision, 11, 34–35, 151, 199, 208, 262, 284–85, 292, 335

Revolutionary War, 13–15, 25–26
Ritz Hotel, liberation of, 281–82
Rivalry, 34, 45, 102–3, 116–17, 118, 124, 143, 158, 171–73, 175, 179–80, 202–3, 204, 205–6, 208, 212, 237, 239, 254, 259, 262–64, 276–78, 278–79, 280, 282–83, 289, 300, 301, 302, 303, 311, 323, 326–28, 333–34
Russian language, 254, 297–98

Salem witchcraft trials, 6, 7
Salvation, 9–10, 16
Saturday Evening Post, The, 261
Saturday Review of Literature, 159, 297
Scandal, 4–5, 106–7, 207, 243
Scientific knowledge, 10, 19–20
Screenplays, 223–24, 232, 237–38, 249–52, 266, 294, 299, 331–32
Scribner's, 146, 199, 200, 258, 261, 290, 291
Scribner's Magazine, 199
Scrupulosity, 48
Sculpture, 55–56, 184, 259
Secession, 283
Sedition, 14–15
Seductions, 152, 197–98, 310, 330
Self-confidence, 206
Self-discipline, 26–27, 48
Self-education, 31, 57, 112, 128
Self-esteem, 11, 29, 41, 67, 73, 94, 109, 111, 114, 166, 168, 169, 187, 202–3, 206, 260–61, 284, 316–17, 328
Self-promotion, 43, 93–94, 96–97, 112, 125–26, 156, 162, 202–3, 310
Self-review, 93–94, 97, 194
Senility, 45–46, 211
Sentimentality, 136, 160–61
Sex, 8–9, 43–44, 106–7, 131–32, 141, 147, 152, 167–68, 197–98, 198–99, 207, 238, 240, 243, 248, 255, 258–59, 265, 285, 288, 302, 310, 319, 320, 329–30, 335
Sexism, 3, 73, 269–70. *See also* Women
Shipwrecks, 74–76
Short stories: sales, 119, 200–201; loss, 275
Show-offs, 126, 207
Shyness, 55, 150
Silences, 41–42, 47–48, 150, 189, 210
Singing, 17, 99, 106, 117, 129, 268
Skating, 47, 199
Skepticism, 92
Skiing, 329
Slander, 7, 33, 89–91, 139, 296
Slavery, 63–64, 89–91, 139–40
Smart Set, 179
Smith College, 292, 340, 341
Smoking, 161, 163
Snobbism, 165, 241, 290
Social conditions, 48–49, 153
Social Credit, 208, 209
Solitude, 104, 160, 189
Song of Solomon, 184
Songs, 227, 301–2
Spanish-American War, 154–55
Spanish Civil War, 301
Spanish language, 286–87
Spectric School, 194, 195
Speechlessness, 150
Spelling, 19, 29, 270
Spiders, 64
Spiritualism, 49–51
Spitting, 246
Sports, 47, 69–70, 206–7, 216–17, 218–19, 219–23, 266, 268, 276–78, 329, 330, 334, 335–36
Stanislavsky method, 235
Stinginess, 156–58
Storytelling, 11, 18, 60–61, 66, 91, 110–11, 113–14, 178–79, 201, 203–4, 241–2
Stubbornness, 177, 247
Students and student life, 5, 26, 177–78, 267–68, 315, 320, 324–25, 339
Suicide, 9–10, 122, 212, 271, 288–89, 339, 341–43
Surveying, 23
Symbolism, 178

Tact, 121
Tall tales, 178–79, 236, 247–49
Tea parties, 41–42, 48, 55, 144, 166–67, 307, 339–40, 340–41
Teaching, 81, 170–71, 175, 176–77, 196–97, 265, 267, 274, 320
Temper, 32, 36, 69, 80, 139, 148, 161, 162–63, 163–64, 165, 178, 246, 278, 283, 285–86, 287, 294, 302, 317, 335

Theater, 71, 235, 264
Translating, 52, 148, 254
Transcendentalism, 36, 71, 72
Travel, 123, 134–35, 149, 268–70, 312–15
Tuberculosis, 70–71
Tuskegee Institute, 139

UFOs, 245–46
Ugliness, 59, 83
University of Michigan, 306, 308, 336
University of Mississippi, 265
University of Nebraska, 159
University of Pennsylvania, 206, 212
University of Pennsylvania Medical School, 196
University of Virginia, 20, 23, 68, 267
Urination, 6, 7, 192–93, 243–44
Utopian communities, 73, 87, 183

Vacations, 190, 267
Vanity, 46, 56, 67–68, 172, 182, 183–84, 300, 321
Vanity Fair, 253
Vegetarianism, 27, 37–38
Visits and visitors, 16, 24, 25, 47–48, 53–54, 55, 56, 77–80, 94, 97, 98–100, 105–6, 116–18, 138, 144, 145, 164–65, 182–83, 187, 191–92, 210–11, 229–30, 245, 249–50, 261–62, 285, 302–3, 321, 325–26, 340–41

Wabash College, 207
Walks, 189–90, 268–70, 335–36
War, 210
War in Italy, 74
Washington *Chronicle,* 97
Washington *Evening Star,* 97
Way Down East, 270
Wealth, 51, 116, 262
William and Mary College, 16
Wit, 12, 109–10
Witchcraft, 6, 7, 329
Woman suffrage, 73, 109
Women, 3, 71, 72, 73, 123, 131–32, 161–62, 198–99, 269–70, 310, 336
Women's College of Georgia, 336
Woodchucks, 83–84
World War I, 162–63
World War II, 168, 169, 281–82, 330
Writer's block, 233, 266

Yaddo, 271, 323
Yale, 9, 26, 27, 301, 307